The Psychology of Writing

The Psychology of Writing

Ronald T. Kellogg

OXFORD UNIVERSITY PRESS
New York   Oxford

Oxford University Press

Oxford New York
Athens Auckland Bangkok Bogotá Buenos Aires Calcutta
Cape Town Chennai Dar es Salaam Delhi Florence Hong Kong Istanbul
Karachi Kuala Lumpur Madrid Melbourne Mexico City Mumbai
Nairobi Paris São Paulo Singapore Taipei Tokyo Toronto Warsaw

and associated companies in
Berlin Ibadan

Copyright © 1994 by Oxford University Press, Inc.

First published in 1994 by Oxford University Press, Inc.
198 Madison Avenue, New York, New York 10016

First issued as an Oxford University Press paperback, 1999

Oxford is a registered trademark of Oxford University Press, Inc.

Library of Congress Cataloging-in-Publication Data
Kellogg, Ronald Thomas.
The psychology of writing / Ronald T. Kellogg.
p. cm. Includes bibliographical references and index.
ISBN 0-19-508139-0
ISBN 0-19-512908-3 (Pbk.)
1.Written communication—Psychological aspects.
2. Cognitive psychology.
3. Psycholinguistics.
I. Title.
BF456.W8K45 1994 401′.9—dc20 93-44667

1 3 5 7 9 8 6 4 2

Printed in the United States of America
on acid-free paper

To Carol

Preface

Interest in the process of writing has grown steadily over the past 20 years. The journey from Janet Emig's (1971) pioneering volume on the composing processes of high school students has been intellectually vigorous and has appropriately attracted researchers from diverse disciplines in the humanities and social sciences. In a relatively short period of time, an impressive literature has emerged on how people go about formulating their thoughts and expressing them in the form of written symbols. After centuries of effort devoted to analyzing and interpreting texts, the contemporary focus on how texts are composed in the first place seems long overdue, particularly to scholars in the humanities and education.

The present book brings my perspective as a cognitive psychologist, rooted in experimental methodology, to the rapidly expanding field of composition research. I initially investigated the cognitive processes called upon in writing because the subject was so woefully neglected by my colleagues. Cognitive psychology not only includes intricate theories and experimentation on speech production, speech comprehension, reading comprehension, and memory, it also includes detailed work on higher-order thinking processes such as problem solving, reasoning, and decision making. It struck me as obvious that a complete psychological account of thinking and language must surely include research on written composition.

With time, it became clear to me that composition research did much more than just fill a gap in the cognitive psychology literature. The study of how people express their thoughts in written form brings together scholars from the humanities, education, and the social sciences in pursuit of a much grander challenge. For the act of writing exemplifies to me the very essence of what it means to be human. Creating meaning through the use of symbols is a ubiquitous human activity. The making of meaning in art, dance, music, and oral and written discourse may well be the defining attribute of our species. The study of writing, then, offers one window through which to view the core of what appears to be a distinctly human mode of thinking.

This book, then, treats the intersection of meaning-making, thinking, and writing from the perspective of an experimentalist and cognitive psychologist. I do not claim to cover the full scope of any one of these topics to the satisfaction of my colleagues in cognitive psychology. The literature on thinking, for instance, is far too broad to tackle in a book focused on writing. Still, a book focused on the intersection of thinking and writing may increase the accessibility of the literature on composition to cognitive psychologists. Although this literature appears in educational psychology textbooks (e.g., Mayer, 1987), it is strangely absent from cognitive textbooks, despite extensive coverage of reading, speech, language, and thinking. One major textbook in cognitive psychology covered writing in one edition but then tellingly dropped it from a subsequent edition (Anderson, 1990a).

Similarly, a full discussion of the many ways that people create meaning in their lives through the shared symbols of culture would take us on perhaps an endless journey through the humanities. The work of semiologists who investigate the full range of human symbol use is far too large to encapsulate in these pages. Indeed, covering even the more limited intersection of meaning-making and writing to the complete satisfaction of scholars from the humanities, education, and the social sciences is probably beyond the scope of any single volume. As we shall see, the nature of writing varies across social and cultural contexts. The collaborative writing in a business setting, for example, differs in process and product from the creative writing of a cloistered poet. A complete account of writing demands a far more detailed consideration of contextual differences than is possible here.

What I do aim to provide here is a theoretical framework that readers from the humanities, education, and the social sciences can use to understand and interpret the composition literature. The framework attempts to do justice to the profound significance of meaning-making as a defining feature of human cognition and to organize the findings on writing in a manner understandable to readers with widely different backgrounds. This work addresses the needs of upper-level undergraduates and graduate students in courses dealing with the psychological aspects of writing. Such courses can be found in departments of English, communications, educational psychology, or psychology. Faculty in any of these departments who pursue or plan to pursue research on written composition should also find the book informative. Finally, I hope that the general reader finds the material accessible, for understanding how people go about creating meaning through the use of symbols enlightens us about a profound characteristic of ourselves.

I thank Joan Bossert, Senior Editor at Oxford University Press, for her enthusiasm for the project, helpful suggestions, and guidance in bringing the book to completion. It has been a pleasure working with all of the editorial staff. I also thank Mike Sharples for his useful comments on the manuscript along with other anonymous reviewers. I have profited from discussions and correspondence over the years concerning writing research with fellow investigators, including Jim Hartley, Bruce Britton, Marcy Lansman, Bob Boice, and John Gould. Secretarial and library staff plus research assistants helped with various aspects of my research and with preparing the manuscript, especially Robin Collier, Ramona Taylor, Mona Brown, Cara Saling, Andy Stewart, Janet McKean, Anne Freeman, and Suzanne Mueller. Lastly, I thank my spouse, Carol, and children, Alicia and Kristin, for their encouragement throughout the duration of this work.

Rolla, Missouri   R.T.K.
November 1993

Contents

The Psychology of Writing

1

Homo Symbolificus

You have to accept the fact that man is not simply *Homo sapiens;* he's *Homo symbolificus*—he's someone who makes symbols.

WALKER PERCY

The student puzzles over a term paper. The professor labors over a monograph. The scientist reports the findings of a recent experiment in an article. The journalist completes a story just before the deadline. The business executive outlines a proposal in a memorandum. The novelist weaves a gripping tale about the human condition. The poet captures a fleeting feeling. The diarist records the events of yet another day. Though their tasks vary widely, each of these individuals confronts the challenge of creating coherent ideas in the private realm of thought and mapping those ideas into the public world of linguistic symbols. In composing a written text, these individuals create meaning for themselves and potentially for their readers. They engage in a special form of thinking—the making of meaning—that may well define one of the most unique characteristics of our species.

The novelist Walker Percy advanced this theme in his remarks at the eighteenth Jefferson Lecture, sponsored by the National Endowment for the Humanities (Coughlin, 1989). Percy argued that "man's unique behavior of language and symbol-mongering eventually must be confronted by science as a natural phenomenon that explains humanity" (p. A7). Although it might be presumptuous to rename our species, Percy's fanciful term *Homo symbolificus* aptly underscores the centrality of meaning-making in human life. Writing, art, music, dance, and other forms of symbol creation and manipulation reveal the very human process of giving meaning to the experience of life.

That meaning-making through symbols defines humanity has long philosophical roots. Charles Sanders Pierce pioneered the field of semiotics in the nineteenth century. His work built upon John Locke's doctrine of signs, which looked upon knowledge as embodied in ideas that are communicated from the mind of one person to another. Locke's work, in turn, echoes ideas as early as Aristotle's (Deely, 1986). Working forward from Pierce's efforts in the modern era takes one through the writings of Ernst Cassirer, Susanne Langer, Nelson Goodman, and Umberto Eco

3

(Gardner, 1982, 1991). For instance, Langer viewed the invention of meanings through symbolization as a basic human need. Gardner (1982) paraphrased Langer this way: "It was a property of the human mind to search for and to find significances everwhere, to transform experience constantly to uncover new meanings" (p. 50). Symbolization and meaning-making, then, are essential aspects of being human.

It is important not to intellectualize meaning-making to the point where only writers and artists play the game. All human beings form opinions, hold beliefs, and express intentions and desires. Speech and gestures comprise two fundamental and pervasive systems of public discourse shared by all members of a given culture or subculture. The level of creativity found in the use of these systems of communicating is marked regardless of socioeconomic status or educational attainment of the culture's members. The constant and universal invention of slang makes this point well, but one need not look far to find other illustrations of symbol creation, manipulation, and communication. One finds humanity busy with the task of meaning-making in bumper stickers, T-shirt logos, tattoos, and graffitti, as well as in the published texts of writers and the displayed works of artists. As Gardner (1991, p. 56) noted:

> Few would question the choice of language as the symbol system par excellence, but it is important to underscore the potency of other symbol systems. Much knowledge is apprehended and communicated through gesture and other paralinguistic means. . . . And various customs, rituals, games, and other social interactions are rife with symbols of various sorts.

This book presents a cognitive psychological account of how people go about the task of writing. In recent years, mathematical cognition and musical cognition have been well represented in journals and books on cognitive psychology, implying a growing interest in how various types of symbol systems are acquired and used. Writing cognition, in contrast, has been virtually ignored in cognitive psychology to date. This has occurred despite intense interest among psychologists in reading and in the production and comprehension of speech, despite over two decades of intensive research on writing processes, and despite the strong influence that pioneering cognitive models of writing (Flower & Hayes, 1980) have had in the humanities and education.

I provide a theoretical framework that organizes the findings of composition researchers and integrates them with the concepts and assumptions of cognitive psychology. The framework I advance should prove useful to individuals with backgrounds in the humanities, education, and the social sciences. The literature on composition represents an amalgam of diverse points of view, methodologies, and disciplinary biases (North, 1987), but I hope to show that cognitive psychology can accommodate the central theses in this diversity.

Inevitably perhaps, theorists have sought to contrast the perspective of their discipline with that taken by another. For example, we find cognitive models of writing pitted against social or cultural models, as if both views were not needed (Faigley, 1986). This book follows from the premise that the cognitive models of writing conceived by Flower and Hayes (1980b), de Beaugrande (1984), Bereiter and Scardamalia (1987), and others can be broadened to integrate and organize what is known about the act of writing.

This chapter provides background on writing, meaning-making, and thinking in the context of cognitive psychology. I set the stage for the theoretical and empirical players who will join us throughout the book. In the first section on meaning-making, I define a critical distinction between personal and consensual symbols. In the next section, I summarize what is meant by thinking in the field of cognitive psychology and argue that the study of writing offers much to a psychology of thinking. Next, I introduce the central idea of how knowledge is represented in the mind of the writer in structures called *schemata,* and how these schemata support the creativity witnessed in writing in particular, meaning-making more broadly, and thinking in all its forms.

The Making of Meaning

At the heart of human nature is the drive to make sense of our world. We do this moment by moment in interpreting our daily experiences. People construct personal, informal models of their experiences much as a scientist constructs public, formal models of phenomena. These models are comprised of symbols that exist both in the private mental world inside one's head and in the public physical world of written texts, works of art, and artifacts of all kinds. It is through the symbols that we create, manipulate, and communicate to others that our experience is rendered meaningful.

Human cultures can be viewed in part as the public records of our strivings to make sense of the world through symbol creation. Cultures evolve continually as new ideas are conceived, new symbols are gestated, and new meanings are born. The survival of new meanings depends on competition and successful adaptation in a manner that parallels the survival of genes in biological evolution (Dawkins, 1976). Civilizations rise and fall, but the ideas and meanings that ring true, useful, and beautiful survive for future generations of humanity.

Csikszentmihalyi (1990) described the two crucial senses in which people make meaning. First, there is the classic sense of reference. What is the meaning of chair? A symbol, such as a word, refers to some object, event, or other form of human experience. Through the construction of complex webs of reference, people order information in their world. Relationships and identity classes emerge through this form of meaning-making. Second, there is the ultimate sense of purpose and significance in life. What is the meaning of life? People construct causal relationships among events such that they lead to some final purpose. Making sense of our experience entails meaning as both reference and purpose. Meaning as reference provides a platform on which to build our theories and tales about the significance of human existence.

Through imitation and other learning processes, people assimilate the attitudes, prejudices, beliefs, and theories of their culture. Such cultural knowledge forms one of several reservoirs of knowledge that an individual draws upon in interpreting and making meaningful the events of life. Creation of symbols always entails, to a greater or lesser degree, the remembrance of what one has learned in the past. Putting a bumper sticker on your car is one variant of meaning-making; writing a letter to the newspaper editor is another. Both reflect the human need to render experience meaningful, though they differ in their demand for originality and in the effort they require.

To say that meaning-making is fundamental to the human mind is hardly novel. This perspective has been thriving for several years in anthropology, linguistics, literacy theory, and philosophy (Bruner, 1990). The roots of this perspective run deep in psychology as well, through the work of Piaget in the 1920s and of Vygotsky in the 1930s. But in psychology the focus has been first on behavior and then on information processing, rather than on meaning-making. The cognitive revolution in psychology in the 1950s and 1960s steered psychology away from the strictures of behaviorism and toward the mainstream concern with symbols and meaning. Yet, psychology rapidly diverged again from its sister disciplines in the humanities and social sciences. Speaking of the cognitive revolution that he and his colleagues at the Center for Cognitive Studies at Harvard helped to spur, Bruner (1990) made the following observations:

> It was, we thought, an all-out effort to establish meaning as the central concept of psychology—not stimuli and responses, not overtly observable behavior, not biological drives and their transformations, but meaning. . . . Its aim was to discover and to describe formally the meanings that human beings created out of their encounters with the world, and then propose hypotheses about what meaning-making processes were implicated. It focused on the symbolic activities that human beings employed in constructing and making sense not only of the world, but of themselves. . . . It would make an absorbing essay in the intellectual history of the last quarter-century to trace what happened to the originating impulse of the cognitive revolution, how it became fractionated and technicalized. . . . Very early on . . . emphasis began shifting from "meaning" to "information," from the *construction* of meaning to the *processing* of information. (pp. 2, 4)

Bruner adopted the interpretive methods of history, anthropology, linguistics, and philosophy in building his cognitive account of mental states, beliefs, intentions, and meaning-making. The empirical methods of cognitive psychology also have an important role to play, I contend. Experimentation in particular, as we will see, can reveal much about the factors that affect how people write and how well they write. Conceivably, composition research may provide a bridge between Bruner's apt theoretical focus on how people create meaning and the strongly experimental orientation of the discipline of cognitive psychology.

Personal and Consensual Symbols

People make meaning by creating, manipulating, and communicating symbols. Symbols can be categorized in many ways, but I find the typology advanced in the context of cognitive psychology by Kolers and Smythe (1984) to be most appropriate here. In a nutshell, Kolers and Smythe underscored the difference between thinking in the private realm of individual consciousness and communicating in the public realm of cultural and social consciousness. Communicating through written text demands a translation from one type of symbol—the personal and private—to another—the cultural and public.

To begin, Kolers and Smythe distinguished between articulated, allographic symbols and dense, autographic symbols. They provided a typology that drew upon and modified Goodman's (1976) philosophical analysis of symbol systems (see Allport, 1984, for a critique of their modifications). Kolers and Smythe use the terms *articulated* and *allographic* to mean that the symbol can be copied precisely. For instance, this book is a copiable collection of symbols in that a true copy exists whenever the letters and spaces between them are placed in proper order. The paper on which it is printed, the color of the ink, and the type of printing press are irrelevant.

Kolers and Smythe described a noncopiable symbol as being *dense* and *autographic.* The unique features of a noncopiable symbol are highly relevant; indeed, they define its essential nature. For example, the original painting of an artist cannot be copied exactly, either by another artist or by technological means. Neither a forgery nor a mass-produced print of a master painting is a true copy of the original, for the precise nature of the surface, the precise colors, and the precise wielding of the brush all matter.

Another important distinction is between consensual symbol systems, which are publicly available to all skilled users, and personal symbol systems, which are privately defined by one person. First, consider consensual symbols. Inscriptions or markings on a clay tablet, on paper, or on a computer display are public in the sense that other people may examine them and interpret them according to agreed-upon conventions. Kolers and Smythe use the term *inscriptions* to refer to consensual symbols that one knows how to extract meaning from or interpret. One knows the rules for inscriptions, in other words. *Marks,* on the other hand, are consensual symbols that one cannot interpret for lack of knowledge of the rules. English words are inscriptions for me, whereas Chinese icons are marks.

Oral and written language are consensual symbol systems that are fundamental to human cognition and are acquired at a relatively early age. In the case of language, young children first master the basic rules of producing and comprehending speech, and then acquire the reading and writing skills. As a consequence of developing literacy, written texts can be scrutinized, comprehended, learned from, and interpreted by the skilled reader. The written text is a consensual symbol system in the sense that it allows the sharing of meanings among members of the culture. Other consensual symbol systems, such as musical, mathematical, and logical notations, may be acquired in addition to language.

Consensual symbol systems include both autographic and allographic types. Speaking, handwriting, dancing, acting, miming, and other human performances are dense and autographic in that each act is unique. If one utters the same statement 100 times, each utterance will be unique, even though the variations are typically subtle and negligible to a listener. One can record a human performance, say on audiotape, in order to capture it in a form that may be copied. The tape then exists as an articulated, allographic symbol that can be copied reliably, but it is not identical to the unique original performance. Audiophiles relentlessly pursue their mission of reproducing—exactly—the qualities of a live performance, knowing full well that a seasoned ear can always hear a difference no matter how technologically sophisticated the copy may be. Other articulated, allographic consensual symbol systems include printed texts, musical scores, choreographic scores, and mathematical equations.

The biological and cultural evolution of our species has resulted in a formidable array of consensual symbol systems. Natural languages, pictures, pictograms, diagrams, and logical, mathematical, and musical notations are consensual in that anyone who has learned a given system can perceive, comprehend, define, and manipulate the symbols. The system of concern here, natural language, is as ancient as it is extraordinary. The evolution of written texts can be traced at least as far back as 8000 B.C. to the use of a simple token system that appears to have been developed for accounting purposes in Sumeria. Schmandt-Besserat (1988) contended that from this beginning the Sumerians developed more abstract writing systems that moved through periods of using impressed markings on envelopes, then impressed markings on tablets, and culminating in the use of pictographs. Sumerian cuneiform script, in turn, evolved from the pictograph system about 2900 B.C. Moreover, the development of writing systems occurred only after many millennia of oral language in the evolutionary history of our species. As Havelock (1991, p. 21) reminded us, "our oral inheritance is as much a part of us as the ability to walk upright and use our hands."

Personal symbols, in contrast to consensual symbols, are "phenomenal events that refer to other objects or events, such as mental images, mental associations, or dreams" (Kolers & Smythe, 1984, p. 294). Only the person experiencing the internal events can properly comprehend and use these symbols. They enable an individual to represent a personal world. They cannot be inspected by others, "nor do they have any status separate from the operation of the cognitive processes that create them" (p. 294).

Sensations, perceptions, images, memories, associations, beliefs, desires, intentions, daydreams, fantasies, and dreams make reference to objects and events in the material world or to other experiences in one's mental world. These products of mental operations are what we mean by *personal symbols*. As you perceive the words on this page, you construct personal symbols that map onto the consensual symbols of the written text. The letters and words themselves do not enter your mental world; instead, the perceptual and memorial systems of the brain process the patterns of light reflecting from the page and generate the personal symbols of visual perceptions, images, associations, and interpretations.

The perceptual operations that the brain uses to construct these private symbols of mental experience can easily be confused with the letters and words that appear on the page. I will return to this point in the next chapter when the constructive properties of cognitive operations and representations are discussed. It is perhaps easier to recognize the crucial difference between the consensual symbols of text and the personal representations by considering the inferences, judgments, interpretations, and meanings that each reader constructs from a text. Depending on the reader's prior knowledge, beliefs, and values, the consensual symbols of a given text can produce widely different interpretations as coded in the reader's personal symbols. The same text—the physical text comprised by public, consensual symbols—

renders a possible infinite number of interpretations—comprised by the private, personal symbols of each reader's mental experience.

The emergence of personal symbols in evolutionary history is surely much older than the history of consensual symbols. Comparative psychologists and ethologists generally agree that the ability to represent or model the environment in some fashion is pervasive in the animal kingdom. Still, the question of whether these representations of the animal mind include conscious personal symbols remains contested. Griffin (1991) and others stated that infrahuman species clearly can think consciously, whereas Kennedy (1992) and others rejected this conclusion as an anthropomorphic error. In the final chapter, I will return to the possibility that humans are not alone in representing the world in the form of personal symbols that enable conscious reflection. The point that needs emphasis here is that personal symbols are viewed as the product of cognitive operations occurring in the nervous systems of biological organisms. They have no existence apart from these operations and certainly cannot be scrutinized in the manner of consensual symbols.

The Communication of Thought

Consensual symbols afford the possibility of communication among people through a common basis of reference. The artist can communicate private experiences and thoughts through the dense, autographic painting or sculpture that may be viewed by others. The novelist similarly can communicate private experiences and thoughts through the articulated, allographic book that may be read by others. For interpersonal communication to succeed, it must be possible to map personal symbols into a consensual symbol system. The mapping, however, is only partial. Through language, for instance, you can gain some insight into another person's private experience, but that is not the same as apprehending it fully and directly yourself.

Kolers and Smythe made the important claim that all personal symbols are inherently dense and autographic. Human experiences as well as human actions, in their view, can never be copied or repeated exactly. Each of us at any given moment experiences a private world that cannot be *precisely* duplicated in another person's mind or even in ourselves at a later moment. The heraclitean assertion that one never enters the same river twice finds expression here. Surely memory allows one to represent similar experiences within oneself across time; perception and learning would not be possible otherwise. Further, consensual symbols allow one to communicate, more or less well, with others regarding the nature of one's private world. But the essential point is that human experience is not precisely copiable.

Kolers and Smythe's claim is not a stranger to psychology. Students of personality will hear echoes of the personal construct theory of George Kelly (1955). A person's history shapes how he or she constructs or interprets the world, and these interpretations are subject to change. Kelly suggested that one could choose to interpret the world differently by building new personal constructs. These constructs are idiographic. People differ in the number of constructs they invent, the way they relate them, and the content of these constructs. Because we each have a unique set of constructs, communication can be strained. Effective communication, in Kelly's view, demands that one see the world through another person's construct system rather than through one's own system.

The task facing the writer is to map in an effective fashion the personal symbols of private thought onto the inscriptions of public communication. This, we will see, is at times a monumental and virtually always a highly demanding cognitive feat. Writers must be able to represent their inner experiences, feeling, beliefs, and attitudes such that they can then be shared and understood in a public forum. Forging the relationship between personal and consensual symbols is difficult and may never be completely successful. This is the crux of the challenge facing each writer.

The Nature of Thinking

Definitions of Thinking

Thinking involves a set of mental skills that create, manipulate, and communicate to others the personal symbols of mental life. This description parallels that of Gilhooly (1982, p. 1), who defined thinking as a "set of processes whereby people assemble, use and revise internal symbolic models." For example, one can model the layout of a city in the mind's eye in order to plan a route to navigate from one location to another. Or one can model the workings of a car to begin to determine what is causing that frighteningly loud noise under the hood. Such models typically embody many personal symbols that refer to what the person knows about both the world and the self. Gilhooly (1982, p. 1) noted that models "may be intended to represent reality (as in science) or conceivable reality (as in fiction) or even be quite abstract with no particular interpretation (as in music or pure mathematics)." These collections of personal symbols allow a person to manipulate ideas, to anticipate the effects of actions, and to think beyond the immediately perceived environment.

A widely used textbook on thinking summarizes numerous definitions of the topic by focusing on three basic ideas (Mayer, 1983). First, thinking occurs internally or mentally but is generally inferred indirectly through behavior. For example, the thinking involved in writing can be inferred by asking the writer to think aloud and by analyzing the text produced. While recent advances in brain-imaging techniques allow one to observe directly that thinking is taking place, the contents of the thought processes still remain private.

Second, thinking is a process that entails manipulating representations of what one knows about the world. The act of composing a text, for instance, involves retrieving information from memory, generating new ideas based on partial information in memory, organizing ideational and linguistic structures, reading source materials and the evolving text, and several other operations. Thinking is typically complex and operationally intensive. Numerous component skills that are the focus of most cognitive research are brought to bear simultaneously on acts of thinking.

Third, what one thinks or knows about a topic is often, though not always, directed at the solution of specific tangible goals. Certainly, a writer's thoughts must at times be goal directed if a text is ever to emerge. But it is equally plain that at times our thoughts drift aimlessly, sometimes in the service of creativity and other times as the result of sheer mental fatigue. Daydreaming and even dreaming serve the writer in creating text, along with directed forms of thinking.

Thinking can be fruitfully viewed as a complex skill that is not inherently different from motor skills (Bartlett, 1958; Kolers & Roediger, 1984). Walking, swimming, riding a bicycle, driving a car, and typing on a keyboard are all highly complex perceptual-motor skills. Each involves numerous component processes, which in turn consist of subcomponent processes. These skills are mediated by hierarchical sensorimotor systems that develop with maturation and practice. In the same way, thinking of all types involves hierarchical cognitive systems. Just as learning to ride a bicycle requires maturation, training, and practice, so, too, does learning to think (e.g., Segal, Chipman, & Glaser, 1985) and learning to write (e.g., Bereiter & Scardamalia, 1987).

Types of Thinking

Directed, undirected, and recurrent thinking comprise three broad classes. *Directed thinking* is goal oriented and rational. When the environment specifies a goal to be achieved in the near future, directed thought works toward it. For example, an on-the-job task might be an order from the boss to complete a routine memorandum on sales projections. The manager assigned the task would take deliberate, direct steps to compile the needed information and produce the document according to the format expected by the boss. I assume here that this writing task has a well-defined goal—a set of specifications of exactly the type of information that should be included and the way it should be presented.

Undirected thought meanders, without progress toward a clearly identifiable goal. Dreaming, daydreaming, and autistic thinking are examples of such thought. Freud (1900) differentiated the primary-process thinking of dreams, characterized by wish fulfillment unconstrained by reality, and the secondary-process thinking of daydreaming, characterized by a respect for reality. Berlyne (1965) employed the term autistic thinking to refer to the often irrational nature of nondirected thinking.

Although some important work has been done on undirected thought (Singer, 1975), the psychology of thinking weighs heavily on the side of directed thinking. The reason for this emphasis stems from the kinds of laboratory tasks used in experimentation. Most problem-solving, reasoning, decision-making, and concept identification tasks studied are characterized by well-defined goals. The entire point of the experimentation is to understand how a person moves in a directed fashion from some beginning point defined in the task to the endpoint. Solving a maze, for example, illustrates the approach.

Recurrent thinking is characterized by repetitious thoughts that may occur while awake or asleep. Recurring dreams, imagining music that "you just can't get out of your head," fixating on a particular solution to a problem, and ruminating about some embarrassing or irritating social interaction are familiar examples. Recurrent thinking can become so pervasive as to lead from the realm of the normal to the abnormal. People suffering from obsessive-compulsive and depressive disorders exhibit a high degree of recurrent thinking. But recurrent thinking may also play a role in the creative work of a writer. A recurring dream, for instance, may force an author to struggle with its meaning and may well become a source of inspiration. Note that a clearly identifiable goal may be apparent in recurrent thinking (e.g., fixation in problem solving) or it may not (e.g., a recurring dream). Outside of abnormal psychology, recurrent thinking has been studied even less than undirected thinking.

Lipman (1991) reviewed the approaches taken to thinking in the humanities and social sciences with the purpose of applying his conclusions to education. He distinguished two general categories of thinking: critical and creative. *Critical thinking* helps one in making judgments because it relies on explicit criteria of what makes for good judgment. For example, a doctor thinks critically in practicing medicine in that the criteria for the the correct diagnosis and treatment of a patient can be taught to and used by the physician. Critical thinking is also self-correcting in that the thinker monitors the process and seeks to steer it toward the truth, which Lipman regards as the megacriterion governing all such thinking. Lastly, critical thinking is sensitive to context. Consider Lipman's example on writing:

> An astute copyeditor going over an essay prior to publication will make innumerable corrections that can be justified by appeal to recognized canons of grammar and spelling. Idiosyncratic spellings are rejected in favor of uniformity, as are grammatical irregularities. But stylistic idiosyncrasies on the author's part may be treated with considerably greater tolerance and sensitivity. This is because the editor knows that the style is not a matter of writing mechanics; it has to do with the context of what is being written as well as the person of the author. (p. 121)

Creative thinking, Lipman concluded, shares many of the same components with critical thinking, but these components take on a different organization and purpose. He contended that "creative thinking could best be defined as thinking conducive to judgment, guided by context, self-transcending, and sensitive to criteria" (p. 193). To begin with, the overriding criterion in creative thinking is meaningfulness, whereas in critical thinking it is truth. Although a concern for truth has its place in creative thinking, the far greater concern is with "wholeness and invention . . . going beyond itself, transcending itself" (p. 193). The self-correcting feature of critical thinking, which aims to take one closer and closer to the truth, diminishes in importance for the creative thinker. Going beyond one's self to invent or discover that which is meaningful is far more important than ascertaining that which is truthful.

Although critical thinking is sensitive to context, creative thinking is fully governed by it. Invention and discovery of meaning are entirely context dependent, in sharp contrast to the determination and specification of truth, in Lipman's analysis. Each context or situation brings with it a set of values that often take the form of contrasting pairs. As creative thinking unfolds, it is molded and governed by these contextual values. Lipman gave the example of a writer to illustrate this contextual force:

> For example, a writer in the process of composing a book may experience the conflict between unity and complexity very intensely. On the one hand, she feels compelled to be faithful to the highly differentiated and complicated subject matter

with which she has to deal, and on the other hand, she wants to present her under-standing of this in the most coherent way she can. So for her a controlling value is the unity–complexity conflict. And as she proceeds, it is evident that she is making definite progress in reducing incoherence to coherence, inconsistencies to consis-tency, and disunity to unity. (pp. 208–209)

Traditionally, a creative act has been defined as one that is original, useful in some sense, and dependent on special training, education, and abilities (Hayes, 1981). Lipman avoided these features in his definition because they focus more on the product of creative thinking than on the process itself. Process and product creativity are two different concepts (Sternberg, 1988). *Process creativity* refers to the ability to apply relevant knowledge inventively to problems at hand. It is as normal to human functioning as is remembering. This does not deny that individuals vary in their ability to apply knowledge inventively. Remembering, too, is a common function, but individuals clearly vary in their ability to remember.

Product creativity refers to the quality and quantity of works judged by others to be original, innovative, useful, and important. Although all people are creative in the process sense, few are creative in the product sense. Anyone can create symbols, but the genius creates symbols that others pay attention to time and again. Product creativity depends not only on individual ability but also on the cultural and societal supports available to an individual (Sternberg, 1988). It occurs only when the right individual lands in the right discipline at the right place and at the right time.

Process creativity is equivalent to Boden's (1990) notion of *psychological,* or *P-creative,* individuals. A person is P-creative when he or she creates an idea that is "novel with respect to *the individual mind* which had the idea" (p. 32). Product creativity, in contrast, is observed only in *historical,* or *H-creative,* individuals. In Boden's terms, the "historical sense applies to ideas that are fundamentally novel with respect to *the whole of humanity*" (p. 32).

A failure to appreciate the distinction between creative thinking in the process sense from creativity as a product has led in our culture to a mythology of creative genius (Boden, 1990; Weisberg, 1986). Creative thinking has been regarded as rare; it has been seen less as a human activity than as a divine one. This notion has ancient roots in the Greek view of the writer or artist being inspired by the Muses. Many a writer today still looks haplessly for the Muse on days when the writing seems to be going badly or not at all.

Writing as a Form of Thinking

I regard thinking and writing as twins of mental life. The study of the more expressive twin, writing, can offer insights into the psychology of thinking, the more reserved member of the pair. Much of what we presently know about thinking stems from observations of how people solve problems with clearly defined goals, such as achieving checkmate in chess. Although such problems may be enormously com-plex, as chess plainly is, they do not capture the difficulties of creating meaning in the form of writing, art, music, and other ill-defined domains of problem solving.

Studies of reasoning and decision-making tasks add another dimension to our understanding, particularly in regard to the errors that frequently occur in thinking processes. Although the studies of well-defined problems, reasoning, and decision making have proved useful, they do not rule out other approaches. The study of writing can at least broaden and, I hope, deepen our understanding.

In their classic work *A Study of Thinking,* Bruner, Goodnow, and Austin (1956) investigated concept identification tasks as "idealized forms of thinking" (p. 246). They argued that all thinking involves and depends on categorizing, which in turn hinges on the human capacity to infer from sign to significate. I certainly have no quarrel with the premise that the study of categorization reveals much about thinking. I do suggest that the study of writing can prove equally fruitful in this regard for at least two reasons. First, writing is a remarkably rich task from a methodological and empirical viewpoint. Second, writing invokes typical elements of thinking. Consider each category in turn.

Methodological Richness

The study of writing has advantages over the study of other types of problem-solving, decision-making, and reasoning tasks. One advantage lies in the richness of the product that the writer produces. By richness I mean that the product includes not only a large quantity of information but also diverse sorts of information. In, say, a deductive reasoning task, the final product is a simple binary judgment: The conclusion is valid or invalid. Even in a complex game like chess, the product is only the record of moves taken by the winner to maneuver the loser into checkmate. Although the number of possible of moves is staggering—outnumbering the number of molecules in the universe (Simon, 1990)—the record is still limited to 64 squares and six kinds of game pieces.

In contrast, the written record can potentially offer what seems like an infinite variety of insights about the thinking of its creator (Witte & Cherry, 1986). For example, in persuasive writing, an evaluation of the quality of the arguments advanced by the composer provides a window on his or her thinking ability. The field of literary criticism seeks in part to expose the writer's thinking through an analysis of the writer's finished text. Moreover, drafts, scribbled notes, outlines, and other products of planning allow one to trace the thought patterns of the writer as well as, and perhaps better than, the so-called final product.

Not only the product of writing is rich; so too is the culture of writing and of writers. For instance, autobiographies of writers and interviews with writers have long been of interest to the literary community and offer an atypical but useful data base for the psychologist. In contrast to standard laboratory tasks, there is great cultural interest in the works of well-known makers of meaning, in writing, music, art, and other creative endeavors.

Another reason for studying writing from a methodological point of view is that its sheer complexity guarantees that many diverse factors will come into play. This book reviews research on knowledge, strategies, tools, rituals, work scheduling, intelligence, anxiety, motivation, and other psychological concepts. All are relevant to a psychology of thinking and writing, but a simpler task may not uncover their significance.

One example of this complexity concerns the types of thinking that play a role in the work of a writer. The study of writing, in contrast to traditional investigations of problem-solving, reasoning, and concept identification, often leads to encounters with undirected and even recurrent forms of thinking. Daydreams, dreams, and repetitive ideas and images that refuse to let go of conscious attention are just as much a part of the writer's life as are well-defined goals and directed problem-solving steps.

Furthermore, writing processes bring into play both critical thinking, as defined by Lipman (1991), and creative thinking. To revise one's thinking on a subject or to edit a manuscript for coherence, clarity, and organization, to take just two examples, certainly calls upon all the critical skills available to the writer. To discover an interesting theme for an essay, to imagine a captivating plot for a novel, to organize a set of arguments that are compelling to the reader—all call upon a writer's creative skills.

Another example of the complexity of writing comes from Bazerman's (1990) work on what it means to be considered an expert writer. He suggested not only that writing is typically an ill-defined problem, but also that it may well be an infinite variety of ill-defined problems. An expert in one domain of writing—novelist, poet, journalist, scientist—is not necessarily even competent in another domain. Each text form requires new ways of inventing and communicating ideas. To illustrate, consider the thinking processes and the written products created by the advertising executive in charge of an ad campaign, the reporter following a late-breaking story, the writer of detective fiction, the life-long poet, the scholarly classicist, or the scientific researcher writing for a technical journal. You can begin to see how the problems of what to include in a text and how to express that content are both numerous and widely diverse.

The complexity and the open-ended nature of written composition can certainly broaden the scope of the psychology of thinking. But these same characteristics suggest that the typical mode of theorizing in cognitive psychology is premature for the level of analysis that I pursue here. My purpose in the following chapters is to provide a rough landscape of the psychological variables relevant to how we construct meaningful thoughts and express these thoughts in written form. I aim to describe the thinking operations that seem to be necessary for the creation of meaning in general and writing in particular. I hypothesize functional relations between psychological factors, such as degree of available knowledge, and writing performance, such as quality of the resulting text. In short, I provide a theoretical framework for understanding the psychology of writing but not a detailed, explicit process model that could in principle be embodied in a computer simulation.

One of the reasons detailed process models and computer simulations have proved successful and popular in cognitive psychology is that researchers necessarily have to examine a specific, well-defined task, often a fairly simple one. To make explicit a step-by-step flow of information across sensing, information storage and retrieval, decision making and information manipulation, and finally motor output, one has to deal with specificity, not generality. The beauty of focusing exclusively on a specific laboratory task is that a computable model can be developed, task performance simulated, and process assumptions falsified by human performance data.

There is no denying the benefits to cognitive science provided by the process model approach. But this approach levies a cost if it excludes alternative theoretical approaches that focus on the richness of psychological variables naturally at work in complex cognition. Knowledge, strategies, tools, rituals, work scheduling, intelligence, cognitive style, anxiety, and motivation will most likely not all find their way—in their various possible forms—into a computable process model. The number of free parameters would sink the simulation. I adopt the modest goal of painting with broad brush strokes a theoretical framework for understanding the complexities of writing as an exemplary form of human thought. The fine delineation of process models can follow later.

Writing as Prototypical Thinking

There are several arguments for the study of writing as a window to a theory of thinking. First, quality writing cannot be achieved without quality thinking. Thinking well may not be a sufficient condition for writing well, but it certainly appears to be a necessary condition. This assertion scarcely needs documentation for those in the college teaching profession who have suffered through a poorly written term paper. A poorly written paper reflects a failure to generate and develop interesting ideas, a failure to arrange these ideas in a coherent sequence, and a failure to consider the needs of the reading audience. A quality paper excels on these and other criteria. Nickerson, Perkins, and Smith (1985) put it this way: "If a person writes well of substantive matters, one tends to believe that that person has the ability to think effectively in a fairly general sense" (p. 252).

Second, writing is a tool for thinking. Writing not only demands thinking, it is also a means for thinking (Nickerson et al., 1985). By writing about a subject, one learns what one thinks about the subject. This property of transforming knowledge is a fundamental component of writing skill that I will return to later. Here the important point is that one can improve one's thinking about a particular subject by writing about it (Horton, 1982). Indeed, the complex logical arguments demanded in legal (Stratman, 1990) and scientific thought (Olson, 1976) may well require the tool of writing. Such arguments must be examined and elaborated to be successful, and the written record permits this in a way that spoken language cannot.

Third, writing involves four cognitive operations that play a role in all thinking tasks. Collecting information, planning ideas in the realm of personal symbols, translating these ideas into the consensual realm of written text, and reviewing ideas and text are fundamental components of writing skill. Most writing tasks demand that the composer attend carefully to all four processes. Given the range of skills called on in writing, we expect that writing often in composition classes and elsewhere will improve the student's ability to think and learn in general (Langer & Applebee, 1987). Indeed, this is partly the motivation for the increased emphasis in education on writing development and on writing across the curriculum (Fulwiler & Young, 1990; Gordon & Braun, 1985a).

Finally, a hallmark of thinking is mental effort and engagement. Thinking and writing do not simply unfold automatically and effortlessly in the manner of a well-learned motor skill, such as typing or riding a bicycle. Further, the writer must monitor and evaluate how well his or her thinking and writing are going. Cognitive psychologists refer to such self-reflective thinking as *metacognition*—thinking about thinking. Saloman and Globerson (1987) characterize the employment of effortful, metacognitively guided processes as a state of mindfulness. Writing a text is a prime example of behavior that demands mindfulness and effortful engagement. Halliday (1987) noted this point as a contrast to speaking: "Writing is in essence a more conscious process than speaking . . . spontaneous discourse is usually spoken, self-monitored discourse is usually written" (pp. 67–69). To be sure, writing tasks vary in their difficulty, and writers may well aim to minimize the degree of effort invested in a given task. But generally, writing anything but the most routine and brief pieces is the mental equivalent of digging ditches.

An interesting comparison of the cognitive effort required by writing tasks and other common laboratory tasks is shown in Figure 1.1 (see Kellogg, 1986b, for details). The scale of cognitive effort of each task was indexed by using interference with secondary-task reaction times. The writer listened for a brief tone generated by

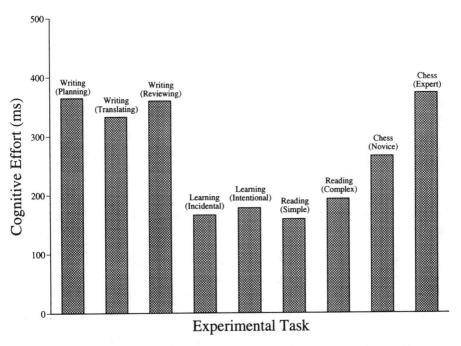

FIGURE 1.1. Cognitive effort for writing and other cognitive operations as indexed by interference with secondary-task reaction time in milliseconds. I borrowed the reading and chess data from Britton's research (Britton, Glynn, Meyer, and Penland, 1982; Britton & Tessor, 1982). All other data are mine. (From Kellogg, 1986b. Copyright © 1986 by the Psychonomic Society, Inc. Reprinted by permission.)

a computer at random times while engaged in the primary task of composing a text. The time in milliseconds required to detect the tone is determined for each planning, translating, and reviewing (collecting was not examined in the experiment). The details of this methodology will be covered later. For now, the point is that the writing operations of planning ideas, translating ideas into text, and reviewing ideas and text consume far more cognitive effort than operations invoked by incidental learning, intentional learning, reading syntactically simple text, or reading complex text. The engagement of novices and experts evaluating moves in the middle stages of a chess game is substantial. But remarkably, the levels of effort measured in undergraduates for fairly simple writing tasks are matched only by those seen among expert chess players engrossed in move selection.

Knowledge Representation and Creativity

The Nature of Schemata

Personal symbols, such as my mental images of a lawn, a tree, and a robin, and consensual symbols, such as the words *lawn, tree,* and *robin,* both refer to world knowledge. The symbol points to what one knows about objects, events, beliefs, and states of the world. What one knows has been described variously in terms of concepts, schemata, schemes, scripts, and frames. Here I adopt *schemata* as a superordinate term that encompasses several specific knowledge representations.

Definitions.   A *schema* is a mental representation of a type of object or event that describes only the general characteristics that define the type; the details of the specific tokens of the type in question are irrelevant and are identified as variables in the schema that assume different values (Stillings, Feinstein, Garfield, Rissland, Rosenbaum, Weisler, & Baker-Ward, 1987). Schemata for lawns, trees, and robins, for example, allow for considerable variations in the individual tokens or examples that fit the general idea. This standard definition must be broadened to encompass more than simply knowledge of physical objects and events. Knowledge of mathematical ideas (e.g., the square root of -1), philosophical beliefs (e.g., free will), and psychological states (e.g., depressive thoughts) illustrate schemata of a nonphysical nature.

Schemata play a major explanatory role in understanding perception, speech comprehension, reading, remembering, learning, and reasoning (Rumelhart, 1980). An early analysis of schemes or schemata came from Bartlett (1932), who defined the idea as follows:

"Schema" refers to an active organization of past reactions, or of past experiences, which must always be supposed to be operating in any well-adapted organic response. That is, whenever there is any order or regularity of behaviour, a particular response is possible only because it is related to other similar responses which have been serially organized, yet which operate, not simply as individual members coming one after another, but as a unitary mass. . . . All incoming impulses of a certain kind, or mode, go together to build up an active, organised setting. (p. 201)

Chafe (1990, p. 80) noted that schemata are "prepackaged expectations and ways of interpreting" that are supplied to a thinker largely through culture. He continued: "Religions, ideologies, systems of education—all provide us with ready-made models we can use for dealing with new experiences" (p. 81). Culture provides us with schemata through learning. We learn by doing, observing, and communicating. Much of formal education consists of learning through oral and written communication enabled by consensual symbol systems. The personal symbols associated with a schema are shaped by the way we learn it. We may all use the word *cow* in consensual communication, but the personal images evoked by that term include the smell of a cow in a barn or the feel of milking a cow only for those with real experience with a cow.

It is useful to think of a schema as generating personal and consensual symbols that refer to properties of the knowledge representation. The schema represents more than any one symbol can convey. From my schema for birds, I can generate many images and associations, albeit the image—robin—and the association—can fly— may come to mind most readily. The schema, then, may be viewed as tacit knowledge that becomes explicit or conscious knowledge only through the generation of personal and consensual symbols. The schema is an unconscious procedure for generating the personal symbols of mental activity, such as perceiving, remembering, imagining, and thinking. It also generates the consensual symbols of communicative activity, such as writing and speaking.

Common Properties.   Before distinguishing each type of schema, the common properties that apply to all schemata require comment. For one, a schema summarizes or represents numerous objects, events, or ideas that differ in one or more ways. The schema groups these and allows the mind to treat them as functionally the same. For example, there is a dizzying number and range of examples that fit one's schema for bird. The variety of birds in the Amazon river basin of South America alone challenges any cognitive structure that promises to represent them adequately. As Attneave (1957) explained, the schema for bird includes information about the dimensions along which birds differ from one another (e.g., size, color, shape of wings). It also includes information about the range of values on these dimensions and the values that occur frequently (e.g., how big can a bird get, and what is the typical or average size of a bird?).

Most, though not all, schemata have fuzzy or flexible boundaries (Rosch, 1973). From the typical instance of a schema—the prototype—there is a gradient of membership. At least for residents of North America, the robin assumes the role of prototype. The turkey lies far out on the gradient from the prototype, and the penguin almost falls off the gradient altogether.

Moreover, a schema is coherent in that it relates well to other schemata; it is embedded in and consistent with people's background knowledge or naive theories about the world (Murphy & Medin, 1985). For example, a person's knowledge of and intuitions about biology dovetail with the bird schema. If one believes that birds breathe, eat, and reproduce, then these abstract theoretical constraints would lead one to reject a robotic robin as not really being a robin. It may look and act exactly like a robin, but if the person knows it is not a biological organism, then it fails to fit the schema. In other words, similarity in perceptual and functional properties provides only a surface-level means of organizing categories. A deep, theory-based level also constrains categorization.

Schemata may be organized hierarchically in some cases. The hierarchy of subordinate (robin), basic (bird), and superordinate (animal) categories is one example (Rosch, Mervis, Gray, Johnson, & Boyes-Braem, 1976). The basic level of categorization—the middle level of the hierarchy—is learned earlier by children and allows a more rapid response in tasks that require people to name the category to which a stimulus object belongs. But such a hierarchy should not lead one to view schemata as static structures of the mind. Bartlett's (1932) original characterization of schema theory argued against the fixed structures of associationist theories in favor of a more fluid, active, and functional form of mental representation (Iran-Nejad & Ortony, 1984).

This fluidity can be seen in Tanaka and Taylor's (1991) evidence that normally subordinate levels of categorization assume the role of basic-level categories for experts in the domain in question (e.g., an ornithologist uses robin as a basic-level concept). Similarly, event concepts that focus on human actions show psychological effects predicted by the assumption that they are organized as subordinate (horror movie), superordinate (entertainment), and basic-level structures (movie). Yet these event taxonomies are certainly not stable because human actions are so multifaceted and flexible (Morris & Murphy, 1990). That people can create a category in an ad hoc manner to fit the needs of the moment illustrates the dynamic and flexible nature of schemata especially well (Barsalou, 1983). People can generate examples of "things to take on a picnic" or "ways to retrieve the keys you just locked in your car"; such categories are surely not stable structures just waiting to be activated in the mind. A schema, then, ought best to be viewed as a dynamic, living structure that continually accommodates new experiences and goals.

Types of Schemata.   *Frames* are schemata that represent the physical structure of the environment. Minsky (1977) proposed this term in his seminal paper on the perception of complex visual scenes such as a room. Besides aiding perception, frames are clearly critical in generating mental maps and other forms of remembering and imagining. The essence of a frame is a detailed structural description, which specifies the features and relations among features that define the physical setting.

Scripts are schemata that represent routine activities. They are always sequential and often involve social interactions. Schank and Abelson (1977) described the restaurant script to illustrate this class. Each script specifies a theme (eating in a restaurant), typical roles (customer and waiter), entry conditions (hungry customer), and a sequence of scenes and actions within scenes (ordering, which involves getting a menu, reading a menu, and so on).

All other types of schemata are generally referred to as *concepts* or *categories*. Two major branches of concepts are identity and equivalence categories (Bruner et al., 1956). *Identity* involves categorization of different forms of the same thing. For example, an identity schema allows one to identify an individual across a life span of changes in appearance due to aging. The self-schema is another example, and one that has been the subject of extensive research in social psychology (e.g., Markus & Wurf, 1987).

Equivalence classes, in which different stimuli evoke a common response, include four types. *Formal* or *rule-governed concepts* specify the features and relations that define membership in the class on an all-or-none basis (Bourne, 1966; Bruner et al., 1956). The definitions of real numbers, gravity, and murder can be specified formally. Such formal concepts lie at the heart of mathematics, science, law, and other disciplines of human thought. Only these abstract creations of the human mind fail to show the fuzzy boundary characteristic of other schemata, though it appears that at least some types of formal concepts show gradients of membership within the rule-governed boundaries (Bourne, 1982).

Natural concepts represent objects and events in the real world. They are characterized by structures based on family resemblances, in which no set of features and relations comprise a sharp category boundary (Rosch & Mervis, 1975). Natural concepts are typically symbolized by a mental image, both for concrete natural entities (e.g., bird–robin) and for abstract human creations (e.g., freedom–American flag).

Ad hoc or *functional concepts* are groupings of objects and events that satisfy a specific task requirement (Barsalou, 1983; Bruner et al., 1956). For example, "things to take on a picnic" or "things for killing that huge spider in the corner" are ad hoc concepts. These are generated on the spot to meet some need.

Finally, *affective concepts* group together stimuli that evoke a common emotional response. Bruner et al. (1956, p. 4) noted that a "group of people, books, weather of a certain kind are all grouped together as 'alike' " and that what "holds them together and what leads one to say that some new experience 'reminds one of such and such weather, people, states' is the evocation of a defining affective response." Affective concepts figure prominently in human development from the preverbal stages of very early childhood to the literature, especially poetry, of adulthood.

Creating and Remembering

The central point to emphasize about schemata is the flexibility they afford human behavior. If knowledge representations are static and rigid, then a thinker who acts on the basis of them gains little over behaving in a rote, stimulus–response fashion. The creative, meaning-making nature of *Homo symbolificus* depends very much on our use of such dynamic forms of knowledge representation. What we know must be continually updated and then stretched to find application in the unique problem that faces us at the moment.

Indeed, all human activities can be viewed as creative if one begins with the observation that a person never perceives or responds in precisely the same way twice (Weisberg, 1986). If an exact match between the current situation and what one knows never takes place, then creativity is always demanded. Ordinary adaptation to constantly changing circumstances requires creativity.

Yet, in an important sense, remembering cannot be disengaged from creating.

The two feed on each other. Creating feeds on memory in that it depends on the availability and retrieval of knowledge stored in the form of schemata. Remembering feeds on creativity in that it depends on the inventive modification of schemata to meet the demands of the present. Every act of creating relies to a degree on memory; in turn, every act of remembering relies to a degree on creativity.

The importance of creativity in memory has been tacitly recognized as fundamental to our understanding of learning and memory at least since the time of Bartlett (1932). He showed, through his research on the recall of prose, how an individual inventively alters original events to conform to schema-based expectations. What is stored in memory represents a creative transformation of the original experience. Furthermore, what is retrieved represents yet another creative transformation, as schemata guide recall in an active process of construction.

Much less well recognized is the importance of remembering in creativity. The literature on creativity has emphasized the departure from old ways of thinking, the novelty of original ideas. Yet, without drawing on past knowledge, without relating new ideas to old ideas, creativity fails. Creativity occurs in the context of knowledge, not in a vacuum. It uses insights of the past as a springboard for new insights.

The degree to which schemata must be flexibly shaped and stretched to find use in the writing problem at hand varies markedly. In some cases, activated schemata can assimilate a problem of what to say or how to say it without modification because the same problem (for all practical purposes) has arisen in the past. The solution to the problem is simply retrieved and applied. For example, a writer may retrieve a learned definition of a concept and use it verbatim in a text. More likely, however, the problem facing the writer requires at least some degree of accommodation of schemata. The writer's knowledge representations must be modified in greater or lesser degrees to be applied to the unique features of the task at hand. Rumelhart and Norman (1978) distinguish three forms of accommodation in the context of learning theory. These forms capture the heart of the matter in writing as well (see Reed, Burton, & Kelly, 1985).

Schemata can be altered in a variety of ways. *Tuning* refers to slight adjustments in schemata that are made on a temporary basis to solve a transient problem. The schemata metaphorically stretch and shape themselves to solve the problem. Returning to the definition example, a writer who paraphrases a previously memorized definition of a concept to fit the precise needs of the text being composed at the moment uses tuning. The tuning of schemata represents an enormously powerful tool for applying what a writer knows in creative ways. It illustrates nicely the flexibility of schemata in meeting ever-changing and unique needs in writing tasks.

But temporary changes in schemata are only one form of accommodation. Existing knowledge structures may be modified gradually and permanently in the face of writing challenges as well. *Accretion* refers to a small but significant change to a schema in response to a writing problem. Over time writers learn new facts, new ideas, and new ways of expressing a concept. Writers' knowledge representations slowly but surely grow in size and complexity throughout all their interactions with the environment, including practice at writing. The writer who encounters and permanently stores in memory a secondary meaning of a term or perhaps a new example of a concept in the course of writing an essay shows accretion.

Finally, a permanent change in schemata may be abrupt and massive, not cumulative and small. A sudden insight can prompt a major *reorganization* of existing knowledge structures. Through learning and reflection the knowledge structures of writers change in size and complexity, not only through accretion but through dramatic restructuring as well. Suppose that a writer encounters a fuzzy example of a concept that does not quite fit existing knowledge representations. Upon reflection, she may creatively see a way to reorganize the structures of several concepts in order to accommodate the new example.

Schemata, then, should be viewed as ideal knowledge representations for the creative enterprises of making meaning. They serve the writer dynamically and flexibly through lively adaptations in the form of tuning, accretion, and reorganization. The bustle of their activity is nicely captured in the following vivid portrait of schemata and the creative imagination painted by Lipman (1991):

> Schemata, as dynamic cognitive structures, react sensitively to the addition or subtraction of an element, in that all the other elements readjust and realign themselves when the change is made. Moreover, they respond holistically to their own internal shifts and alterations. We can therefore conceive of an individual mind as containing countless such schemata, some moribund, some stirring sleepily, and some seething with activity—even though none of this is in the field of awareness. For example, it may be that during sleep many of these schemata are as busy as factories, each churning out vast amounts of novel images and ideas, not for immediate use, perhaps, but to be retained for eventual use—in dreams or in art or in the formation of hypotheses or in any of an endless number of applications . . . it is not our funded experience alone that we bring to bear upon new perceptions or thoughts, but this superfund derived both from past experience and ongoing imaginative activity. (p. 202)

Overview

To conclude this opening chapter, the schemata or knowledge representations revealed by cognitive research are well tailored for the creative endeavors of *Homo symbolificus*. I have suggested that cognitive research on thinking has much to offer the study of meaning-making in general and writing in particular. At the same time, the study of written composition broadens the cognitive psychology of thinking and language.

The next two chapters develop a theoretical framework. First, in Chapter 2, I present the components of writing skill, such as planning, attention, and memory. Then I turn to the manner in which writers interact with their environment—ranging from the physical dimensions to the cultural dimensions—in the creation of a text. Finally, I discuss the constructive and narrative aspects of symbol creation and manipulation.

In Chapter 3 I examine the intellectual resources and constraints brought into play in the act of writing. These include the writer's knowledge, methods of using knowledge, and personal qualities that give individual character to the expression of knowledge. The writing process is plastic in that it changes shape, depending on complex interactions among intellectual resources and constraints. These variations do not necessarily affect how well a writer thinks and communicates, however. Writing performance theoretically depends solely on the usage of knowledge. Fluent, effective writing emerges when knowledge of many types is available, accessible, and applied inventively.

Chapters 2 and 3, then, provide a theoretical framework for reviewing and integrating the composition literature. I do not provide an exhaustive review, for the literature is too large and growing too rapidly. Rather, I select representative studies to give the reader an understanding of the factors that affect how one writes and how well one writes. Chapter 4 covers work on what a writer knows and how his or her knowledge affects the process of writing and writing performance. Chapter 5 summarizes personal qualities that modulate writing performance, such as intelligence and motivation. Chapter 6 addresses a key aspect of method—namely, strategies for retrieving and applying relevant knowledge to the task at hand. Chapter 7 addresses the tools used by writers, with a focus on the word processor. Chapter 8 expands the discussion of tools to encompass idea processors or computer systems designed to boost a writer's use of relevant knowledge. Chapter 9 completes the method review with a discussion of work schedules, rituals, and the role of one's environment in writing performance.

Chapter 10 brings together the key themes of this book and briefly considers their applications. I conclude by attempting to find a place for the creator of symbols in a world of intelligent creatures and devices. Speculations about human, animal, and artificial intelligence bring the book to a close.

2

An Analysis of Meaning-Making

Writing and rewriting are a constant search for what one is saying.

JOHN UPDIKE

Appearing in collections of interviews with well-known writers (e.g., Cowley, 1959; Plimpton, 1984, 1989) is a motif of active construction. The process of making meaning is not typically a neat and tidy matter of retrieving prefabricated personal symbols from long-term memory and then translating these into the consensual symbols of written text. Instead, more often the process is a struggle to generate and shape ideas, with the translation from the personal realm of thought to the public realm of text spurring further invention and insight on the part of the writer (Murray, 1982). As E. M. Forster wrote through a character in a novel: ''How do I know what I think until I see what I say?''

This chapter presents three ideas that are indispensable in understanding writing. These ideas integrate issues and concerns that have received more or less attention in the various disciplines of the humanities, social sciences, and education. Although the ideas are diverse, I aim to show that all three are at home in a cognitive psychological framework. I regard them as necessary elements of any theory that explains the human process of creating meaning. After reviewing these ideas, I proceed in the following chapter to link the nature of the writing process with measures of writing performance.

I begin with the idea that complex cognitive activities can be understood in terms of the interaction of simpler component processes that are hierarchically organized. This is a common assumption of cognitive theories, and it accomplishes much in the domain of writing. Writing and other meaning-making activities depend on the component processes of collecting knowledge, planning ideas, translating ideas into text or other consensual symbols, and reviewing ideas and text. Next, I turn to the cyclical interactions between writers and their environment. That cognition is situated in the environment, including its social and cultural aspects, is central to recent work in education and psychology. Effective writing depends on numerous cycles of learning, composing, and reflecting on both what one has learned and what one has written. I conclude with a look at the constructive and narrative properties of conscious thinking, drawing from research in both psychology and the humanities. I examine the hypothesis that the personal symbols of consciousness are organized by a narrative system. The constructive narrator drives the human mind in a continual process of finding meaning in everyday experience.

Components of Writing Skill

Writing Processes

Phase versus Process.   Prewriting activities that precede a first draft, composing a first draft, and revising subsequent drafts are considered here as different *phases* of product development rather than as separate writing processes (Sommers, 1979). I recognize that a writer need not always move forward in a linear fashion through these phases, such as when a finished draft is completely discarded and the writer begins anew. Some writers may at times truncate the prewriting phase and begin drafting soon or immediately after taking on a writing assignment. Others may at times extend the prewriting phase and then compose a first and final draft. Prewriting, first draft, and subsequent draft phases are merely convenient markers for discussing the evolution of a document from incipient ideas to final product.

Within each phase of product development, the writer engages in numerous activities. As shown in Figure 2.1, the term *writing process* refers to collecting information, planning ideas, translating ideas into text, or reviewing ideas and text (see Hayes & Flower, 1980). These processes occur repeatedly throughout all phases of writing. Collecting and planning are certainly important features of the prewriting phase, but they can and do recur during an advanced draft of a text. Translating

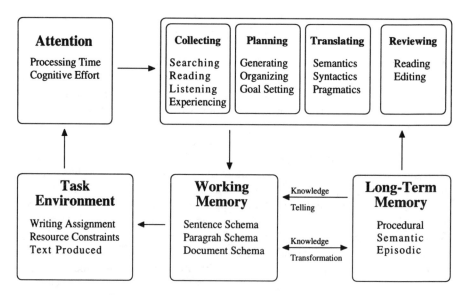

FIGURE 2.1. Cognitive components of writing skill.

ideas into sentences certainly occupies a writer's attention in composing a first draft. But translation may enter into prewriting as well, as some writers put down in their notes sentences that they come back to later in assembling a draft. Reviewing ideas and organizational plans and editing errors in drafted text dominate the multiple revisions that a document may undergo. Yet reviewing certainly can enter into the composition of a first draft and often plays a central role in the prewriting phase as a writer reviews the mental and written plans generated to date.

Collecting information involves searching bibliographic indexes, reading, source materials, and experiencing events such as hearing a lecture. Collecting requires gathering and scrutinizing consensual symbol systems and transforming the knowledge into personal symbols for subsequent use in thinking and writing. Later I will argue that the inventive use of available knowledge is a necessary condition for effective thinking and writing. The collection skills of searching, reading, listening, experiencing, and learning are, therefore, fundamental to a writer's success.

Planning involves creating and organizing ideas and setting goals to achieve during composition, such as choosing an appropriate tone for a given audience. Planning typically occurs in the mental domain of personal symbols. A writer might sit staring blankly into space, looking almost catatonic, while personal symbols are created and organized. The nature of these personal symbols can range from images and abstract ideas to trial sentences or pre-text held in the mind's eye for inspection (Flower & Hayes, 1984; Witte, 1987). Writers may also externalize their plans on paper, using consensual symbols but with the intent to communicate only with themselves, not with an audience.

For example, a writer might draw a sketch, jot down key words, or produce a handwritten outline. In these cases, planning involves consensual symbols that are more likely to be inscrutable marks than comprehensible inscriptions. That is to say, the symbols probably cannot be interpreted by most observers who examine them. Yet, regardless of how interpretable the consensual symbols used to record the writer's plans might be to others, the key point is that the symbols hold meaning for the writer alone. The writer had no intention of communicating with a reader through such notes, lists, outlines, or doodles.

Plans establish boundaries that often prove useful in translating ideas into sentences. Yet, the boundaries are fuzzy and allow for ambiguities and inconsistencies in ideas. Planning allows the writer the freedom to explore ideas in a tentative fashion, without the need to commit prematurely to a particular line of thought or style of expression. The ambiguities may be resolved later in the processes of composing sentences and revising.

Flower and Hayes (1984) noted that the products of planning fall along a continuum ranging from nonverbal imagery to textual representations that show greater linguistic content and a larger number of the formal constraints of prose. For example, text-based representations such as individual propositions, word images, and the ''gists'' of multiple related propositions come closer to actual text than the images of a daydream or a pictorial sketch of the relations among ideas. Moreover, the notes that writers might externalize for their own use in the planning process can come quite close to formal prose. In the mental realm, trial attempts to formulate sentences in the head, which Witte (1987) defined as pre-text, are obviously close to the sentences generated on paper or on a computer display. Semantic and syntactic operations come into play, which at least partially invoke the process of translating personal ideas into the public world of consensual symbols. Flower and Hayes correctly stressed that writers must recode the nonverbal representations of thinking into representations that ultimately result in standard text. The final step in this recoding invokes a complete translation of personal symbols, as the writer attempts to communicate with an audience through formal, polished prose.

Translating ideas into text refers to the syntactic, semantic, and pragmatic operations involved in sentence generation. Translation involves mapping personal symbols onto the consensual symbols of written discourse with the intention to communicate. Without translation, thinking is limited to creating and manipulating symbols in the private world of the writer. Communication occurs in the public world of culture only by dint of translation. The writer struggles to ensure that syntactic rules are followed, semantic distinctions articulated, and pragmatic considerations of discourse followed.

Finally, *reviewing* involves reading the evolving text, evaluating the text or plans for text (both written and mental), and editing errors. Reviewing provides the check on how well one has collected, planned, and translated. Reviewing involves working with personal symbols (e.g., Is this idea adequate?), consensual symbols (e.g., Is this sentence grammatical?), and their relations (e.g., Does this sentence convey my intent?). In reviewing, the writer tries to adopt the potential reader's point of view. The aim is to preview the meaning that readers will derive from the text and to match it with the writer's intentions.

A Fuzzy Process Distinction.   The separation of planning and translating borrows from research on speech production. There a distinction is drawn between planning at a preverbal, conceptual level and then translating into linguistic expression. Operations of translation—for example, lexical access and syntactic construction—occur only after planning (Bock, 1982; Schriefers, 1990). This separation, however, was challenged by Nystrand (1982, 1986, 1989) in the case of writing. He contended that resources of language actually shape the cognitive operations of planning rather than occurring after the fact (see also Smith, F., 1982).

I agree with Nystrand's unease about neatly separating planning and translating, but I disagree that the distinction is useless. Nystrand was surely correct in contending that discourse knowledge shapes the planning process. Planning can often proceed by way of inner speech. We privately narrate in the form of inner speech about past, present, and future experiences. Vygotsky (1962) emphasized that speech and thought converge in the course of cognitive development, despite their separate roots in early development.

Certainly, the pre-text discussed by Witte (1987) demonstrates that a planning operation in the mental realm can call into play the semantic and syntactic operations of translation. Note, though, that the pragmatic concerns of shaping the text for a particular audience are not crucial in pre-text, nor must the writer slavishly follow the semantic and syntactic conventions of formal prose. As Witte noted: "Pre-texts are, in short, 'the last cheap gas' before writers commit themselves to extended written text" (p. 398). The production of a written text, then, demands translation in its fullest sense of shaping personal symbols into a consensual symbol system that carries meaning for others.

Admittedly, some types of apparently externalized plans are difficult to distinguish from the products of translation. After all, if the writer uses consensual symbols as opposed to some idiosyncratic means of putting thoughts on paper, then one must consider whether the product has undergone translation. At one extreme, a writer may create notes in the form of full sentences that later find their way almost verbatim into the final document. Such notes clearly are the product of translation. At the other extreme, the writer may draw doodles, vague diagrams, or highly personal, cryptic notes that clearly reflect planning operations—but they communicate something only to their creator. John-Steiner (1985) provided several interesting examples of such cryptic, externalized plans. The cited diagrams of Darwin used in developing *The Origin of Species* and the notes of Virginia Woolf used in developing a work of fiction can be scrutinized by others, but they fail to communicate much, if anything. Between these two extremes lie cases that could arguably be viewed as products of planning or translation. The voluminous laboratory notes of Thomas Edison provide many examples of clear-cut external plans, translated sentences, and cases that fall on the fuzzy boundary between planning and translating (Rosenberg, Israel, Nier, & Andrews, 1991).

The Case for a Distinction.   Despite the difficult fuzzy cases of pre-text and externalized plans that include phrases and sentences, I still maintain that the distinction between planning and translating is worth drawing. To begin, despite Vygotsky's emphasis on the role of inner speech in thinking, he made it clear that inner speech is very different from external speech. Inner speech takes a highly abbreviated form comprised mostly of predicates and freed from the syntactic and semantic constraints of external speech; it is personal speech that need be intelligible only to its creator. To quote Vygotsky (1962):

> Inner speech is not the interior aspect of external speech—it is a function in itself. It still remains speech, i.e. thought connected with words. But while in external speech thought is embodied in words, in inner speech words die as they bring forth thought. Inner speech is to a large extent thinking in pure word meanings. It is a dynamic, shifting, unstable thing, fluttering between word and thought. (p. 149)

Moreover, the emphasis Nystrand placed on the linguistic nature of planning overlooked the other forms that planning can take. It is possible to plan visually, with little if any verbal content (Arnheim, 1986; Weiskrantz, 1988). At least for some individuals, such visual thinking can occur in states of focused attention, as well as during daydreams and dreams in both children and adults. Indeed, John-Steiner (1985) documented the centrality of purely visual planning in artistic and scientific creativity, including the well-known example of Einstein using visualization in formulating the theory of relativity. Gardner (1983) contended that thinking through visual symbols of the mind is a system of intelligence completely independent of verbal thinking.

Finally, schemata representing forms of knowledge other than discourse knowledge shape planning. For example, knowledge of the domain about which one is writing also shapes the planning process. The number and sophistication of ideas that one can generate are plainly constrained by what one knows about the topic. Thus, discourse knowledge is not privileged in its role of shaping how a writer plans.

The distinction between planning and translating, though fuzzy, retains value for one overarching reason: It highlights the gulf between personal and consensual symbol systems—between thinking privately, on the one hand, and communicating publicly, on the other. In order to communicate thoughts, images, and other personal experiences, one must transform them into consensual systems that may be heard or seen by others and interpreted.

The process of generating a sentence is invoked by an intention to communicate in a social context. That is not the case when one is merely thinking about ideas or about ways to organize them. Translation is the conversion of thoughts into well-formed ''strings'' that convey meaning to others. The syntactic, semantic, and pragmatic requirements of these strings differ, depending on whether the message is spoken or written. But in either case, the intention is to communicate through publicly shared symbols.

The planning–translation distinction is also useful in characterizing different strategies used by writers. As we see in Chapter 6, the approach that writers take to compose first drafts varies. Some plan, translate, and review in rapid sequence or perhaps simultaneously in an effort to generate a highly polished draft. Others forgo reviewing altogether when composing their first draft. In the absence of theoretical distinctions among processes, the diversity in strategies would go undescribed.

Behavioral and Emotional Components

Brown, McDonald, Brown, and Carr (1988) partitioned discourse production into three major sets of components: formulation of discourse, overt behavioral output, and monitoring of output. The components shown in Figure 2.1 elucidate the cognitive skills involved in the formulation of discourse and the monitoring of output in the sense of reading and editing for syntactic, semantic, and pragmatic problems. The reviewing process could also be invoked to monitor output in other ways, such as checking for adequate legibility of handwriting or maintaining a high rate of typing speed. Figure 2.1 omits, however, the behavioral components noted by Brown et al. (1988) and the affective components that must enter the picture. I take up the role of emotion in Chapters 3 and 5. Behavioral components, on the other hand, receive much less attention, and the reason for this deserves comment at this point.

The chief behavioral components in writing involve the sensorimotor systems that mediate handwriting, typing, speaking, and dictating. Gould (1980) distinguished speaking, in which the writer composes a message that will be listened to, from dictating, in which the writer composes a message that will be read. Besides these primary behaviors, there are numerous other secondary activities involved in writing. For example, collecting information requires a wide range of behaviors that are implicated in finding materials in a library, searching a computer data base, or taking notes on a lecture. Although typing and handwriting play a role in these behaviors, other sensorimotor skills such as walking, reaching, grasping, looking, and listening are just as important. Planning and, to a lesser degree, collecting, translating, and even reviewing can take place during any possible human activity. Long walks, jogging, taking a shower, and other activities that allow attention to be focused completely on, say, planning are common examples. This range of behaviors suggests that an accounting of them is better left to a book on sensorimotor control than to a book on writing.

Another reason for my decision to skirt a full consideration of behavioral components comes from the findings reported by Brown et al. (1988). They examined the allocation of attention to discourse formulation, behavioral execution, and monitoring during handwriting. They studied writers transcribing paragraphs with instructions to stress speed or legibility, in some cases with a concurrent demand to perform a listening task. They also examined either transcription of a perceived text or reproduction of a text recalled from memory after varying amounts of study, again either with or without a concurrent listening task. The text was much less available to the participant when it was necessary to recall it from memory after only a brief period of study compared to transcription of a text available for reading. Measurements of legibility, writing rate, amount of text reproduced, and spelling suggested the degree to which attentional resources are shared among formulation, execution, and monitoring. Brown et al. assumed that the stress placed on speed versus legibility manipulated aspects of execution and perhaps monitoring, whereas the transcription of available information versus reproduction from memory manipulated aspects of discourse formulation.

The results indicated that the effects of text availability and type of stress on the rate of handwriting were independent. But the effects of these variables on accuracy of performance (e.g., legibility and misspellings) were not independent. Brown et al. concluded that formulation and execution draw on a common pool of attentional resources, with formulation taking a higher priority when task demands overload the writer.

That motor execution and discourse formulation draw jointly on attentional resources is significant. It suggests that a careful analysis of how writers record their thoughts may bear fruit by lessening attentional overload. If dictation, word processing, typewriting, and writing in longhand vary in their demands, then writing performance may vary across tools, a possibility that will be examined in Chapters 7 and 8. However, it must be pointed out that transcription and reproduction of a text from memory are not the same as original composition. It may be that the attentional demands of formulating discourse in original composition dwarf those of motor execution.

That formulation has a higher priority on attentional resources than does execution, even in the transcription and reproduction tasks, justifies the focus of this book on the cognitive and affective components of writing rather than on the behavioral components. There are many interesting questions about motor control in the tasks of handwriting, typing, word processing, and dictating. But they merit examination primarily because they shed light on the fundamental issues surrounding the motoric control of behavior in general. Such issues lie outside the scope of this book.

Attention

Collecting, planning, translating, and reviewing depend on the retrieval of relevant information and skills from long-term memory and, in some cases, from external memory sources. The writer's knowledge must be brought to bear on the task. The writer achieves this by allocating limited attentional resources to each process. A central assumption of cognitive psychology is that a person's ability to attend to multiple sensory inputs, mental processes, and motor outputs is limited. Both time and cognitive effort must be allocated to a mental process unless it can operate automatically, independent of the limitations of attention.

Processing time is the amount of time spent attending to a particular process. *Cognitive effort* is the degree of available attentional capacity that is momentarily allocated to the process. They need not covary. For example, I have found that, at least in certain writing tasks, translating demands the most processing time but the least cognitive effort (Kellogg, 1987a). Generating sentences appears time-consuming, but it can proceed in a more automatic manner compared with planning and reviewing.

Task Environment

The task environment shapes the allocation of attention. It includes the intended audience, the writing assignment that specifies the topic, the reason for writing, and the rewards and punishments associated with doing a good or poor job. It also includes the resource constraints, such as the number of collaborators, the amount of time before the deadline, and the availability of secretarial assistance and computer-based aids for writing. Finally, the task environment includes the plans and text that the writer has already produced on an assignment; further allocations of attention to the task depend in part on how much text has been produced and how well. Writers read the text produced thus far, for example, and its style and content then constrain what they will add next (Kaufer, Hayes, & Flower, 1986).

Memory

The structure of long-term memory presumably includes procedural, semantic, and episodic knowledge (Tulving, 1985). Writing clearly involves numerous procedures, ranging from high-level planning to the muscular movements of handwriting or typing. Semantic knowledge is essential not only in the production of language but also in the realms of thinking, symbol creation, and symbol manipulation. Finally, episodic knowledge is the immediate product of all collecting operations and forms a reservoir of vignettes that find their way into written expression. All three types of knowledge must be represented in an adequate theory of writing; the issue of whether they comprise truly separate memory stores falls outside my concerns here.

Collecting, planning, translating, and reviewing can be viewed as procedural skills that are part of long-term memory. All knowledge available to the writer about the topic, the prospective audience, and the language are also stored as schemata in long-term memory. Clearly, individuals differ in the amount of knowledge available and in how well they retrieve and maintain it in working memory. For instance, sentence generation and reviewing should proceed more smoothly for a writer who is high in verbal ability than for one who is low. Similarly, generating ideas should be most fruitful for the knowledgeable and creative writer.

Working memory holds material recently attended to and provides a work space for thinking, learning, and remembering (Baddeley, 1986). The knowledge retrieved through collecting, planning, translating, and reviewing must be held temporarily for further manipulations. For instance, in translating an idea into a sentence, the subject must be held in working memory in a sentence schema while the predicate is constructed. Similarly, a paragraph schema must be maintained as supporting sentences are added to a topic sentence. In planning, a writer might maintain a mental document schema or outline of the entire document in working memory. In Chapter 6, I return to this document-level schema in considering the effects of prewriting strategies.

In contrast to long-term memory, working or short-term memory is severely limited in the number of words, phrases, or "chunks" of material that it can hold simultaneously (Baddeley, 1986). With space for only five to nine chunks, the component of working memory serves as a limitation as well as a resource to writers. Britton, Burgess, Martin, McLeod, and Rosen (1975) noted that the skill of writers and the demands placed upon them by particular tasks relate directly to what they hold in this memory component:

> What has just been written, and what is still to be written, can only be held there to a very limited extent. For someone just learning to write, the number of words in the short-term memory may be even fewer, for he often needs to have letters there as separate items. The fluent writer, however, can hold not only whole words and phrases, but meanings as well, and possibly general intentions (which can scarcely be thought of as items), so that it is much easier for what is written to have coherence. If, on the other hand, the teasing out of the thought becomes particularly difficult, all the resources of short-term memory may have to be concentrated on a few words. That is when a writer may lose the track of his thoughts, omit or repeat words, misconnect or blunder in some way. (p. 45)

Knowledge-Transforming

Bereiter and Scardamalia (1987) described a knowledge-transforming model of adult writers that characterizes the construction assumed to occur in working memory. It includes a knowledge-telling component in which the writer retrieves content from memory, tests its appropriateness to the topic and type of composition, and then generates a sentence. The authors distinguished between *content knowledge,* which is knowledge about the specific domain being written about, and *discourse knowledge,* which is linguistic knowledge applicable to any topic. These forms of knowledge, plus a mental representation of the writing assignment, are resources and constraints on the knowledge-telling process. Once the writer identifies the topic and genre, he or she searches long-term memory for relevant information and then constructs sentences expressing the information. This search-and-then-translate or think-

and-then-say procedure is repeated until the writer cannot think of any more appropriate ideas.

Bereiter and Scardamalia viewed writing as an act of problem solving. Specifically, the writer must explore options and decide on solutions as to what to say and how to say it. The possibilities and mental steps taken in exploring these possibilities constitute what cognitive theorists metaphorically call a problem space. Bereiter and Scardamalia identified two such problem spaces, one for matters of content and one for matters of rhetoric. As part of planning, the writer actively sets goals for the composition, goals both of content and of rhetoric. Problems of belief and knowledge are solved in the content space, and problems of achieving the goals set for the composition are solved in the rhetorical problem space. Interactions between these problem spaces comprise reflective thought in writing as the writer struggles in working memory with what to say and how to say it. These interactions result in extensive changes in both the content and rhetorical problem spaces. The act of writing is one of intense reflective thought that transforms both what the writer wants to say and how he or she chooses to say it. Knowledge is thus transformed as a result of reflective thought while writing. The writer's thoughts can progress from inchoate glimmers to focused beams.

Bereiter and Scardamalia (1987) devote much of their book to documenting the developmental progression from writing as purely knowledge-telling to writing as primarily knowledge-transforming. They offer convincing evidence that children and other novice writers are limited to knowledge-telling. Talented young students, college students, graduate students, or "people at advanced levels in any intellectual discipline" engage in knowledge-transforming. Bereiter and Scardamalia perceive a continuous shift from knowledge-telling to knowledge-transforming with development in writing skill. The cyclical relations among reflecting, writing, and learning are fundamental to the making of meaning as we shall see.

The Cycle of Cognition

Knowledge transformation in writing, as described by Bereiter and Scardamalia (1987), illustrates a more general feature of cognition: the cyclical nature of perceiving, learning, and thinking. Neisser (1976) proposed a cycle of perception to explain the role of exploration and anticipatory schemata in picking up information about objects and events in the environment (Figure 2.2). *Perception* refers to a cycle of interaction among mental schemata, overt exploratory behavior, and information available in the environment.

Schemata direct exploration of the environment by anticipating certain kinds of information and then seeking that information. The exploratory behavior, in the form of eye, hand, and other body movements, samples the available information about objects and events in the environment. The informational cues picked up from the environment may, in turn, modify the schemata, changing future anticipations. The Piagetian notion of *accommodation* refers to cases in which the information picked up modifies the schemata that initiated the exploration. *Assimilation* refers to cases

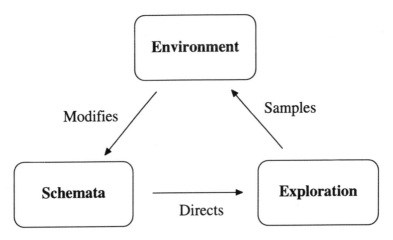

FIGURE 2.2. The cycle of cognition. (Adapted from Neisser, 1976.)

in which the sampled information confirms the original expectations or is forced to fit those expectations.

Neisser (1976, p. 66) doubted that much is gained by modifying the information rather than the schema. He theorizes that only schemata modifications make much sense from the standpoint of achieving accurate perceptions of the environment and developing cognitive abilities. I share his doubts but retain the use of the term *assimilation* to identify cases in which original expectations are confirmed sufficiently to render modifications unnecessary. I view assimilation as a theoretical ideal endpoint of a continuum ranging from no modifications to radical modifications of schemata.

Neisser's cycle addressed the physical aspects of perceiving objects and events. Its scope can be readily broadened, I believe, to include the social and cultural aspects of perception, as well as thinking and other forms of cognition. The environment from which an individual samples information includes the task, social, and cultural environments, as well as the physical environment. For example, in attending a party, we not only perceive the physical objects and events, but we also generate expectations about what we will do at the party, who will be talking amicably with whom, and what time we should gracefully exit.

Furthermore, some of the objects and events of the multifaceted environment include consensual symbol systems, such as written and spoken language. For example, a reader may sample from a text to modify schemata in the process of learning a discipline. Of critical importance here, a writer may sample from his or her own draft of a text to modify the ideas that generated the text in the first place.

Schemata construct anticipations about the physical, social, cultural, and task environments. These anticipations direct exploration of the environment, at all of its levels, in an effort to sample information. The extracted information may then modify the schemata if the knowledge structures must accommodate to the situation. *Assimilation,* as I am using the term, means that the sampled information confirms the expectations generated by the schemata driving the cycle. Perceiving and think-ing proceed through a cycle of interaction among mental schemata, exploratory behavior, and the environment.

For example, part of the task environment includes the rhetorical and content problems posed by a writing assignment. Schemata representing discourse and con-tent knowledge generate expectations that the writer uses to guide exploration of the problems at hand. Exploration involves sampling information about, say, the prob-lem of how to organize a section of text. The anticipatory schemata either assimilate the sampled information or accommodate it through modifications of varying degrees. The cycle continues as long as the writer continues to think about and modify knowledge schemata that address the organizational problem in the task at hand.

Situated Cognition

Neisser's cycle and my extension of it underscore that thinking is neither a passive nor a detached activity. Thinking involves an interaction between the person and the environment, just as perception does. Every act of thought is presumably situated in a particular context of physical, social, cultural, and task constraints.

Greeno (1989) also noted the importance of interaction between the thinker and the environment: "thinking . . . can be considered as a relation involving an agent in a situation, rather than as an activity in an individual's mind" (p. 135). He illus-trated this point with a study by Scribner (1984), who examined dairy workers filling product orders for delivery trucks. The workers filled drivers' orders for various products that came in different-sized containers. The containers, in turn, came in cases, with the number of containers per case varying across products. The workers were given a form that specified, in a special notational system, the number of cases and the number of containers that must be added or subtracted for each product. Instead of symbolically solving the problem with paper-and-pencil calculations that added items to or subtracted them from whole cases, the workers manipulated the containers themselves. They used partial cases efficiently by interacting with actual objects in the environment. Scribner contended that such active engagement with the environment achieved optimal solutions in nearly all of the situations observed.

The notion that perception and thought represent complex interactions between a person and the environment is a persistent one in cognitive psychology. Powers's (1973) elegant analysis of feedback and feedforward mechanisms in perception and behavior foreshadowed the cycle of perception advanced by Neisser (1976) and the situated cognition idea reviewed by Greeno (1989). Also, Bandura's (1978) work on reciprocal determinism in social learning theory clearly implies that all human activity is situated in an environmental context. All these ideas reinforce the view that thinking, as well as perception, occurs through cyclic interaction with the task, physical, social, and cultural environments. The process of thinking both changes the environment and is changed by the environment through feedback.

The Case of Writing

Writing and other meaning-making activities illustrate the cycle of cognition as well as, if not better than any other form of thinking. Zwilich (1985) nicely summarizes how the cycle of cognition proposed here applies to meaning-making activities in musical composition: "Inspiration engenders product which, in turn, engenders more inspiration. . . . All the written arts work this way" (p. 30).

The knowledge-transforming aspect of writing exemplifies the nature of the cognitive cycle and situated cognition. The writer is presented with a task environment consisting of a writing assignment, an audience, a deadline for completion, and other constraints. As the writer begins to think about the task, the need to collect additional information becomes clear. This prompts behavior designed to find the needed information, such as tapping a computer data base or searching for a book or article in the library. The information search and other forms of collecting feed back to the planning operations, resulting perhaps in an attempt to translate incipient ideas into text.

The written text, created through the typing or handwriting behavior of the author, becomes part of the task environment. The text produced at any point actively reshapes the task initially perceived by the author, and the nature of the writing problem shifts as the text develops. Thus, the writer's thinking and behavior change the physical and task environments.

But at the same time, the writer's knowledge of the topic is transformed as a consequence of having converted private thoughts into a public symbol system. Such transformation occurs even when others do not read the text and provide external feedback to the author, although the availability of such feedback from the discourse community certainly fuels the transformation process. So, the information collected as part of writing together with the text produced act to change the writer's knowledge and points of view.

The writer samples information from the social environment in particular. Schemata model the anticipated readers' attitudes, beliefs, and knowledge of the topic and language. Schemata representing the writer's rhetorical knowledge direct the exploration of the social environment and, in turn, are modified by the sampled information. Depending on how well the writer knows a particular audience and how extensively he or she explores the environment, the rhetorical schemata may be either fine-tuned to solve the problems at hand or radically reorganized.

Some task environments, particularly those involving computer networks, call for collaboration with other writers, adding yet another social element to the process (Barrett, 1989). Each collaborator's knowledge representations offer another source of information that may be explored by others. Indeed Rubin (1988) contended that virtually all writing is collaborative in nature in that writing involves conversation with others. Such conversation can be plainly seen when two people correspond with each other through letters or electronic mail. Multiple authors converse as well in the process of producing a jointly authored text. Further, conversation often serves as a source of ideas for generating or revising a text. Rubin (1988) noted that even the sole author typically discusses a piece with others, receives feedback from peer review, and benefits from the comments of a succession of editors on the way to publication.

Writing as a Social Act

The cycle of cognition, then, captures a prominent theme of the composition literature: Communication, whether written or spoken, is a social and cultural act. The social nature of writing can be seen in several ways. For one, both oral and written communication depend on an interplay between the creator of a message and the receiver if communication is to succeed (Olson, 1977). The precise form that this interaction takes differs with the medium, but some commonalities can be easily observed. For example, Grice's (1989) cooperative principle of conversation is relevant to writing as well as speaking. Readers assume that writers seek to communicate their thoughts clearly, to state all that readers need to comprehend the text but no more, and to make statements that are relevant to the topic at hand.

Another indicator of the social nature of writing is that writing performance depends to some degree on the social skills of the writer (Rubin, 1984). For example, a composite measure of social cognitive ability, which included, among other things, the ability to take the perspective of others into account, was responsible for about 35% of the variance in the quality of narratives written by fourth graders (Rubin, Piche, Michlin, & Johnson, 1984). Methodological shortcomings in such studies, as North (1987) argued, may have led to an inflated estimate of the importance of social cognitive ability. The specific measure of social cognition employed and the specific demands of the writing task certainly matter (Kroll, 1985). But the conclusion that good writers must be capable of envisioning an audience and using relevant schemata to simulate the reactions of readers to their text cannot be seriously challenged.

Moreover, the reasons for writing and the rewards for doing so are interwoven in a complex social fabric involving, in many cases, school or work settings (Odell & Goswami, 1984, 1986). The writer is always situated in a linguistic community with shared interests. The words of Frederiksen and Dominic (1981) aptly characterize writing as an act embedded in a social and cultural context:

> The context or *situation* in which a person writes can exert a strong influence on writing processes. The writer's perception and interpretation of the situation can influence the purpose for writing as well as the writer's awareness of what function the writing will serve. A particular situation can also influence how writers perceive relevant information, how they construct meaning, and how they determine the distance they want the written *voice* to have from the topic, the message and the audience. (pp. 13–14)

An important theme of the next chapter is the centrality of knowledge availability and use in writing. Maimon (1986) reminded us that the earliest uses of the term *knowledge* in written English carry the notion of acknowledgment or debt to the ideas of other thinkers: "Public utterance can become knowledge when speakers or writers understand how to acknowledge their debts to the words of others. Such acknowledgement does more than create context; it creates a shared world" (p. 89).

Moreover, discussions between writers and readers have been shown to be a fruitful source of ideas (Staton & Shuy, 1988). Not only can writing be distinguished by sorting it on the basis of its intended audience (Rafoth, 1985), but writing may be evaluated in terms of the degree to which it satisfies the needs of this audience (Odell, 1981).

Although the social nature of writing deserves emphasis, attempts to reduce writing to either a purely social process or a purely cognitive process occurring inside the head of an individual author are misguided (Carter, 1990). Witte (1992), for example, argues persuasively against such reductionism in his call for ''a culturally viable theory of writing, one that is sensitive to both the social and the cognitive and one that allows the relation between thought and language to be understood productively'' (p. 261). The cycle of cognition presented here effectively represents both points of view in a single theoretical construct and seems consistent with the general outlines of the constructivist view of writing proposed by Witte. My purpose here has been to show that concepts from cognitive psychology—the components of writing and the cycle of cognition—are fully consistent with writing theories that recognize both the functioning of an individual mind and the functioning of the social and cultural environment.

The Constructive Narrator

The components of writing skill and the cycle of cognition are two of the three essential elements of meaning-making. The third element addresses the difficult matter of how the stream of conscious thought is constructed. We have seen that knowledge representations in the form of schemata are continually active. In states of alert directed thought, undirected daydreaming, and the twisted dreams of sleep, the mind remains an active constructor of personal symbols. Moment by moment, a person perceives, reflects, imagines, and dreams. The manner in which the personal symbols of consciousness are constructed and organized is fundamental to the psychology of writing, meaning-making, and thinking.

The Constructive Nature of Consciousness

As explained in Chapter 1, schemata construct the personal symbols that comprise the stream of conscious awareness. Tacit knowledge becomes explicit through this process of construction. In the undirected thinking of dreams and daydreams, it is relatively easy to recognize the constructive aspects of consciousness. In flights of fantasy the mind ''sees'' or ''feels'' things that are not physically present. The novelist lost in a daydream about the characters in her book is clearly constructing an inner reality. In directed and recurrent forms of thinking, too, the constructive nature of schemata is certainly not obscure. For example, the essayist struggling with how to organize a concluding paragraph in the most persuasive way constructs many possible versions and evaluates in his mind or on paper the best choice.

In perception of objects and events, however, the constructive activity of schemata is often harder to see. Arguments have raged in cognitive psychology about the extent to which perception is a constructive activity. This is not the place to debate these matters. But I do think it is worthwhile to consider briefly the constructivist approach to perception as a way of making concrete the notion that schemata construct personal symbols in all forms of conscious cognition.

Let us begin with Neisser's (1976) discussion of how visual perception proceeds by way of construction using *anticipatory schemata.* The perceiver constructs anticipations about what will appear in the optical array—that is, the pattern of light reflected off objects that enters the eyes. These anticipations direct active exploration of the environment, through eye and body movements, in an effort to pick up the expected information. *Anticipatory schemata,* to use Neisser's terminology, guide this detection of information.

Neisser clearly described the constructive process, but he left out the result of the construction. He noted that ''what is constructed is not a mental image appearing in consciousness where it is admired by an inner man'' (p. 20). I disagree. The result of construction *is* a mental image, a personal symbol. But there is no need for a person to view this symbol; such a regress explains nothing. The personal symbol is the conscious experience. Neisser mistook the double identity of consensual symbols, which exist as symbols and as physical marks to be inspected, for personal symbols (Kolers & Smythe, 1984). Personal symbols exist only as mental experience, not as some medium for a person or homunculus to inspect.

That personal symbols are actively constructed by schemata can be seen in two ways. First, even when optical information about an object is fleeting, degraded by noise, or otherwise extremely impoverished, perception of the object can succeed. Findings of this sort strongly suggest that the perceptual system can construct accurate personal symbols from inadequate optical information. Shepard (1990), for example, noted that the visual system is highly adept at constructing correct perceptions of faces, cliffs, snakes, and other biologically pertinent stimuli from minimal cues.

Second, visual illusions reveal that the processes used in perception are highly constructive. Although such illusions are rare, they nonetheless reveal perceptual processes that operate in ecologically valid contexts (Shepard, 1990). For instance, the artful depth illusion rendered by Roger Shepard in Figure 2.3 illustrates the construction of what appear to be two creatures of markedly different sizes; they are in fact identical in size. Because texture gradients wrongly suggest that the upper creature is at a greater distance than the lower creature, the constant retinal image size gives rise to constructions of different consciously perceived sizes.

Another compelling feature of the constructive nature of perception and thought can be found in the same figure by Shepard (Figure 2.3). Many observers perceive terror on the face of the lower creature and anger on the upper creature. In other words, a causal connection between the two figures is easily inferred. With some reflection, one might even begin to weave a tale about the reason for the chase. Let us now discuss how the mind spins stories so readily with so little provocation.

The Narrative Structure of Consciousness

Homo symbolificus loves a good story. In fact, *Homo fabulans* may be the most accurate identifier of our species because we create, manipulate, and communicate

FIGURE 2.3. The constructive aspect of consciousness, illustrated by Roger Shepard's (1990) Terror Subterra. (From Shepard, 1990. Copyright © 1990 by W. H. Freeman and Company Publishers. Reprinted by permission.)

symbols most often by weaving them into tales (Howard, 1991). Storytelling and myth making appear in all human cultures (Campbell, 1988). From a very early age, stories captivate children. Reading a story to children or viewing a story on television with them reveals how easily their attention is held—longer than for almost any other stimulus (Howard, 1991). The classic fairy tales, whether they are read or presented in cartoons or films, convey the essential images and myths of Western culture. Bettleheim (1976) articulated how the stories of Hansel and Gretel, Cinderella, Rapunzel, and others portray the grand issues of good versus evil, love versus hate, and life versus death. Exposure to these stories, Bettleheim suggested, is critical to moral development.

Bruner (1990) reminded us that the study of narratives has a long and significant history in disciplines such as linguistics, anthropology, and philosophy, as well as literature and composition. Cognitive psychologists to date have focused on the importance of narrative schemata in reading comprehension and memory (e.g., Mandler, 1984), in the production of oral discourse (Chafe, 1990), and in the thought processes involved in reaching decisions (Pennington & Hastie, 1988). But the proposal of a constructive narrator as a fundamental element of meaning-making assumes that narration is much more central to human cognition than these cognitive theories suggest.

Specifically, a fundamental narrative system organizes the personal symbols of human consciousness. I shall refer to this system as the *narrator,* using Calvin's (1990) terminology. The narrator coordinates the entry into conscious awareness of the personal symbols generated by a multitude of schemata that are active simultaneously at a tacit, unconscious level. It constructs the contents of conscious thought by taking the personal symbols generated by active schemata and placing them in a sequential and causal pattern. Such an organizing system plainly involves multiple component processes and neural mechanisms; I refer to them collectively as the narrator.

Narrative texts have long been viewed by scholars in the humanities as analogs to conscious experience (Stanzel, 1984). The narrator of a story observes and evaluates the actions of the characters and events. This indirect form of literature contrasts with the direct form of drama, where the mediacy of the narrator is absent. In keeping with the Kantian tradition, the mind does not directly apprehend the world. It does so only through the mediacy of the personal symbols generated by schemata and organized as narrative.

From the field of psychology, Sarbin (1986) described the importance of the narrator in what he called the *narratory principle.* For him,

> human beings think, perceive, imagine, and make moral choices according to narrative structures. Present two or three pictures, or descriptive phrases, to a person and he or she will connect them to form a story, an account that relates the pictures or the meanings of the phrases in some patterned way. (p. 8)

Calvin (1990) emphasized the narrator's function as a spinner of scenarios. Gazzaniga (1985) labeled such a narrative system the *interpreter* and emphasized its function as a creator of social beliefs. Whereas Gazzaniga located the interpreter in the left, dominant hemisphere of the brain, Calvin took pains to show that no physiological center of consciousness need exist to account for the psychological center that we experience.

Though I borrow Calvin's term for simplicity, I do so with some reluctance. I fear that terms such as *interpreter* and *narrator* carry with them a homunculus. The narrative system forces a temporal sequence and causal organization on the personal symbols generated by simultaneously active and diverse schemata. The personal symbols generated by these and ordered by the narrator *are* the stream of conscious experience. They are not consensual symbols that are viewed by some little person in the head.

The term *narrative system* also carries excess baggage from the field of discourse processing. I do not equate the narrator with the detailed schemata that guide the comprehension and production of folktales, fables, short stories, novels, and other narrative forms. The cognitive structures for handling the setting, theme, plot, and resolution of conflict (Thorndyke, 1977) and the mechanisms for establishing causal chains (Trabasso & van den Broek, 1985) in the processing of narrative texts are plainly developed for specific reading and writing tasks. The narrator of consciousness, in contrast, is both more general and more rudimentary than these text structure representations.

I will return in Chapter 10 to the relationship between the narrator and the development and use of schemata for processing narrative discourse. I suggest that the narrative structure of consciousness provides the basis for children learning narrative text structures at an early age and for the *relative* ease with which narratives are written. We find extensive development of intricate narrative schemata, tuned to each unique form of storytelling encountered in the oral and textual traditions of a given culture. The narrator is not the same as these schemata, but it in theory provides the seed for their growth.

Coherence, Sequence, and Causality.   The hypothesis advanced here is that the narrator both motivates one to seek meaning and enables one to make meaning. The constant stream of thoughts, fantasies, perceptions, and memories—the personal symbols generated by a host of simultaneously active schemata—are placed in a narrative structure. The story structure inherently demands the need to make sense, to find coherence, to seek meaning. Narrative structure enables meaning-making, first, by providing a sequence of events, episodes, or experiences, and, second, by establishing causal connections among those experiences.

Stories provide a structure for making sense of life experiences. The human ability to reflect on experience carries with it a drive to weave the fragments of passing thought into a coherent whole. The narrator motivates the search for meaning and coherence by spinning scenarios and constructing tales. The evolutionary development of a rudimentary narrative system must be seen as fundamental in the biological and psychological history of our species. The characteristically human acts of meaning-making seen in storytelling, dance, art, music, and writing would not occur without the functioning of the narrator.

The narrator imposes a sequential order of events in time. At any given moment, parallel, simultaneous events occur in both the outer world of the environment and the inner world of the mind. In order to render this experience meaningful, the narrator forces a serial order on the events selected for conscious apprehension. Even though complex plots may emerge in conscious content, with juxtapositions of imagined, recalled, and presently perceived events, a sequence unfolds.

The evidence that two events never occur simultaneously in consciousness is compelling (Baars, 1988). Certainly parallel mechanisms can process multiple simultaneous sources of information and stimulation, but they do so automatically and unconsciously. Rapid attentional switching or time sharing enables a person to recognize and consciously process two channels of information presented aurally, visually, or in both auditory and visual modalities (Kahneman, 1973). Without time sharing, one of the channels registers in sensory memory and receives only unconscious, automatic processing.

Two simultaneous sensory events are either merged as a single event, perceived sequentially, or perceived selectively by ignoring one of them. It appears that the psychological moment or interval in which simultaneous events are in some fashion integrated lasts for roughly 100 milliseconds. Multiple events occurring within this integration interval of conscious attention must be fused into a single–compound event; delayed to form a sequence of first one and then another event; or masked, with one event blocking the conscious registration of another (Blumenthal, 1977).

The narrator discovers or establishes causal relations among the events that comprise the sequential stream of consciousness. The narrator seeks to establish causal connections as a way of rendering experience meaningful. And the narrator seeks to explain why events unfold as they do, providing a causal glue for holding together perceptions, memories, and fantasies about the future. The causes may or may not be veridical in the sense of bearing up to external scrutiny. What is important is that the narrator provides the individual with a story that makes sense. In the absence of a properly functioning narrator, perceptual, memorial, and imaginal events would seem random and experience meaningless.

Clinical psychologists have analyzed the importance of the stories that individuals construct about their experiences (Howard, 1991) and the idiosyncratic causal links that they establish (Beck, 1991). The studies of social psychologists, too, have documented the richness and complexity of the method by which a person attributes credit and blame for life events (Peterson & Seligman, 1984; Taylor & Brown, 1988). Attribution theory lies at the heart of social psychology (Myers, 1987); it deals in essence with the functioning of the narrator in the realm of social relations. Finally, developmental psychologists have suggested that narratives are central to the moral life and growth of children (Bettleheim, 1976; Vitz, 1990). These diverse areas of investigation point to the influence of the narrator on our psychological health and well-being.

Self-Talk and Narration.   The work of the narrator in imposing sequence and a network of causal relations often results in a linguistic running commentary on experience. Jaynes (1976) characterized this commentary well:

> Seated where I am, I am writing a book and this fact is imbedded more or less in
> the center of the story of my life, time being spatialized into a journey of my days

and years. New situations are selectively perceived as part of this ongoing story, perceptions that do not fit into it being unnoticed or at least not remembered. More important, situations are chosen which are congruent to this ongoing story, until the picture I have of myself in my life story determines how I am to act and choose in novel situations as they arise. (pp. 63–64)

Jaynes suggested that we see ourselves as the central character in the stories of our lives and build a coherent account of the causes of perceived events and reasons for our behavior. Support for this notion comes from Klinger's (1990) investigations of everyday thinking and daydreaming that reveal the nearly constant nature of self-narrating processes. Participants were interrupted in daily activities by a beeper and asked to report on their thoughts. Klinger found internal chatter 75% of the time, with 50% of the reports yielding fairly complete statements of running commentaries and 25 percent yielding at least a few words. Klinger summarized his findings as follows:

> We talk to ourselves continually, even when we seem to be quiet. Even the reputedly taciturn Scandinavian-American Minnesotans who made up a large part of our beeper sample chattered away to themselves most of the time. . . . The single most common feature of daydreams and other thoughts is self-talk. We hear an unexpected sound and say to ourselves, "What the heck was that?" We walk along appreciating the nice weather, and comment to ourselves, "What a nice day!" We play through our minds an image of a friend. We see him in our daydreams smiling and talking and we think in nearly so many words, "I wonder if he'll visit. I wonder if he really cares about me." (p. 68)

While agreeing with Jaynes's view of narratization, and while welcoming Klinger's results, I wonder about limiting narration to linguistic commentary. The personal symbols of conscious experience certainly are often linguistic in nature, particularly in reflective thought, when the mind comments to itself about various internal or external phenomena. But conscious contents include perceptual, memorial, and imaginal experiences that are coded in visual, auditory, tactile, and other nonlinguistic personal symbols. These sequences of symbols can tell a story in the same way that a silent film can convey a plot without language. To take a simple example, we can see causal relations between moving visual elements as one launches, drags, or deflects another (Michotte, 1963). Even reflective thought can proceed in a highly visual, nonlinguistic manner (Arnheim, 1986; Gardner, 1983; John-Steiner, 1985; Weiskrantz, 1988).

Jaynes preferred to classify these nonlinguistic experiences as something other than consciousness. He then proceeded to deny that consciousness is necessary for learning, reasoning, and thinking. I prefer a more inclusive view of what comprises the contents of consciousness. Not only is perception part of consciousness, but a compelling case can also be made that, in Baars's (1988) words, "perception is certainly the premier domain of detailed conscious experience" (p. 96).

Another example of highly visual narratives occurs in the undirected or recurrent thought of daydreams and dreams. The alternative state of consciousness in dreaming, in particular, yields sequences of visual, auditory, and tactile events that may or may not be accompanied by verbal commentary. The criteria for establishing causal relations relax in this state as the events unfold in sometimes bizarre and possibly incoherent ways. The narrator tries, sometimes futilely, to link events that burst into the sequence.

Seligman and Yellen (1987) suggested that a dream represents an attempt to integrate streams of personal symbols of unrelated visual images, on the one hand, and often unrelated emotional episodes, on the other. The dreamer constructively integrates the visual and emotional streams in perhaps the only manner possible, as a loosely structured, surprising story.

Summary

In conclusion, the human ability to create a meaningful world relies on at least three core ideas. The constructive narrator drives the meaning-making process in the most fundamental sense. The structure of consciousness itself is shaped by a narrative system that imposes a sequence and a coherence upon personal symbols. At an unconscious level, many schemata are active in both the waking and the sleeping mind. The personal symbols that they generate must be lined up and causally related for their appearance in the mind's eye of awareness. Without this coherence there would be no meaning at all.

The cycle of cognition accounts for the manner in which meaning is created only through interaction between a person's mind and his or her environment. Meaning-making in general and writing in particular are not merely solitary, isolated events. Writers must be engaged in their environment, in all of its facets, both social and cultural.

Finally, the components of writing and meaning-making provide a window on the cognitive processes used to think in the realm of personal symbols and to write in the realm of consensual symbols. Information processing models in cognitive psychology routinely describe the components of the task environment, attention, working memory, and long-term memory. Here we have focused on the processes that play a vital role in meaning-making activities in particular. Collecting knowledge in many forms, planning ideas, translating ideas into sentences, and reviewing ideas and text are essential components, as are the knowledge-telling and knowledge-transforming modes of using the knowledge stored in long-term memory.

3

Process and Performance

Writing is easy. All you do is stare at a blank sheet of paper until drops of blood form on your forehead.

GENE FOWLER

The previous chapter sketched some necessary elements of meaning-making and writing. This chapter develops the functional relations among the writing process, performance measures, and intellectual resources, such as the degree of available knowledge. Writing well requires concerted effort and concentration, the marshaling of many intellectual resources, and the skilled negotiation of numerous constraints.

I begin with a discussion of the three types of intellectual resources and constraints that a writer must manage. Broadly defined, these are knowledge, personality, and method. Next, I define ways of tracking the process of writing and ways of measuring writing performance in terms of quality, fluency, and productivity. I distinguish structuring and restructuring the writing process from amplifying the writing performance. Knowledge, personality, and method variables partially define the writer's task and therefore often structure the writing process. Writers attend differently to collecting, planning, translating, and reviewing to meet the specific demands of the task at hand.

How well writers perform—measured, say, in terms of the quality of the products they produce—depends on factors that directly affect the use of relevant knowledge. Knowledge must be available, accessible, and inventively applied by writers for the resulting text to attain a high level of quality. Further, writers must be motivated by the task to invest substantial attention in collecting, planning, translating, and reviewing. Although some factors both restructure the process and amplify performance, the two issues must be judged independently.

Dimensions of Intellectual Resources and Constraints

Nickerson (1981) and Perkins (1987) characterized intelligence and thinking skills in terms of three dimensions of intellectual resources. Intelligence as content or

47

knowledge refers to the role of domain-specific knowledge in thought. Studies of expert–novice differences in problem solving point to domain knowledge as a critical intellectual resource. Intelligence as methods or tactics refers to the role of strategies in retrieving and applying knowledge to a given intellectual problem. Studies of both general problem-solving strategies and heuristics situated in the context of specific domains of problem solving illustrate the method factor. Finally, intelligence as power refers to neurological fitness or "raw brain power," in Perkins's terms. The speed of encoding, pattern matching, and other basic cognitive components varies with neurological fitness. Studies of reaction time as an indicator of intelligence predate the relatively recent focus on domain knowledge and strategies for using that knowledge.

Nickerson and Perkins characterized domain knowledge, strategies, and power as three potentially independent sources of variation in intellectual functioning. Here I extend their analysis and suggest that the three are special cases of broader resource dimensions that must be addressed in a theory of writing skill. Moreover, some cases provide as much of a constraint on writing as a resource for writing.

Knowledge

What a writer knows has occupied the attention of several scholars (e.g., Faigley et al., 1985; Fredericksen & Dominic, 1981; Nystrand, 1982). Here I briefly touch on aspects of knowledge and discuss the theme in greater depth in Chapter 4. My purpose is not to reproduce what others have documented about the specific schemata possessed by writers. Instead, I aim to characterize the scope of a writer's available knowledge and then examine how his or her use of that knowledge determines the writing performance.

Applebee (1982) differentiated the writer's knowledge of topic, language, and audience. The topic of a writing task may well bring several domains of knowledge into play. An understanding of basic scripts, concepts, and frames about world knowledge serves as a cultural and disciplinary background for topic knowledge. The intended audience must also be understood by the writer. At a general level, audience knowledge reflects an understanding of the sociocultural environment in which a document is created (Rafoth & Rubin, 1988). At a more local level, the characteristics of individuals or small groups to whom a document is addressed are relevant. The age, knowledge, beliefs, attitudes, and preferences of the targeted audience have implications for how a document is written.

Alexander, Schallert, and Hare (1991) suggested a typology of knowledge that applies generally to thinkers and learners, not just to writers. I prefer their categories because the connection to the cognitive psychology of thinking, language, learning, and knowledge representation is plainer than that of Applebee's (1982) typology. Alexander et al. distinguished among conceptual, sociocultural, and metacognitive knowledge.

All thinking tasks—problem solving, reasoning, and writing—depend on knowledge embodied in concepts, frames, and scripts, and on the consensual symbol systems of language used to express such knowledge. Alexander et al. referred to all this as *conceptual knowledge. Sociocultural knowledge* is the social background or context against which we discuss and think about conceptual knowledge. A concept, particularly an abstract concept such as responsibility or freedom, means different things in different cultural contexts. The connotations vary with the culture. Thinking proceeds through a filter of *sociocultural knowledge.* Finally, *metacognitive knowledge* is the knowledge one has about what one knows. Knowledge about knowledge regulates how one approaches and accomplishes tasks.

Clearly, a writer employs conceptual, sociocultural, and metacognitive knowledge in the act of composing. Applebee's (1982) topic and language areas of knowledge represent subsets of conceptual knowledge, as discussed more fully in the next chapter. Knowledge of the audience represents a combination of conceptual knowledge, especially those aspects concerned with the pragmatics of linguistic symbol systems and sociocultural knowledge.

A long-standing distinction in philosophy and psychology is between *declarative* and *procedural knowledge:* to know X versus to know how to do X. One influential proposal in cognitive psychology further divides declarative knowledge into *episodic* and *semantic* forms (Tulving, 1985). Consider what a writer knows about typing on a word processor. He or she possesses procedural schemata that support the sensorimotor aspects of manipulating the keyboard and the cognitive aspects of knowing the software commands, for example. In addition, the writer knows the meaning of the term *word processor* and the many semantic relations it shares with *computer, typewriter,* and other concepts. Finally, the writer knows the look, feel, and other experiential qualities of the specific word processor sitting on the desk before her; each episode or personal encounter with a word processor, dated by time and place, may also be represented in memory.

The earlier distinction among conceptual, metacognitive and sociocultural knowledge involves both procedural and declarative ways of knowing. Conceptual knowledge, for instance, draws upon procedural, semantic, and episodic memories. To write an essay about word processors, one must draw upon knowledge of how to use a word processor, its semantic links to related ideas, and specific experiences.

Still another distinction among forms of knowledge and memory bears on writing skill. *Tacit knowledge* operates outside of a thinker's conscious awareness. For example, the rules of grammar are apparently learned during early childhood and used throughout life with little, if any, conscious understanding. Essentially the only time attention focuses on syntactic rules is in formal classroom instruction in grammar, especially in learning a foreign language. Certainly, the production of oral and written discourse occurs through tacit use of grammatical rules. *Explicit knowledge,* in contrast, is consciously represented and reflected upon in the form of a personal symbol. As noted in Chapter 1, schemata generate personal symbols that enter the flow of conscious experience, making explicit what was once only tacit.

Work on memory has contrasted measures of *explicit memory,* which rely on conscious recollection of knowledge representations, and measures of *implicit memory,* which rely on priming knowledge representations (Richardson-Klavehn & Bjork, 1988). For example, a researcher might present a person with a long list of words that includes the term *stylus.* Later in the experiment the person may be asked to recall the words, an explicit measure of memory, or to decide as rapidly as possible whether an item is an English word in a list of words and nonwords, an implicit measure of memory. The time to make this lexical decision is reliably less when the word in question, *stylus,* appears earlier in the experiment and primes the decision. This result occurs even when the person can neither consciously recall nor recognize having seen *stylus* earlier in the experiment.

As writers plan, translate, and review during composition, they consciously recall past vignettes, phrases from books read, quotations, and literally thousands of other forms of information and knowledge. But an even vaster resource and a more profound influence on writing skill remains outside of conscious reflection. All past experience potentially primes or shapes the content of what writers say and the skill with which they say it. Indirect influence of tacit knowledge is common in writing, as well as in other thinking tasks. What emerges on the page reflects the author's unconscious as well as conscious knowledge and intentions.

Method

Method includes the strategies, tools, work scheduling, environment, and rituals used by a writer to retrieve and manipulate knowledge (Kellogg, 1986a). Prewriting strategies (e.g., outlining) can be distinguished from drafting and reviewing strategies (e.g., composing a rough versus a polished draft).

The writer may translate thought into language with a variety of tools, as noted earlier in our discussion of motor functions in writing. Handwriting, typing on a word processor or typewriter, and dictating to a machine or person represent diverse ways of putting thought into written text. Whether the choice of tool matters raises interesting questions about how discourse is formulated, as well as questions about motor output.

When a writer works, for how long, and how frequently are scheduling aspects of method. A writer's productivity must surely be related to scheduling, at least in the obvious sense that one who procrastinates constantly cannot produce. The environments selected by writers and the rituals used to inspire them to work effectively are also conceivably related to writing performance. Method, then, must be viewed as much more than simply a description of the mental strategies employed in the production of text.

Personality

Personality refer to several dimensions of individual differences that are theoretically relevant to writing. Although many personal factors might be included here, four seem most pertinent. Intelligence, motivation, cognitive style, and anxiety are rich sources of individual differences among writers. The power metaphor cited by Nickerson (1981) and Perkins (1987) captures what Sternberg (1985b) defined as componential intelligence. Individual differences in basic information-processing capacity influence how well people collect, plan, translate, and review.

But intelligence is only one source of individual differences that carry implications for the writing process and writing performance. Motivation to write must be addressed (e.g., Amabile, 1983). Cognitive style (e.g., Baron, 1985) requires attention as well. Finally, the personality dimensions of anxiety and fear play prominent roles in all human endeavors, writing included (e.g., Rose, 1985).

Tracking the Process of Writing

Measurement of Processing Time

Alternatives. Measurement of how attention is allocated to collecting, planning, translating, and reviewing is essential but controversial. The use of verbal or think-aloud protocols is one common technique. The writer learns to say aloud the thoughts that enter his or her mind. It is a form of immediate and undirected retrospection. The writer must not mull over personal thoughts and recode them for the record. The experimenter must not suggest to the writer the types of statements to make. As long as the writer's thoughts are in a form that can be vocalized readily without altering the nature of the process, then the think-aloud technique can be an extremely useful tool (Ericsson & Simon, 1980).

Thinking aloud undeniably provides a detailed record of the thought processes invoked in writing. Despite its usefulness in identifying writing processes and uncovering other aspects of composing (Hayes & Flower, 1980, 1983), the method is by no means flawless. One potential problem is that the extensive record of thought processes gives the theorist a free hand in selecting and interpreting the writer's statements to support a theoretical point. Hartley (1991) observed that the manner in which Flower and Hayes (1980) developed their model of the writing process from the verbal protocols was never entirely clear. Indeed, North (1987) cited their model as a prime example of the Formalist approach to theorizing, which relies more on the intuitions and insights of the theorist than on the evaluation of empirical evidence.

A related difficulty with the extensive record produced by thinking aloud is that the collection and analysis of verbal protocols are too tedious for large numbers of writers to be tested. Verbal protocol studies typically analyze only a handful of writers. The method is impractical for use in experimental designs with adequate statistical power that can detect significant effects of the variables manipulated in the experiment (North, 1987). For example, a comparison of developing an outline as a prewriting strategy versus starting a first draft without one requires more than five or six participants to determine whether this variable reliably affects the quality of the resulting text.

Moreover, thinking aloud adds an obvious additional demand to the already heavy demands imposed by composing itself. Talking aloud as one plans, translates, and reviews adds another motor demand to the handwriting or typing demands already present. Rymer (1988) commented that the technique may only be suitable for experimental assignments because its intrusive nature discourages professionals from thinking aloud while engaged in real work. Of the nine scientists studied by Rymer, only five were willing to try thinking aloud while composing a scientific paper. Two of these declined to participate immediately, and another tried but soon quit because he found the method too intrusive. Yet another tried for several sessions, but his protocol included only the words he had drafted, long pauses, and occasional explanations of his silence. With Rymer's blessing, this individual also dropped out, leaving but one scientist who could provide a good verbal protocol while writing on the job.

An alternative approach avoids the problem of intrusion completely. The writer can simply be videotaped and, if composing on a computer, a record of every key-stroke can be made (Lansman, Smith, & Weber, 1990). The time spent in the planning mode of a computer-based writing system can be compared with the time spent in the sentence-generating mode, for example. Further, analysis of the pauses while writing longhand (Matsuhashi, 1982) or typing on a word processor (Bridwell-Bowles, Johnson, & Brehe, 1987) affords useful insights into the composition process. An extension of this approach is to record the individual behaviors and interactions of writers engaged in collaborative writing (Hawisher, 1992).

A recording of overt behavior does not unambiguously identify whether an individual is planning, translating, reviewing, or even daydreaming during a pause. A pause should not necessarily be viewed as time for planning only. Because authors can spend over 70% of their writing time pausing (Matsuhashi, 1987), the use of some form of introspection affords a clearer view of the writing process than pause analysis alone. Naturally occurring verbal protocols that emerge from discussions among collaborators provide one such form of introspection that should be easier for writers than standard think-aloud instructions.

A third approach to tracking the writing process employs a directed form of retrospection (Ericsson & Simon, 1980). With this technique, the writer is trained to identify her thoughts in terms of only a few experimenter-defined categories. I have used this technique extensively to estimate the percentage of time spent on planning, translating, and reviewing in experimental tasks. The writers are interrupted at random times during the composition session and prompted to retrospect about what they were just thinking. The percentage of times that a particular process category is named provides the estimate of the time devoted, on average, to that process. A similar technique was fruitfully employed by Schumacher, Klare, Cronin, and Moses (1984). But instead of collecting the data during composition, they showed a videotape of the session to the writer, who then tried to remember what he or she was thinking during any pause lasting for at least 10 seconds.

With both versions of directed retrospection, the experimenter trained the writers to identify their thoughts as best fitting particular categories. I employ only four to keep the writer's task simple since the retrospection occurs during composition: planning, translating, reviewing, and other. Schumacher et al. (1984) used 11 cognitive categories (e.g., global planning) and 4 grammatical categories (e.g., punctuation and capitalization); because they delayed the retrospection until after composition, they were able to present the writer with a more complicated set of selections.

One advantage of directed retrospection is that it probably interferes less with writing processes than does thinking aloud. At least it should interfere less when one complies with the think-aloud instructions to vocalize all thoughts as they occur. If the writer chooses when to vocalize, waiting for convenient breaks in thought patterns, then the think-aloud procedure may well be less intrusive than being interrupted at random by the experimenter. Of course, the sketchy, halting verbal protocol is not especially informative. The responses of directed retrospection are easier to collect and analyze in large enough numbers to satisfy statistical power considerations.

The chief disadvantage of directed retrospection is that the resulting data are markedly less rich in detail compared to those produced using verbal protocols; the writer is forced to choose from among only a few possible categories of thinking processes. Also, directed retrospection is more intrusive than videotaping the writer and analyzing pauses in composition (Matsuhashi, 1982) unless the retrospection is delayed until after composition. Of course, by then the writers may have forgotten exactly what they were thinking during a pause even with the aid of a videotaped record.

Directed Retrospection Analyses.   Further, directed retrospection assumes that writers can reliably distinguish among the categories defined by the experimenter. For example, are the categories of planning, translating, and reviewing as meaningful and valid to the research participants as they are to theorists and experimenters? In addition, the value of directed retrospection hinges critically on demonstrating that the method does not interfere unduly with the process of writing. I have addressed these issues in two experiments (Kellogg, 1987b).

To examine the interference question, I compared the performance of a group of college students who reported using directed retrospection while writing and a control group who wrote uninterrupted. To ensure adequate statistical power for the comparison, I tested 30 subjects in each condition and found no significant differences in the time spent writing, the number of words produced, the words produced per minute (WPM), or the judgments on various scales of document quality. In fact, the means on all measures of efficiency and quality were practically identical.

The validity question concerns whether writers used the response categories correctly, that is, as the experimenter trained them to use the categories. Ideally, one would obtain a perfectly accurate record of what a writer thinks about while composing. Then, both the experimenter and the writer would examine this record independently and categorize each thought as an example of planning, translating, reviewing, or other. Agreement in these categorizations would indicate that the subject used the terms *planning, translating, reviewing,* and *other* in the manner intended by the experimenter. Of course, obtaining an accurate public portrayal of the personal symbols of a writer's thoughts is theoretically impossible. The closest I could come to this ideal validation procedure was to use a verbal protocol obtained with think-aloud instructions as the best available record of what the writer was thinking. This was less than ideal because the writer probably gave less information than he or she was thinking, making it harder for the experimenter to categorize appropriately each segment of the verbal protocol.

I asked twelve college students to think aloud at one-minute intervals while writing; they spoke into a tape recorder whatever they were thinking about at the moment. Typically they reported a few phrases or a sentence or two. The experimenter immediately determined whether the writers reported thoughts best representing planning, translating, reviewing, or other, and then gave a confidence rating on the accuracy of this categorization on a 3-point scale (1 = not sure, 3 = very sure). The writer had no knowledge of how the experimenter classified each segment of the verbal protocol. After the writing was finished, the experimenter taught the method of trained introspection (this took 10–15 minutes) to the writer and then played the recording of the verbal protocol. The writer tried to categorize the reported thoughts just as the experimenter had earlier. I waited until after the verbal protocol was obtained before training the writers so as not to bias what they said while thinking aloud. This delay, however, probably made it harder for them to remember the context of their statement.

If the writer and the experimenter usually agreed in their categorization, then the method of directed retrospection probably yielded valid insights into the writer's actual writing processes. On average, 73% of the writer's categorizations matched the experimenter's. This level of agreement is substantial when one considers (1) the memory loss that probably occurred during the 10–15 minutes between the times when the subject finished the writing task and started listening to the verbal protocol and (2) the difficulties the experimenter had in categorizing some of the fragmentary statements made in the verbal protocols.

Relevant to this second point, I found significantly higher confidence ratings given by the experimenter for cases where the participants agreed with the experimenter ($M = 2.35$) than when they disagreed ($M = 1.66$). This finding suggests that the cases of disagreement may well have reflected the experimenter's uncertainty about how to assign categories to another person's verbal protocol. Presumably an individual can better classify his or her own thought than someone else's. To summarize, the writer's reported categories using directed retrospections appear to be reasonably valid reflections of his or her actual thought processes.

Measurement of Cognitive Effort

The momentary allocation of available attentional capacity defines cognitive effort. The term *cognitive engagement* perhaps better describes the idea and avoids the unfortunate overtone of struggle. When an individual is fully absorbed in a task that matches his of her skill level, the person enters what Czikszentmihalyi (1990) calls a *flow state*. He describes this subjective experience as effortless despite the deep level of momentary attentional capacity invested. Because of its traditional use in the literature of cognitive psychology, I retain the term *cognitive effort* and use it as synonymous with *cognitive engagement* (Saloman & Globerson, 1987). Later, I try to determine when cognitive engagement produces a sense of struggle and when it produces a sense of effortless absorption.

Cognitive effort has been measured in several ways. One of the most common is the use of secondary task reaction times (Kahneman, 1973). This technique assumes that spare capacity not required by a primary task such as writing will be directed to the secondary reaction time (RT) time task. In my writing studies, baseline RT data are first obtained when the participants focus attention exclusively on a simple RT task. Then, on a variable interval schedule, auditory signals are presented while the writer composes. Whenever he or she hears a signal, the writer says "Stop" into a microphone as rapidly as possible and the RT is recorded. The instructions emphasize focusing attention on the primary writing task. The increase in dual-task RT over baseline or single-task RT reflects the degree of cognitive effort devoted to writing. An interference score representing dual-task minus single-task RT indexes cognitive effort.

Other measures of cognitive effort include primary task difficulty, subjective ratings of task difficulty, and several physiological measures including sinus arrhythmia, evoked brain potentials, respiration rate, and pupil diameter. The details of the extensive literature on the measurement of cognitive effort are beyond our needs here (e.g., Kahneman, 1973; Moran, 1982; Navon, 1984; Wickens, 1984). One key lesson emerging from this work is that the various measures do not necessarily correlate. Each measure is sensitive to different parameters and contributes a slightly different perspective on the concept of mental workload. Ideally, then, multiple measures would be taken. Alternatively, an index should be adopted as a standard, allowing comparisons across experiments and laboratories. Secondary-task RT has effectively become the standard in cognitive psychology, whereas several measures are used in ergonomics, the discipline of designing technology with human factors in mind.

Another key lesson is that two tasks may interfere with one another for structural rather than capacity reasons (Kahneman, 1973). For example, two tasks requiring the visual system will interfere more with each other than two tasks using different modalities, even when the cognitive effort demands in the two cases are identical. Multiple resource theories of attention have been developed from this basic notion of structural interference. Wickens (1984), for instance, proposed that attentional resources are allocated according to perceptual modality (seeing versus hearing), processing codes (spatial versus verbal), and stages of processing (perception versus response execution).

In studies of writers composing in longhand or on a word processor, structural interference can be minimized by using an auditory rather than a visual RT probe. The secondary probe requires a different sensorimotor system than the writing task itself. Response execution to the probe must not interfere with the writer's handwriting or typing. A vocal response serves well in these cases, though if dictation were under investigation, a manual RT response would be in order.

Measures of Writing Performance

Quality

Quality, fluency, and productivity are distinct measures of writing performance. *Quality* refers to judgments about how well a document communicates or achieves its purpose with its intended audience. The question of how one defines quality has vexed scholars at least since the time of Plato's *Phraedus*. In the case of writing, the values held by the reader hold considerable sway over the judgment of quality in writing. But assuming that judges share the same cultural and linguistic value systems, intensive research over the past two decades suggests that readers can be trained to agree reasonably well on the quality of a written document (Huot, 1990).

Much of the progress in text evaluation has been driven by a national concern over the poor writing skills of students graduating from high school during the 1970s and 1980s. Passing a writing proficiency test has been adopted by some states as a requirement for graduation (Freedman & Calfee, 1983). The quality of written composition is also increasingly being used as a critical benchmark by colleges and universities, both as an entrance requirement and as an assessment of the success of the college or university curriculum in teaching thinking and writing skills. At the same time, dissatisfaction with indirect tests of writing skill, such as a multiple-choice examination on grammar and usage, has grown. Direct assessment of a sample of writing is presently in wide use (Huot, 1990).

All forms of direct assessment are challenged by the enormous variety of texts that people create. Hartley (1991) noted that text evaluation must be considered in light of the different purposes of texts, the different audiences to which they are addressed, and the different genres in which they are composed. Witte (1992) illustrated this variety nicely in the following ethnographic "snapshot" of one type of professional at work:

> During a particular day, a civil engineer works on seven distinct "projects"—all of which either presently exist as drafts of "letters," "reports," or "proposals," or will take one of those forms. As he attends to various aspects of these projects, the engineer, among other things, (a) calls an attorney for a city's planning department about the status of a pending zoning ordinance, (b) writes a note instructing his personal secretary to call a bonding company in order to find out "specifics" about the "performance record" of a construction company, its owners, and its principal subcontractors, (c) makes several lists of changes to be made on three sets of "blue lines" he reviews, (d) writes two entries for "meetings" on his desk calendar after talking with four people on the telephone, (e) "writes" a "subroutine" to compute the appropriate site for a wastewater "trunk line" through a proposed housing development that he describes as "topographically troublesome," and (f) gives another secretary oral instructions for "making" (i.e., labeling) a set of file folders. At different times during the next 4½ months, the documents—all but two incorporating more than one symbol system—related to each of the seven projects are completed. (p. 245)

Direct assessment involves an objective analysis of the textual properties, a subjective judgment by the reader of the text, or a behavioral index of the reader's judgment of the text. Witte's (1992) example shows that a system for assessing one type of writing may not be at all appropriate for another type. Here the focus will be on analyzing texts comprised solely of linguistic symbols and usually multiple paragraphs, not brief notes and certainly not signs and labels. Yet even with these restrictions, the variations in types of text structures between, say, narrative and persuasive texts raise difficulties in common measurement.

Another difficulty in measurement concerns reliability. Interjudge reliability is generally higher, often markedly higher, for objective than for subjective measures. The complexities of subjective judgments of text quality cannot be denied, particularly when a single holistic rating is assigned to a text (Charney, 1984).

Freedman and Calfee (1983), for example, proposed a model that specified seven personal characteristics of the rater and five characteristics of the task environment that affect how the rater reads the document, evaluates it, and articulates his or her evaluation. The personal characteristics include reading ability, world knowledge, expectations, values, the purpose of the evaluation, productive ability (i.e., ability to articulate a decision), and the audience for the evaluation. The task environment includes the time of day, length of task, type of text, the physical environment, and the kind of training and supervision provided. With so many factors at work, it should not be surprising that two readers may disagree on how to judge the quality of a text.

It would be a mistake to abandon subjective measurement, however. The judgment of a reader is essential to quality measurement given that writing is situated in a social context. Objective analysis decontextualizes the text. It moves the text a step away from a real audience. At best it assesses characteristics that correlate with reader acceptance and admiration, such as the use of a readability formula. A writer's success in converting personal symbols into communicative language cannot be fully indexed in the absence of a reader who actively tries to comprehend and interpret the text.

Subjective Measures. The three main forms of assessing the quality of a document using a judge are primary trait, analytic, and holistic (Huot, 1990). *Primary trait scoring* assumes that the rhetorical situation dictates the specific characteristics that exemplify a quality text. For example, if the task instructions asked the writer to describe a typical Wednesday as a student at the University of Missouri–Rolla, then the text would need to present a coherent chronology of events for the student. The primary traits, therefore, are highly specific and must be derived for each writing assignment.

Analytic scoring begins with several properties that presumably are essential for good writing and assigns a quality judgment based on the number of these properties shown in a sample. The content, organization, effectiveness, idea development, word usage, grammar, punctuation, spelling, and other properties might be examined and tallied. Analytic scoring is time-consuming but is the most reliable of the three methods. However, its reliability is not substantially greater than that of the more efficient holistic rating. The latter is therefore recommended for testing large groups of writers (Huot, 1990).

Holistic scoring provides the rater's general impression of the overall quality of the writing and is certainly familiar to teachers and professors. Holistic scoring can shade into analytic scoring in that one might identify two general dimensions that are then rated on, say, a 7-point scale. Each dimension subsumes several analytic properties that may correlate strongly. In my work, I have found that diction, grammar, punctuation, and other stylistic properties correlate highly, leading to my use of a single dimension of style. Holistic scoring is both the most economical and the most popular system, and its reliability compares favorably with that of other techniques (Faigley, Cherry, Jolliffe, & Skinner, 1985; Huot, 1990). It is reported in most of the literature cited in this book.

Objective Methods. It is also possible to index quality by analyzing the objective properties of the text. The Writer's Workbench is one of several automated text analysis systems that flags certain errors and compiles statistics on several criteria (Macdonald, Frase, Ginrich, & Keenan, 1982). Spelling, punctuation, occurrences of the same word twice, poor and sexist diction, and split infinitives are checked and errors marked in an analyzed document. The style is assessed in various ways. Numerous statistics, such as average word, clause, or sentence length; the number of simple, compound, and complex sentences; the percentage of abstract words; and the number of passive constructions, are compiled. Then some of these numbers are used in various readability formulas. Finally, the statistical profile can be measured against benchmark documents of a particular genre that have been subjectively rated as superior in quality.

Another approach to objective analysis is to apply theories of text structure, initially developed in reading research. For example, Kintsch's (1974) propositional analysis offers a formal system for representing the micro- and macrostructure of a document. This has proved useful in describing in detail the difference in idea development between a document composed by an expert on a subject and one composed by a novice (Voss, Vesonder, & Spillich, 1980). Britton, Gulgoz, and Tidwell (1990) used Kintsch's formalization in developing a revision system that aims to capture more accurately the author's intent in modifying a document. A related method is to analyze a text into *idea units,* which are defined as a group of propositions related to a single argument, fact, or opinion, and their organization (Graesser & Clark, 1985).

Still another objective approach is to analyze a text for coherence by marking what Halliday and Hasan (1976) referred to as *cohesive ties.* Local ties reflect links between adjacent sentences, and remote ties reflect links between a sentence and an earlier, nonadjacent sentence such as a topic sentence. The presence of many such ties creates a cohesive text. Local and remote ties establish connections between information already in the text and new information, satisfying what is called the *given–new contract* of discourse processing (Clark & Clark, 1977). Of course, there are several linguistic devices for achieving such links. They include referential ties such as pronominal anaphora, lexical ties such as paraphrasing, and inferential ties that link sentences on the basis of real-world knowledge. Syntactic ties, such as the use of conjunctions, also achieve linkages.

A similar approach, called *feature analysis,* has been used to distinguish between immature and mature forms of writing in developmental studies (Sharples, 1985). Features are defined at three levels of text structure: word and phrase, clause and sentence, and text section. At the word and phrase levels, mature writing features abstract nouns and multiple modifiers, for example. Immature writing both lacks these positive features and includes speech idioms and ambiguities that stem from a young writer's inability to foresee places where the reader may fail to comprehend. At the sentence level, the mature writer uses relational words, adverbial phrases, apposition, and ellipsis to coordinate ideas, whereas the immature writer simply uses the word *then* to relate ideas. The knowledge-telling mode of writing discussed by Bereiter and Scardamalia (1987) accounts for this feature of immature writing, as ideas are retrieved from memory and immediately expressed, punctuated in a sense by *then.*

At the level of major sections, chapters, or whole texts, mature writers organize ideas according to conventional structures, such as comparison/contrast, problem/solution, pyramid ordering of the main point followed by increasing elaborations, or story grammars (Sharples, 1985). In the terms used here, the mature writer draws on diverse schemata for structuring documents created for different purposes. The immature writer fails to organize effectively and appropriately for the purpose of the text. Such writing features arbitrary ordering, tangled ideas, and chains of associative thinking. Again, such features are consistent with a knowledge-telling as opposed to a knowledge-transforming mode of writing.

Behavioral Measures.   Bruce, Collins, Rubins, and Gentner (1982) defined text quality, or in their term *objectives of communicative acts,* along four dimensions: comprehensibility, memorability, enticingness, and persuasiveness. These properties can be used as the basis for analytic scoring by experts. Memorability, in particular, suggests an obvious alternative. The reader's ability to recall a text can define operationally the property of memorability. Similarly, performance on a Cloze reading test in which the reader must guess words that are omitted from the text can index comprehensibility (e.g., "The waiter uncorked the bottle and poured the _____ into his glass."). Measurements of attentional involvement, such as secondary-task reaction times, can index the enticingness of the text. Finally, shifts on scales of attitudes or behavioral changes after reading a text can be used to index persuasiveness.

Schriver (1989) described responses by the reader as *reader-focused* measures of evaluating text quality. Concurrent tests evaluate quality while readers are engaged in the act using Cloze tests, other performance tests, and through verbal and behavioral protocols. For instance, asking readers to think aloud as they read and comprehend the text is one form of concurrent testing. Retrospective tests include surveys, focus groups, and reporting of critical incidents on textual problems.

Subjective, Objective, and Behavioral Relations.   Several studies have sought to find objective cues in the text that predict subjective judgments or behavioral measures. But the relationships obtained are often complex. For example, Reed (1989) found that the average number of words per sentence relates in a curvilinear manner to quality judgments. A linear equation accounted for only 18% of the variation in quality judgments. Too few or too many words were judged harshly, whereas between 8 and 23 words per sentence were given good ratings. The wide range limits the usefulness of this measure as a primary index of quality. Similarly, the total number of words in a document usually correlates moderately with quality judgments. But as Freedman and Calfee (1983) noted, longer length is not necessarily an indicator of superior idea development if redundant padding appears.

To establish causal relations between objective text characteristics and subjective ratings, Freedman and Calfee manipulated four theoretically relevant traits by careful rewriting of essays. They manipulated idea development, organization, sentence structure, and mechanics, citing Kintsch's (1974) hierarchical system of text analysis as the basis for their selection. In rewriting the essays, they retained the main propositions of the original but strengthened in some cases and weakened in others, say, the degree of idea development. Their results showed that development had the strongest effect on holistic ratings of quality, followed by organization and mechanics. The main effect of sentence structure was not statistically significant. Interestingly, they found interactions with the organization factor. If an essay was well organized, then it received superior ratings only when sentence structure and mechanics were strong. However, if it was poorly organized, then the strength of sentence structure and mechanics mattered little. The emphasis on content and organization as the chief predictors of holistic ratings has been confirmed by some researchers (Breland & Jones, 1984) but disputed by others (Rafoth & Rubin, 1984).

Cohesive ties, too, relate to quality judgments. Witte and Faigley (1981) found that high- and low-quality essays differ in the number of such ties that are present in the expected manner. The effect sizes in this and the earlier-cited studies were not such that one could safely abandon direct writing assessment in favor of text analysis. Rather, subjective ratings, precisely because they are colored with the values and interpretations of readers, comprise the primary assessment of quality. Text analysis measures are useful adjuncts in revealing why some texts are judged better than others, and they reflect on the processes used to create the text.

The relations between subjective or objective measures and behavioral measures are still less well understood. The most heavily researched area is the relation between readability formula and measures of learning. Presumably, highly readable texts, based on the use of common words and simple text structure, should be easier to comprehend and retain. Klare's (1963) early review of studies, however, raised serious doubts about the validity of this assumption. A later model of reading proposed by Klare (1976) contended that the lack of control over reading skill and the reader's motivation may well account for the dismal results of earlier studies. Yet, even with these variables accounted for, Duffy and Kabance (1982) found little benefit in learning from text based on revisions guided by a readability formula.

A more promising line is to apply a detailed theory of reading comprehension, such as that proposed by Kintsch and his colleagues (Kintsch & van Dijk, 1978; Miller & Kintsch, 1980), to the writing and revision of texts. Britton, Van Dusen, Glynn, and Hemphill (1990) tested documents using a computer program based on Kintsch's model to enumerate the locations where inference by readers is demanded to establish coherence. The number of such locations correlated significantly and negatively ($r = -.80$) with a measure of text recall.

Britton, Gulgoz, and Tidwell (1990) extended Kintsch's model to a "principled revision" of text. They repaired the locations flagged by the program as demanding inference on the part of the reader. Then they compared the revised text with the original, along with a text revised in accordance with a readability formula, on measures of free recall and multiple-choice recognition of factual information. As predicted, free recall doubled for readers given the principled revision compared to the original text.

Moreover, Britton, Gulgoz, and Tidwell derived a graphic mode of representing the cognitive structure intended by the author of the original text. They did so by selecting 12 important terms from the text and then constructing all possible paired combinations of them (66 in all). The author, plus seven experts on the subject of the text, rated each pair for relatedness on a 7-point scale. They then applied a network statistical analysis to the 66 ratings to derive a graphical representation of the intended text structure. They compared the shape of this intended structure of the text with the shapes garnered from readers' relatedness ratings of the same 12 terms.

Britton and his colleagues found that the principled revision yielded a mental representation for readers that correlated reliably with the intended structure ($r = .5$). However, the original text failed to do so. This implies that Kintsch's objective text analysis program is related positively with what readers actually learn from a text. The result also suggests the value of Kintsch's program as an automated revision aid.

Another result warrants emphasis. Britton himself subjectively evaluated the original text and repaired it using his knowledge and skill about how to write well. The new version he called a *heuristic revision.* Strikingly, the heuristic version not only resulted in free recall double that of the original, it also supported superior performance on the multiple-choice recognition test of factual learning relative to all other versions of the text. Finally, readers developed a mental representation from the heuristic revision that correlated best of all with the original ($r = .6$). These findings taken together suggest that the subjective judgment of a skilled writer provides an added edge to the revision process that cannot at present be matched by a highly sophisticated objective analysis using Kintsch's reading model. Of course, the skill level of the writer is critical; subjective judgments do not necessarily lead to improved text (Duffy, Curran, & Sass, 1983).

Conclusion. The relations between subjective quality judgments and measures of reader behavior are largely uncharted waters. Numerous promising research routes beckon. But for now, I contend that subjective quality ratings are an indispensable component of text evaluation despite the disagreements between judges that occur. The relatively low interjudge reliabilities that obtain with quality judgments ($r = .5$ to $.8$) trouble experimentalists accustomed to reliabilities at the $.9$ level. But the value-laden nature of the term *quality* makes disagreement in judgment inevitable, if not desirable. Judges need to be trained to ensure that documents are rated on the same criteria. But procedures that train judges to agree completely are possibly contrived and misguided; they eliminate the very value differences that objective measures of text analysis lack.

In addition to subjective judgments, objective analysis methods should be employed. The potential of automated revision based on Kintsch's reading model (Britton et al., 1990; Kieras, 1989) illustrates the benefits of continued work on objective text measures. Finally, much more attention needs to be devoted to behavioral measures of readers, a conclusion also advanced by Schriver (1989). She argued, however, for the advantages of reader-focused measures over other ways of assessing text quality. I prefer to regard quality as an ill-defined concept with subjective, objective, and behavioral measures serving as characteristic rather than defining properties. The employment of all three measures provides a better view of text quality than that afforded by any one alone.

Fluency

Fluency is taken here to mean verbal fluency, the rate at which words are generated in constructing sentences. The average number of WPM is the standard measure of verbal fluency (Gould, 1980). This is based on the total amount of time devoted to the production of a certain number of words. However, average WPM obscures the fact that written language production occurs in bursts and pauses. The study of when pauses occur and for how long has proved useful in portraying the nature of the writing process (Matsuhashi, 1987). A fine-grained analysis of production rate during particular bursts would provide an especially accurate picture of fluency.

Fluency is a measure of writing ability distinct from quality. Fluency, based on average WPM, and quality, based on judges' ratings, are only moderately correlated; a recent study in my laboratory obtained an $r = .43$ for style ratings and $r = .50$ for content ratings. Producing language rapidly need not imply that the sentences and paragraphs are effective and coherent for readers.

Fluency at a particular subprocess can be isolated. For example, ideational fluency is the rate at which an individual generates ideas (Guilford, 1967). Caccamise (1987) measured ideational fluency and found that idea generation increased with the degree of domain-specific knowledge about the topic. Translating or reviewing fluency could be isolated by counting rates of original sentence generation only or rates of revising drafts, after pauses for planning and reading were excluded.

Productivity

Productivity refers to the number of finished documents that a writer produces over a long time frame. School and business settings in which documents are completed and sent to recipients without review are useful locales for studying pure productivity. A pure measure of productivity excludes peer and editorial review because such review depends partly on quality. Also, the measurement of publication rates is vexing. Problems raised by multiple authorship, the length of the document, and the stature of the publisher, among others, cloud the interpretation of this dependent variable. Still, productivity is a fundamental characteristic of writing performance, and several survey studies have examined it (Boice & Johnson, 1984; Hartley & Branthwaite, 1989; Kellogg, 1986a). In the publish-or-perish world of academics, for example, writers must be capable of composing quality texts with a high rate of productivity.

The relations among productivity, quality, and fluency are probably positive but moderate, though I have not seen a study that measures all three. In reviewing the literature on quality and productivity relationships using the number of times scholars cite an article as the measure of its quality, Simonton (1988) found correlations ranging between .47 and .76. Even so, writing well or writing rapidly does not guarantee a high rate of productivity.

Completing a document depends on sustained effort, as well as on quality and fluency. Consider the tortoise and the hare as writers. The one who completes the race most often might be the writer who works at the task slowly but surely. Productivity certainly hinges on how much time and effort the writer devotes to working. But a writer's ability to retrieve and apply personal knowledge to the task is also relevant. Quality and fluency certainly depend on skill at retrieving and applying knowledge. But one can argue that such skill is critically dependent on having devoted extensive practice, time, and effort to writing. Across a variety of cognitive skills, deliberate practice plays a pivotal role (Ericsson, Krampe, & Tesch-Römer, 1993).

Process and Performance

Performance Amplification

Quality, fluency, and productivity concern the product of writing. How good is the text? How rapidly does it emerge from the writer's mind? How many products suitable for readers are completed in a given time frame? Taking as a baseline unskilled writers who score poorly on all three measures of writing performance, the question arises as to the ways their performance might be amplified. *Amplification* refers here to gains in the quality, fluency, or productivity of writing.

Process Restructuring

A separate question concerns the flow of the skill itself—the process rather than the product of writing. I use the term *process* here and elsewhere as a mass noun; as we have seen, many processes and subprocesses comprise the overall writing process, just as many trees comprise a forest. The allocation of processing time and cognitive effort to collecting, planning, translating, and reviewing varies from task to task and from writer to writer. The task constraints and the method of composition used by the writer structure the nature of this allocation of attentional resources. I define *quantitative restructuring* as a change in attentional allocation caused by some specific task or method change.

No single normative pattern of attention allocation can be identified; hence, the term *quantitative restructuring* gains meaning only in a specific context. For example, how does the use of a prewriting strategy restructure the process of writing relative to forgoing prewriting? Or how does composing on a computer restructure writing relative to composing in longhand?

Restructuring is a relational concept in another way as well. It concerns the relative degree of processing time or cognitive effort allocated to, say, planning versus reviewing. For example, the use of a polished-draft strategy restructures the process relative to the use of a rough-draft strategy by increasing the time devoted to reviewing before finishing a first draft. Quantitative restructuring captures shifts in the distribution of attention to component processes.

The term *qualitative restructuring* captures changes in the way a process unfolds as a consequence of task or method variations. Not only does the amount of attention given to processes change, but how that attention is used may also change. For instance, the use of a word processor instead of pen and paper might alter the qualitative nature of reviewing during the composition of a first draft. Because it is so easy to produce a clean first draft, the writer might be more compelled to correct spelling errors, punctuation, and other local mechanical errors while composing. When a factor alters the detailed nature of a writing process, I refer to the phenomenon as *qualitative restructuring*.

Relative Automatization

Changes in the absolute level of attention devoted to writing concern automaticity. *Automatization* signifies a relative reduction in the cognitive effort or processing time demanded by the process. For example, as a writer's skill in treating a particular topic increases, the effort needed in collecting, planning, translating, and reviewing decreases. It is not a question of redistributing attention differently but rather of attending less to all component operations.

The traditional use of the term *automatic performance* implies that little if any attention is required. This term comes from the study of simple cognitive processes and from motor skills. Effortless performance occurs fluidly in a unified manner when it is automatic. Effortless skill appears to be encapsulated, with interaction among its components no longer visible.

I employ the term automatization to refer to a relative decrease in the effort invested in all component operations. The notion of effortlessness is excess baggage in the case of writing. As noted in Chapter 1, writing is typically highly effortful. Automatization lessens but does not eliminate the cognitive demands. A writer's skill cannot be so great that the act of writing is as effortless as skilled typing. Consider three reasons for this claim.

If a writer effortlessly translates personal symbols into consensual symbols, then it is very unlikely that he or she has taken the perspective of a reader approaching the text afresh. One of the hardest aspects of reviewing is to shift from the world of the writer to the world of the reader. The writer must anticipate places where the reader may fail to make an inference or may disagree with a line of reasoning. Effortlessly produced consensual symbols are more likely to be cryptic than communicative.

Second, McCutchen (1988) argued that component processes, such as planning, translating, and reviewing, must interact even for the skilled writer. For example, generating sentences must be constrained by the goals of the writer. Translation, therefore, cannot proceed separately from the goal-setting operations of planning. While the interaction among components may become less transparent with increasing skill, it does not become invisible even for an expert. The interaction among component processes demands at least some cognitive effort.

Third, all but the most routine writing task pose unique challenges. A particular task confronts the expert and novice alike with specific content and rhetorical problems. Having written about a familiar topic, or in a certain genre, or to a particular audience eases the way for future writing. But it is unlikely that a previously created schema can be effortlessly reproduced or modified slightly to cope with the problems of a new writing task. The writer must struggle with the fresh problems posed by the task at hand.

Economy of Effort

Although writing is never effortless, writers often seek to make it so. Unless people are motivated to seek outstanding performance, they settle for satisfactory performance with the least cost. Writers economize effort and "satisfice" performance when they seek a satisfactory product with the least possible investment of processing time and cognitive effort. A writer's best work emerges only after the maximum investment of attention to the task.

Economizing effort is an old idea in psychology and biology (Anderson, 1990b; Bruner, Goodnow, & Austin, 1956; Harris, 1979; Newell & Simon, 1972). Bruner et al. described how this principle manifested itself in the concept identification tasks that they investigated. Their participants adopted strategies that minimized the load placed on attention and memory even if it meant less than optimum performance. Similarly, Newell and Simon examined satisficing in the context of selecting a move in a problem-solving task. To satisfice meant to accept the first move meeting prior expectations or needs. The satisficing heuristic follows from the view that people lack sufficient information or cognitive capacity to process available information to perform optimally. In the present context of writing and meaning-making, the term *satisficing* implies a motivational factor as well. Writers satisfice not only because of informational and attentional constraints, but also because the task at hand fails to motivate them to excel.

Panel A of Figure 3.1 illustrates relative automatization, the theoretical pattern expected when writers with varying degrees of expertise satisfice performance and economize effort. The panel indicates an increasing but nonlinear curve for quality and a decreasing curve for effort as the degree of knowledge available to the writer increases. Higher levels of knowledge enable the writer to automatize the process, partially, thus minimizing effort. The more a writer knows, the more likely it is that he or she has already solved some of the rhetorical and particularly the content problems involved in developing a document schema. The writer satisfices and economizes effort rather than engaging the task fully. For various reasons, the motivation to become fully engrossed in the task and produce a superior document is lacking in this case.

Numerous perceptual-motor and cognitive skills have revealed the pattern shown in Panel A, including typing and solving routine mathematics problems (Logan, 1992). As individuals practice more and acquire more expertise, their performance keeps improving but shows clear signs of diminishing returns, fitting a mathematical curve called a *power function*. At the same time, the attention they devote to the task decreases as they automatize their performance. Many factors may well limit the ability of individuals to continue to improve, but the one I focus on here is motivation. Specifically, if the task is extremely interesting and the person is motivated to practice the task in a deliberate manner for many years, one should see a different pattern.

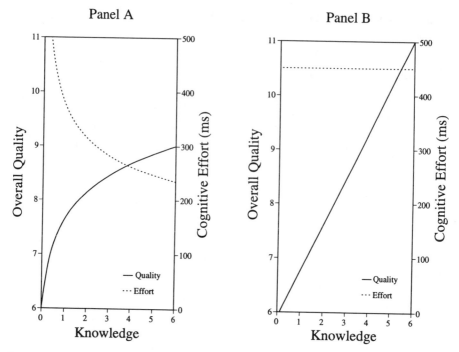

FIGURE 3.1. Automatization (Panel A) and performance amplification (Panel B) as available knowledge increases. (From Kellogg, 1993. Copyright © *Composition Studies*, Texas Christian University. Reprinted by permission.)

Creative Flow and Affect

Amplifying performance to peak levels requires that an individual fully invest processing time and cognitive effort in the task at hand. All available knowledge must be brought to bear, and the writer achieves this through total absorption in the task. In a phrase, the writer must abandon economizing effort and became totally engrossed in the process of making meaning. Csikszentmihalyi and Csikszentmihalyi (1988) referred to such absorption as a *flow state* and suggested that it occurs only when the demands of the task evenly match an individual's knowledge and skills. I suggest that amplification of writing performance to superior levels occurs during states of creative flow, when task demands and skill levels match and writers lose themselves in their work.

Panel B of Figure 3.1 illustrates the theoretical pattern of amplification with a linear increase in quality and a constant, high level investment of cognitive effort as knowledge increases in availability. A decrease in cognitive effort with a high level of general knowledge does not occur because the writer fully engages the content and rhetorical problems. Instead of satisficing, the writer becomes fully dedicated to the task and aims to achieve a superior product. Writers at times use their knowledge as best they can to amplify performance rather than to reduce effort demands.

Positive affect is central to flow states (Csikszentmihalyi and Csikszentmihalyi,

1988). A feeling of enjoyment, at times bordering on euphoria, comes with attentional absorption. Clarity of purpose, high motivation, and a belief that one is in control of the work are also commonly experienced in flow states.

Mismatches between task demands and skill levels can result in two negative affective states. When the task is too easy, an individual readily becomes bored. When the task is too difficult, frustration and anxiety result. Obviously, high levels of writing performance are not possible when a task lies beyond one's knowledge and skill levels, and the person feels frustrated and anxious. Performance may be adequate on easy writing assignments simply because the individual's skill is so much greater than the task demands. But it may be difficult to achieve inspired writing on such easy tasks because of the boredom they engender.

Although a creative state of flow typically brings with it positive emotions, it would be an overgeneralization to suppose that this must always occur. A writer's abilities certainly may fluctuate with such factors as fatigue, hunger, and time pressure. At the same time, the demands of a writing task may fluctuate as the writer moves from, say, a content problem in which past knowledge provides a ready solution to one that forces reorganization of numerous schemata. The precise match between abilities and task demands will therefore wax and wane. A writer might well be fully absorbed in a writing task, showing a high degree of attentional involvement, and still encounter moments of boredom or frustration (Ochse, 1990). I use the term *creative flow state* to indicate the state in which the writer is fully engaged in the task rather than economizing on effort. For the most part, writers have positive emotions during creative flow, but temporary fluctuations will occur. Extended periods of boredom or frustration, in contrast, are not consistent with flow states.

Knowledge Usage and Writing Performance

As we will see in later chapters, the writer's strategies, tools, work environment, work scheduling, rituals, intelligence, cognitive style, and other factors shape how a particular writing task is approached. Quantitative and qualitative restructuring of the process are the norm; hence, the term *writing process* is inherently vague. Further, of all possible variations in the writing process, no one of them emerges as the best way to produce quality documents, to compose fluently, or to be a highly productive writer.

Gorell (1983) aptly compared the various ways that one can produce quality writing to the various ways that one can make a tasty Mulligan stew, concluding: "The problem is that the writing process is so complex and varied, as much current useful research is showing, that discusssions of *the* process seem to exhibit the zeal, but also face the futility of the medieval alchemist" (p. 273).

To cut through the complexity, it is necessary to ask some key questions about the relation between alternative writing processes and measures of writing performance. Which of the many factors that restructure the process also amplify performance? Are there factors that amplify performance that have no discernible influence on the process? In short, what are the constraints on producing high-quality text fluently and productively? These questions are as important as those concerned with variations in the writing process alone.

I approach these process–performance questions armed with a simple hypothesis in an effort to see how far it can take us. Ultimately, how well a writer composes is solely a function of how well the writer brings relevant knowledge to bear on the task at hand. Knowledge usage is the key to understanding the skill level of a writer as opposed to the way the process of writing unfolds. The task facing a writer, as well as the intellectual resources and constraints that the writer brings to the task, structure the time and effort given to the process. Here we consider whether only a subset of the factors that shape the process also affect knowledge usage and, hence, performance.

Conditions for Knowledge Usage

The use of conceptual, discourse, and metacognitive knowledge requires four conditions. Knowledge must be (1) *available* as a result of past learning, (2) *accessible* at the time it is needed in the writing process, and (3) *applied* inventively to the rhetorical and content problems posed by the task environment. A lifetime of experience and education merely creates the potential for effective writing. The knowledge needed for a particular writing task must also be retrieved from memory and applied inventively to the unique content and rhetorical problems at hand. The fourth condition is *motivational*. An expert writer may be capable of retrieving and applying vast reservoirs of knowledge to a task, but will do so only if motivated to engage the work with full effort and absorption. Later chapters address the literature on these four conditions in detail. We will examine them in studies on the availability of a writer's knowledge, the writer's personality, and the methods that the writer uses to retrieve and apply what he or she knows.

Retrieval and Application of Knowledge.   I turn to the principles developed in cognitive research on attention, learning, and memory to illuminate how aspects of the writer's personality and method of composing affect knowledge usage and performance. The first principle is the empowering effect of *concentration*. A basic finding in regard to human attention is that people have trouble doing more than one task at a time (Kahneman, 1973). If one of the tasks can be handled automatically, with little if any attention required, then people can succeed. Through extensive practice, one can drive at 65 miles per hour on a freeway and carry on a conversation at the same time. But if both tasks demand attention—as when the conversation turns to an argument and the driving turns to rush-hour traffic—then one must concentrate on one or the other.

As already discussed, the operations of writing generally demand attention. To activate the schemata that a writer needs at a given moment in composition, and then to tune or even reorganize them creatively to address the unique problems at hand, concentration is needed. Yet as also noted, collecting, planning, translating, and reviewing occur throughout all phases of document development and interact with each other extensively (McCutchen, 1986).

The concentration principle suggests that the pattern of allocating attentional resources should be restructured to avoid the problem of overload or the scattering of attention. The demands of juggling the four operations of collecting, planning, translating, and reviewing can readily overload the writer's limited attentional capacity (de Beaugrande, 1984; Flower & Hayes, 1980b). Advantageously restructuring this juggling act in an way that enhances concentration on fewer operations at any one time should enable a writer to better retrieve, manipulate, and creatively use content and discourse knowledge. Moreover, personal qualities of the writer that enable intense concentration, such as intelligence and a reflective cognitive style, should similarly foster the use of available knowledge.

The second principle involves *organizational strategies*. It is well documented in the memory literature that organization aids the retrieval of episodic information (e.g., Einstein & Hunt, 1980). Moreover, research on semantic memory assumes that knowledge organization is critical (Chang, 1986). If a strategy produces an organizational schema relevant to the task, then content and possibly discourse knowledge incorporated into the organizational schema should be more accessible to the writer while composing. For example, creating an outline during prewriting yields a linear, hierarchical document schema that the writer can rely on as a knowledge retrieval aid during composition of a first draft. The organization of the topics to be covered should facilitate retrieval of relevant, domain-specific knowledge, for example.

The third principle is *encoding specificity*. This principle claims that the retrieval conditions should be matched as closely as possible to the conditions existing at the time of memory encoding or initial learning. To illustrate the idea, having heard a lecture in a particular room, students should be able to retrieve the material they learned later on somewhat better if tested in the original lecture room compared to a new environment. Although the principle evolved from research on episodic memory, Day's (1992) results suggest that it extends to semantic memory as well. This powerful principle of memory accounts for findings of (1) recognition failure, in which learning and retrieval cues are matched or mismatched (Tulving & Thomson, 1973); (2) environmental dependency, in which the learning and retrieval environments are manipulated (Smith, Glenberg, & Bjork, 1978); (3) state dependency, in which the state of consciousness involved in learning and memory is manipulated through drugs (Eich, 1980); and (4) mood dependency, in which emotional states are manipulated experimentally (Bower, 1981).

The encoding specificity principle should prove useful in understanding the conditions that work for or against a writer's effectively bringing relevant knowledge to bear on the task. For example, the use of rituals to set the proper context for writing can be interpreted in this light. If a writer's thoughts about a document originated with a physical location, a state of mind, or in the presence of particular music, conversation, objects, events, or people, then re-creation of the original thinking context ought to facilitate retrieval.

Motivation. The final condition for effective knowledge use is the motivation to engage the writing task fully. When will writers be satisficing and economizing effort, and when will they engage the task fully? The importance of the task surely matters. Outstanding works of literature, science, art, politics, and so on would not exist without skilled experts devoting maximum time and effort to the tasks that they deem important (Ericsson, Krampe, & Tesch-Römer, 1993). Regardless of skill level, I assume that tasks vary in importance to the writer. Typically, extrinsic rewards and punishments control the level of perceived importance. An essay assigned in the context of a laboratory experiment for which the writer receives extra credit in a general psychology course undoubtedly is perceived by most participants as low in importance. The same assignment placed on the Scholastic Aptitude Test (SAT) or American College Testing (ACT) examination becomes highly important.

Still, extrinsic forms of motivation may be surprisingly weak in comparison to intrinsic forms (Amabile, 1985). Writers who show strong intrinsic motivation may be the most likely to enter a flow state and not settle for merely satisfactory performance. Understanding completely which writing assignments attract a writer's interest and spark a high level of intrinsic motivation may be beyond any theory. But the importance of intrinsic motivation in writing can hardly be overstated. Scardamalia and Bereiter (1991) noted that "even the most mundane writing tasks, made deliberately simple so as to be accessible to novice writers, seem to elicit creative effort from experts" (p. 173). Some topics may prompt an expert to refashion the task into a challenging form that evokes a state of creative flow.

4

Knowledge

For a writer, of course, everything is grist for the mill, and a writer cannot know
too much. Sooner or later everything he does know will find its uses.

Louis L'Amour

I turn now to a further treatment of the types of knowledge that writers possess and
to empirical studies of how knowledge affects process and performance. I focus on
studies that add flesh to the theoretical skeleton of the opening chapters. First, I
examine further the knowledge typology introduced in the previous chapter in light
of research showing how each type of knowledge relates to writing performance.
Next, I consider the issue of knowledge availability by asking how one educates and
prepares a writer. Knowledge availability influences writing even when the writer is
unaware of the knowledge, the third topic considered here. Fourth, I turn to studies
that document how knowledge restructures the process of writing. Finally I consider
the distinction between amplification and automatization.

Types of Knowledge

Types of Knowledge

As explained in Chapter 3, Alexander et al. (1991) described three forms of knowledge that a writer draws upon. They distinguish among sociocultural, conceptual,
and metacognitive knowledge. *Sociocultural knowledge* refers to tacit understanding
of basic beliefs shared with members of one's family, community, ethnic group, and
national culture. Knowledge of the world and knowledge of language comprise *conceptual knowledge*. Alexander et al. view all experiences as passing through a filter
of tacit sociocultural knowledge. Such knowledge may be made explicit in the form
of personal or consensual symbols, but when cultural knowledge becomes the focus
of attention, it is indistinguishable from other forms of conceptual knowledge. Lastly,
metacognitive knowledge refers to knowledge about the self, tasks, strategies,

and plans and goals. Broadly speaking, it encompasses all knowledge about knowledge.

Conceptual knowledge has two major divisions, as shown in Figure 4.1. We will examine these divisions separately in what follows. The first division, *content knowledge,* concerns physical, social, and mental aspects of the world. Such knowledge becomes increasingly formalized in the subcategories of domain knowledge and discipline knowledge. Text quality measures of content, idea development, organization, factual communication, and the like depend crucially on content knowledge. To illustrate the differences among embedded levels of content knowledge, Alexander et al. (1991) noted the case of human biology. The high school student who studies body parts in a text on human anatomy learns more precise distinctions and acquires a greater depth of understanding that is characteristic of the second division, *domain knowledge.* As knowledge of a domain deepens and widens further, and as the domain itself acquires a history of development and scholarship, a discipline appears. A medical student studying human anatomy learns at the discipline level.

Content Knowledge

Several studies document the relation between domain-specific knowledge and performance. First, Voss, Vesonder, and Spillich (1980) compared the narrative accounts of a baseball game composed by writers judged to be either well or poorly versed in knowledge about the game. They employed Kintsch's (1974) propositional analysis on the texts to discover the similarities and differences between the two classes. The results showed that the novices generated the same number of macrostructure propositions (i.e., units reflecting the main ideas of a text as opposed to

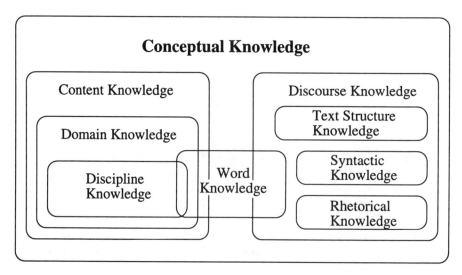

FIGURE 4.1. Conceptual knowledge (From Alexander, Schallert, & Hare, 1991. Copyright © 1991 by the American Educational Research Association; Reprinted by permission).

supporting details) as did the experts. Thus, the main events of the game found their way into the narratives of both classes. They differed markedly at the micro level of propositions, however. The experts incorporated many more detailed ideas into the texts compared to the novices. Presumably, the texts of the novices would have received poorer content quality ratings than would those of the experts, but subjective quality assessment was not done.

Caccamise (1987) measured the ideational fluency of college students on two topics, one familiar and the other unfamiliar. She asked the students to think aloud while they generated ideas as a prewriting task. She found a negatively accelerated relationship in the cumulative number of ideas generated across time. Increasingly fewer new ideas occurred during the latter phases of her task. The curve was especially steep on the unfamiliar task, as the students quickly exhausted their supply of ideas. There were fewer ideas on unfamiliar topics than on familiar ones, and those ideas were less well organized.

The studies by Voss et al. and by Caccamise illustrate two approaches to examining knowledge effects. One way is to hold the topic constant and compare individuals who know more or less about it. Another way is to study the same individuals on topics that are more or less familiar to them. A third way is to study the same individuals on the same topic but provide more or less information about the topic as part of the task environment (Kellogg, 1990). College students in my laboratory were provided with the writing topic only (T), the topic plus several relevant ideas to use in an essay (TI), or the topic plus ideas plus a possible organizational structure for an essay (TIO). The three conditions mirrored different levels of schemata development on the topic.

The overall quality of the essays increased systematically across the T, TI, and TIO conditions for writers who used no prewriting strategy. The same result occurred for writers who used a clustering strategy in which they diagrammed a network of ideas and their relations during prewriting. But for writers who outlined during prewriting, the T, TI, and TIO conditions failed to differ reliably. This result will be returned to in Chapter 6 in discussing the effects of prewriting strategies.

The availability of domain-specific content knowledge helps writers plan text in two ways, judging from Langer's (1984) work. Langer measured how much students knew about a topic by asking them to free-associate in response to key words, jotting down whatever words entered their minds. Judges then evaluated their responses in terms of quantity (ideational fluency) and quality (the degree of organization among ideas), as well as a combined measure (fluency of well-organized ideas). All three measures correlated reliably but modestly with ratings of essays composed by the students. Thus, topic knowledge helps writers both generate a large number of relevant ideas and organize them effectively.

Rowan (1990) also obtained reliable but modest correlations between the degree of domain-specific knowledge possessed by writers and a measure of quality in an explanatory writing task. The participants first read a document that explained five basic properties of light and historical information about the discovery of these properties. Then they wrote a text that explained these properties to a particular audience. The technical accuracy of the resulting texts and the degree to which the texts proved adaptive to the needs of the assigned audience were coded by judges.

Accuracy correlated reliably with the number of semesters of high school science ($r = .27$) and with the number of hours of college physics taken by the writers ($r = .16$). Given the large sample size (over 150 participants), these relationships were statistically significant, but the effect sizes were modest at best. The adaptiveness of the tests correlated only with the number of high school science semesters, and weakly at that ($r = .18$).

Thus, on both theoretical and empirical grounds, it is clear that writing skill depends on much more than domain-specific knowledge. Another caveat about the effects of such knowledge comes from the findings of Rosenberg and Wright (1988). They examined ideational generation in a task similar to those used by Caccamise (1987) and Langer (1984). Their participants received either a familiar or an unfamiliar topic sentence for a short story and then wrote down in 15 minutes all the ideas that entered their minds. Next, they reread their lists of ideas, added to and deleted from the lists as appropriate, bracketed related ideas, and marked all the main ideas as opposed to details.

For one pair of familiar ("The bride kissed the groom") versus unfamiliar ("The farmer dropped the knife") topic sentences, the results showed greater ideational fluency for the familiar sentence. However, the ideas generated were not more related and integrated relative to those surrounding the unfamiliar sentence. Furthermore, the results showed no differences for a second pair of familiar ("The doctor cured the patient") versus unfamiliar ("The judge fired the janitor") sentences. Rosenberg and Wright stressed the high degree of variability in their data, both between the sentence content conditions and among the individual writers assigned to any given condition. They speculated that these variations arose because some individuals in the familiar condition elected to construct a novel scenario from their topic sentence instead of using existing schemata. At the same time, some individuals in the unfamiliar condition assimilated the topic sentence to familiar schemata, which had the effect of augmenting idea generation. How the participants chose to use available knowledge, regardless of how much they knew, affected the experiment's outcome in interesting ways.

Discourse Knowledge

Lexical and Syntactic Knowledge. *Discourse knowledge* refers to knowledge about language and its uses. Text quality measures of style, language usage, punctuation, mechanics, rhetorical skill, sentence complexity, textual cohesiveness, and the like depend crucially on discourse knowledge. It equates with Applebee's (1982) categories of language and audience knowledge in his discussion of what writers must know. Discourse knowledge operates at the word, sentence, paragraph, and text levels. At the word or lexical level, such knowledge overlaps with content knowledge in the sense that the consensual symbol of the word refers to a schema that represents content knowledge about objects and events. The more words a writer knows, the more opportunities he or she has to choose the right word in a particular context. Vocabulary development and diversity in word choice relate positively to the quality ratings given to their samples (Grobe, 1981).

Another aspect of discourse knowledge is understanding the syntactic rules for combining words into meaningful propositions and sentences. Syntactic rules define the acceptable and unacceptable strings of words in a language. The coherence of a paragraph depends in part on the use of syntactic ties between independent clauses (Haliday & Hasan, 1976). The use of conjunctions, for instance, illustrates such cohesive ties. An extensive literature shows that the complexity of syntactic structures used by writers increases as they mature and learn how to write (e.g., Crowhurst & Piché, 1979). Yet this literature does not support a clear relation between judgments of writing quality and degree of syntactic knowledge (Huot, 1990). For example, Nold and Freedman (1977) measured 17 syntactic variables and correlated them with holistic quality judgments on writing samples of college freshmen. With the exception of the use of final free modifiers, none of the variables predicted quality ratings. As we will see, syntactic knowledge is only one means for providing textual coherence and effective composition.

Text Structure Knowledge.   Texts vary in structure according to their aims and uses. Theorists have offered various classifications of text structures (e.g., Britton, Burgess, Martin, MacLeod, & Rosen, 1975; Kinneavy, 1971; Meyer, 1975). One long-standing classification is Alexander Bain's distinctions among narrative, descriptive, expository, and persuasive types of text (DiPardo, 1990). Although I will refer in this section and elsewhere to studies that manipulate the type or mode of discourse, it is important to recognize that the boundary between one mode and another is fuzzy and that writing assignments often call for a blend of various modes. The writer's ideas and aims, rather than the defining rules of a particular mode, ought to guide the structure that a text assumes. As DiPardo (1990) reminded us:

> Rhetorical tradition has too often distorted issues of intention and purpose by setting up unnatural distinctions, devising categories and components that are said to be useful for both describing and teaching the art of written discourse.... The need thus emerges to look at writing as a flexible, many-faceted phenomenon involving divergent and ever-shifting goals, engaging the whole self in all its interwoven dimensions—the cognitive, emotional, social, and spiritual. (pp. 66–67)

Knowledge of the prototypical structure of a mode of discourse is important in the comprehension and recall of text (Kintsch & van Dijk, 1978; Thorndyke, 1977) and in text production (Hillocks, 1986). Moreover, explicit instruction on text structures amplifies students' writing quality (Gordon & Braun, 1985b).

Knowledge of text structure includes the means for organizing the topical information in a text. The various types of text structures differ in the degree of syntactic complexity that they typically require. In reviewing the literature on this point, Hillocks (1986) concluded that persuasive and expository texts tend to exhibit more complex sentence structures than narratives. However, all these modes of discourse share a need for coherence at both the local and global levels. Haliday and Hasan (1976) identified several cohesiveness ties that operate on a semantic as well as a syntactic level. Through the repetition of words, paraphrasing, and use of pronouns, one can link an independent clause to the one that preceded it. In this way, each sentence elaborates the one that precedes it, establishing a strong sense of local coherence. Learning the means to link information locally is necessary for the developing writer (Englert, Stewart, & Hiebert, 1988; McCutchen, 1982).

Sentences must do more than relate locally to each other, however. Each sentence must develop the topic as a whole, thus contributing to the global coherence of the text (Kintsch & van Dijk, 1978). Witte (1983) concluded that a writer's use of global links that organize and deliver information to the reader is essential in the production of high-quality text. A text that develops a topic in a globally coherent manner, as measured by a method that Witte called the *Functional Sentence Perspective,* received high scores for holistic quality. Syntactic measures, such as the mean number of words per clause, failed to distinguish high- versus low-quality texts and global coherence. Sullivan (1987) advanced this theme by showing that writers' sophistication in using devices to introduce new information and relate it to given information, thus developing the topic across an entire text, figured prominently in how well their essays were rated for quality. Like local coherence, knowledge of the means to attain global coherence grows with the maturity of the writer (Englert & Hiebert, 1984; Wright & Rosenberg, 1993).

Rhetorical Knowledge.   Lastly, rhetorical knowledge concerns an understanding of the audience of a text. The writer adopts different styles and assumes different tones to achieve various rhetorical effects with various audiences. Although writers may compose texts only for themselves, they typically address the needs of the intended readers. Rhetorical knowledge, then, is vital to a writer's ability. It should not be conceived as mere polish, with other aspects of discourse knowledge comprising the substance of writing skill. Certainly in the case of persuasive and expository writing, the author must adapt the text to a specific audience for it to be effective (Rafoth, 1985; Rubin & Rafoth, 1986).

Writers of high school age know how to tailor their syntax to the demands of their audience (Crowhurst & Piche, 1979). Bracewell, Scardamalia, and Bereiter (1978) found that specifying the audience for writers in grades 4 and 8 had no impact on the frequency of generating statements that provide a context for the reader. By grade 12, however, knowing to whom they were writing increased the number of context-creating statements. Flower and Hayes's (1981) concluded that the timing of pauses in writing is typically determined by rhetorical planning needs. Analyses of verbal protocols revealed substantial pauses when expert writers pondered the needs of the audience and the writers' purposes and goals. Finally, Rowan (1990) reported a small but reliable correlation between her measure of audience knowledge and scores of the adaptiveness of explanatory essays ($r = .13$).

Concern with knowing the audience has been important to orators and composers since antiquity. Aristotle and Cicero devoted much attention to the attitudes and emotions of audience members, breaking them into social groups that hold varying expectations. Even so, Faigley et al. (1985) noted that "we still do not understand how successful orators or writers come to a sense of audience and use that awareness" (p. 81). Echoing this sentiment, Hillocks (1986) noted, in his review and meta-analysis of the literature, that a writer's use of rhetorical knowledge remains an important topic for research. He asked the following unanswered questions that still require further research:

Do writers hold some sort of audience in mind as they write? If so, how specifically
developed is the image? To what extent is the image a composite which includes
the writer's own memories of experience as audience? . . . When and how do writers
decide to elaborate, simplify, clarify? (p. 90)

This is not to say that interesting work has failed to shed light on these questions.
Rafoth (1988), for example, argued that audience awareness is a highly interactive
component of writing. Writers do not simply envision a group of readers, infer the
nature of their attitudes and beliefs, and imagine how they might respond to the
evolving text. They also share substantial amounts of knowledge with their readers
in the form of cultural norms and domain-specific knowledge. Writers attempt to
steer readers in new ways of thinking by skillfully linking new ideas to shared old
ideas. A text that tells readers only what they already know and expect fails to
persuade, inform, or entertain. Instead of *audience,* Rafoth prefers the term *discourse
community* to capture the dynamic way in which writers, readers, and texts interact.
Consistent with this view, Langer (1984) found that a writer's sense of audience is
enhanced by having a substantial amount of background knowledge on the writing
topic. Further, attending to the audience while drafting has been shown to yield
poorer-quality texts than waiting until revision (Roen & Willey, 1988). While drafting, the writer gains a personal voice without worrying to excess about the reader's
reaction. It must be added, though, that Rafoth (1989) observed both good and
poor writers among college freshmen delaying their concern with audience until
revision.

Metacognitive Knowledge

When people reflect on what they know and what they can do, they engage in
metacognition, or thinking about thinking. Flavell, Miller, and Miller (1993) and
Alexander et al. (1991) conceptualized metacognition in terms of self-knowledge,
task knowledge, and strategic knowledge. *Self-knowledge* involves awareness of how
well one performs various tasks, especially relative to the abilities of others. Such
knowledge might well influence a writer's motivation levels in particular tasks,
depending on their assessment of whether success is likely. The self-schema is
widely recognized as critical to both intrapersonal processes of perception, memory,
affect, and emotion and interpersonal processes of social perception, social strategies,
and feedback processing (Markus & Wurf, 1987).

Throughout cognitive development, people assess the demands that tasks place
upon them—that is, they develop *task knowledge.* The relative difficulty of different
types of writing assignments, for example, comprises part of what a writer knows
about the task environment. Knowledge of the materials that are relevant to a particular writing assignment is another aspect of task assessment. Knowing where to
turn in collecting information needed for completion of the task is crucial. The
strategies, tools, and work schedules adopted by writers vary with their assessment
of the difficulties that lie ahead. Besides reflecting on the task environment, writers
reflect on the physical, social, and cultural environments in which the act of composition is situated. To illustrate this with a well-known example, when Salman

Rushdie (1989) composed *Satanic Verses,* he surely reflected on the risks of casting Islam in a poor light, in the opinion of the fundamentalist Muslim world.

Metacognition also includes *strategic knowledge,* or awareness of the strategies that help one to retrieve and apply knowledge. This strategic aspect of metacognition refers not to skill in using the strategy itself, but to the ability to evaluate when a strategy is needed, to select an appropriate strategy, and to monitor the effectiveness of the chosen strategy. The costs and benefits of various strategies must also be understood by writers if they are to allocate their attention effectively given the demands of the task at hand. For example, outlining as a prewriting activity may be worth the effort for certain writing tasks but not others. Skilled writers use what they know about themselves, about tasks and materials, and about strategies to navigate their way through the sea of challenges confronting them in writing.

Metacognitive knowledge comes slowly in development through countless cycles of cognition, in which a person explores the environment and modifies schemata (Flavell et al., 1993). Schemata that represent aspects of other schemata must be developed to enable one to think about one's own cognitive processes.

Karmiloff-Smith (1986) fruitfully conceptualized the development of metacognition in terms of progressively generating explicit representations, which are consciously accessible and usable, from implicit, tacit representations. A child's gradual awareness of grammatical rules illustrates such development. Three-year-olds can label ungrammatical sentences as ''silly'' (e.g., ''Ball me the bring''), suggesting that tacit schemata are functional (Gleitman, Gleitman, & Shipley, 1972). Only later, by about age 7 or 8, do children begin to identify particular rules in the sense that they can list multiple examples of a specific rule. Still later, at age 9 or 10 at the earliest, children gain awareness of the rules, generating explicit personal symbols that may be reflected upon from tacit schemata. As metalinguistic development proceeds, the older child can verbalize the grammatical rules and refer to them abstractly, independent of concrete examples.

A major movement in the teaching of all language skills, including writing, flies under the banner of *language awareness* (James & Garrett, 1992). The range of instructional exercises used with this label are too broad to characterize adequately here. They address the needs of learning to speak and write in a foreign language as well as in one's native tongue. Yet all the exercises emphasize the development of explicit awareness about language and its uses. Awareness of the cognitive, affective, and social aspects of language all receive emphasis.

Sharples (1985), using computer technology, designed a teaching system that encouraged explicit learning of linguistic rules. Children using his system developed a vocabulary of linguistic terms and examples of various grammatical rules. At the same time, they generated and modified sentences through a set of exercises and games. After completing this initial phase, the children applied their knowledge of language to creative writing. The second phase took children ''through the levels of text from sentences to story by creating simple descriptions, linking them together into a descriptive environment, and then forming this into a narrative essay'' (p. 84). Other activities in the second phase further developed an explicit awareness of discourse knowledge.

Although Sharples noted individual differences among the 11-year-old children in his study, he found the computer-based teaching system to be effective in advancing their writing skills. Most students in the treatment group interacted well with the computer and profited from the experience. Only one of the children in the control group, who happened to come "from a family of avid readers and theatre-goers" (p. 108), matched the progress made by those for whom the computer interactions were fruitful. Sharples and Evans (1992) further advanced their approach, based on feature analysis and metacognition, to teaching creative writing in children aged 9 and 10.

Bereiter and Scardamalia (1987) suggested ways to hasten metacognitive awareness in young writers who have progressed to the point of being able to represent knowledge explicitly, as described by Karmiloff-Smith (1986). These include teaching children to think aloud and asking students to tell others how to do a particular writing task. Scardamalia, Bereiter, and Steinbach (1984) reported that such methods lead to an increase in the amount of reflective thinking shown by sixth-grade writers.

Gordon (1990) evaluated the effect of explicit instruction in story structure on the metacognitive awareness of sixth graders using a pretest-posttest design. Throughout the school year, the teacher explained the role of setting, plot, and resolution in narrative texts; analyzed stories using diagrams; used thinking-aloud exercises during reading and writing; and taught students to question themselves during comprehension and composition. Similar instruction focused on expository text structures. Gordon reported that throughout the year, students developed more elaborate schemata for narrative and expository texts. Further, they showed an increased awareness of having access to a variety of meaning-making strategies during reading and writing, though only a few shifted to greater use of self-monitoring strategies. Raphael, Englert, and Kirschner (1989) also concluded that direct instruction is beneficial and isolated some specific metacognitive skills that are learned from alternative instructional formats.

A study on metacognition and writing in teenagers was reported by Durst (1989). High- and low-ability 11th-grade students composed aloud in two experimental sessions. In one session, they wrote an analytic essay that called for marshaling evidence to support a thesis. In the other, they wrote a chronological summary essay based on their reading of history passages. Interestingly, the students monitored their composing processes and assessed their understanding of the topic markedly less in writing the summaries. The analytic essay demanded knowledge-transformation, whereas the summary essay permitted knowledge-telling (Bereiter & Scardamalia, 1987; Haas, 1990); the former type of task invokes greater metacognitive activity than the latter. Monitoring took many forms in writing the analytic essay. Both high- and low-ability writers devoted substantial time and effort to calibrating the demands of the task, assessing their domain-specific knowledge of the topic, and monitoring the effectiveness of their writing strategies.

Multiple Measures of Knowledge

Rosenberg, Lebovitz, Penningroth, and Wright (1992) assessed the quality of expository texts written by college students and related it to two discourse knowledge indexes. They administered a test designed to tap a writer's knowledge of what makes a text globally coherent; the test required the ability to identify sentences that help develop a topic. They also measured reading comprehension, which provides a broadly defined index of discourse knowledge. Another measure in the study concerned the writer's planning ability. The authors' results showed reliable correlations between essay quality and reading comprehension ($r = .46$), knowledge of global coherence ($r = .39$), and planning ability ($r = .30$). A multiple regression analysis showed that all three predictive measures combined accounted for 30% of the variation in quality ratings.

Accounting for nearly a third of the variance in writing quality is impressive, given the large individual differences that characterize writing research. The results reported by Rosenberg et al. (1992) raised the possibility of doing incrementally better by including measures of domain-specific knowledge and discourse knowledge. To this end, I borrowed the baseball knowledge quiz and the narrative writing task used by Voss et al. (1980) and added a persuasive writing task concerned with salaries in major league baseball (Kellogg, 1992). The ACT examination provides a separate score for verbal ability, as does the SAT. The ACT English score indexed discourse knowledge in the study. Scores on such standardized tests reflect the availability of certain aspects of discourse knowledge, especially word and syntactic knowledge. Specifically, they aim to assess an individual's proficiency in diction, spelling, grammar, punctuation, syntax, and sentence order (Charney, 1984).

Overall quality scores, representing the sum of analytic scores on content and style, correlated reliably with the ACT English scores ($r = .39$) and with the baseball knowledge quiz ($r = .57$) for the narrative task. Combining both measures in the multiple regression analysis showed that 38% of the variance in quality judgments could be explained. For the persuasive task, the ACT ($r = .53$) and the quiz ($r = .43$) scores correlated reliably with overall quality; jointly the measures accounted for 40% of the variance in quality judgments.

Note that domain-specific knowledge proved more important in the narrative task, whereas the ACT index of discourse knowledge dominated in the persuasive task. The degree of relationship is moderate but is nevertheless encouraging relative to other results in the literature. For instance, Rowan's (1990) multiple regression analyses showed 23% of the variance in scores of accuracy of explanations accounted for by two measures of domain-specific knowledge and three measures of discourse knowledge (plus a measure of audience knowledge). The adaptiveness of the explanatory essays proved still more elusive, with only 12% of the variation in scores explained by the multiple regression model. Conceivably a study that combined the measures of reading comprehension, knowledge of global coherence, planning ability, verbal knowledge, rhetorical knowledge, domain-specific knowledge, and metacognitive knowledge might account for a substantial degree of variance. As we will see later in this chapter, though, this possibility hinges on using writing tasks that motivate writers to amplify their performance. If they economize effort and satisfice quality instead, then linear relationships among these measures would not be expected to account for high degrees of quality variation.

The Preparation of Writers

High levels of experience with and education about a subject are both necessary for the writer to be regarded as an expert. Only then will there be a rich network of content, discourse, and other forms of knowledge. Scripts, frames, formal concepts, affective concepts, and all other types of schemata encode the procedures, meanings, and episodes of the writer's learning experiences. How much knowledge has been acquired and how will both be reflected in the schemata available to an individual writer.

For example, affective concepts are available to someone who experienced, say, combat in the Vietnam War that are impossible to acquire through books, lectures, or films. Also, the vividness of personal symbols acquired through primary experience cannot be matched by secondary media. On the other hand, books and lectures are ideal for learning formal categories that are often difficult to pick up through isolated experience with examples. For instance, everyday experience with falling objects and inclined planes does not help, and may work against, acquiring the formalizations of physics (Caramazza, McCloskey, & Green, 1981).

Anecdotal Evidence

One way to document the importance of knowledge availability in writing is to consider what well-known authors report about their preparation for their craft. Education through formal and informal means are essential to the writer. As Henry James advised, "Write from experience and experience only," but "Try to be one of the people on whom nothing is lost" (Bartlett, 1992). James Michener engaged in extensive library research for his writing but also emphasized the importance of experience in building sufficient domain-specific knowledge. He put the matter well in the following quotation (King, 1990):

> I try to do everything I write about. I go oystering in the Chesapeake. I go crabbing. I climb mountains, and I've gone across deserts. I think I should be viewed as a literary Baptist. I believe in total immersion. I think that unless your head is underwater, you really ain't been baptized. (pp. 191–192)

Similarly, Jack London prepared himself for writing *Call of the Wild* by dropping out of school at age 14 to work in a cannery. He "took odd jobs on the tough Oakland waterfront, raided oyster beds in San Francisco Bay, then joined harbor police . . . traveled on a seal boat to Japan, worked in a jute mill, and wandered the country as a hobo" (Weil, 1992, p. 2T).

Reading extensively is another trait of the writer, as Louis L'Amour (1989) made clear in his autobiography, *Education of a Wandering Man*. He recounted the hundreds of books that he digested as part of his development as one of the most prolific of all American writers. His reading list while riding the rails or taking passage on a freighter to the Orient as a young man surpassed even the Great Books curriculum of the 1930s. He literally read everything he could get his hands on and went to great lengths to find the classics of Western literature.

John Barth, too, immersed himself in the classics, as he explained in the following interview (Plimpton, 1989):

> The great guides were the books I discovered in the Johns Hopkins Library, where my student job was to file books away. One was more or less encouraged to take a cart of books and go back into the stacks and not come out for seven or eight hours. So I read what I was filing. My great teachers (the best thing that can happen to a writer) were Scheherazade, Homer, Virgil, and Boccaccio; also the great Sanskrit taletellers. I was impressed forever with the width as well as the depth of literature—just what a kid from the sticks, from the swamp, in my case, needed. (p. 4)

Truman Capote also revealed his reading compulsion; when asked in an interview whether he read a great deal, he responded (Cowley, 1958):

> Too much. And anything, including labels and recipes and advertisements. I have a passion for newspapers—read all the New York dailies everyday, and the Sunday editions, and several foreign magazines too. The ones I don't buy I read standing at news stands. I average about five books a week—the normal-length novel takes me about two hours. (p. 293)

Of course, the reading habit is hardly unique to fiction writers. A remarkable illustration may be found in Professor Harold Bloom of Yale University, whose productivity as a literary critic is outdone only by his reading proficiency (Lehman, 1986). Professor Bloom claims to read and absorb up to 1,000 pages per hour. Given that this rate translates to about 3.6 seconds per page, skepticism is natural. However, the remarkable scope of the literary anthologies that he has edited, numbering 800 volumes, lend credence to his claim. His original introductory essays for the anthologies fill about 25 volumes alone. Such work required vast reading, no matter what the rate.

Empirical Evidence

A variety of biographical studies have concluded that at least 10 years and often 20 years of experience is needed for an individual to attain the status of an expert. Simon and Chase (1973) studied chess experts in detail and commented that all international chess masters have been intensely engaged in the art of the game for at least a decade. Gustin (1985) reported a similar finding for exceptional research mathematicians.

Hayes (1981) examined musical composition, the domain closest to text composition that has been studied in this way. Strikingly, he found that the average time needed between the initiation of musical education and the creation of an outstanding composition is 20 years. Contrary to popular belief, child prodigies such as Mozart required extensive practice in composing and immersion in the field of music prior to creating a truly eminent work, as judged by music experts. The early compositions of such prodigies fail to meet the criteria for outstanding quality.

What can be said about the activities that must transpire during the decade or two needed to attain expertise? Ericsson, Krampe, Tesch-Römer (1993) marshaled an impressive array of evidence that expert performance in any domain represents the end result of highly effortful and sustained activities designed to attain excellence. They called such activities *deliberate practice.* Outstanding performance in domains as diverse as athletics and music depends equally on intensive, prolonged, deliberate practice, often beginning in childhood. The individual must manage to maintain the motivation to practice and excel, on the one hand, and to avoid burning out and losing interest, on the other.

A series of studies examined the developmental antecedents of creative individuals in science, leadership, and other domains. Simonton (1988) reviewed this literature and drew several interesting conclusions regarding cultural enrichment, role models, and formal education. First, parents of creative individuals are often financially secure enough to provide a culturally and intellectually stimulating environment, ''as revealed by respectable home libraries, magazine subscriptions, and artistic or mechanical hobbies'' (p. 111). Several studies document a correlation between intensive reading in childhood and success in adulthood. Besides reading, active exploration of the environment is encouraged by parents of future achievers.

The need for an intellectually stimulating environment certainly does not end at childhood. Rich social interaction through conversation with family, friends, and other writers spurs creativity for some mature writers. Samuel Johnson and the Bronte sisters readily come to mind as classic illustrations. Yet, equally remarkable writers, such as Balzac and Joyce, managed or perhaps depended on social isolation (Boorstin, 1992).

Second, the odds of an eminent figure emerging in a field increases with exposure to other eminent figures who serve as role models. Simonton suggests that these role models may either be *paragons* who are admired from a distance or *mentors* who personally guide an emerging genius. For instance, the chances of winning a Nobel Prize are better for those who have studied with a previous laureate than for those who have not (Zuckerman, 1977).

Simonton warns against imitating role models too closely, however. Creative development calls for emulation, but only to a degree. A well-known example of overdoing imitation is the lackluster careers of Rembrandt's students, who followed the master's style so meticulously that distinguishing Rembrandt's work from that of his students poses challenges. None moved on to achieve distinction in their own right by developing their own unique styles. Seeing beyond one's predecessors by standing on the shoulders of giants, to use Newton's image, requires stepping on role models at some point.

Third, the role of formal education and creativity is complex. Several studies have shown that succeeding in school fails to predict later creative performance. Einstein's disdain for formal instruction, even in mathematics, characterizes this outcome. On the other hand, in science at least, the most creative practitioners acquired their doctorates at an early age and usually completed both their undergraduate and graduate education at prestigious universities (Zuckerman, 1977). Yet it is not uncommon for creative individuals to make substantive contributions to their field before completing their doctorates. For example, Einstein wrote revolutionary papers in 1905 while working in a patent office, rather than in the laboratories and lecture halls of the University of Zurich.

Interestingly, the most famous case of contested authorship turns in part on whether a formal education is a necessary condition for greatness as a writer. For two centuries, debates have raged about the true identity of Shakespeare. Scholars have contended that Francis Bacon, Edward de Vere, and an astonishing 56 other candidates may have been the Bard, not William Shakespeare of Stratford. A central argument against the man from Stratford is the absence of any records that Shakespeare attended grammar school and widespread agreement that he did not study at a university. Surely, the greatest dramatist of Western culture could not have been an uneducated commoner, some claim.

Yet, Matus (1991) points out that the venerable Ben Jonson had only a few years of basic schooling, let alone a university education, before going to work, most likely as a bricklayer. Moreover, the grammar school records of Jonson's attendance no longer exist; only a few biographical notes verify that he received any formal education at all. Conceivably, literary genius can develop from experience and informal education alone. Both Jonson and Shakespeare were clearly men of the theater with prodigious experience in the staging of drama.

Simonton (1988) explained—correctly, I think—that the question is not whether education enhances creativity. The answer is clearly affirmative. Rather, the question is whether formal schooling competes with self-instruction as a viable form of education. Again, the answer is affirmative, he believes. From primary school to graduate school, gifted individuals devote themselves to various intellectual hobbies, including, as noted earlier, extensive reading. Not surprisingly, creative graduate students spend markedly more time on independent research and self-initiated study than unproductive colleagues, for example (Chambers, 1964).

For most individuals, the value of formal education in developing a reservoir of knowledge and skills should not be underestimated. A recent study documented that, on the whole, formal schooling has a large, positive impact on the intellectual capital of a nation after controlling for the effects of home background (Husen & Tujinman, 1991). Longitudinal data on intelligence test scores gathered in the Netherlands and Sweden were analyzed using linear structural relations models. It was found that the educational attainment of youth was accounted for by home background and by child IQ measured at age 10. Home background failed to influence adult IQ, measured at age 20, once child IQ and formal schooling were held constant. Schooling, in contrast, did directly influence adult IQ, holding constant the variations in home background and child IQ.

Implicit Memory and Knowledge Access

Some of the knowledge that writers draw upon exists as the printed sources of other authors. Britton et al. (1975) noted that a writer copies from others in many ways, including verbatim quotations, expansions or summarizations, presentations of alternative points of view that differ from those of the writer, and mimicking the stylistic voice of another. These forms of copying generally proceed with full awareness on the part of the writer.

But much of what a writer knows, particularly discourse and sociocultural knowledge, exists only in tacit form. For example, sentence patterns as well as cultural beliefs are shared by members of the same discourse community and are drawn upon freely by all, without conscious awareness. The same sort of unconscious copying may also occur with specific sentences, facts, and arguments—forms of domain-specific knowledge. When it does, however, the author is subject to the charge of plagiarism.

Cryptomnesia refers to the belief that a thought is novel when in fact it is a memory (Brown & Murphy, 1989). The phenomenon can lead to inadvertent plagiarism if a writer fails to acknowledge unwittingly an earlier source due to the failure to recognize his or her own thoughts and words as unoriginal. In some cases the writer borrows from the words of others, as did Daniels (1972), who confessed to inadvertent plagiarism as follows: "I have certainly been aware that I had an extraordinary ability to remember material when I wanted to, but I have never before realized that I did it unconsciously" (p. 125). In other cases the writer borrows unknowingly from his or her own published work. As Skinner (1983) lamented: "one of the most disheartening experiences of old age is discovering that a point you have just made—so significant, so beautifully expressed—was made by you in something you published a long time ago" (p. 242).

Cases of apparently inadvertent plagiarism surface regularly in newspaper and magazine publishing and in the music industry. Punitive actions sometimes result, as in the case of the editor dismissed after years of service for a major newspaper after failing to recognize that the words in her editorial had been published elsewhere or the copyright infringement ruling against George Harrison for unwittingly reincarnating the tune "He's So Fine" by the Chiffons in the form of "My Sweet Lord."

In a seminal laboratory analogue of cryptomnesia, Brown and Murphy (1989) had groups of four students take turns generating examples of categories (generate). Then each student in the group tried to recall the examples that he or she generated (recall old), under instructions to not name items generated by others. Finally, they generated additional examples (recall new), again with instructions to duplicate neither their own nor others' earlier responses. On the recall old test, 75% of the participants produced at least one plagiarized item and, on the recall-new test, 70% did so. Self-plagiarized items, the thorn of Skinner, were rare in the laboratory task; nearly all items were lifted from other students.

The pattern of results in the three experiments reported by Brown and Murphy indicated that plagiarism occurred more frequently in written tasks than in oral tasks. Having heard material, one is more likely to plagiarize it when writing than when speaking. Whether the reverse pattern occurs after having read material remains to be seen. But based on their results alone, writers may be especially susceptible to borrowing unknowingly ideas they have gained through lectures, discussions, and other forms of aural input. In addition, their results indicated that high-frequency responses and those from orthographic as opposed to semantic categories were most likely to be plagiarized. The implications of the former outcome are straightforward;

ideas that are expressed frequently—that are "in the air"—are especially open to borrowing. The latter outcome may imply that shallow, superficial matters of how things look or sound are more susceptible to plagiarism than deep, semantic matters of what things mean. But a broad generalization of this type is premature.

The mutual interdependence of creativity and recall was highlighted in the opening chapter. The writer's task clearly calls for the full generative power of language. Duplicating sentences is the exception to the rule; virtually all sentences are unique, which is in part what makes the translation process of discourse production so creative. The planning of ideas clearly also demands creativity from the writer, with the quality of a document depending in some ways on the uniqueness of ideas that it contains. At the same time, though, the writer cannot create without an extensive reservoir of knowledge. That knowledge must be made accessible, either consciously or unconsciously, and then applied inventively to the problems that arise in composition. The phenomenon of cryptomnesia demonstrates how even what seems to be a wholly creative effort has links to previously stored knowledge.

Knowledge and the Writing Process

Qualitative Restructuring

Bereiter and Scardamalia (1987) developed their ideas about knowledge telling and knowledge transforming by observing the different ways in which children and knowledgeable writers generate ideas. Because young writers know relatively little about specific domains, they experience great difficulty in generating usable ideas. Even college students, in comparison to experts in an area such as biology or economics, suffer from idea bankruptcy when planning text (Graesser, Hopkinson, Lewis, & Bruflodt, 1984). Whereas an expert might generate far too many ideas to be included in a text, the novice strains to generate enough to begin and quickly laments, "I can't think of anything else to say."

By the age of 12, most children have developed knowledge telling, in which the writing assignment is converted into a topic. Then memory is searched for information relevant to the topic, and the retrieved idea is translated into a sentence. This process continues until no more ideas can be found and composition ceases. The expert, in contrast, sets goals for the text and generates ideas that satisfy these goals. The interactions among collecting, planning, translating, and reviewing are sophisticated as the expert struggles with the problems of content and rhetoric. Of course, the development of knowledge transforming hinges on multiple factors, but the greater topic knowledge of the expert is certainly a key factor.

Several studies have examined how the processes of collecting, planning, translating, and reviewing differ for the expert writer compared with the novice. Qualitative changes in the nature of the writing process with growth in expertise are readily observable. For one thing, the strategies used by experienced writers include a concern for the rhetorical situation that is not seen in the writing of novices (Flower & Hayes, 1980a). Based on an analysis of verbal protocols, Flower and Hayes reported that expert writers generated 67% of their ideas in response to rhetorical goals related to the novel writing task. Novice writers, in contrast, generated 83% of their ideas in response to the writing topic.

In reviewing the literature on how planning differs between experts and novices, Hayes and Flower (1986) suggested that thinking more carefully about rhetorical concerns is only one of three key differences. Another is that expert writers draw upon schemata for sentences, paragraphs, and entire documents (e.g., Schumacher, Klare, Cronin, & Moses, 1984). Having written extensively in a given genre, for example, alters qualitatively how a writer plans a new document. Certain elements of the format take shape when the writer retrieves already developed schemata.

The writing assignments confronted by experts are not amenable to following a formula, however. As argued here, a highly knowledgeable writer may elect to settle for satisfactory performance and automatize, to a degree, the demands of planning and other operations. But to achieve the expert's best level of work, the demands of writing operations must remain stringent. Simply retrieving well-tuned schemata fails to yield the necessary quality. Even so, the expert can draw on problem-solving strategies that are unavailable to the novice. Hayes and Flower (1986) identified this difference as the third important way that the planning of an expert appears different from the planning of a novice. Both may devote the same time and effort to writing, but only the expert can invest attention in sophisticated problem-solving strategies that yield sophisticated texts.

Hayes and Flower (1986) proposed three specific problem-solving strategies employed by experts. The expert knows how to define the goals of the writing task in a way that is at once both demanding and manageable. The expert, through the reflective procedure of knowledge transformation, constructs an elaborate plan for a document involving many goals, subgoals, and constraints. Finally, the expert understands and uses the metacognitive strategies of monitoring the process and directing attention to specific aspects of planning, such as generating ideas versus organizing.

In some respects, translating ideas into sentences appears qualitatively the same for experts and less skilled writers. Both types of writers usually construct sentences from left to right in a part-by-part manner (Kaufer, Hayes, & Flower, 1986). Roughly 75% of the sentence parts mentioned in a thinking-aloud protocol were included in the actual text of both types of writers. The key difference observed by Kaufer et al. was that the experts generated more words per part and longer documents overall.

This outcome is not surprising, given Hunt's (1965) landmark study and the many studies that followed it. Hunt examined how the sentence structures of writers change with experience and instruction. The minimal *terminal unit,* or *T-unit,* refers to a main clause and all of its added modifiers, including subordinate clauses. Hunt found that across Grades 4, 8, and 12, the average number of words per T-unit and the average number of words per clause increased reliably. Moreover, Hunt found changes in the types of clauses employed. Adjectival clauses doubled in frequency between the 4th and 8th grades, and doubled again between the 8th and 12th grades. Noun clauses also increased with grade level, albeit less dramatically.

At still higher levels of expertise, Faigley (1979) reported that T-units, clauses, and modifiers were all reliably shorter for college students than for professional writers. The professionals wrote between two and five times as many base words as modifiers, depending on the type of modifier, compared to the college students.

Of course, a major development in writing skill is learning the rules of spelling, punctuation, handwriting, and other mechanics of consensual symbol systems. Translating ideas into text is a qualitatively different operation when one must struggle with these low-level production concerns than when they come automatically. Children have not yet mastered such production rules, and the need to focus on mechanics contributes to poor performance (Perl, 1979). Still, developmental studies by Bereiter and Scardamalia (1987) raise doubts that poor writing performance in young children is due primarily to a preoccupation with mechanics. Instead, they point to the crucial shift from a knowledge-telling to a knowledge-transforming strategy.

The nature of reviewing also differs with the expertise of the writer. Faigley and Witte (1981) analyzed texts revised by college freshmen, advanced college students, and expert adult writers. The advanced students made the most changes. They made about the same number of corrections that altered the meaning of the text as did the experts, but nearly twice as many nonmeaning changes as well. The freshmen made nearly all nonmeaning changes. The experienced writers were more likely to alter the ideas and organization of a document, whereas the novices viewed editing only in terms of mechanical corrections and word choice (see also Stallard, 1974).

Bracewell, Scardamalia, and Bereiter (1978) pointed to another interesting qualitative difference between 8th- and 12th-grade writers. The revisions made by the younger writers lowered the quality of their texts far more often than they raised quality. The 12th-grade writers had reached the point where their revisions helped more than they hurt.

Finally, Hayes, Flower, Schriver, Stratman, and Carey (1985) observed that experts detected 1.6 times more problems in an error-ridden text than did novices. Further, the experts were 1.7 times more likely to be able to diagnose the nature of the problem. Experts therefore are best positioned either to detect a problem and immediately rewrite the sentence or paragraph, on the one hand, or to detect the error, diagnose its nature, and revise accordingly, on the other hand.

Quantitative Restructuring

As the content and discourse knowledge available to a writer grows, the pattern of allocating attention to writing operations also changes. The most striking illustration of this may be found in the transition from knowledge telling to knowledge transformation (Bereiter & Scardamalia, 1987). The young writer focuses almost exclusively on generating ideas, evaluating in a rudimentary way the appropriateness of the content, and then translating the ideas into sentences. Setting goals and organizing ideas—two critical elements of mature planning—are lacking. Reading the text as it evolves and editing at multiple levels of textual structure are also lacking. The only hint of time and effort devoted to reviewing occurs when the writer checks the appropriateness of ideas retrieved or created from memory. As the writer matures, more time and effort are shifted from generating sentences to all aspects of planning and reviewing.

Yet even the 12th-grade or college student fails to devote extensive time and effort to prewriting (Emig, 1971; Pianko, 1979). The exhaustive collecting of information and planning that often characterize mature adults engaged in an important writing task are rarely seen in students carrying out school assignments. In particular, the development of written plans during prewriting are relatively uncommon, according to Emig (1971). She noted, however, that some of the students she studied were more likely to invest in planning during prewriting on self-initiated writing projects compared to school assignments. Similarly, Graves (1983) stated that when students select topics of their own choosing for school assignments, they devote more time to revision than when the teacher assigns the topic.

Zbrodoff (1985) examined prewriting time in the laboratory for students and adults given a story-writing assignment. She varied the time the writers were allowed to work on their stories from 2.5 to 20 minutes and measured how long they delayed before starting a draft. Interestingly, as the allowed time increased, the adults gradually increased their prewriting time. The 5th- and 10th-grade students began almost immediately to generate sentences, regardless of the time constraints. In another set of conditions, Zbrodoff imposed no time limit but required the stories to be 6 to 48 lines in length. The adults waited more than six times as long as the younger writers before drafting and waited longest in the 48-line condition. Clearly, then, planning time and effort, at least during the prewriting phase, increase as individuals develop.

A similar shift can be seen in the time given to reviewing. The Pianko (1979) study showed that college freshmen devoted a scarce 9% of the total time spent on a writing project to reading and editing. This result predated the introduction of word processors into schools and universities. The new technology certainly invites students to read and revise their papers throughout many drafts. But as will be discussed in detail in Chapter 7, most students typically do not accept the invitation (Theismeyer, 1989).

In summarizing the literature on how expertise alters the attention given to reviewing, Hayes and Flower (1986) first cautioned that the task environment strongly affects the amount of reviewing done, regardless of how much the writer knows. Then they added: "In general, though, it appears that the more expert the writer, the greater the proportion of writing time the writer will spend in revision" (p. 110).

In a series of three experiments, I tried to isolate the restructuring of processing time and cognitive effort for content knowledge, on the one hand, and certain aspects of discourse knowledge, on the other. Two of these experiments examined the pattern of attentional allocation for writers who were high or low in domain-specific topic knowledge (Kellogg, 1987a). The experiments differed in the manner in which topic knowledge was manipulated, but the results did not vary. Writers in both knowledge conditions spent slightly more than 50% of their time translating across all phases. Again, in both conditions, the amount of time spent planning decreased across phases, whereas reviewing time increased. Moreover, for both high- and low-knowledge writers, cognitive effort was allocated more to planning and reviewing than to translating. Although there was a marked difference in the absolute level of effort expended in the two knowledge conditions, the pattern of allocation was the same. High-knowledge writers devoted less effort than low-knowledge writers, but they did so uniformly for planning, translating, and reviewing.

The third study, reported briefly in Kellogg (1993), involved participants at four levels of verbal ability based on their percentile scores from the ACT English subtest. Group 1 ($n = 17$) included students with a percentile score less than 56; Group 2 ($n = 16$) included those with scores ranging from 56 to 71; Group 3 ($n = 17$) ranged from 71 to 89; and Group 4 ($n = 19$) ranged from 90 to 99.

Based on directed retrospective reports, all writers devoted more processing time to translating ($M = 52\%$) than to either planning ($M = 26\%$) or reviewing ($M = 19\%$). An analysis that examined each third of composing time (10 minutes) showed that planning time decreased and reviewing time increased as writing progressed. Translating time, on the other hand, was relatively constant across the phases of writing. This interaction of process by phase was statistically reliable. Of key concern here is that verbal knowledge failed to interact with process. The three-way interaction of process by phase by knowledge level was also unreliable. Writers at all four levels of verbal knowledge allocated processing time in essentially the same fashion.

The cognitive effort analysis revealed significant differences among the types of process, with translating ($M = 364$) demanding less effort than either planning ($M = 413$) or reviewing ($M = 414$). These values are the mean RT interference scores in milliseconds. As with processing time, the main effect of knowledge level was nil in the case of cognitive effort. The interaction of knowledge and process also failed to approach significance.

Thus, my efforts to isolate how particular types of knowledge quantitatively restructure the writing process have proved disappointing. The pattern of allocating attention to planning, translating, and reviewing remains uniform, regardless of the writer's verbal and topical knowledge. The pattern does vary somewhat from experiment to experiment, however, particularly for the measure of cognitive effort. The demands of the task environment clearly shape how a writer allocates processing time and effort. One task may demand a greater focus on planning, while another may emphasize reviewing, for instance.

The literature reviewed earlier also clearly showed that as writers develop and mature—augmenting all aspects of their knowledge base—they shift attention from nearly purely sentence generation to a mix of planning, translating, and reviewing. I interpret these shifts as a response to the different task environment, as perceived and defined by the expert compared to the novice. For example, the task demands facing a child employing the knowledge-telling strategy are less complex than those facing an adult trying to transform knowledge through the act of writing (Bereiter & Scardamalia, 1987). Stated generally, as writers acquire more and more knowledge, they define complex task environments that *demand* extensive planning and reviewing. The entire constellation of content and discourse knowledge enables writers to define more complex tasks. Gains in one type of knowledge alone, such as those examined in the studies described above, apparently fail to have any measurable impact.

Knowledge, Amplification, and Automatization

Domain-Specific Knowledge

That writing performance depends on how much the writer knows about the topic is both intuitively obvious and easily documented, as shown earlier in this chapter. More surprising are the results that suggest little if any relation between the quality of a text and the writer's command of the subject matter. For instance, Conte and Ferguson (1974) asked high school seniors to compose a letter to a brother, sister, or best friend in which they urge against the use of drugs. They compared writers who used drugs with those who were nonusers. Their ratings of the letters revealed no reliable differences, despite the fact that the users knew much more about the topic than the nonusers. One interpretation of this outcome is that the drug users were not motivated by the writing prompt to engage the task fully. They may have satisficed performance and economized effort, so that their letters proved to be no better than those from writers with less topic knowledge.

Further, Langer (1984) reported only a modest positive correlation between how much students knew about a topic and holistic quality judgments of texts written on the topic in a school assignment ($r = .30$) and the teacher's marks on the papers ($r = .16$). Only the former correlation was statistically reliable, and even that dropped to $r = .25$ when the confounding effect of general academic knowledge was separated statistically from topic knowledge. It may well be that the school assignments studied by Langer failed to motivate the highly knowledgeable writers to use their full effort. Performance amplification is expected only when gains in degree of knowledge are accompanied by high investments of time and effort. The meager percentage of variance ($r^2 = 6.25\%$) in holistic scores accounted for by topic knowledge in Langer's study could reflect a pattern of relative automatization. The highly knowledgeable writers may have written only slightly better texts but expended markedly less cognitive effort than those with less knowledge. This nonlinear relationship between knowledge level and text quality would deflate the correlation coefficient.

A study from my laboratory examined differences in topic knowledge and measured cognitive effort (Kellogg, 1987a; Experiment 1). The data were collected after the shooting down of a commercial Korean airplane by the former Soviet Union. Following this incident and a proposal by the United States to ban Soviet flights to New York, the Soviets countered with a proposal to move the United Nations to more neutral territory. The task was to write a persuasive essay on why the United Nations should remain in New York. A test of general knowledge about the history and purpose of the United Nations assessed the degree of domain-specific knowledge. As anticipated, all subjects knew at least a fair amount about the United Nations, but there were individual differences in how detailed their knowledge was. The subjects were divided into high- and low-knowledge groups using a median split procedure. In reality, the two groups might better be considered as moderate- and high-knowledge groups.

Content quality in this study was measured by having judges rate the documents on a 7-point scale in terms of language usage, organizational coherence, idea development, effectiveness of persuasion, and mechanics. I summed the mean scores on these scales to index overall quality (Figure 4.2). Quality is plotted on the left axis and cognitive effort, indexed as an interference score in milliseconds (ms), on the right. Both the low- and high-knowledge groups failed to differ in terms of overall quality. However, the high-knowledge group devoted significantly less cognitive effort than did the low-knowledge group. This outcome occurred for planning, translating, and reviewing, as noted earlier.

Thus, increasing levels of knowledge did not augment document quality. The low-knowledge writers knew enough about the United Nations to achieve a satisfactory level of performance, nearly on par with the high knowledge writers, but only the low-knowledge writers had to work very hard to attain this level of quality. The high-knowledge writers developed a document schema relatively effortlessly and still achieved a satisfactory product. I interpret these results as illustrating the concept of relative automatization. This outcome would be clearer if three or more degrees of topic knowledge were examined and cognitive effort measured, allowing one to plot a curve that can be fit to the pattern predicted for relative automatization.

More interesting, though, is the question of what motivates writers to engage a task with full effort. First, knowing too little about a topic presumably discourages a a writer from even attempting to engage a task fully. Presumably, students know more about topics that they choose to write about compared with those assigned to

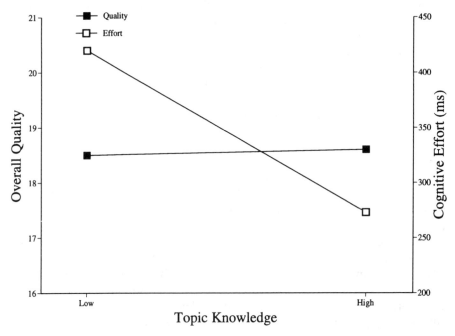

FIGURE 4.2. Content quality and cognitive effort as a function of domain-specific knowledge. (From Kellogg, 1993. Copyright © 1993 by *Composition Studies*, Texas Christian University. Reprinted by permission.)

them by teachers, and thus are more motivated to revise and find their own voice with self-selected assignments (Graves, 1983). Gradwohl and Shumacher (1989) compared topics that sixth graders wanted to write about with those they preferred not to write about and those assigned by teachers. Their results confirmed that the children knew significantly more about the "want topics" compared with the "don't-want topics" and "teacher topics." Interestingly, the latter two types failed to differ, suggesting that teachers may at times find the very assignments that students know little about and have no motivation to engage.

Second, specifying the audience for writers can also heighten their interest in the task and the amount of effort that they devote to it. Redd-Boyd and Slater (1989) studied college students engaging in a persuasive writing task under conditions of an imaginary assigned reader, a real assigned reader, and no assigned reader. English teachers and the assigned readers rated the texts. Specifying an audience had only a small beneficial effect on the assigned readers' ratings and no effect on the teachers' ratings. But an examination of questionnaire data showed that, regardless of condition, some writers envisioned an audience anyway. These data showed that the writers who thought of someone like the assigned reader were much more likely to persuade the assigned reader compared with those who did not. The questionnaire and interview data also showed that assigning an audience boosted the students' engagement in the task.

Third, the external rewards and punishments should matter. I presume that if a student's entire course grade in a political science course depended on the quality of the essay on the United Nations composed in my lab, then I would see amplification not automatization. The writer's characteristics—particularly achievement motivation and intrinsic motivation to write—should also affect the writing, as the next chapter shows.

Discourse Knowledge

The experiment described earlier, in which degree of verbal knowledge was manipulated, shows how the degree of knowledge can strongly affect performance. The documents written by students were judged in terms of style and content quality on 7-point scales. Style quality is more at issue in the case of verbal knowledge, whereas the content of a document is more affected by topic knowledge. Still, I summed both ratings to yield an overall quality score. That way, comparisons between how topic knowledge affects performance differently than verbal knowledge do not get lost in worries about different measurement scales. The means for overall quality are plotted along with cognitive effort scores in Figure 4.3.

The results document the phenomenon of amplification of performance. Overall quality increased linearly and cognitive effort was uniform as verbal knowledge increased. The level of effort was high, comparable to the levels obtained in earlier studies on writing and playing chess (see Figure 1.1).

Several researchers have examined the relation between standardized test scores of verbal knowledge and the quality of writing samples. Indeed, the predictive power of the tests served to validate their use on a national scale. Godshalk, Swineford, and Coffman (1966) found that the verbal subtest of the ACT correlated reliably

THE PSYCHOLOGY OF WRITING

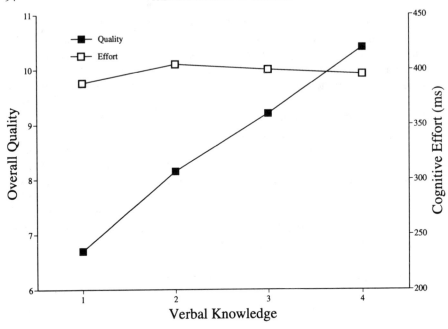

FIGURE 4.3. Overall quality and cognitive effort as a function of verbal knowledge. (From Kellogg, 1993. Copyright © 1993 by *Composition Studies*, Texas Christian University. Reprinted by permission.)

with holistic scores on student essays. They reported correlation coefficients of at least .70. Culpepper and Ramsdell (1982) examined several types of standardized tests and found correlations ranging from .52 to .74. Stiggins (1982) reviewed the literature existing to date and concluded, without equivocation, that verbal knowledge test scores correlate positively with the quality of written texts. Thus, there is compelling evidence that as the availability of verbal knowledge increases, writing performance increases.

The data in Figure 4.3 show a clear linear relationship. But it should not be inferred that domain-specific knowledge always shows automatization, whereas discourse knowledge shows amplification. The central issue, in my view, is whether the task motivates the writer to devote full effort. The next study shows that a pattern consistent with automatization can be obtained among writers differing in verbal knowledge, at least when the task calls for narrative composition (Kellogg, 1992).

I tested 61 college students who had taken the ACT on both a persuasive and a narrative task in a group design situation that precluded the collection of reaction times. Half received the narrative task first and half the persuasive task. I borrowed the narrative prompt from Voss, Vesonder, and Spillich (1980) and asked participants to compose an account of a half inning of a major-league baseball game. For the persuasive prompt I used the controversy over major-league salaries. In the 1992 season, nearly half of all players in the National and American leagues earned more than $1 million. The persuasive task called for the writers to compose an editorial that argued for a cap of $1 million, a salary that should be reserved for the best players. They were to argue that the salary inflation caused by the arbitration process used in salary negotiation is bad for baseball and must be stopped.

I split the 61 subjects into quartiles based on their ACT English subtest scores ($n = 14$ to 16). As in my other studies on these questions, style ratings proved more sensitive to verbal knowledge and content ratings more sensitive to topic knowledge. But to provide a common scale for comparisons, I summed the two measures to yield overall quality. Shown in Figure 4.4 are the quality scores (recall that cognitive effort scores were not collected) for the two writing tasks as a function of available verbal knowledge. The narrative curve fits the pattern of automatization. In the persuasive condition, the quality measure increased linearly with degree of verbal knowledge. Without the cognitive effort scores, a firm conclusion is premature. Still, the results in Figure 4.4 suggest that verbal knowledge can support automatization in a narrative task.

Moses (1986) reported a related finding in a study that varied knowledge of text structure. He examined first-year journalism students who either had or had not taken the course in news reporting. The experimental task called for writing obituaries. The text structure for this concise genre was taught in the news reporting course. Based on think-aloud protocols and judges' assessment of videotapes taken during composition, Moses concluded that the writers with high genre knowledge—that is, those who had taken the course—showed reliably less rhetorical planning and goal

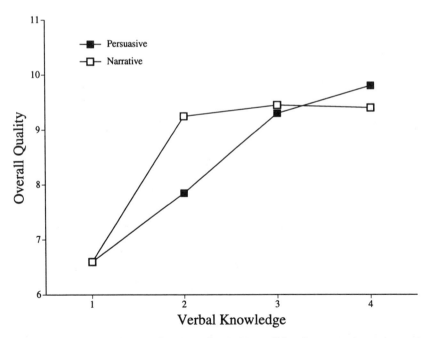

FIGURE 4.4. Overall quality as a function of verbal knowledge for persuasive and narrative composition. (From Kellogg, 1993. Copyright © 1993 by *Composition Studies*, Texas Christian University. Reprinted by permission.)

setting than those in the low-knowledge condition. Presumably the high-knowledge writers drew upon a schema for carrying out this task and achieved a satisfactory result with less investment in planning.

At this juncture, there is little doubt that domain-specific topic knowledge and verbal knowledge contribute powerfully to the quality of writing. Less certain are the precise conditions under which each type of knowledge supports automatization, on the one hand, or amplification, on the other. Further studies on different types of text structures, and variables affecting the writer's interest in the topic and motivation to engage the task fully, are needed.

5

Personality

I don't believe for a moment that creativity is a neurotic symptom. On the contrary, the neurotic who succeeds as an artist has had to overcome a tremendous handicap. He creates in spite of his neurosis, not because of it.

ALDOUS HUXLEY

I use the term *personality* to refer to the personality dimensions that theoretically mediate thinking and writing skills. I seek to understand how these personality dimensions affect the availability, accessibility, and creative application of knowledge in intellectual tasks.

Personality, as I use the term here, serves as both a resource for and a constraint on meaning-making activities. Perkins's (1987) notion of raw intellectual power is certainly one such personal resource, and I will review it here under the heading of componential intelligence. Three other categories seem essential as well: motivation, cognitive style, and anxiety. These factors either facilitate or inhibit a writer's ability to retrieve and creatively apply knowledge. They differentiate both how writers go about their work and how well they succeed.

In approaching this territory, I should make clear at the outset that I am not seeking to define the *creative personality.* Such a concept suggests that only certain people are creative, a view at odds with the whole notion of *Homo symbolificus* as the makers of meaning in one domain or another. I take guidance from Frank Barron (1988), who sought to describe how the motivation and style of persons—the self—influence how they go about creating meaning in their life. He denied the existence of a creative personality per se:

> Creative people come in all shapes and sizes, all colors and ages, and all sorts of personality types. There are introverts and extroverts, maniacs and depressives and manic-depressives, schizophrenics and hysterics, sociopaths and good citizens—in brief, a wide variety of temperaments among people who are especially creative. It is not, in my judgment, the personality type that makes the difference, but the self. To the self I ascribe motivation and style, the choice of meaning, and the *making of meaning*, in work, career, and life course. (p. 94)

Barron saw opportunities for creative acts everywhere in the lives of human beings, not just in work in general and certainly not just in the work of writers, artists, scientists, and others for whom the term *creative genius* is typically reserved.

> One's life itself is there to create. Family, friends, and associates, personal style, inner experience, general behavior, dress, character—these are creations in the opportunity available to us all as human beings. (p. 95)

Intelligence

Perkins (1987) described the importance of raw *intellectual power*. By this he meant the neuronal capacity for and speed of information processing. The notion that mental speed is central to intelligence can be traced to the earliest psychometric studies of intellectual functioning and continues to enjoy support (Eysenck, 1987). Jensen (1987) reported a series of studies showing a correlation between speed on a choice-RT task and standard IQ measures. He noted that individual differences in the RT intercept in the task correlate strongly with the RT intercepts found in both Sternberg's short-term memory retrieval task and Neisser's visual search tasks. Further, Ahern and Beatty (1979) found that students with higher SAT scores exhibited less pupillary dilation than those with lower scores, meaning that they expended less cognitive effort to solve problems at all difficulty levels. Thus, one interpretation of intelligence must include the notion of neuronal efficiency or power to process information.

The concept of intellectual power is only one aspect of intelligence, of course. Perkins (1987) also considered intelligence as content knowledge and as tactics or strategies. I expanded on these concepts to formulate the broad categories of intellectual resources and constraints, namely, knowledge, method, and personality. Other theorists have broadened the notion of intelligence to include human acts that traditionally have not been regarded as intellectual. Gardner (1983) brought musical, bodily, social, and intrapersonal skills into the discussion, as well as the more familiar topics of verbal, mathematical, and spatial skills.

Sternberg's (1985b) triarchic theory distinguishes componential intelligence from contextual and experiential intelligence. *Componential intelligence* refers to the speed and accuracy of encoding, pattern matching, retrieval from memory, and other basic mental operations. *Contextual intelligence* concerns mental activity directed to purposive adaptation to the environment, as well as the selection and shaping of environments. Finally, *experiential intelligence* addresses the ability to cope with novel task environments in a flexible, creative fashion. It also concerns the ability to automatize mental processes with practice and the development of expertise.

It is clear that intelligence, broadly conceived, is identical to the subject matter of this book on thinking. But intelligence, taken in the narrow sense of intellectual power, is a source of individual differences among writers that should properly be treated in this chapter along with motivation, style, and anxiety. A consideration of

Sternberg's (1977, 1985b) componential intelligence illustrates how this narrowly conceived notion of intelligence bears on writing.

Componential Intelligence

Sternberg defines a *component* as an elementary process for operating upon symbols or objects. These processes deal with the sensory input of information, internal manipulation of representations, and translation of representations into motor output. The parameters of each component include duration, difficulty, and probability of execution. That is, components vary in their speed, probability of proper execution, and probability of executing at all.

Sternberg distinguished meta-, performance, acquisition, retention, and transfer components. *Metacomponents* control the course of action in thinking and monitor the success of the selected path. These are the executive functions needed in planning and decision making, and they are likely to be critical in writing skill.

Performance components actually execute a strategy for thinking. The execution of prewriting planning strategies or first-draft translation strategies varies in success with individual differences in performance components. *Acquisition components* are learning operations and figure in the acquisition of new knowledge and skills, including strategies for how to think effectively. Obviously, the development of writing skills and the ability to collect information depend on these components.

Retention components retrieve knowledge and skills as thinking occurs. They determine whether a writer's available knowledge is accessible when it is needed in composition. Finally, *transfer components* generalize knowledge from one thinking task to another.

Sternberg (1977) successfully applied the componential approach to the study of inductive reasoning, in which a probable conclusion is inferred from information provided in the premises. Analogies (a lawyer is to a client as a doctor is to a ?) are an extensively investigated form of inductive reasoning. Pictorial, geometric analogies and closely related matrix problems, as well as verbal analogies, have been studied. Similarly, series completion problems (3, 4, 6, 9, ?) using numbers, words, pictures, and other stimuli are another common inductive reasoning task. Lastly, classifications (Which word does not belong with the others? *cat, dog, horse, fish*) illustrate another version of induction.

Taking analogies as prototypical of inductive reasoning, Sternberg developed a detailed model of the components involved. Specifically, he theorized that the reasoner (1) encodes the terms of the analogy, (2) infers the relation between lawyer and client, to use the example given earlier, (3) maps the relation between the first and second halves of the analogy (individuals who provide professional services), (4) applies a relation to the second half that is the same as that found in the first half (to whom does a doctor provide services?), and (5) responds with the answer of patient. He assumed that response latencies would depend on the additive and linear combination of the duration associated with these components. Moreover, he tested a model in which the inference component (2) was exhaustive, whereas the mapping (3) and application (4) components were self-terminating. The data strongly supported this model, accounting for a striking 92% of the variance in response times for people–piece analogies and 86% of the variance for verbal analogies. A similar model for error rates performed less well for the people–piece problems (59%) and not at all well for verbal analogies (12%). Still, the speed of responding, if not the accuracy, can be nicely accounted for in terms of componential intelligence.

Sternberg's choice of components has been criticized by Neisser (1983) on several grounds. First, the components are numerous and tailored to each specific task; they lack the parsimony and generality that one would like. Second, the metacomponents are vague and out of place with the elementary operations identified as performance components. Third, the tasks and experimental designs used by Sternberg may encourage research participants to adopt componential strategies. The high correlations observed in Sternberg's studies may be at least partially traced to demand characteristics. These criticisms may well be valid. My purpose in this section is to show that the rather vague notion of raw intellectual power can be reformulated into a precisely articulated model. On that score, Sternberg's model is unassailable.

Relation to Writing

The more intellectual power the writer brings to bear on the task, the better. This is so for several reasons. Because of the superior operation of acquisition components, the highly intelligent writer possesses a larger pool of available knowledge. The intelligent writer presumably collects the most information, both in the sense of day-to-day learning across a lifetime and in short-term searching for specific information needed on a writing assignment.

Retention components are responsible for retrieving the writer's knowledge. The more intelligent the writer, the more likely retrieval will occur rapidly and correctly when it is needed. Another link with knowledge access is through metacomponents. The executive functions of selecting an appropriate strategy and monitoring its effectiveness are critical in writing. The more intelligent the writer, the more likely that he or she will adopt effective strategies. Performance and transfer components yield individual differences in how well the writer executes the fundamental operations of collecting, planning, translating, and reviewing.

Relevant Research

Despite a voluminous literature on intelligence testing, studies examining the relation between intelligence and writing performance are remarkably scarce. Nearly all of the traditional tests of intelligence, such as the Weschler and Stanford-Binet, separate verbal scales from nonverbal scales. Also, theories of intelligence dating back to Thurstone (1938) have given a prominent role to verbal comprehension and verbal fluency. But surprisingly, writing and text production have been relatively slighted in intelligence research.

The neglect may stem from the unimpressive results of existing studies (Percival, 1966). Correlations between intelligence test scores and writing performance are reliable but weak ($r = .20$). An amusing example comes from the story that the mathematician Poincaré scored so poorly on the Binet intelligence test that he would have been classified as an imbecile were it not for the 500 papers and 30 books that he had published (Ochse, 1990). MacKinnon (1978) concluded that .40 is the expected relation between intelligence and creative production in general. But above IQs of 120, there is little relation between test scores and productivity.

This weak relationship certainly does not encourage a view that componential intelligence is critical to writing ability. Yet, it does not rule out that tests geared specifically to the assessment of the components of information processing would reveal strong relationships. For example, a more encouraging result came from a study on the relation between performance on the Wechsler Adult Intelligence Scale-Revised (WAIS-R) and the U.S. Air Force Criterion Task Set (CTS) (Gilliland, Schlegel, Dannels, & Mills, 1989). The latter is comprised of nine tasks that tap perceptual, thinking, and motor skills. The thinking or central processing tasks include linguistic processing and grammatical reasoning, along with four other tasks less relevant to writing (memory search, continuous recall, mathematical processing, and spatial processing). The results indicated lower RT on the central processing tasks for high WAIS-R individuals relative to low WAIS-R ones. The data were not reported separately for the grammatical reasoning and linguistic processing tasks.

Hunt (1987) has shown that tasks requiring storage and manipulation of symbols are performed much better by those with high levels of verbal knowledge. As we saw in detail in Chapter 4, the availability of verbal knowledge strongly influences the quality of text production. Hunt's results are still more encouraging for the view that information processing components provide an important source of individual differences among writers.

Benton, Kraft, Glover, and Plake (1984) provided additional evidence that componential intelligence correlates with writing ability. They investigated short-term memory for letters, iconic memory for letters, and tasks requiring the manipulation and reordering of letters, words, and sentences. They selected good and poor writers by taking college students who scored at the top and at the bottom on three measures: ACT English scores, ACT composite scores, and grade point averages. They found that the good writers manipulated symbols in short-term memory faster than did the poor writers. The two groups were equivalent on tests of iconic memory and on the short-term retention of letters.

Daiute (1984) examined how short-term memory capacity for digits and sentences related to the ability of individuals to generate multiclause sentences in first drafts. The correlations varied across ages, but taking the results as a whole, there was a small but reliable positive relationship for sentence memory ($r = .31$). Digit span, on the other hand, failed to yield a correlation different from zero.

A direct test of the relation between componential intelligence and creativity in writing comes from a report by Sternberg and Lubart (1989). They investigated creativity and asked New Haven, Connecticut, residents to produce two drawings, two advertisements, two scientific problem solutions, and two creative stories. A panel of peer judges evaluated each piece of work for creativity, novelty, appropriateness to topic choice, integration of diverse elements, technical goodness, aesthetic value, and effort (Amabile, 1983). A composite measure of creativity was based on these scales. Several measures of individual differences were used as predictors of creative performance, including a test of fluid intelligence and a test of componential intelligence. The latter assessed individual differences in selective encoding of information, selective comparison of stored facts, and selective combination of previously separate facts. Across tasks and intelligence tests, the correlation coefficients with creative performance ranged from .51 to .61, all highly reliable.

Motivation

Earlier I argued that the time spent writing is the chief determinant of productivity. A productive writer must devote many hours, days, months, and years to the craft. Fluency and quality writing require not only devoting time to the task but engaging it fully. I have stated that motivation largely governs whether writers enter a state of creative flow and perform to their full potential. In this section, I consider various forms of motivation in relation to writing.

Achievement Motivation

McClelland (1961) addressed the facet of personality that compels some persons in our society to achieve more than others. The inclination to engage in a particular activity is as important as the ability to carry out the activity. Atkinson and Raynor (1978) formalized the role of motivation in achieving success in a multiplicative relation among three variables. The tendency to achieve success (T_s) is a product of the motive to succeed (M_s), the subjective probability that performing a task will lead to success (P_s), and the incentive value or attractiveness of succeeding (I_s), that is, $T_s = M_s \times P_s \times T_s$. The importance of the need for achievement in accounting for task success rates has been extensively documented by these and other authors.

The specific prediction that achievement motivation increases the time spent on a task and productivity has received attention. For example, French and Thomas (1958) studied the persistence of Air Force personnel in solving a complex problem. Those with a strong need for achievement were more likely to solve the problem than those with a weak need. Moreover, those with a strong achievement motivation were more likely to continue working on the problem until the experimental time limit was reached. Publication rates of scientists and engineers in an industrial research setting has been shown to correlate significantly with the degree to which they felt committed to or involved with their work (Pelz & Andrews, 1976).

The Need to Write

Achievement motivation surely plays a role in the success of prolific writers. But there may be a more specific need that drives many who spend hours a day, every day composing text. Is achievement motivation alone able to account for Isaac Asimov's almost unbelievable productivity? He had published over 100 books by age 50 and nearly 400 more before his death at age 72 ("Transition," 1992). His topics included science fiction, literary criticism, psychology, mathematics, mysteries, poetry, humor, and American history. Or consider Harold Bloom, the literary critic. His sweeping review of essentially the whole of literature consists of a series of anthologies numbering at least 800 volumes (Lehman, 1986). Bloom's introductions to the volumes fill about 25 books. The director of the 16-member publishing staff for the series, Patricia Baldwin, says of Bloom's productivity: "Harold can turn out an introduction faster than our staffer's turn out jacket copy" (p. 56). Balzac, Dickens, Chesterton, Simenon, and others add to the list of extraordinarily prolific writers who manifestly had a strong need to write.

Published work by famous authors is not the only reason for postulating a specific need to write. Such writers often dispose of as much material as they publish (Ruas, 1985). Joseph Heller, Scott Spencer, and E. L. Doctorow report in interviews that they may write a book numbering hundreds of pages and then trash it all and begin anew. Among nonprofessional writers, compulsive letter and diary writers further reflect the need of people to compose.

Writing is an especially powerful meaning-making activity. By reflecting on the recent past, as in composing a diary entry or a letter to a friend or relative, the writer relates and develops the significance of the events. Writing provides an opportunity for seeking meaning in our day-to-day existence that might be lost if left to other, less visible forms of thinking. In addition, reflecting on what we know, as in writing an essay, results in a transformation of that knowledge. The writer learns what he or she thinks about a subject for the first time through the act of composing. The act is one of self-discovery as much as it is one of communication with others. As Green and Wason (1982) noted: "Any kind of serious writing involves a confrontation with the self because it creates an object which is both a part of the self and a part of the world of ideas" (pp. 51–52).

The need to write could well be regarded as a natural, albeit highly specific, form of motivation. Making meaning defines our species, and writing affords a vehicle for this function. Kubie (1958) speculated that the need to write is indeed universal. The reason adults differ so widely in the intensity of this drive stems from formal education, Kubie argued. The evaluation anxiety of imposed writing assignments and grades presumably represses in some individuals the need to write.

A similar sentiment has been expressed by an extraordinarily prolific writer, Joyce Carol Oates. Her comments in an interview correctly underscore that the need to write is healthy, natural, and certainly not pathological (Dembo, 1983). She answered a question about whether her writing productivity reflected compulsive behavior this way:

> I assure you there is very little compulsive about my life, either in my writing or otherwise. I believe that the creative impulse is natural in all human beings, and that it is particularly powerful in children unless it is suppressed. Consequently, one is behaving normally and instinctively and healthily when one is creating—literature, art, music, whatever. An excellent cook is also creative! I am disturbed that a natural human inclination should, by some Freudian turn of phrase, be considered compulsive—perhaps even pathological. (p. 353)

William Goyen shed further light on the need to write (Plimpton, 1989):

> I can't imagine *not* writing. Writing simply is a way of life for me. The older I get, the more a way of life it is. At the beginning, it was totally a way of life excluding

everything else. Now it's gathered to it marriage and children and other responsi-
bilities. But still, it is simply a way of life before all other ways, a way to observe
the world and to move through life, among human beings, and to record it all above
all and to shape it, to give it sense, and to express something of myself in it. Writing
is something I cannot imagine living without, nor scarcely would want to. Not to
live daily as a writing person is inconceivable to me. (p. 34)

Intrinsic Motivation

Amabile (1983, 1985) has suggested that extrinsic motivation, such as financial
rewards or social recognition, is actually detrimental to creative activities. *Intrinsic
motivation,* defined as interest, enjoyment, satisfaction, and the challenge of the work
itself, is instead viewed as critical for creativity. When external rewards such as pay,
grades, awards, and other forms of social recognition motivate the thinker, the result
is presumably less creative, contends Amabile. The extent to which an individual is
predisposed or shaped by the task environment to focus on external motivation may
affect the creativity of thinking and writing.

A remarkable study by Amabile (1985) supports the intrinsic motivation principle in writing. Creative writers were solicited from a university community. They
regularly committed time to creative writing tasks, either for course work or for
publication. After establishing a baseline reading on the creativity of the writers
using a poem-writing task, the participants were randomly divided into three groups.

The extrinsic group read and thought about a list of external reasons for writing
(e.g., the market for freelance writing is expanding, one best-selling novel can make
an author financially secure, teachers and parents encouraged writing as a career).
The intrinsic group read and thought about a list of internal reasons for writing (e.g.,
enjoyment of self-expression, writing achieves new insights, enjoy playing with
words). These lists were studied for only 5 minutes. A control group was also
included that was not exposed to either list of reasons. Then three groups all composed a second poem, which was evaluated by 12 poets for its creativity.

The three groups did not differ in creativity on the first poem, as expected. But
they did differ on the second poem in the predicted direction. The intrinsic and
control groups' means were equal in creativity, whereas the extrinsic group's mean
was markedly less than both. This implies that, normally, creative writers tended to
be intrinsically motivated. Strikingly, only 5 minutes of pondering extrinsic reasons
for composing disrupted this fundamental intrinsic motivation and caused a decrease
in creativity, an important aspect of the poem's quality.

Sternberg and Lubart (1989) offered a different interpretation of such studies.
They suggested that the critical issue is the extent to which an individual is task
focused by either intrinsic or extrinsic factors. By task-focused they mean devoting
time to the task, rather than thinking about the goals or the end result of having
completed the task. I elaborate their interpretation by noting that the writer must
engage the task fully, enter a state of creative flow, rather than simply put in the
time.

Intrinsic motivators (e.g., enjoyment) may generally prompt a person to focus
on a task either because they are less salient or, conversely, more integrated with

task completion; extrinsic motivators (e.g., fame) are highly salient and more likely to produce a goal-focused mindset. The key, then, is engaging the task with a committed investment of time and effort, a viewpoint consonant with the theoretical framework adopted here. As Sternberg and Lubart noted, for some tasks and individuals (e.g., financial investors), extrinsic rewards such as money may be most motivating, whereas for others (e.g., poets), intrinsic rewards are more important.

More negatively, Ochse (1990) cautioned that Amabile's (1983) results may apply only to laboratory situations in which extrinsic rewards are modest and short-term in scope. Ochse contended that "one should be wary, therefore, of generalizing the rather simplistic conclusions of this type of research to explain the creative achiever's tendency to stubborn labor" (p. 135).

I concur with most aspects of Ochse's critique of the work on intrinsic motivation, but by no means do I think we can do without the concept. The notion that people are intrinsically motivated to attain goals that are within the reach of their abilities is a central premise of performance amplification and flow states (Csikszentmihalyi, 1990). This is not to say that only intrinsic interest in the work compels devotion to writing tasks and the state of creative flow. As I will discuss, extrinsic rewards and punishments of many kinds can also accompany the deep level of task engagement that I see as necessary for creating meaning through writing and other art forms.

Further, flow states and deep absorption may be necessary for superior work, but by no means does this imply that all the time and effort engaged in writing fit the flow concept. People may economize effort even on demanding aspects of tasks. Cleary (1991) found that student writers often procrastinate until the night before an assignment is due and, by that point, have no choice but to economize effort and and satisfice performance. One student captured the feeling: "Millions and millions of times I thought, 'Here I am [the] last night. It's agony, and I'm sick of staying up the night before. . . . I'm going to write it and get it done. I don't care what kind of grade'" (p. 498). Cleary attributed this common state of affairs to a lack of intrinsic motivation to engage the school assignments. The extrinsic motivators of good grades and pleasing the teacher sufficed for advanced writers, but standard and basic writers had neither extrinsic nor intrinsic reasons for laboring with the required intensity over a school assignment.

Also, Ochse (1990) accurately observed that "creative production is likely to include some rather boring as well as some excessively demanding experience—some relatively easily attainable subgoals and some which are at least temporarily beyond the creator's grasp" (p. 140). My primary contention is that amplification of performance requires, at many if not most points in the writing process, the flow state of total absorption.

Extrinsic Motivation

Despite Amabile's (1985) intriguing results, and while recognizing the power of intrinsic motivation, I am reminded of Samuel Johnson's wise statement that "no man but a blockhead ever wrote except for money." Extrinsic rewards have driven many a poet and novelist every bit as intensely as they have driven investment bankers and stockbrokers. Truman Capote (1959) put it this way:

> Well, I can't imagine anything *more* encouraging than having someone buy your work. I never write—indeed, am physically incapable of writing—anything that I don't think I will be paid for. (p. 290)

Scientists and humanists in the academy may appear, at first blush, to stand above such a crass attitude simply because so much academic writing (e.g., a journal article) brings no direct compensation. But it certainly does bring indirect compensation in the form of salary offers and in opportunities for attracting grant support. Of course, money is not the only extrinsic motivator. Social recognition from peers and readers may well be a still more potent form of reward. Conversely, fear of the rejection and criticism of peers should the writer fail constitutes a compelling form of negative reinforcement.

Ochse (1990) reviewed the literature on the role of extrinsic satisfactions that derive from producing creative work. Developing a reputation as a skilled creator is clearly important. Ochse noted that "creators aspire to win fame and self-esteem by seeking recognition and admiration from discerning people whose opinion really matters" (pp. 144–145). Egoism, jealousy, even bitter acts of aggression against competitors can be witnessed in any literate community of writers, scientists, artists, and other creators of meaning. Such social striving does not exclude the importance of working for money. Instead it joins forces with the financial incentive.

Cognitive Style

Dimensions of Style

Cognitive style refers to a stable disposition to behave in a certain way when performing a mental task. Several such traits have been investigated, including field independence, breadth of categorization, impulsivity, mental self-government, and globalization (Baron, 1985; Sternberg, 1988a). I include in this section a review of Jensen and DiTiberio's (1989) application of Jungian personality traits to the psychology of writing. Styles, like other personality traits, are thought to be partially situation specific (Baron, 1985). For example, an individual may be highly field dependent, unable to ignore irrelevant aspects of the optical array, only when driving a car and less field dependent in other situations. The consistency in behavior owing to a style may be manifested more across time in a given situation than across situations at a given point in time. An individual's style is also thought to be partially under voluntary control, at least in some theoretical approaches. With sufficient motivation and effort, one might adopt a different style to adapt better to current situations.

Baron (1982, 1985) has developed systems for categorizing styles based on a task analysis of thinking. Thinking arises in response to a problem, a situation in which a person is in doubt about how to proceed, usually in pursuit of a goal. An initial phase of thinking is a *search for possibilities*, such as hypotheses, alternative solutions, or ideas. These possibilities must be evaluated, prompting the thinker to conduct a *search for evidence*. Search for goals, use of evidence, and other phases can also be delineated. Styles can then be defined in terms of deviations from the optimum degree of time and effort devoted to each of these phases.

For example, the search for possibilities, evidence, and goals may be done in varying degrees. Presumably, there is some optimum range of time and effort that should be devoted to search operations, depending on the nature of the problem. The ideal thinker tends to fall within that range. Impulsive individuals, in contrast, fall short of the range, failing to search extensively. Reflective individuals devote substantial time and effort to searching. The net result is that, in choice situations, impulsive individuals respond rapidly but inaccurately, while reflective individuals respond slowly but accurately.

Reflective versus Impulsive Style

Because writing demands reflective thought while struggling with content and rhetorical problems in working memory, the impulsive–reflective style is of special interest here. I presume that a reflective style best serves the writer in most aspects of collecting, planning, translating, and reviewing. Granted, being overly reflective might hinder a writer's fluency or productivity, especially if it leads to procrastination. Further, strategies such as free writing, which call for spirited, uninhibited language production, may be workable only for impulsive individuals. But in general, the writing task, perhaps more than any other, calls for a reflective cognitive style.

Baron suggests that style is under the thinker's control and is therefore modifiable through instruction. However, in the absence of corrective measures, he views people as impulsive by nature, economizing effort in their haste to respond. Baron (1985) speculates about the reason for the tendency toward impulsiveness:

> One reason is that the costs of search—in time, effort, and lost opportunities—are usually immediate, while the benefits of extra search are usually far in the future. For example, a student who does her homework carefully, giving even the most difficult problems her best effort while missing her favorite TV show, will reap the rewards of this diligence on the final exam and beyond. When it comes to thinking about moral matters, the only reward will be a clear conscience for having thought a matter through. The asymmetry in the costs and benefits of thinking will thus in general cause impulsiveness, if people are overly influenced by the immediate as opposed to the distant. (p. 383)

Research on how reflective and impulsive adults differ in the way they compose and in how well they compose is needed. Existing developmental evidence suggests, first, that impulsiveness decreases with increasing age and intelligence test scores (Messer, 1976). Second, Messer controlled for IQ and found that impulsive students do less well on assignments in general. Third, Bereiter and Scardamalia (1987) found that reflective thought develops as young writers mature and make the transition from a knowledge-telling to a knowledge-transforming form of composition. Further, they described studies in which sixth graders were trained to manifest more reflective thought in composing through the use of cues that prompt self-questioning, by modeling reflective thought for the student, and by directly instructing students in the use of planning strategies. Their results were consistent with other research demonstrating that reflectivity can be trained, at least in experimental tasks (Baron, 1985).

Sternberg's Intellectual Styles

Sternberg (1988a) adopted government as a metaphor in describing several cognitive styles that are potentially relevant to creating, thinking, and writing. He began with the three functions of government in differentiating legislative, executive, and judicial styles. A *legislative style* refers to devising rules, procedures, and ideas; an *executive style* is concerned with implementation; and a *judicial style* evaluates the soundness of rules and determines whether they have been followed. For instance, in the investment world, a legislative stylist develops investment products from scratch (Sternberg & Lubart, 1989). The executive stylist implements ideas created by others, such as a broker who buys and sells investment products. The judicial stylist prefers to evaluate how well the market is doing, rather than actually developing or running the market.

Sternberg suggested that creative people tend to prefer the legislative style. From the present theoretical perspective, however, inventively applying knowledge to writing problems comprises only the final of three necessary steps. The availability of knowledge in the first place and the accessibility of that knowledge in the second show no apparent preference for one style of mental self-government over another. Further diluting the relevance of these three styles for writing performance is that the task invokes planning, translating, and reviewing. Whereas the legislative style may give one an edge in planning, the executive style may facilitate the implementation of plans, the translation of personal symbols into consensual symbols. Obviously, the judicial style suits reviewing well.

In sum, then, for creating texts and other consensual symbol systems, I see little reason for predicting that legislative stylists should do best on a holistic or analytic measure of quality. The Sternberg and Lubart (1989) investigation of creativity in the production of drawings, creative stories, advertisements, and scientific problems supports this analysis. They found no correlation between a legislative preference and creativity scores.

Two other dimensions of mental self-government, to continue with the metaphor, are the conservative–progressive and the global–local polarities. The conservative maintains traditional approaches, whereas the progressive seeks innovation. Sternberg and Lubart proposed that progressives are more creative, but their results failed to support this prediction. I interpret this null result as consistent with a framework that emphasizes the availability, accessibility, and creative application of knowledge in writing tasks. Whereas the progressive succeeds with innovative applications, the conservative ensures that the lessons of the past are not forgotten. Successful performance in writing, problem solving, reasoning, and decision making relies on a complex interaction of remembering and creating, each feeding on the other.

I do concur with Sternberg and Lubart's suggestion that creativity demands the ability to alternate between global and local styles. The global style prefers the broad problems, whereas the local style prefers the narrow, detailed aspects of a task. Surprisingly, the authors found a negative correlation ($r = -.35$) between global preference and overall creativity. Perhaps the constraints of laboratory tasks, in which topics are suggested and problems defined, favor the local style. Gruber (1974) offered evidence that creativity outside the laboratory, in the real world, requires people who first seek out large, broad problems.

Barron's Personal Styles

Frank Barron's (1988) classic work with the Symbolic Equivalence Test provides the most telling evidence on the importance of style factors. This 30-minute paper-and-pencil test examines skill in transforming a stimulus image (e.g., leaves being blown in the wind) into possible symbolic equivalents (e.g., a civilian population fleeing chaotically in the face of armed aggression). The test scores the number of acceptable but not original responses and the number of original responses. Acceptable responses are assigned a score of 1, 2, or 3, depending on how apt they are, and original responses receive a score of 4 or 5, depending on their degree of originality. Barron (1969) reported a high correlation between test scores and an independent assessment of verbal creativity of several groups selected to differ in this regard. For example, a group of famous writers, known to be high in verbal creativity, scored best on the Symbolic Equivalence Test, followed by famous architects, a distinguished group of mathematicians, and so on. Moreover, test scores for individuals correlated with external criterion ratings of creativity, judged relative to all others in the relevant professional group.

Extensive research with the Symbolic Equivalence Test and other assessment tools led Barron to conclude that creativity stems from a personal style that includes a tolerance for ambiguity, a willingness to resist group pressure and to form independent judgments, a preference for complexity coupled with a drive to find an underlying simple order, and a willingness to take risks and seize opportunities (Barron, 1969, 1988; Barron & Harrington, 1981). Sternberg and Lubart (1989) examined some of these personal styles in their work and reported positive correlations between overall creativity and tolerance for ambiguity, individuality, and willingness to take risks.

MacKinnon (1978) also stressed the individuality of those recognized for their creative work in their disciplines. Introversion and limited social engagement characterize such creative people. Self-sufficiency and initiative in pursuing lines of work are typical traits. Barron's tolerance for ambiguity, drive for simplicity, and willingness to take risks also find converging support in MacKinnon's work on the intellectual style of scientific and artistic creators. Such people find excitement in ideas and aesthetic pleasure in creating or discovering the simple, elegant principle that underlies apparent complexity.

Jungian Traits

Jensen and DiTiberio (1989) explored the implications of Jungian personality theory for the psychology of writing. Carl Jung described four bipolar dimensions of personality traits that are linked closely with the cognitive styles discussed previously. Jung (1921) offered a cognitive approach to the field of personality, one that viewed differences among individuals in terms of their cognitive-affective styles of processing information.

The first dimension is introversion versus extroversion and concerns the individual's orientation to life. The introvert focuses on the subjective inner world, whereas the extrovert looks to the objective external world. The second dimension concerns ways of perceiving and distinguishes sensing versus intuitive types. The sensing type gathers concrete, detailed sensory data, whereas the intuitive type imagines abstract possibilities, looking first for the gestalt, the overall impression, rather than the details. The third dimension concerns ways of judging and distinquishes thinking versus feeling types. The thinking type makes decisions on the basis of principles and regard the process as highly objective, whereas the feeling type emphasizes the highly subjective nature of decision making and enters personal values into the process. The fourth dimension concerns orientation to the outer world and distinguishes judging versus perceiving types. The judging type tries to structure the world in order to accomplish goals, whereas the perceiving type prefers to examine and understand the world as it is.

Jensen and DiTiberio employed the Myers-Briggs Type Indicator (MBTI) to identify the style or type of each of the participants in their studies. They then related these types to the writing process, citing case studies to support their arguments. For example, Jensen and DiTiberio identified a sensing type who struggled with composing a master's thesis because of his tendency to gather too much factual data. Each fact seemed as important as the next. As a result, he found it difficult to interpret and categorize the data and form overviews. An intuitive type in their study had no difficulty developing categories and interpreting data by composing generalizations. He did, however, fail to see the need to cite specific facts and quotations to back up his interpretations. The abstractions of intuitive writers therefore may not convince readers. Interestingly, Jensen and DiTiberio (1989) contended that "teachers (especially intuitive teachers) often perceive that intuitive types are better writers than they actually are, in part because they can write abstractly" (p. 55).

Thinking types presumably depend on structure in the composition process and are most likely to turn to mental or written outlines. The thinking types can overdo such structuring, worrying more about grammatical and logical format than about communication. "As a result," Jensen and DiTiberio noted, "their essays may be clear and structured but also dull, similar to the archetypical dry, academic treatise" (p. 62). Feeling types write well only when the topic interests them greatly. The words of one feeling type illustrate the phenomenon of amplification: "The conditions I write best under are when I know a lot about the subject and I can express my total feelings on the subject" (p. 62). If an uninteresting topic is assigned or selected, feeling types fail to live up to their potential as writers. Jensen and DiTiberio claimed that for this reason, the grades of feeling types fluctuated greatly during a semester-long composition course.

Judging types are great planners and implementers. Rarely do they fail to make a deadline. But they may stick too closely to their plans, fail to research a topic adequately before beginning, and hastily make decisions about style and content.

Later, in revising their first draft, judging types find the need to expand, clarify, and qualify their initial statements. Perceiving types, on the other hand, immerse themselves in the domain of their assignment, with too little regard for narrowing the topic and meeting deadlines. As one such graduate student put it: "Data collection is easy; writing is hard" (Jensen & DiTiberio, 1989, p. 70). Perceiving types fill entire rooms with books, articles, and notes, yet still believe that there are always more facts to gather in order to achieve the desired level of comprehensiveness.

Additional research, particularly experimental investigations, must be done before strong conclusions may be reached regarding cognitive styles. The personal styles examined by Frank Barron, the reflective style studied by Robert Baron, and the Jungian personality types explored by Jensen and DiTiberio appear especially promising in understanding writing and other tasks of meaning-making. Styles probably modulate the ability of an individual to learn and expand available knowledge, retrieve relevant knowledge when it is needed, and apply the knowledge creatively to current problems. I suspect that they play an especially powerful role in distinguishing individual differences among highly intelligent people. In other words, individuals with IQs greater than 120 show no clear correlation with creative production (Hayes, 1981). The cognitive styles of these individuals may become more important and IQ scores less so once the raw intellectual power reaches this threshold. Documenting how styles impact writing performance and the allocation of attention to writing processes is a rich area for future research.

Anxiety

Nickerson (1988–89) noted that anxiety plays a mixed role in intellectual pursuits. On the one hand, anxiety and fear of failing can motivate people to perform useful activities. On the other hand, anxiety can paralyze the thinker or at least produce detrimental effects on thinking operations.

The role of anxiety in writing is an especially interesting issue because emotionally the task can be intensely engaging. A purely cognitive model—or even a social-cognitive model—is inadequate for the behavior of writing (Brand, 1989). Motivational and affective factors weigh heavily. Green and Wason (1982) even contended that the fundamental problem in writing is affective, concerning attitudes about openness and trust.

Openness refers to the freedom to gain access to our own thoughts and feelings. In other words, the writer must be willing to explore personal symbols in an uninhibited fashion. *Trust* refers to the toleration of exposing our thoughts and feelings on paper. In other words, the writer must be willing to translate personal symbols into consensual symbols without fear. Openness, then, is most closely tied to generating ideas and trust to translating them into words.

Writing involves emotional risks in the process and emotional benefits in the product. The work is arduous in emotional turmoil as well as in mental effort. But once a document is completed, especially a major project that meets with approval from readers, the document becomes a source of immense pride. This dual nature of affect in writing was captured in a quotation attributed to the novelist James Jones: "I hate writing. I love having written."

Lowenthal and Wason (1977) asked academic writers how they felt about the job, and most reported this mixed but intense response (e.g., "Writing is a very hard grind—the good times come along only on the back of sweat and tears"). A few found nothing good about the experience (e.g., "Writing is like 'being sick' "), and a few took great pleasure in it. One recalled a statement from Hemingway that "the only two things he had ever enjoyed were writing and making love."

Hartley and Branthewaite (1989) surveyed productive British psychologists on their writing habits, attitudes, and feelings. A cluster analysis of their responses revealed two types of writers from an affective viewpoint. *Anxious* writers felt more obligated to write, were less happy about writing, felt it was harder than it used to be, experienced more self-doubt, and enjoyed it less than *enthusiastic* writers. Most of the writers in the sample of highly prolific academics were enthusiastic (63%), and 23% were anxious.

Brand (1989) reported the most comprehensive series of studies on the emotions of writers. One version of the Brand Emotions Scale for Writers (BESW) measured the temporary emotional states that might come and go during composition. Another form of the BESW measured the enduring emotional traits that consistently described the emotional condition of a writer whenever they composed. The trait, then, was a persistent feature of the individual's personality as a writer, as opposed to a transient feeling. Brand investigated a broad population of adult writers, ranging from college students to professionals, including English teachers.

For college students drawn from psychology and English classes and those sampled from advanced expository writing classes, a common pattern of emotions characterized the states typically experienced just before and after composing. These students felt reinterested, happy, anxious, adventurous, and excited prior to beginning an assignment. After finishing, the participants typically felt relieved, satisfied, interested, happy, adventurous, excited, inspired, and affectionate. Positive feelings predominated at both points in time, but they intensified after writing. In contrast, the professional writers and English teachers maintained a steady emotional state before and after writing, though again virtually the same rank order of positive emotions emerged. The English teachers differed from the professional writers primarily in that the intensity of positive emotions was less both before and after writing.

As for the trait-scale data, the professionals and English teachers normally experienced positive emotional traits. Curiously, the college students experienced shifts on these scales, suggesting that for them at least the scales were not tapping a stable dimension of their personality as writers. As the school term wore on, the students tired of the writing assignments and this resulted in their trait scores turning less positive.

In theory, writing performance should depend partly on emotional factors. On the one hand, the time spent absorbed in the task of meaning-making, and hence productivity, ought to relate directly to the degree of positive affect associated with it. The writer who enjoys the task and finds emotional satisfaction in completing documents that are read by others ought to spend the most time engaged in writing and in amplifying the writing performance. On the other hand, the writer who suffers anxiety about writing and about having others read the resulting product is likely to avoid the task if possible. Procrastination, fretful attempts at writing, and complete avoidance, or *writer's block,* are consequences of anxiety.

Another result of negative affect is that it probably hampers the retrieval and application of knowledge in the course of writing. If the task arouses anxiety, then the defense mechanism of repression may limit access to the very content and discourse knowledge needed to complete the task. Further, arousal beyond the optimum level called for in complex intellectual tasks probably impairs effective retrieval of knowledge. Even if anxious writers successfully retrieve the relevant knowledge, their ability to apply it creatively to the rhetorical and content problems at hand should suffer. Both retrieval and application should suffer if the writer suffers from a breakdown of concentration or attentional overload brought on by frustration and fear. The evidence on anxiety, procrastination, repression, and creativity in writing supports these claims, though not unequivocally.

Writing Apprehension

Apprehension about writing is widespread enough and strong enough to make procrastination virtually universal. Lowenthal and Wason (1977) reported that starting a task was judged difficult by all of the respondents in their survey and was viewed as the single most difficult part of writing by 30%. Boice and Johnson (1984) found that 34% of their sample of university faculty reported moderate to high anxiety about writing.

Others have examined apprehension among student writers. Freeman (1983) reported from a survey of college students that 45% found writing painful, 61% found it difficult, and 41% were lacking confidence in their ability to write (Freedman, 1983). For all groups examined by Brand (1989), anxiety was the most common of the negative emotions experienced. Consistent with the prediction that a high level of anxiety interferes with knowledge access is a study by Daly (1978). He found that degree of writing apprehension, assessed by self-report on a questionnaire, was negatively correlated with the quality of documents written by the students.

Daly's conclusion has been called into question by subsequent research, however. First, Brand (1989) reported that both students and professionals experienced only moderate levels of frustration, fear, and anxiety and that these negative emotions were not affected by the act of composing itself. Second, Kean, Glynn, and Britton (1987) examined verbal aptitude as well as writing apprehension in predicting writing quality. As expected, higher degrees of verbal knowledge were associated with higher holistic quality ratings of the letters written in their task, and with lower rates of punctuation and spelling errors. Interestingly, though, the authors also found that verbal aptitude and anxiety were inversely related. In Experiment 1 of their work, a time constraint was placed on the experimental task and a significant negative correlation between anxiety and quality was obtained. A multiple regression analysis suggested that this effect was unimportant once verbal aptitude was taken into account. That is, low verbal aptitude may cause writing apprehension, but it is the lack of knowledge, not the apprehension, that affects writing quality.

In Experiment 2, the time pressure on the students was eliminated. Kean et al. found that anxiety and quality were not even correlated under such circumstances. This result militates further against the notion that anxiety directly influences the accessibility of relevant knowledge during writing.

Before rejecting the hypothesis that retrieval failure due to anxiety may affect writing quality, it would be interesting to examine professional writers, all of whom are highly knowledgeable about the language. If it could be shown that those who experience high anxiety write less well than those who do not, then the hypothesis would find some support. Also, it should be noted that a review of the literature indicates varying degrees of negative relations between verbal aptitude and writing apprehension, including nonsignificant ones (Daly, 1985).

Finally, anxiety about writing can be viewed as a state as well as a trait. If it could be shown that writers at any given level of verbal aptitude perform better when they are calm than when they are anxious, then the accessibility hypothesis would gain strength.

The results reported by Cleary (1991) show just such a pattern. She employed extensive interviews, composing aloud, and classroom observation to investigate the effects of negative emotions and moods on the writing performance of 40 eleventh graders. Of the total sample, 32 students exhibited inability to concentrate on writing, in some cases for prolonged periods of time. This was due to (1) "overburdened conscious attention exacerbated by frustration," (2) "distressing life situations," (3) "threat in the writing environment," and (4) "lack of intrinsic motivation" (p. 485). The first three reasons demonstrate plainly the manner in which anxiety disrupts the retrieval and application of knowledge and at times brings all writing to a halt.

Nearly a third of the sample identified attentional overload as a serious problem. For example, at one time or another, particular assignments in school frustrated the students so much that they gave up altogether. The diligent, grade-conscious students, when faced with such difficult assignments, "would continue in agony when pressed by a deadline because the consequences of not completing the assignment were too great" (p. 487). Composing aloud revealed one such student trying to generate ideas, organize them, puzzle over word choice, and worry about the teacher's reaction—all at the same time. Numerous erasures accompanied audible sighs and groans as this writer struggled to retrieve and apply content and discourse knowledge.

Nearly a third of the writers experienced deaths in their families or other, less devastating distress in romances, friendships, or family. The emotions connected with these events continually interrupted the writers' attempts to compose and meet deadlines. One student blocked completely when asked to write a satire on her semester-long topic of Zionism. This occurred because of the painful feelings of losing her grandfather recently and her sister's decision to move to Israel. The instructor would not allow a change of topic for one student. To write anything connected with her religion at that time would have been difficult, but a satire proved impossible.

Another student reported trouble with a paper because of another life event:

> That paper took me longer to write than . . . anything else I've done in my whole life because that day I had gotten a lot of trouble from seniors. The funny thing is I really cared what these seniors felt about me. . . . I'd gotten thrown in a trash can . . . , and then trash dumped all over me, and then thrown into the pond in the back. . . . I was really upset. I went home and I sat and I tried to write that [paper]. And I wrote a sentence down, but I would stop and think . . . and would go, "OK, what would be a good word to start off with that sentence,["] and I'd start thinking . . . zoom off to what happened. It was just frustrating that I couldn't get it done, . . . that I couldn't block it out. (p. 492)

Nearly two-thirds of the students showed disruption of concentration in response to a threat in the writing environment. One advanced writer perceived the comments (e.g., "You have some talent, don't lose it") and grade (a C on his first paper) given by his teacher as highly threatening. In composing aloud, this writer's fear of the teacher was evident: "He can't stand colloquialism . . . like 'hand in hand' . . . it is not a personal relationship anyway . . . let's try this. . . . I can see his correcting pen all over this" (p. 494).

Remedial, average, and advanced student writers perceived the teacher as a threat, losing concentration and in some cases the motivation to write. Persistent criticism, Cleary concluded, is a "pervasive and serious problem for developing writers" (p. 495).

Writer's Block

Rose (1984) reported that about 10% of the college students had writer's block, meaning that they avoided the task altogether. These students tended to follow rigid, maladaptive rules that disrupted successful writing. For instance, one blocked writer developed overly elaborate plans that lengthened the prewriting stage to several days. Then, with only a few hours left for creating a draft, the student found it impossible to translate the complex plan into a short essay.

The frequency of blocking among academic or professional writers is difficult to determine. However, about half of all graduate students finish their Ph.D. requirements A.B.D.—"all but dissertation" (Monaghan, 1989). Some of them seek professional assistance to overcome their block (Bloom, 1985). Boice and Johnson (1984) observed a significant negative correlation between reported scholarly productivity and degree of writing anxiety among university faculty. Remarkably, even among a sample of productive British psychologists, 12% reported an inability to write at times for motivational/emotional reasons (Hartley & Branthwaite, 1989).

Boice (1990) has tried to help anxious academic writers by forcing them to translate their thoughts into text, disallowing planning and collecting alone. A common way to procrastinate is to plan, analyze, and collect information, rationalizing that one is making progress. Though these operations are necessary, they clearly are not sufficient. An influential philosopher, Karl Marx, apparently suffered in this regard. Myers (1991) reported the depth of procrastination exhibited in Marx's work:

Marx, an angry and often irascible man, also was a born analyst, so much so that his endless analyzing got in the way of his efforts to convert his extensive notes into books. Volume 1 of "Das Kapital" came out in 1867, after 18 years of work; the other two volumes had to be finished by Friedrich Engels, his friend and collaborator, after Marx died in 1883. (p. 10)

Boice (1985) designed a program to help professors with writer's block. The publish-or-perish world of academia spurs anxiety among faculty that can lead to blocking at some time. Without question, those who persistently block perish. Boice investigated differences in the self-talk of blocked and nonblocked faculty. His participants recorded their thoughts on note cards during the initiation and completion of writing sessions. Over 5,000 examples of self-talk were collected and sorted. Boice identified seven categories of thoughts: work apprehension, procrastination, dysphoria, impatience, perfectionism, evaluation anxiety, and rules.

Work apprehension (thoughts about the difficult, demanding nature of writing) and rules (thoughts about maladaptive formulas for writing, such as "Good writing must be spontaneous and clever") occurred about equally often among blocked and nonblocked writers. Procrastination (thoughts that justify avoiding or delaying writing) was much more common among blocked (90%) than among nonblocked (55%) writers. Dysphoria (thoughts reflecting burnout, panic, or obsessive worries), impatience (thoughts of achieving more in less time or imposing unrealistic deadlines), perfectionism (thoughts reflecting an internal critic who allows no errors), and evaluation anxiety (thoughts about fears of rejection) also afflicted the blocked writers more often.

Such statistical findings are interesting, but they cannot compete with the self-report of one writer in conveying the depth of anxiety that plagued him. Van Brooks conveyed it best in "Opinions of Oliver Allston," as quoted by John-Steiner (1985):

In thirty years of writing, I have not gained an ounce of confidence. I begin each new book . . . with a sense of impotence, chaos, and desperation that cannot be overstated. I always feel that I am foredoomed to failure. Every day I begin my work with the same old feeling that I am on trial for my life and will probably not be acquitted. (p. 77)

Writer's block is a real phenomenon, though its extent cannot be readily calibrated. Given the heavy investment of cognitive effort and emotional resources in writing long, complex assignments, it would not be surprising if nearly everyone who has put pen to paper has not experienced temporary if not prolonged blocking. Perhaps only Isaac Asimov avoided at least a few days of procrastination ("Transition," 1992). Asimov reportedly worked seven days a week and "wrote as fast as he could type, 90 words per minute, never suffering a blocked minute" (p. 85). His astonishing legacy of books makes it difficult to brush aside this claim as fanciful. I turn now to a discussion of the affective nature of creative flow, a state that Asimov surely experienced, if anyone has.

Creative Flow

Csikszentmihalyi and Csikszentmihalyi (1988) proposed that when the demands of the task match the person's level of skill, a flow state potentially emerges. *Flow* refers to being in tune with the environment, experiencing enjoyment or even euphoria, clarity of purpose, a sense of mastery, high intrinsic motivation, and total absorption in the task. Typically, time is distorted and hours seemingly fly by when one loses oneself in the work.

The flow state provides a phenomenological description of a person operating at a peak level of performance. Cognitive effort and processing time are fully invested, with the aim of maximizing performance. Economy of effort is sacrificed to peak performance. The task at hand is fully engaged, and relevant knowledge is retrieved and applied creatively to problems as they arise. Concentration or expenditure of cognitive effort is maximal, but interestingly, the person experiences a sense of effortlessness, ease, and enjoyment. Struggling is unnecessary. It comes when the task exceeds available, accessible skill. Anxiety and frustration are the consequences. Alternatively, when skill exceeds task demands, boredom results.

Massimini, Czikszentmihalyi, and Delle Fave (1988) administered questionnaires to widely diverse populations around the world to learn the conditions associated with flow states. In 40% of their samples, the flow experience was triggered by the activity itself. The second most common way of entering the state was by concentrating and avoiding distraction (13%). The need for a high degree of intrinsic motivation was reported by 9%. The two most common phenomenological dimensions were a sense of well-being and positive affect (50%) and the satisfaction of using one's skills well (20%).

Both anxiety or overarousal and boredom or underarousal should be associated with poorer writing performance. Quality, fluency, and productivity ought to be amplified when the writer achieves a state of creative flow. Larsen (1988) reported several case studies of student writers that were consistent with this view. His anxious writers procrastinated, felt confused, lacked concentration, and worked inefficiently in marathon sessions. His bored writers lost all sense of personal challenge and engagement once the prewriting activities of collecting information and planning were completed. Translating their plans into text and carefully reviewing their work held no excitement. The drafting process for them was mechanical and offered no new problems to solve. Instead of creatively engaging the task, the bored writers routinely cranked out a mediocre piece of work just to get it done. Instead of time flying by, the writing process was drudgery and time crawled.

Further evidence comes from studies of productivity in science. Roe (1952) described 64 eminent scientists in terms of "a driving absorption in their work" (p. 25). The productive, successful scientist "works hard and devotedly at his laboratory, often seven days a week" (p. 22). Roe further noted that these scientists "have worked long hours for many years, frequently with no vacations to speak of, because they would rather be doing their work than anything else" (p. 25). In a similar vein, Csikszentmihalyi (1990) reported interviews with surgeons who admitted an addiction to their work, who found that "anything that takes them away from the hospital—a Caribbean vacation, a night at the opera—feels like a waste of time" (p. 155).

Simon (1974) found that productivity correlates positively with the time engaged in work, noting that successful researchers typically work 8 to 10 hours per day, 300 to 335 days per year. Simonton (1988) summarized the absorption shown by prolific scientists by reminding us of Michael Faraday's motto: "Work, Finish, Publish."

Peak performance in thinking and writing, then, appears to occur during states of creative flow. Anxiety, on the one hand, and boredom, on the other, are generally detrimental. I emphasize here that at various stages of working on any project, anxiety and boredom are bound to occur in even the most prolific and profound writer. My point is not that such emotional states never occur for the writer who amplifies his or her performance. Rather, amplification of performance, the positive affect of creative flow, must occur, and the more often, the better.

The link between creative flow and performance amplification runs counter to the traditional theme that creativity and psychological disorders go hand in hand. The alcoholism and depression of William Faulkner and Ernst Hemingway or the bipolar affective disorder of Virginia Woolf and Vincent Van Gogh are common examples. Andreason (1987) and Berman (1988) provided convincing documentation of the links between depressive and obsessive disorders and genius in arts and letters. Moreover, the popular image of the tormented genius suggests that neurotic anxiety or even psychosis somehow benefits the artist. A careful analysis reveals a much more complicated relation, however.

Kubie (1958) presented several convincing case studies of the destructive side of psychopathology. He documented that fear, guilt, obsessions, and other anxiety states can palpably diminish creative production. Beeman (1990) explained that the creative lifestyle carries with it risks, much like those confronting a tightrope walker. Reward and encouragement for artistic efforts are rare. Those few who attain recognition during their lifetime are then under pressure to continue to improve while simultaneously being taken away from their work for publicity efforts such as book promotion tours. Beeman saw alcoholism, drug addiction, and certain forms of mental illness as avenues of escape from the difficulties of a creative lifestyle, escape that might well be unnecessary if society supported and encouraged creativity.

Beeman studied the life and work of Virginia Woolf to understand the dynamics of creativity and mental disorder. She noted:

> the drive to create is not at all times a benevolent dictator but can push the artist beyond his or her constitutional limits. When this occurs, some sort of breakdown is inevitable; either a somatic illness intervenes or a psychiatric disturbance or relief may be sought through alcohol and drugs. In the case of Virginia Woolf, there was the imminent threat of manic-depressive psychosis. (p. 141)

Csikszentmihalyi (1990) echoed Beeman's analysis in his conclusion that cultural expectations and the difficult social role of writers probably account for the relationship between mental disorders and creativity. The criticism that creators inevitably face can overwhelm some individuals. Typically, intense anxiety and fear are purely destructive. At best, such negative emotions might drive an individual to work to avoid failure in the eyes of others. Emotional insecurity can spur creative production, but at the same time, unhappily, it spurs self-dissolution. The well-established link between psychopathology and creativity arises, then, because both are caused by emotional insecurity (Ochse, 1990).

Alcoholism, drug addiction, and various mental illnesses eventually ravage the creator afflicted with them. The rate of destruction may be slow, as in alcoholism, or fast, as in suicidal depression. Either way, the illness destroys the creator. One cannot help but ponder how much more Faulkner, Hemingway, Van Gogh, and Woolf could have contributed to humanity, given their remarkable knowledge and talent, had they been blessed with more hours of creative flow and fewer hours of emotional torment.

6

Strategies

I have never thought of myself as a good writer. Anyone who wants reassurance of that should read one of my first drafts. But I'm one of the world's great rewriters.

James A. Michener

Few topics in writing research engender as much controversy and produce such differing views as the value of various strategies for applying a writer's knowledge. Expert opinions on prewriting strategies, for example, range from recommendations to use elaborate notecard systems arranged and embedded in complex patterns to foregoing prewriting altogether. Views on strategies for composing first drafts and revising subsequent drafts are equally at odds with each other.

The theoretical framework proposed here contends that the value of a strategy should be directly related to its promotion of better retrieval and application of knowledge. I hypothesized three ways for achieving this in Chapter 3. One way is to restructure the allocation of resources to reduce overload. Greater concentration on fewer processes ought to aid knowledge retrieval. Another way is through organization. Any strategy that organizes the writer's knowledge should aid its retrieval. Finally, methods of writing that reactivate cues associated with the original encoding of knowledge should also aid retrieval and use.

Flower (1981) divided strategies into weak and strong groups. Interestingly, what separates the two groups is attentional overload: Weak strategies promote it and strong strategies alleviate it. Weak strategies are perfect first drafts, trial-and-error sentence generation, waiting for inspiration, and words looking for an idea. Flower's analyses of verbal protocols of writers struggling with the process yielded these four types. As noted, the difficulty with the perfect-draft approach can be interpreted in terms of attentional overload. The other three approaches also fit this interpretation. Trial-and-error sentence generation refers to the process of combining words almost randomly as alternative expressions of the same idea. The multiple translation of the same idea quickly overloads attentional capacity and short-term memory.

Waiting for inspiration characterizes writers who think about the document extensively but never begin translating personal symbols into consensual symbols.

They wait until the words start flowing because they know exactly what they want to say or until the entire piece can be seen clearly in their minds. Again, thinking until one knows exactly what one wants to say overloads limited attentional capacity.

Finally, words looking for an idea occur when the writer focuses on sentence generation to the point that linguistic form runs ahead of content knowledge. Writing "although," "not only," or "but" and then stopping suggests that the translation process overwhelmed attentional capacity, leaving none available for planning content. Flower notes that such a writer "has let the momentum of language itself direct composition" (p. 38).

Powerful strategies include *brainstorming,* saying to oneself "What I really mean is . . ." (WIRMI), using notations rather than sentences, and satisficing. In each case, the purpose is to reduce the demand on attention. Brainstorming frees the writer to generate ideas, without concern for their organization or how to express them. WIRMI allows the writer to focus on the thought rather than on how it is expressed in consensual symbols. The polished prose can come later. Notational devices are vague consensual symbols that can be inspected by others but not necessarily understood (John-Steiner, 1985). Flow charts, trees, boxes, arrows, and other notes ease the load on attention and working memory, yet allow the writer to keep moving. Finally, satisficing, in Flower's scheme, means using an imperfect idea or expression in order to get on with the writing. Satisficing obviously aims to alleviate attentional overload.

This chapter reviews studies relevant to these theoretical claims. It is convenient to categorize strategies according to two broad phases of product development: prewriting and first-draft revision strategies. I do so while recognizing that the development of a document need not always follow a linear path through these phases and that the four fundamental processes rarely if ever do so.

The binary division is also crude and a bit arbitrary. Prewriting could easily be partitioned into subphases from early vague thoughts about a document to the formation of detailed plans. As Stotsky (1990) noted, the writer's preparation for drafting includes "the working out of ideational content through internal verbal thinking or through note-taking, outlining, other scribbing, and even talking to others" (p. 52). The prewriting phase involves a wide variety of collecting, planning, translating, and reviewing activities. Still, the division of strategies into those invoked during prewriting versus those invoked during the various stages of drafting is appealing and manageable. It recognizes an important break between thinking about writing and putting together a draft. As we saw in the previous chapter, that leap to drafting can pose a formidable psychological barrier for many writers. This barrier serves a convenient purpose in discussing strategies as well.

Prewriting Strategies

Before a writer begins the initial draft of a document, he or she may spend anywhere from a few minutes to several years engaged in thinking, note taking, locating sources, reading, toying with ideas and their organization, revising arguments, and several other so-called prewriting activities. They are so called only because they frequently occur extensively before a writer begins a task of any difficulty. But as noted previously, such collecting, planning, translating (such as filling in a sentence outline, as well as other forms of drafting), and reviewing can occur during any phase of writing right up to the final draft.

Murray (1985) graphically described what he called the *essential delay* of the writer. Extensive prewriting activities do not necessarily imply writer's block, according to Murray. He suggested that professional writers must accumulate vast amounts of information that must be digested and understood before effective writing can begin. They collect so much information that "its sheer abundance makes the need for meaning and order insistent" (p. 221). Murray recalled the wisdom of E. B. White on prewriting: "Delay is natural to the writer. He is like a surfer—he bides his time. Waits for the perfect wave on which to ride in" (p. 219).

Listing, Clustering, and Outlining

The strategies used by a writer in collecting information and reflecting upon it in the very early stages of prewriting, before a specific writing task is even envisioned, are difficult to categorize. But once the writer begins to focus on a specific writing assignment, three types of prewriting can be readily identified. Each of these can take place entirely in the writer's head, without any translation of personal symbols into the consensual symbols of text. Alternatively, each can result in an external record, one that can be referred to and reflected upon by the writer.

The first prewriting strategy is *clustering* or *networking ideas and their relations.* This consists of noting ideas visually as nodes of a network and, in some cases, marking the links between nodes as relations between ideas. Several iterations in constructing the network or cluster may be needed. Rico (1983) referred to such an ideational network as a *cluster,* while Fields (1982) used the term *pattern notes.* The technique is best viewed as a brainstorming tool that may help writers generate ideas in the early stages of prewriting. It is important to point out that the resulting network may suggest the relations among ideas, but it lacks a hierarchical or even a linear organization. Buzan (1991) proposed a related strategy, called *mind maps,* but his networks allowed for the formation of hierarchical relations.

The second prewriting strategy is *listing ideas.* As ideas are generated they are noted, either mentally or in some external medium. Specific relations to previous or subsequent ideas may or may not be noted. The order in which the ideas are placed in the list can reflect, sometimes after several attempts to build the list, the order needed for the text. Listing, then, provides a linear organization for the prewriting plan.

The third prewriting strategy is *outlining ideas and their hierarchical relations.* This consists of noting ideas in terms of a hierarchy of structural relations. Super-ordinate and subordinate relations are made explicit, as well as the functional relations that are represented in networks or clusters. The formality of the outline can range from the classical system, with Roman numerals, capital letters, Arabic numerals, and lowercase letters, to personal, idiosyncratic, casual methods. Outlining also includes the graphically oriented tree diagram technique for representing the information. Like the other strategies, outlining may require several iterations. When completed, the outline, by definition, must provide both a linear and a hierarchical plan for drafting the text. This assumes that the outline serves as a guide for generating the text as opposed to a device for developing and structuring ideas alone. The appearance and detail of the document vary with the outlining style.

My argument in favor of prewriting strategies rests on the assumption that they enhance the access and application of knowledge. By planning extensively before drafting, the writer can concentrate on translation and reviewing while composing drafts. Prewriting strategies restructure attention in a way that should alleviate attentional overload. They help eliminate what Collins and Genter (1980) called downsliding, becoming entangled in local problems of text processing when attention should be focused on global planning and rhetorical goals. By eliminating the need for extensive planning during drafting, the juggling act becomes less rigorous. Moreover, listing and outlining provide an organizational structure for a document before drafting begins. This organization should help writers to retrieve detailed knowledge needed during composition. As Murray (1985) noted, the sheer abundance of information needed by a writer strains effective retrieval and use without the help of an organizational scheme.

An opposing viewpoint is readily derived from work emphasizing the interactive nature of writing processes. There is strong evidence that writing is nonlinear and recursive: Collecting, planning, translating, and reviewing interact extensively during the development of a text (de Beaugrande, 1984; Kennedy, 1985; McCutchen, 1988). In an influential book on writing methods, Elbow (1981) warned against trying to outline before beginning to write. He suggested that outlining may be worthwhile when one already knows which ideas should be included in a text. But for most writing tasks, the quality of writing and the fluency of language production should be enhanced by forgoing prewriting and beginning immediately the creation of a rough first draft in which collecting, planning, translating, and reviewing interact extensively (see also Smith, F., 1982).

Prewriting strategies may interfere with the knowledge transformation that occurs as a writer thinks through a document (Horton, 1982). Such a view is consistent with an opportunism model of planning (Hayes-Roth & Hayes-Roth, 1979). Outlining may prevent the writer from exploiting opportunities that arise during the interaction of collecting, planning, translating, and reviewing.

At this juncture, it is important to remember that the use of a prewriting strategy does not imply that all interaction among collecting, planning, translating, and reviewing ceases. Rather, the degree of interaction varies. All four processes are probably still invoked during the first draft and subsequent draft phases, but less planning is expected when a prewriting strategy is used than when it is not. In other words, opportunities from interaction can still be exploited during composing, but there should be fewer such opportunities when a prewriting strategy is adopted. Whether such a loss is important is the question.

It is also important to realize that the use of a prewriting strategy does not necessarily interfere with knowledge transformation. Certainly one way, and perhaps the best way, to transform knowledge is by translating vague personal symbols into text, however ragged it may be at first. But knowledge transformation can conceivably occur entirely in the head, without putting sentences on paper. Mentally listing ideas or visualizing clusters or outlines is another approach to rethinking what one thinks about a topic. Alternatively, one may engage in the same types of planning on a computer or on paper, without actually beginning a draft. Whether knowledge transformation proceeds better in some or all tasks by prewriting or by drafting is another important question.

Field Research and Case Studies

Research on outlining is limited, and apparently on listing and clustering it is virtually nonexistent. Emig (1971) and Pianko (1979) observed that few high school and college students do any written planning during prewriting on school assignments despite exposure to formal writing instruction, which at that time encouraged outlining. This was true of both good and poor student writers, indirectly supporting the interaction hypothesis (Stallard, 1974). Two studies tested whether high school and college students received better grades on papers for which they had prepared a written outline; they found at best only a marginally significant advantage for outlining (Branthwaite, Trueman, & Hartley, 1980; Emig, 1971).

Studies of more experienced writers engaging in longer writing assignments reveal a somewhat different picture. Stotsky (1990) concluded that case studies and surveys of professional writers show that they generally use some type of written outline, formal or informal, before beginning a draft.

For example, Bridwell-Bowles, Johnson, and Brehe (1987) observed eight graduate teaching associates who had published within and outside academia as they learned to use word processors. They classified the writers as *Beethovians or Discoverers* versus *Mozartians or Executors* on the basis of their use of prewriting strategies. Beethovians engaged in few prewriting activities and preferred to compose rough first drafts immediately in order to discover what they had to say. The Mozartians engaged in extensive planning during prewriting, such as creating outlines, and then executed as polished a first draft as possible. Some writers were classified as combinations of these extremes. Because the writers were learning to use a new writing tool, inferences cannot be drawn about which type of writer produced the best documents. It was interesting that the Mozartians found the word processor more compatible with their approach than did the Beethovians.

In a related case study, Lansman, Smith, and Weber (1990) monitored nine graduate students and eight professional technical writers as they composed on a new authoring system called the WRITING ENVIRONMENT. The system supports writing processes by offering a Network Mode for idea generation and exploration, a Tree Mode for organization and global editing, an Edit Mode for sentence generation and local editing, and a Text Mode for other types of editing. By providing separate modes, the WRITING ENVIRONMENT can track the time devoted to each as the writer's attention shifts from one mode to the next.

Of interest here are the results of Lansman et al. on the distribution of planning time. Few of the writers studied did nearly all of their planning (Network and Tree modes) before beginning to draft. They were clear-cut Mozartians. A few others were clear-cut Beethovians, alternating the two planning modes and the two writing modes throughout composition. The largest group of participants fell between these extremes. Using a quantitative index of how planning was distributed, Lansman et al. found that the majority of participants did most of their planning during prewriting. The correlation between this index and holistic quality ratings was nonsignificant.

However, there was a significant, and surprisingly negative, correlation between total time spent planning and holistic quality ($r = -.44$). Lansman et al. interpreted this finding in light of the extraordinary amount of time that some of their participants spent planning. All participants spent 90 minutes learning to use the Writing Environment. Some found the novelty of the Network and Tree modes perhaps too inviting. They spent more time than was practical exploring their use, leaving too little time for writing a draft. Many of the reports in the study included headings produced in the Network or Tree modes, with no associated text. Lansman et al. suggested that there is probably some optimal amount of planning for a given writing assignment, and that their participants tended to exceed that limit. Further experience with the Writing Environment may reduce this problem and alter the correlation between planning time and quality.

Kellogg (1986a) surveyed science and engineering faculty about their writing methods to determine which if any were correlated with productivity. Productivity was indexed by summing the number of published journal articles, books, technical reports, and grant proposals and reports over a 3-year period. Various weighting schemes were explored for books published, but there were too few ($M = .29$) for it to make much difference how they were weighted. The mean overall productivity was 16.3 (SD = 9.54). The frequency with which the respondents used a particular method in writing technical material was assessed on a scale ranging from "Never" (1) to "Always" (7).

The correlation between written outlining and productivity was significant and positive ($r = .27$). I divided the respondents into four groups on the basis of their response to the outline question and a question about how often they tried to create a polished first draft. The median response on each scale was used as the dividing point. The mean productivity of the participants in each of the four conditions is plotted in Figure 6.1. The use of a prewriting strategy of outlining clearly made a difference in a direction predicted by the knowledge-usage framework. Hartley and Branthwaite (1989) corroborated this result, stating that the productive writers they studied worked out a plan for the document before beginning a draft. Whether the writers aimed to create a rough or polished first draft made no difference, a point that will be discussed later in the chapter.

To summarize, the observational and field research give a mixed view of the value of prewriting strategies. The only strong, positive effect is the correlation between outlining and productivity. The studies that yielded null or negative results all suffer from low statistical power, using in most cases only a handful of participants. It is possible that a small positive effect could go undetected outside of a well-controlled laboratory experiment designed with adequate statistical power.

Laboratory Experiments

Restructuring and Concentration. I designed a series of experiments to examine the role of prewriting strategies. Laboratory experiments, of course, suffer from a

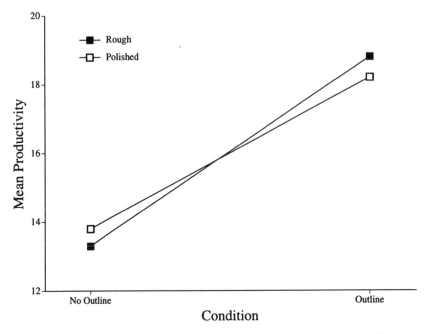

FIGURE 6.1. Reported productivity of science and engineering faculty. (Adapted from Kellogg, 1987b. Copyright © 1987 by Sage Publications. Reprinted by permission.)

lack of ecological validity by selecting a small number of writing topics and forcing participants to write under laboratory conditions. Still, their virtues outweigh these vices.

Kellogg (1988) used directed retrospection and secondary-task RT data to measure processing time and cognitive effort devoted to planning, translating, and reviewing. As in other studies using these methods, collecting was ignored by requiring the writer to compose a business letter without source materials. Experiment 1 examined four conditions defined by the factorial combination of drafting strategy (rough versus polished) and prewriting strategy (outlining versus no outlining). Experiment 2 compared mental versus written outlines. Those in the no-outline, control condition began composing immediately after receiving their task assignment. The participants in the written-outline condition devoted 10 minutes of prewriting to developing a formal outline using Roman numerals, capital letters, Arabic numerals, and lowercase letters as needed. Those in the mental-outline condition did the same but entirely in their heads; they were not permitted to put their outline on paper. The writers worked until they were satisfied with the overall quality of their documents, which averaged about 28 minutes of writing time.

These experiments tested the hypothesis that outlining restructures the allocation of processing time during composing to reduce attentional overload. By allowing the writer to concentrate on fewer operations, I expected knowledge access, and therefore performance, to improve.

The results in Figure 6.2 portray the pattern of allocating processing time across

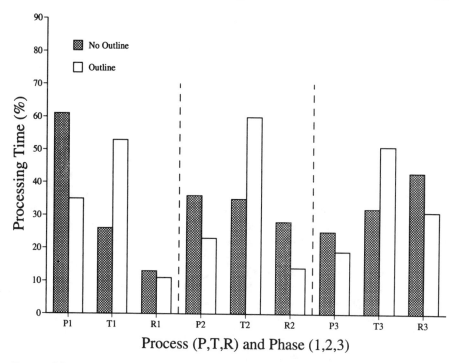

FIGURE 6.2. Processing time in a letter-writing experiment for planning (P), translating (T), and reviewing (R) as a function of prewriting strategy. (From Kellogg, 1988. Copyright © 1988 by the American Psychological Association. Reprinted by permission.)

the first, second, and third phases of writing time in Experiment 1. The interaction of condition and process was reliable, as was the three-way interaction of condition, process, and phase. As predicted, the writers who did not outline devoted more planning time during the first two phases of composition than those who did. Those who outlined, either mentally or in writing, concentrated substantially more on translating.

The overall quality of the documents was affected by this restructuring effect. In both experiments, the participants in the outline conditions achieved quality scores that were reliably higher than the scores of those in the no-outline condition. Analytic scales for usage, coherence, idea development, and communicative effectiveness all showed this superiority for outlining. Mechanics, in contrast, revealed equal scores for control and outline conditions. Although the participants spent about the same amount of time drafting, regardless of condition, their fluency also depended on whether they outlined. Calculation of the number of words composed per minute of drafting time showed reliably greater fluency for those who outlined during prewriting.

Interestingly, Experiment 2 revealed no significant difference between mental and written outlines. This implies that the external representation itself is not responsible for the benefits of outlining. The external representation of a written outline could free space in working memory for other information needed in writing. For the 200- to 300-word documents studied here, though, this was not the case. A long document, on the other hand, most likely would favor a written over a mental outline. Stotsky (1990) correctly pointed out that, in contrast to studies of students writing essays of fewer than 350 words, studies of students and professionals composing lengthy documents show that written outlines serve a critical function.

Organization.   I manipulated the demands of the writing task directly to explore the boundary conditions of the outlining effect and to examine the role of organization (Kellogg, 1990). The participants were given the Topic only in the T condition. They were given the Topic plus 14 relevant Ideas for possible inclusion in their essay in the TI condition. Those in the Topic plus Ideas plus Organization (TIO) condition received a suggested organizational scheme for their essay in addition to the ideas and topic. The scheme divided the essay into an introductory paragraph in which the writer could describe the issue and the purpose for writing, a section in which specific points are addressed, and a conclusion in which the most important points are summarized and possibly the writer's own position is stated. It was suggested that the specific points could be organized by first presenting the pros and then the cons, and that each category could begin with practical reasons first, emotional or psychological reasons next, and general, abstract, or philosophical reasons last. The TI and TIO instructions emphasized that the ideas and organizational scheme were only suggestions; participants were free to use or not use any or all of the suggestions.

The demands of the task decreased across the T, TI, and TIO conditions to the extent that the participants made some use of the suggestions. The TI writers had less need to generate ideas but still had to organize them. Thus, since part of the value of outlining comes from the organizational boost that it gives to knowledge access, I expected to see higher performance for those who outlined first relative to control writers in both the T and TI conditions. The writers in the TIO condition, on the other hand, had an outline handed to them, in essence, prior to starting the prewriting phase. The topic knowledge they needed was available and accessible in the control and outline conditions. I expected to eliminate the superiority of outlining in the TIO case.

In this study, I again used a no-prewriting control condition. It can be fairly argued that another type of control is also needed. Perhaps the time spent prewriting helps the writer to prepare for composition in a general way that has little to do with aiding knowledge retrieval through concentration or organization. Perhaps writers need to "warm up" to their task. The clustering condition I included formed, in essence, an ideal control for this possibility. Clustering required the writers to engage the writing assignment during prewriting, but the brainstorming technique did not yield a plan with the organization demanded by text. For these writers, the difficult processes of ordering ideas and establishing goals for the text still had to occur exclusively during the drafting phase. In fact, the large number of ideas and relations generated through clustering may even add to the planning burden once drafting begins. The writer must sort out good ideas from bad ones, as well as organize them coherently. Thus, clustering should not allow the writer to restructure attention to aid concentration on translating, nor should it provide an organizational crutch of any kind.

The data for overall quality (a combination of analytic scores on content and style) are shown in Figure 6.3. That the demand manipulation succeeded is indicated by the pattern for the no-prewriting control condition. The writers used the ideas and organization provided, at least when they were forced to begin drafting immediately. The essays in the TIO condition were rated best, followed by those in the TI condition, with the T essays considered the worst. Other detailed analyses of the text content also showed that the writers used the ideas and organization offered them.

More important, the benefit of outlining was substantial in the T condition and still robust in the TI condition. I succeeded in eliminating the outlining effect completely in the TIO condition. The clustering condition failed to differ reliably from the no-prewriting condition in all cases. An analysis of the prewriting plans showed that clustering included more ideas than outlining. But the greater number of ideas generated with clustering did not improve the quality of the document itself. I strongly suspect that the brainstorming spurred by clustering can help writers during earlier stages of prewriting. But the important point here is that clustering does not lead to a concentration or organization effect. It provides a useful control, then, in ruling out nonspecific warmup effects in studies of prewriting strategies.

Theoretically, then, outlining helps writers to retrieve and apply knowledge. It does this at least partly by allowing writers to concentrate on translating because they have already generated and organized ideas before composition. In addition, the hierarchical structure of an outline helps writers to retrieve (certainly) content and (perhaps) other knowledge when it is needed during composition. That is, organization as well as concentration may account for the benefits of outlining. To separate the two, I included a list condition in my final experiment. Writers in this condition listed ideas in the numerical order that they planned to use in drafting the text. I expected the list writers to concentrate on translating better than the no-prewriting control and clustering writers. But those in the list condition lacked the full organizational benefits of a hierarchical plan. They had only linear organization to aid them in knowledge retrieval. I predicted, then, that quality judgments for the list condition should fall between the control and outline conditions.

College students wrote an essay about the pros and cons of professionals joining an "antigreed club." The assignment was taken from writing-sample problems used on the Law School Admissions Test (Bobrow, 1979) and was used in Experiment 2 of Kellogg (1987a). The subjects were tested in several small-group sessions and randomly assigned to the no-prewriting control ($n = 15$), cluster ($n = 16$), list ($n = 19$), and outline ($n = 19$) conditions. Two judges agreed reliably in their assessments of content and style quality on 5-point scales, and as in other studies, I averaged their ratings.

The mean overall quality judgments (sum of content and style) appear in Figure 6.4 for the four conditions. As in Kellogg (1990), the clustering technique resulted in documents judged equal in quality to those produced with no prewriting at all. As predicted, the list condition fell short of the quality observed in the outline condition but well above that found in the other two conditions. The observed differences

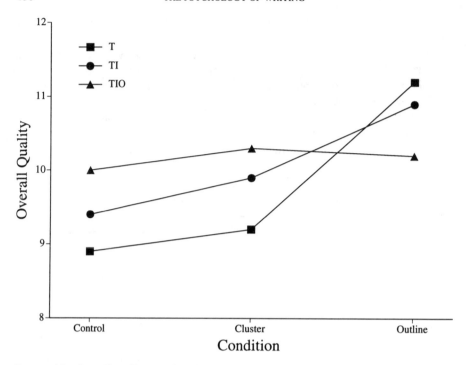

FIGURE 6.3. Overall quality as a function of task demands and prewriting strategy. (Adapted from Kellogg, 1990. Copyright © 1990 by the University of Illinois Press. Reprinted by permission.)

were statistically reliable. I interpret this pattern as compelling evidence that the benefits of outlining derive from two components. First, there is the concentration effect examined in detail in Kellogg (1988). Second, there is the organization effect explored in Kellogg (1990).

Conclusions and Limitations

For student writers composing 200- to 300-word essays in a single sitting, the laboratory evidence convincingly demonstrates that outlining in advance improves the quality and fluency of writing. This result is given greater generality by the survey work showing that science and engineering faculty who outline frequently tend to be most productive. The results support the suggestion that outlining can aid knowledge accessibility both through the restructuring of attention and through the memory aid of organization.

But it would be unwise to conclude that outlining is always useful. The work on task demands clearly shows this not to be the case when the writer already has plenty of ideas that are well organized. Presumably there is no need to improve knowledge accessibility through restructuring or organization in such cases. The mixed bag of

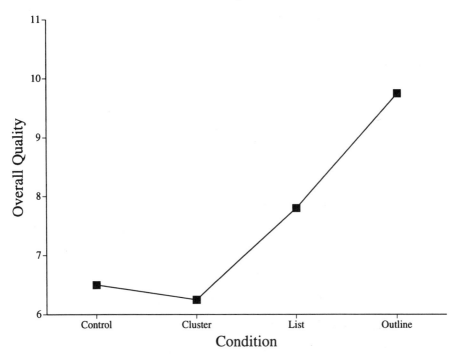

FIGURE 6.4. Overall quality as a function of prewriting strategy. (From Kellogg, 1993. Copyright © by *Composition Studies,* Texas Christian University. Reprinted by permission.)

results from field studies is likely due to variations in the task demands investigated. Note that the field study showing the benefits of outlining came from faculty doing actual technical writing, where creating and organizing ideas are clearly needed.

At the opposite extreme, creating an outline during prewriting may be unwise when the writer has few if any good ideas on a topic. Galbraith (1992) reported that outlining decreased the number of new ideas that emerged when writers later drafted an essay relative to the number that emerged when writers immediately composed a rough draft. The availability of the outline impeded the information of new ideas when writers planned and translated freely, without concern for organization or quality of expression. This cost of outlining might well outweigh the benefits when the writer cannot readily formulate novel and interesting ideas during prewriting. The benefits of concentration and organization during drafting would not amount to much if the outline contained too few ideas of sufficient complexity and number to support a high quality document.

Another caveat concerns the detail of outlines. Few participants in the laboratory studies created more than two levels of depth. On the one hand, the writing prompts used in the laboratory may not require a deeper outline. On the other hand, it may be too difficult to plan in advance a deep outline with, say, four or five levels, even on lengthy real-world writing assignments. It may be that such detail can only be achieved after composing a first or even a final draft. For a similar reason, it might be difficult to generate a sentence outline without already having composed.

The relative order of clustering, listing, and outlining fits the expectations based on the importance of organization in creating a final, readable document. But to denigrate the value of clustering is premature. The data show a brainstorming benefit: Clustering yielded more ideas than outlining (Kellogg, 1990). This would be particularly important during very early stages of prewriting, when the writer is struggling with inchoate notions. Available evidence in no way suggests that clustering is useless to a writer who is struggling to come to grips with a lengthy and challenging professional writing assignment early on, long before a draft is even contemplated. A writer who is thinking about writing a book, for example, may produce numerous clusters or networks. If a task could be designed that measures performance at such a stage, linear and hierarchical organization might be found to impair rather than aid the writer.

First-Draft Revision Strategies

From Polished Draft to Free Writing

Once the writer begins a draft, attentional allocation may involve one of three strategies. A *rough draft strategy* calls for the writer to focus on collecting, planning, and translating during the first draft phase, with little or no concern for reviewing. The writer deliberately avoids criticizing the quality of the draft, saving all editing for a second or third round. The aim is to produce text, however ragged, without attending to critical reviewing.

Free writing is a term used by Elbow (1981) to denote an extreme version of the rough draft strategy. In free writing, the process of translating ideas into text is not interrupted by either collecting or reviewing. Even planning is minimized; the writer translates whatever ideas occur at the moment, without bothering to organize his or her thoughts. The aim is to compose text as rapidly as possible, translating, in essence, a stream of consciousness. The initial draft resulting from this process may well have something in common with the stream-of-consciousness writers who adopted a variant of free writing for composing highly original fiction (Boorstin, 1992). For genres that demand clear organization and expression, as well as adherence to standard style requirements, further drafts are required as the writer fleshes out the original draft. Elbow regards the strategy as essential for enabling the writer to achieve a distinctive and powerful voice.

The third strategy is a *polished-draft* approach. The writer attends to collecting, planning, translating, and reviewing as the first draft unfolds. An attempt is made to produce polished prose. Following this strategy in no way eliminates the need for subsequent drafts. Especially with long, complex documents, it would be nearly impossible to compose a final, polished manuscript in one draft. But the point is that the writer attempts to polish the text, worrying about word choice, spelling, and sentence structure, as well as higher-level concerns.

Flower (1981) included the polished- or perfect-draft approach in her list of weak strategies. She noted that "if your ideas are not fully formed and you need to concentrate on purpose, content, or organization, it makes little sense to try to juggle the demands of polished prose at the same time" (p. 41). Even so, a highly accomplished professional, William Zinsser, swears by the polished-draft strategy. Zinsser (1983) compared his polished draft writing to bricklaying. Beginning with the first sentence, the foundation of the document must be erected, brick by brick, until the entire edifice stands strong.

The type of first-draft strategy employed determines when a writer reads and edits text. But specific revising strategies can be identified in terms of the level of changes made. Global revising concerns the macrostructure of a text. Are the ideas and their organization well developed? Local revising concerns the microstructure. Is a particular sentence expressed well? Are the word choice and spelling correct? It is assumed that both levels of revision must be carried out by a skilled writer (Hayes & Flower, 1986).

From a knowledge usage perspective, the concentration effect discussed in connection with prewriting strategies again applies. The strategies require different patterns of attentional allocation. The polished-draft strategy requires the writer to juggle all processes simultaneously. Free writing focuses on translating whatever ideas are generated in whatever order, with little regard for careful sentence construction and no regard for reviewing. Free writing, therefore, should most help writers to retrieve the knowledge they need to translate ideas into sentences because that is the sole focus of their attention. The writer is totally absorbed in playing with ideas by writing about them. Knowledge transformation is naturally encouraged by this approach. One problem with free writing is that discourse knowledge must eventually be brought to bear on the final product. Another is the ease with which writers digress from a line of thought or even from the topic at hand. Free writing, therefore, demands a task environment that allows the composition of multiple drafts.

Previous Research

Glynn, Britton, Muth, and Dogan (1982) provided the most compelling evidence that draft strategies support quality writing by allowing concentration on fewer operations at once. They found that planning is adversely affected when writers attempt to plan, translate, and review at the same time. Glynn et al. examined the number of arguments generated by students in a persuasive writing task while manipulating, via instructions, the number of processes juggled. The unordered-propositions (U) condition encouraged the writers to focus exclusively on generating ideas. The ordered-propositions (O) condition prompted them to generate and organize their ideas. The mechanics-free (M) condition added the requirement of translating their organized ideas into rough-draft sentences. Lastly, the polished-sentences (P) condition encouraged careful reviewing of the sentences while generating sentences and planning. An analysis of the total number of arguments produced on a preliminary draft revealed a significant effect of instruction condition, with the conditions ranked as shown in Figure 6.5. The more the writers were required to do, the fewer arguments resulted.

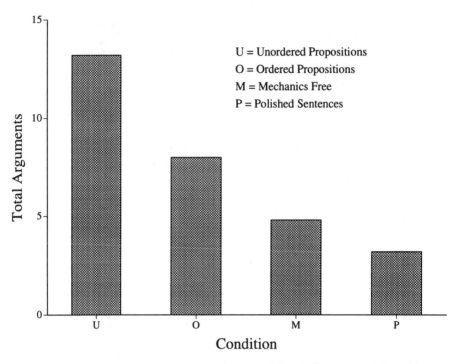

FIGURE 6.5. Total arguments generated as a function of first-draft strategy. (Adapted from Glynn, Britton, Muth, & Dogan, 1982.)

Quality judgments of the final draft were not collected; it is unclear whether ideational fluency relates directly to document quality. However, the number of sentences, the number of clauses per sentence, and the number of punctuation and spelling errors in the final draft were the same across conditions. The only textual characteristic that differed was the number of arguments presented per sentence. The polished-draft condition yielded a lower mean on this measure than did the other three conditions.

Another experiment on this subject comes from my own laboratory (Kellogg, 1988; Experiment 1). College students first learned numerous facts about a fictitious controversy regarding busing systems for the handicapped, organized and integrated these facts, and wrote a letter arguing in favor of a particular system. Using directed retrospection, the experiment provided evidence on the restructuring of processing time under different strategy conditions. Writers in the rough-draft condition received instructions to compose a draft freely at first, with the chief aim of getting their thoughts on paper rather than worrying about how well they were expressed. After this initial effort, they were to go back and focus on the manner of expression, adding, deleting, and revising as needed. In contrast, writers in the polished-draft condition received instructions to compose a polished draft, with the chief aim of expressing their thoughts as well as possible from the beginning. They were to add, delete, and review from the first phrase or sentence they wrote. The experimenter instructed all participants to work on their letters until they were satisfied with their quality, with no time constraints.

The amount of processing time devoted to planning, translating, and reviewing clearly differed between draft conditions. Specifically, in the early phase (the first third of writing time), there was a marked difference in the time devoted to reviewing between conditions. The polished-draft writers juggled planning, translating, and reviewing, whereas the rough-draft writers concentrated on planning and translating. Given this restructuring, one would expect less attentional overload in the rough-draft group and better performance.

But this was not the case. Fluency was only slightly greater, and not reliably greater, for the rough-draft condition; quality judgments were essentially equal for the rough- and polished-draft conditions. A weakness of this study is that multiple drafts over two or more writing sessions were not examined. The restructuring of time within a single session of writing through the rough-draft strategy may be a relatively weak manipulation. It could be that composing a rough draft for the entire first session, with no regard for reviewing until the manuscript is picked up later and revised in a subsequent draft, is necessary to detect an advantage.

The multiple-session explanation cannot readily account for the results of Gould, Conti, and Hovanyecz (1983), who manipulated strategies in a study on writing with a simulated listening typewriter. Managers dictated business letters in which they tried to convince the receiver of their views (e.g., asking for money for a project; recommending relocation of one's office). With the help of a hidden typist rather than a voice-recognition system, the dictated words appeared on a video display terminal. The writers were instructed to follow a rough-draft or a polished-draft strategy while composing; in both cases, they were allowed to make changes in a second draft session. They reported that a rough-draft strategy supported greater fluency during composition compared with a polished-draft strategy. Still, the documents were judged to communicate most effectively when a polished-draft strategy was used.

Hartley and Branthewaite (1989), in their survey of productive British psychologists, asked how frequently the writers produced a single draft with very few, minor changes. They found that this factor correlated significantly with productivity in completing books. If it can be assumed that such writers were polishing this single draft as they composed it, then this could be taken as evidence in favor of the polished-draft approach. Another factor also correlated with book productivity, however: the frequency of rewriting to turn a rough first draft into a more polished version. These results suggest that both strategies can be effective, but it should be mentioned that neither item correlated with productivity for book chapters and technical articles. Kellogg (1986a) also found no relation between first-draft strategies and productivity among science and engineering faculty.

Further adding to the confusion regarding drafting-revising strategies are the case studies of nine scientists reported by Rymer (1988). She interviewed all scientists and asked them to compose a scientific paper while thinking aloud. Interestingly, only five were willing to even try, and only one of the five mastered the technique well enough to provide usable data. On serious professional tasks, the requirement to express all thoughts aloud undoubtedly places a serious obstacle before those trying to engage the task fully, enter a state of creative flow, and amplify the quality and fluency of writing. The one scientist who successfully gave a complete protocol adopted a free writing strategy, followed by seemingly endless revisions. This strategy can alleviate attentional overload by ignoring at first extensive planning and reviewing, allowing the writer to vocalize his personal thoughts while drafting.

Rymer reported that the drafting habits of the nine scientists ranged from the "spew and revise" of free writing to the "perfect first draft" approach. The subject who adopted this polished-draft strategy devoted a significant amount of time and effort to prewriting. Thus, the attentional overload problems encountered by many during a first draft were avoided altogether. Consider the report of this individual, whose first drafts are virtually identical to the finished product:

> what I tend to do in writing up a paper is do a fair amount of thinking about it before I actually start writing ... and I prepare graphs before I start writing, so I will have an idea what I want to have in my paper ... then I find generally that writing goes very quickly, and I just sit down and write, and I don't look back in general, as to what I've written, until I've reached the end of the paper. (p. 219)

Future Directions

Owing to the differences among the studies just reviewed, definitive conclusions about drafting-revising strategies are premature. A systematic analysis of first-draft strategies in combination with other method, knowledge, and personality factors is needed. I suspect that the cognitive style and possibly other personality dimensions may strongly predispose a writer to prefer one drafting strategy over another. For example, I would not be surprised to find that an impulsive style might better match with free writing, whereas a reflective style might best suit the polished-draft strategy. Consistent with this view, Galbraith (1992) found that low self-monitors, who express virtually all they feel in an impulsive fashion, generated their ideas best when composing a rough draft. Their idea production was poor when asked to plan by taking notes during prewriting. Interestingly, high self-monitoring individuals, who worry about how they present themselves to others, showed the opposite pattern. For them taking notes in advance yielded more novel ideas compared to composing a rough draft directly.

Task Environment and Strategies

The knowledge-usage point of view suggests that prewriting and first-draft revision strategies are potentially worthwhile because they improve access to and application of needed knowledge. Thus far, this point has been made without regard to the constraints imposed on the writer by the task environment. But there are three ways in which the value of strategies may hinge on the specific task facing the writer.

Multiple Drafts

First, there is the issue of multiple drafts. Many tasks call for writers to compose a document in one or, at most, two drafts. Routine business letters and memoranda fit this category. Writing in schools, such as answers to essay questions, lab reports, and even papers prepared out of class, often fit as well. Most laboratory studies on writing also investigate writing in only one or two drafts. The predictions about the value of strategies in aiding access to relevant knowledge are clearly defensible for such tasks. The writer must retrieve the necessary knowledge in one or two sittings. Failure to do so cannot be compensated for at a later date.

But when a writer has the luxury of returning to a document on several if not many occasions, the criticality of following a particular strategy is less clear. If an idea was omitted, or an organizational scheme jumbled, or a sentence mangled in one draft, then it can always be corrected in a subsequent draft. A prewriting strategy combined with either free writing, a rough-draft strategy, or a polished-draft strategy would probably offer equal knowledge access over multiple drafts. So would beginning without any prewriting, as long as one adopted free writing or a rough-draft strategy on the first draft. The only strategy combination that might hamper a writer in a multiple-draft situation would be no prewriting and a polished first-draft approach. But even then, a writer who is willing to toss away major sections or even entire drafts of a document may be able to retrieve the knowledge needed given enough time to work on the task.

Generally, whenever a document is especially long or complex, multiple drafts are required. If the final document is to be done well, then adequate time must be given to permit several drafts. Documents that are especially important also fit this category. In such cases, the choice of strategy may matter less.

Time and Resource Constraints

A document may be long and complicated, but that alone does not guarantee that multiple drafts can overcome strategy deficiencies. First, writers are famous procrastinators. Perhaps a high-quality document could be produced in, say, 10 drafts, using almost any combination of strategies. But people rarely allocate the time needed to complete more than, say, five drafts (more about this in Chapter 7). Given that a deadline is approaching and one is limited in how many drafts are feasible, strategy choice may be important even in multiple-draft tasks.

For multiple drafts to be feasible, one of two resource conditions must be met. The writer must use a word processor on the second draft, if not the first. Redoing a draft on a typewriter or by hand is prohibitive. Certainly young writers (Daiute, 1985), and most likely writers of any age, enjoy word processors so much because they take the pain out of creating multiple drafts. Alternatively, the writer must have secretarial help. Without a word processor or a secretary, even tasks that should be done in multiple drafts will probably be done in as few drafts as possible.

Conditions of Knowledge Usage

The evidence reviewed in Chapters 4, 5, and 6 suggests that a writer's usage of knowledge depends on the knowledge being available, retrieved, and applied successfully to the content and rhetorical problems in the task environment. Prewriting strategies plainly show that retrieving and applying knowledge can be influenced by

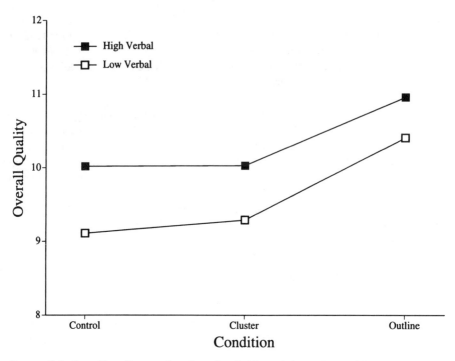

FIGURE 6.6. Overall quality as a function of verbal knowledge and prewriting strategies. (From Kellogg, 1993. Copyright © 1993 by *Composition Studies,* Texas Christian University. Reprinted by permission.)

concentration of attention on relatively few writing operations at any one time and by the power of organization. I end this chapter with a final study showing that the effects of knowledge availability are independent of the effects of outlining as an aid to knowledge access and application.

In this study, 151 college students were tested in several small group sessions. They wrote on the two topics used in Experiment 2 of Kellogg (1987a), with about half assigned to each in the three prewriting conditions tested. The students were randomly assigned to either a no-prewriting control condition, a cluster condition, or an outline condition. Using percentile scores on either the ACT English or SAT Verbal subtests, I split each strategy group into two halves: low and high verbal knowledge using the 71st percentile. The exact number of participants in each cell in the design varied slightly throughout this procedure ($n = 22$ to 27).

The results for overall quality are shown in Figure 6.6. As in other studies, average ratings from two judges were used, and content and style were rated separately. Style ratings showed a larger effect of verbal knowledge and of prewriting strategy than content ratings. Still, even a summation of the two drives home the importance of knowledge usage in writing performance. The overall difference between high- and low-verbal writers was reliable. Moreover, as in past studies, the outline condition achieved reliably higher ratings than both the control and cluster conditions. These variables did not interact reliably; the pattern of differences among strategies was statistically the same for both low- and high-verbal writers.

The lack of interaction shows that a full understanding of knowledge usage demands an accounting not only of how much a writer knows but also of how well he or she brings it to bear on the task at hand. Outlining helps writers to retrieve and apply what they know, regardless of their level of verbal knowledge. In the next two chapters, I examine how the tools used by a writer may affect knowledge usage.

7

Word Processors

The word processor is God's gift, or at least science's gift, to the tinkers and the refiners and the neatness freaks. For me it was obviously the perfect new toy.

WILLIAM ZINSSER

Interest in tools used by writers mushroomed with the advent of the word processor. The past decade or so has brought a revolution in the craft of writing. In a remarkably brief period of time, the technology of writing moved from the manual typewriter through line-based text editors on mainframe computers to word processors on powerful personal computers and still more powerful workstations.

What has been written about writing on a word processor expresses an unqualified ardor about the power of computer-based composition. This was particularly true in the early years of personal computer development as students, teachers, and professionals explored the new writing tool. To illustrate, consider Moran's (1983) evaluation of the word processor:

> You can imagine what the word processor has done for me. Now the words fly up the screen, not ink on paper but images that, with a single keystroke can be erased, filed, moved, changed. "Nothing permanent here," I feel. "What I'm putting up on the screen is just images; no need to worry." And so the editor retires to the sidelines, allowing the creator to produce language, both good and bad. The editor is recalled later, at the appropriate time, to cut, paste, add, delete . . . I produce more, and I produce that more with less effort. (p. 113)

This chapter considers whether there is a basis for such enthusiasm from the standpoint of psychological theory and whether the research to date backs up the anecdotal claims. The questions concern the various ways that word processors alter both writing processes and the final product. The answers to these questions will have no bearing on whether people will use computers as writing tools. Writers have already embraced word processors (Dorner, 1992). Such technology is already an integral part of our business and educational institutions. It is rapidly entering our home lives as well. Witness the proposals to develop a National Information Infrastructure "that would connect all Americans within the next 20 years" and "bring digitized text, video, and audio to every business, factory, school, and household in the country" (DeLoughry, 1993a, p. A17). Still, the answers may influence how computers as writing devices are designed for effective use. After considering the word processor in this chapter, we turn to various augmented writing devices—what I generically call *idea processors*—in the next chapter.

Cognitive Technologies

Cognitive technologies, such as written languages, have long been thought of as amplifiers of mental functioning (Brown, 1985; Bruner, 1966). Computers appear to be particularly powerful amplifiers of our natural abilities, allowing us to do tasks more effectively and efficiently. This clearly holds for numerical processing; only the exceptionally gifted mathematician or strange savant talented only in mental calculations is capable of numerical processing that comes even close to the speed and accuracy of a digital computer. But whether computers amplify performance in writing and other complex thinking tasks is less certain.

Performing mathematical operations with paper and pencil or, worse yet, in the head strains the information processing capacity of people. Attentional and working memory limitations put a person at a disadvantage relative to a computer in, say, dividing a seven-digit number by a five-digit number. The algorithm can obviously be carried out faster and more accurately by a machine. But it would be misleading to assume that a word processor can do the same for writing. The writing task demands the making of meaning, not simply the processing of linguistic information. The insert, move block, word wrap, margin set, and other operations performed by a word processor automate the secretarial or clerical demands of putting words on a page. Even a powerful desktop publishing system partly automates the layout and graphic design of a text. But the design process itself still calls for creative thought on the part of the human user. The difficult demands of creating ideas, organizing them, and generating sentences that effectively convey one's thoughts remain for the writer using even the most sophisticated word processor on the most powerful workstation available today. Therefore, a word processor might be better viewed as a smooth, highly automated typewriter and typesetter rather than as a tool that aids the writer in the difficult challenge of creating meaning.

Computers may still have profound effects on writing even if it turns out that they do not amplify writing performance. Pea (1985) proposed that computers do not simply amplify our mental functioning. Rather, they change the tasks we do by reorganizing cognitive processes. Pea argued that the qualitative changes in mental functioning that take place when computers restructure tasks are the key to understanding the effects of cognitive tools. Restructuring results in different allocations of attentional resources in the task environment shaped by the computer.

Norman (1989) developed this restructuring notion by emphasizing that the total system of human, task, and artifact or tool must be considered. He suggested that cognitive tools may enhance performance, but only indirectly. They do not directly enhance human ability; rather, they change the nature of the task in a way that leads to superior performance. By contrast, some tools, such as a megaphone, act as true amplifiers of human ability. The content and form of the human voice are unaffected by the megaphone, yet the vocal intensity is augmented.

Norman also contended that, by definition, cognitive artifacts are representational devices that intervene between the human and the world. Through the symbol system of a computer program, the human interacts with the real world via a virtual world. The task is necessarily altered in consequence. Norman speaks of a gulf between the human's goals and intentions and the object and task. Appropriate design of the artifact, on the one hand, and increasing skill through mental effort and training, on the other, are ways of bridging the gulf when using a cognitive tool. But a tool is rarely so well designed, and the user is rarely so expert, that the task is not somehow restructured by using the tool. One would anticipate, therefore, that the use of computers for writing and thinking would restructure the allocation of attentional resources to fit the modified task.

Norman illustrates his point with an example offered by Bodker (1989) of a writer trying to enter a footnote using Microsoft's word processing software for the Macintosh computer (WORD). Before the writer can enter the footnote, Word requests a confirmation and decision about the form of the footnote. Although the software needs this information, it asks for it when the writer would normally be thinking about the content of the footnote, not its format. Thus, the tool controls when the writer attends to this aspect of composing. Similarly, Hawisher (1989) noted the need for children to shift from an insert mode to an edit mode to make corrections with the early BANK STREET WRITER, a requirement that discouraged recursive translating and reviewing.

The present theoretical framework emphasizes that restructuring and amplification are independent issues. Aspects of a writer's method or personal dimensions of the writer can restructure the allocation of attention to fit new task demands without necessarily causing any changes in performance. The link between restructuring and amplification hinges on whether the writer's knowledge is made more accessible than usual. A case has been made in Chapter 6 that prewriting strategies change the way a writer works and that these strategies influence performance. Although the tool used alters how a writer composes, it must be asked whether the alteration has any implications for performance.

Three hypotheses have been advanced to predict performance gains for writers using word processors. One is that fluency should increase with a word processor because sentence generation can proceed rapidly, without worrying that the text is permanent and unalterable (Daiute, 1985; Lutz, 1987). The word processor may help writers by making the text malleable. This view assumes that writing with a pen or typewriter is constrained by the messiness of making changes compared to a word processor. If one adopts Elbow's (1981) position that a free-writing strategy produces powerful writing, then one could anticipate benefits in quality as well as fluency.

A second hypothesis is that word processors are best suited for integrating planning and translating (Catano, 1985; Ransdell, 1989). The notion is that writers often lose incipient ideas while they are thinking because of the demands of transcribing them physically using a pen. The word processor may help writers make ideas visible and therefore retainable. Presumably, verbal and ideational fluency and the development of high content quality should be amplified using a word processor because this tool best matches the fluidity of thought.

The third hypothesis, advanced by many, is that word processors increase the time and effort given to revision and thereby improve the quality of the finished text (e.g., Bernhardt, Edwards, & Wojahn, 1989; Dauite, 1985). The word processor presumably encourages writers to edit as they compose a draft. Furthermore, the ease of altering a text enables writers to continue revising texts over numerous drafts, presumably more than would be possible without the technology.

A Knowledge-Usage Viewpoint

A word processor undoubtedly restructures the allocation of processing time and cognitive effort even if it does not amplify performance. As Pea (1985) and Norman (1989) have argued, the structure of essentially any task is altered by the tool used to do it, and there is no reason to posit writing as an exception to the rule.

As for whether the word processor amplifies writing performance, it is fruitful to consider its impact on how well writers use their knowledge. The first observation concerns the simple notion of time on task. One must engage in the task if knowledge is to be used. Procrastination and other pursuits preclude the use of available knowledge. The nature of the tool used could affect time on task if the writer enjoys composing with a particular tool. One would expect productivity to be amplified by a tool that encourages the author to write long and often.

Whether there are intrinsic properties of handwriting, typing, dictation, or word processing that generate positive emotions and moods in most writers is unknown, but I doubt it. Tool preference probably is idiosyncratic. For example, for a writer who likes fountain pens and hates typing, the feel of a favorite fountain pen in hand would outweigh the technological advantages of a word processor. The intense interest in designing portable computers that allow one to enter information with a pen or by voice suggests that typing on keyboards is disliked by more than a few. On the other hand, a psychologist who has authored several textbooks confided in me that she typed every word on an electric typewriter. James Michener typed his work on a *manual* Olympia typewriter. With that 25-year-old machine, "using only two fingers, he has pecked out millions of words" (Nicklin, 1993, p. A27).

Many, if not most, writers today prefer a word processor, even if the keyboard could use some improvement. A colleague at another university recently complained that he finds it very difficult to write without his word processor now that he has used it for several years. I interpret his attachment as a ritual that spurs him to spend time on the task, think, and create. As we will see in Chapter 9, tools can become part of a writing ritual, along with aspects of the environment (e.g., writing only in a study at home late at night) or behavioral patterns (e.g., writing only after jogging 5 miles). The key point here is that one can be attached to virtually any tool, regardless of whether that tool directly improves writing performance.

Second, the availability of knowledge is important to usability, given that the writer spends time on the task. This factor is irrelevant, however, to a comparison of handwriting, typing, dictation, and word processing. The availability of knowledge does not fluctuate with the tool used to translate personal symbols into consensual symbols. The next chapter considers computer-based knowledge systems that are intended to do just that. For example, a system that analyzes text for readability and detects spelling and grammatical errors could help a writer with deficient language skills.

Third is the issue of accessibility and application of knowledge. From the standpoint of the theory advanced here, a word processor would need to make a writer's knowledge more accessible for it to have a major impact on the fluency and quality of writing. Again, putting aside, for the moment, idea or knowledge processors that are explicitly designed to enhance retrieval of relevant knowledge, I do not see why tool choice should matter. Knowledge represented in long-term memory and in external sources must be retrieved and applied by the writer through mental operations. Collecting, planning, translating, and reviewing are the crux of discourse formulation. Writing performance would be expected to suffer only if a particular tool consumed substantial attention that would otherwise be given to these component writing processes (Brown et al., 1988).

The notion that writers often lose ideas when using a pen, but not when using a word processor, is a plausible but unconvincing argument. It assumes that writers often lose ideas when using a pen because writers can plan and translate text at a rate that exceeds the motor abilities of handwriting but not of typing. This may be true for some writers at inspired moments or for those using a free-writing strategy, but as a general rule, it seems highly suspect. Planning and translating are generally highly effortful, controlled operations that proceed too slowly in general, not too rapidly, for the pen to match the pace.

Joram, Woodruff, Bryson, and Lindsay (1992) proposed that word processors may distract writers from remembering, thinking, and creating, resulting in poorer-quality texts relative to those produced by handwriting. They stated that word processors encourage revision, but only at a surface level (e.g., spelling corrections). Paying extra attention to surface corrections may reduce the time and effort given to deeper forms of reviewing, as well as collecting, planning, and translating. The proposal of Joram et al. takes the hypothesis that word processors best support revision and turns it on its head.

From the knowledge-usage viewpoint, it may be necessary to distinguish a subset of writers who lack ready access to knowledge of the language and who need to revise extensively. Another subset may better use their knowledge because the text they create is more visible to them in print than in handwriting, with fewer ideas lost in translating. The word processor may be ideal for these two subsets. Another subset of writers with high levels of verbal ability, in contrast, may be more likely to devote too much attention to reviewing at the expense of other critical processes, as suggested by Joram et al. (1992). However, I prefer at the outset the straightforward assumption that tool choice fails to affect knowledge use, writing quality, and fluency. At most, it may have an indirect effect on productivity; writers may like to compose on word processors for various reasons, including ease of revision, and may therefore compose longer and more frequently with them.

Seminal Research

Gould pioneered research on the effects of tools on writing in a series of studies (e.g., Gould, 1978, 1980, 1981). He studied executives, managers, and other office personnel in various letter-writing tasks. He measured the quality and fluency of writing with different tools and videotaped the writer to assess the process by means of pause analysis. *Reading time* refers to segments when the writer read previously created text. *Generating time* reflects actual speaking, dictating, typing on a text editor, or handwriting. *Planning time* is the time remaining when the writer was not writing or reading.

Consistent with the knowledge-usage framework, Gould found no differences among the tools in the quality of texts produced. But Gould (1980) also concluded that writers were more fluent using dictation and speaking compared to handwriting. Handwriting, in turn, supported greater fluency than writing on a text editor (Gould, 1981). These rankings are based on WPM during composition by the author, while ignoring that a secretary is needed to transcribe dictated and spoken text and that handwritten text may need to be retyped before it is read.

Gould compared the amount of time spent pausing but not reading, which he equated with planning, across the different tools. He concluded that planning requires about two-thirds of total composing time, regardless of the tool used. Thus, although writers could dictate letters in less time than they could handwrite or text-edit them, the proportion of time devoted to planning remained constant. Selecting a different tool, then, did not restructure how the writer allocated processing time to planning.

Amplification of Performance

Gould's early work involved a line-based text editor. It predated the full-screen editors used today in personal computers and advanced workstations. The question arises, then, as to whether his conclusions withstand the results of recent research on word processors. First, studies examining amplification will be presented, followed by evidence on restructuring.

Laboratory Studies

Card, Robert, and Keenan (1984) duplicated Gould's letter-writing procedures with a full-screen, display-oriented editor. They tested eight research professionals who had considerable experience with the Bravo word processor used in the study. They found that the writers were equally fluent on the word processor (12.2 words per minute) and in longhand (12.0 words per minute). This result argues against the position that writers lose fewer ideas when translating with a word processor. It is difficult to argue this position if writing fluency does not vary with the tool.

An expert judged the letters in terms of style, mechanics, and content, as well as rank ordering them in terms of holistic quality. The differences always favored the handwritten letters, but they were not statistically reliable. The word processor led to markedly more modifications than did handwriting (23.3 versus 5.0). Interestingly, 73% of the extra modifications appeared to have been done to improve the text. Yet only about half of them actually improved text quality, according to the expert, and some of them lowered it.

Haas (1989), too, voiced concern that Gould's rather dismal conclusions about computer-based writing might be related to his use of line editors. Haas was also interested in differences between personal computers and advanced workstations. The large screens of workstations, as well as their power and speed, could make them more useful as word processors than personal computers are.

Haas found that experienced professionals wrote documents that were judged as poorer in content quality on personal computers relative to longhand. Judgments of mechanics, a key component of style quality, showed no differences. Interestingly, the advanced workstation fared better than the personal computer in terms of content quality. But it was no better than writing longhand. Moreover, the three tools supported equally fluent writing in her study, confirming the results of Card et al. 1984).

Ransdell and Levy (in press) investigated college students' writing of narrative and persuasive letters using longhand and personal computers. Regardless of the type of text, the handwritten compositions received reliably higher judgments of holistic quality than did those written on a word processor. The students made the most revisions when using the word processor, but the majority of these were corrections of errors in spelling and typing. In fact, when these minor changes were not considered, Ransdell and Levy found that the handwritten letters contained the most revisions affecting the meaning of the text.

Haas (1989) attributed the weak performance observed with personal computers to the small size of their screens. Earlier evidence indicated that it is harder for writers to grasp the overall structure of a text when scrolling it on a small screen; paper provides a better *sense of the text* (Haas & Hayes, 1986). Difficulties in getting a clear sense of the text could plainly hinder effective writing.

As an aside, Hansen and Haas (1988) discussed the page size, legibility, system speed or responsiveness, and tangibility requirements of a well-designed word processor. By tangibility they mean the degree to which the state of the system is visible to the user and readily modifiable. For example, tangibility would be enhanced if a writers could immediately apprehend the location of the current screen in a document. To achieve this, Hansen and Haas suggested displaying a rectangle that represents the full length of the document and an elevator image that represents the position and amount of text currently on the screen.

Hansen and Haas regarded paper as highly tangible because the text "is laid out in particular places on each sheet of paper, the sheets are stacked together, and the user can move sheets from the unread stack to the finished stack" (p. 1083). To duplicate the manner in which paper provides the writer with a clear physical overview of the text, Eklundh (1992) devised a system with multiple windows wherein each window corresponded to a page. As each page filled, a new blank page appeared on the screen. Writers could then stack the pages or spread them out much as they would with paper. Eklundh aimed to keep the position of a sentence on a page fixed until the writer actively modified it. Initial findings indicated that the visibility of a page on the screen aided the writers in grasping a global perspective of the text. Further, the writers seemed to prefer having the pages immediately adjacent to the current page plainly visible and more distant pages neatly stacked.

Returning to the germane laboratory studies, two experiments conducted with college students also yielded no evidence that word processing amplifies performance (Kellogg & Mueller, 1993). Both fluency, measured in WPM, and quality judgments of content and style were examined. The means for several variables are shown in Table 7.1. In the first experiment, the style judgments were slightly less positive for documents composed on the word processor relative to longhand. This finding was apparently related primarily to the greater number of spelling errors found in the word processor condition. A detailed analysis of the cohesiveness ties included in the documents (Halliday & Hasan, 1976; McCutchen, 1986) showed no differences between tool conditions. The number of local and remote ties was statistically the same in both conditions. Fluency was unaffected by tool use as well, a result consistently found in all but Gould's seminal study with line editors.

A second experiment replicated and extended the first by comparing longhand with word processing by either highly experienced (high condition) or moderately experienced users (low condition). The level of experience markedly affected fluency and quality, with the moderately experienced users doing much more poorly. However, the highly experienced users merely brought their performance up to the level obtained by those writing in longhand.

The laboratory experiments discussed thus far yield results consistent with the knowledge-usage predictions. Word processors and pens are equally effective "output devices." Neither demands so much attention for output that discourse formulation suffers as a result (Brown et al., 1988). Less experienced users of word processors do perform more poorly than highly experienced users. Without a great

TABLE 7.1. Measures of Writing Quality Under Longhand and Computer Conditions

Condition	Measure of Document Quality							
	Style Quality	Content Quality	Words per Sentence	Spelling Errors	Grammatical Errors	Local Ties	Remote Ties	Unsuccessful Ties
Experiment 1								
Longhand	4.6	4.6	20.4	3.6	9.1	25.3	1.1	0.5
Computer	3.6	3.9	21.4	6.4	10.1	21.5	0.8	0.8
Experiment 2								
Longhand	4.2	4.3	18.6	3.6	6.9	27.2	1.7	1.0
Low experience	3.3	3.3	18.3	4.7	5.6	22.0	1.4	0.4
High experience	4.5	4.3	21.0	3.3	6.0	30.1	1.4	0.2

Note: n = 16 in Experiment 1; *n* = 23 In Experiment 2.

Source: From Kellogg and Mueller, 1993. Copyright © 1993 by Academic Press Ltd. Reprinted by permission.

deal of practice on a word processor, the writer undoubtedly is distracted from the critical processes of collecting, planning, translating, and reviewing. Further, it appears that the design of the word processor can distract the writer from critical processes in discourse formulation. But the superior design of the workstation yields performance no better than that obtained with a pen.

A final experiment by Joram et al. (1992) adds an interesting wrinkle to these conclusions. They manipulated the writer's knowledge and skills (advanced versus average eighth-grade writers), the tool (pencil versus word processor), and drafting strategy (compose as usual versus delayed revision). As noted earlier, they anticipated that the word processor may distract writers from critical aspects of discourse formulation because it focuses attention on editing surface features during composition of a first draft. They hypothesized that instructions to delay all revisions to a second session may avoid this problem and allow the writers to use the power of the word processor to revise documents extensively, resulting in superior documents relative to handwriting.

Joram et al. found no reliable differences in the rated holistic quality of papers produced with word processors and handwriting. However, the judged creativity of the texts provided an interesting interaction. The researchers regarded the creativity judgments as a better measure of their hypothesis that the word processor might interfere with planning and translating. For advanced writers, this appeared to be the case. When these writers were instructed to compose as usual, their papers achieved higher creativity scores when written with a pencil relative to a word processor. When instructed to delay revision, this difference vanished and in fact reversed very slightly. The average writers appeared to compose the same way, regardless of instructions, and showed little if any difference in creativity across tool conditions.

The quality ratings reported by Joram et al. fit with the simple prediction of the knowledge-usage hypothesis. The creativity results for the advanced writers suggest that one can detect a negative impact of using a word processor, provided that one uses a measure sensitive to disruptions in generating and organizing ideas. Before modifying the knowledge-usage hypothesis that the tool makes no difference, I would like to see these results replicated with larger samples. Joram et al. studied seven advanced writers using word processors, assigning only three of them to the delayed-revision condition. It may be that these three were the most creative, regardless of the tool and strategy they employed.

Field Research

Numerous studies have been done in school settings to evaluate the impact of word processors in composition classes. One early suggestion was that word processors are ideally suited for children who devote considerable attention to the motor demands of handwriting (Daiute, 1985). The word processor, it was suggested, might lower the motor demands of writing because handwriting had not yet been automatized for younger writers. Shifting attention from the mechanical aspects of writing may then allow greater concentration on the thinking aspects of the task (Bangert-Drowns, 1993). This presumes that typing consumes less attention than handwriting in young writers. Following this line of reasoning, a voice-input system, a so-called listening typewriter, might prove even more beneficial to children than a key-based word processor.

As Hawisher (1986) noted in her review, however, the methodology of the relevant field studies varied from case studies and surveys to informal exploratory designs. Few investigators used identical posttest conditions for the experimental and control groups.

Theismeyer (1989) further criticized the researchers in this area for generalizing from case studies and small samples; relying on students' attitudes, feelings, and beliefs about word processors rather than measures of performance; and failing to control for the inevitable Hawthorne effect of introducing an innovation into the classroom. When no clear support of amplification can be observed in well-controlled laboratory studies, concerns about the soundness of the methodology used in the field studies are intensified.

Theismeyer feared that the seemingly positive results are temporary and illusory, based on his reading of the literature and his experience in teaching composition on computers. He put it this way:

> after an initially favorable response to the fun of playing with the technology, and the inevitable "Hawthorne effect" by which any innovation in a work situation initially raises productivity and morale, students are no more likely to start their papers before the eleventh hour, and most take minimal advantage of the machinery to promote revision of their work. Left to themselves, the hundreds of students I have observed do little more with a word processor than they would have done with a typewriter. In fact, many do less. Before computers, student writers might compose a rough draft by hand, mark it up for revision, then polish it while typing the final draft for submission. The word processor's ability to produce clean-looking copy allows today's student to submit what is in effect a rough draft, modified only by a few on-screen changes. (pp. 85–86)

Moreover, in a series of reviews, Hawisher (1986, 1987b, 1989) comprehensively analyzed comparative studies, case studies, and ethnographic studies carried out while teaching composition in school. Although some studies found improvements in quality with word processing, the majority found no advantage. For example, Hawisher (1987a) investigated college students who were learning revision strategies, and alternated the use of a pen or typewriter and a word processor. Trained readers evaluated the quality of both the first and final drafts of their documents. Comparisons between compositions done on a word processor with the typed or handwritted documents showed no differences in quality. Hawisher's reviews and one by Cochran-Smith (1991) agree that word processing results in longer texts with fewer mechanical errors. But the quality judgment data fail to show that the word processor is superior to longhand.

One review of the instructional field studies suggested that word processors amplify writing performance (Bangert-Drowns, 1993). The review included 32 studies comparing two groups of students receiving comparable writing instruction, "differing only in that one group was allowed to use the word processor for some phases of the writing process" (p. 74). Nearly two out of three studies reported an advantage for the word processor group on a measure of holistic quality, yet in only fewer than one out of three cases was the difference statistically reliable. The average effect size was a difference of .27 standard deviations favoring the word processor group over the longhand group. Though this is a small effect, it proved significantly greater than zero. The improvement in quality had no relation to the students' grades. Moreover, it bore no relation to the duration of the instructional program, which is perplexing if the word processor per se directly amplifies writing skill.

The effect size was reliably greater for studies including remedial instruction for basic writers (.49) relative to average writers (.09). Further, the basic writers benefited more uniformly from their experience with word processors; the average writers showed substantial variation in the effects of such instruction. These outcomes, taken together with the lack of any effect of the duration of the instructional program, led Bangert-Drowns (1993) to suggest an indirect motivational explanation for the value of word processors. The technology may spur basic writers to "engage in writing tasks more wholeheartedly" (p. 88).

Perhaps well-designed word processors in the hands of highly experienced users would amplify the quality of writing, but only to a small degree. It may be that previous studies lacked sufficient statistical power to detect very small effect sizes. The field experiment reported by Owston, Murphy, and Wideman (1992) is intriguing. They studied eighth-grade students using a Macintosh computer. The students had over 1.5 years of experience in writing with the computers, and a pretest showed the level of proficiency expected for children of that age (only a few typed with all 10 fingers). The researchers employed a large sample size ($n = 68$) and a repeated measures design in which each student composed expository essays both on the computer and with pen and paper. This design maximized the chances to detect significant differences by having the participants serve as their own controls.

The differences in mean quality ratings for the on-computer and off-computer groups, respectively, were reliable for 6-point scales of competence (3.88 versus 3.57), focus (3.68 versus 3.38), support (3.57 versus 3.27), and mechanics (3.99 versus 3.65). Ownston et al. attributed the higher scores for computer-written papers to the extensive experience the students had with computer-based writing and with the graphical interface of the Macintosh. While I do not deny that these factors are critical, the careful design of their experiment, which ensured a high degree of statistical power, may have been equally important.

Another field study included 146 college students in a computer-based English composition class and another 194 in a regular composition class (Bernhardt et al., 1989). Each student wrote an impromptu essay or a first draft, which was then followed by a revised essay. Those in the computer classes had the option of using the computer or longhand to revise their essays. Despite the large sample size, Bernhardt et al. detected no reliable differences between the computer and regular groups on either the impromptu or the revised essays. Interestingly, though, the computer group composed worse impromptu essays and better revised essays. Regardless of the group, the students improved the quality of their essays in the revised version. However, for those in the computer group who elected to use the computer for revision ($n = 112$), the gain was reliably greater than for those who revised on paper.

Bernhardt et al. concluded that the computer benefited revising skills but noted that the ease of revision may have encouraged the computer-based writers to draft poor-quality first drafts.

Summary

The knowledge-usage framework outlined earlier is in the awkward position of predicting the null hypothesis of no differences among tools. The small but reliable quality improvements reported by Ownston et al. (1992) certainly make one hesitate to accept the null hypothesis. Still, the generally negative picture from field and laboratory studies together best supports the contention that tool choice makes no difference in determining how well a writer composes. Further research is warranted, but to date the results are discouraging for hypotheses that predict strong and reliable effects favoring word processors.

Specifically, the idea that sentence generation can proceed rapidly because the writer does not worry about the permanence of the text is weakened by the finding that fluency does not vary between word processor and longhand. Further, the hypothesis that word processors best integrate planning and translating has not fared well. It predicts that writers are generally more fluent on a word processor than in longhand. Though some individuals might well be, the experimental literature rejects this prediction for most writers. Given that no differences in fluency occur, it seems unlikely that writers forget ideas more often when writing in longhand. I will return to this notion in the next chapter in discussing the listening typewriter. This voice recognition system gives the writer both the immediate visual feedback of the word processor and the low motor demands of a dictation system. Possibly this is a tool that matches the fluidity of thought. It may also be worthwhile to try instructional programs that teach students to view text on a word processor as ''fluid and as closely allied to thought and speech'' (Bangert-Drowns, 1993, p. 89).

Finally, the word processor may encourage frequent and extensive revision. In the next Section, we will consider how the word processor alters the process of composing. But the hypothesis that such revision necessarily supports higher-quality writing does not enjoy strong support. In fact, the alternative hypothesis—that constant revision detracts from creative writing—appears to be equally worth examining in future work, given the intriguing results of Joram et al. (1992).

Restructuring

Pea (1985) and Norman (1989) have argued that computers invariably restructure tasks. Theoretically, it should be no surprise that writers deploy attention differently when writing with a word processor than when using a pen, even if performance in the two cases is identical. Yet, Gould's results (1980, 1981) suggested that writers attend to planning about two-thirds of the time, regardless of which writing tool they use. Does this conclusion still stand after more than a decade of further research?

A Matter of Measurement

First, it is important to note that Gould defined planning as pauses in generating sentences that were not spent reading text. In terms of the four operations defined in Chapter 2, these pauses could have included translating as the writer pondered how to phrase a particular idea. The pauses could also have included editing operations; after reading already generated text, the writer might have paused to revise a sentence or paragraph. The time spent actually generating ideas, organizing ideas, and setting goals regarding the text could easily have been less than Gould's estimate and may have varied across tools. There is no reason to doubt that pauses in generating sentences and reading occupy two-thirds of writing time, but that does not rule out the possibility that tools restructure writing tasks.

A study by Lansman et al. (1990) confirmed the suspicion that planning time per se is less than pausal analysis suggests. They studied writers using an enhanced word processing system that included planning modes of creating networks and trees. They tracked the time spent in these and other modes. Like Gould, they studied experienced writers. Lansman et al. found that only 28% of writing time on average was spent in the planning modes of the system.

The trained retrospection method I have used yields estimates very close to those reported by Lansman et al. To review, with my method, writers are interrupted periodically by a tone as they compose. After saying ''stop'' to trip a voice-activated relay for measuring RT, they press a button indicating whether they were planning, translating, or reviewing at the moment they heard the tone. Earlier, they were trained to identify their thoughts in these categories (or in an unrelated category for those that did not fit). Estimates of processing time are derived by calculating the percentage of time that the writers report each process.

Although the writers' strategies affect the overall values, the range suggests that far less than two-thirds of the time is spent planning. Typically, in my studies, 25–35% of processing time is allocated to planning, an estimate consistent with the results of Lansman et al. Translating demands the most processing time, taking 40–60%. The least time is devoted to reviewing, typically 20–25%.

The Possibility of Qualitative Changes

Another question raised by Gould's conclusions is whether tools restructure writing processes qualitatively even if quantitative measures show no variations. For example, is planning done the same way when composing on a word processor versus with a pen? Measures of processing time and cognitive effort may show no tool effect, but retrospective reports or verbal protocols may reveal important qualitative differences in how attention was used in the two cases. Qualitative as well as quantitative restructuring should be examined.

The two experiments from my laboratory referred to in the section on amplification were designed to address the question of qualitative as well as quantitative restructuring (Kellogg & Mueller, 1993). Directed retrospection and secondary RT indexed processing time and cognitive effort, respectively. Qualitative changes were measured by asking college students, after finishing their essays, to complete questionnaires on the nature of their planning, translating, and reviewing operations, as well as other points of interest. The students wrote on IBM PCs using Writing Assistant, a simplified word processing program with which they had experience.

An increase in RT over baseline reflects the cognitive effort demanded by writing. The interference scores for planning, translating, and reviewing are shown in Figure 7.1 for the students who wrote in longhand and those who used a word processor. As I found in previous studies, translating was reliably less effortful than planning and reviewing. But of special interest here was the significant interaction between writing tool and writing process. There was essentially no difference between tools in the effort devoted to translating. In contrast, the word processor involved more cognitive effort than writing in longhand for both planning and reviewing.

The results in Figure 7.1 plainly show that the use of a word processor quantitatively restructures the writing process. When our writers planned and reviewed on a word processor, they concentrated on the task more intensely than they did with longhand composition. The greater effort or engagement seen in this condition is especially interesting in light of the failure to observe any difference in writing quality or fluency. The process clearly had changed, but performance had not.

The other measure of attention, processing time, was estimated by computing

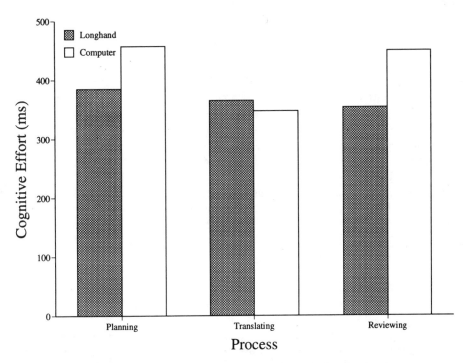

FIGURE 7.1. Cognitive effort devoted to writing processes under longhand and computer conditions. (From Kellogg & Mueller, 1993. Copyright © 1993 by Academic Press Limited. Reprinted by permission.)

the percentage of times that the writer reported using each process during the first, second, and third 10 minutes of writing. The results showed that the students allocated most of their processing time to translating and about equal amounts to planning and reviewing. Moreover, planning time and, to a lesser degree, translating time reliably decreased across phases, whereas reviewing time increased.

Writers attended for about the same amount of time to each process, whether composing with a pen or a word processor. There was one exception, however. During the initial phase of drafting, those writing on the computer reported more reviewing time than those using longhand.

Thus, the results showed substantial quantitative restructuring of cognitive effort and, to a mild degree, of processing time. Qualitative restructuring was revealed from the postwriting questionnaires. Students in the computer condition reported a reliably higher mean rating than those in the longhand condition on the question concerning how much their reviewing involved changes in mechanics, such as spelling, grammar, and punctuation. Thus, writing on a word processor restructured the time spent reviewing during the early phase of drafting and the qualitative nature of reviewing.

Other local changes at a deeper level of analysis (e.g., voice change and word substitution) were equally frequent in both writing tool conditions. In addition, the frequency of reviewing at a global structural level (e.g., rearranging paragraphs and reorganizing mental plans) and altering global changes in content (e.g., modifying old ideas and generating new ones) were statistically equal across writing tool conditions.

Participants were also asked to indicate which, if any, of their usual writing habits were omitted during the experiment. Two outcomes suggest that writing on a word processor alters the planning process. Omission of doodling and drawing was checked by 38% of the writers in the computer condition and by only 6% of those in the longhand condition, a reliable difference. Omission of note taking was checked by 88% of those in the computer condition and by only 31% of those in the longhand condition, again a reliable difference.

A second experiment separated students who were highly experienced with word processors, based on self-report, from those who were only moderately experienced. Different writing assignments were used to increase the generality of the results of the first study. From the present theoretical framework, I expected that the restructuring effects would be at least equally pronounced, if not more so, for the highly experienced users. This followed from the assumption that the nature of word processing per se causes these qualitative and quantitative changes.

An alternative hypothesis is that the highly experienced writers would not restructure the writing process at all because they would have mastered the word processor as a writing tool. With practice they may have learned to allocate attention just as they would with pen and paper.

The cognitive effort data replicated the first experiment, with the computer writers devoting significantly more effort to planning and reviewing compared with the longhand writers. If anything, the highly experienced writers showed the largest restructuring effects, though they did not reliably differ from the less experienced writers. Effort given to translating was uniform across conditions.

Processing time data revealed the same patterns observed earlier. There were reliable differences between the highly experienced and longhand writers in reviewing time during the initial and middle phases of drafting. Highly experienced users in particular, then, spend more time reviewing during the early phases of composing. The questionnaire results showed that the computer writers polished their writing at the level of local mechanics as they composed. They showed a greater local focus on spelling, grammar, and punctuation compared to those using pen and paper. This was especially true for the highly experienced users.

Comparisons with Earlier Work

The above results are consistent with Gould's (1980) conclusion that planning time is invariant across tools. However, the cognitive effort devoted to planning, as well as its qualitative nature, clearly varies with the writing tool used. These points corroborate the conclusions reached by Bridwell-Bowles et al. (1987) from case studies of skilled writers doing actual writing. They, too, reported that the word processor alters the nature of planning, particularly for those who employed the Beethovian discovery method of composing. These individuals use free-writing or rough-draft strategies, composing in an effort to discover what they think about their assignments. These drafts are then laid out, marked up, cut up, and annotated with arrows, doodles, and comments. Composing on the word processor interfered with this highly visual form of planning based on earlier drafts, notes, and graphical markers (see the results of Haas, 1990, below).

The Mozartian execution method of composing, in contrast, called for extensive planning during the prewriting phase. These writers planned both mentally and externally, using pen and paper, the structure of the text in varying degrees of detail before sitting down to the word processor to compose a relatively polished first draft. Bridwell-Bowles et al. noted that the Mozartians found the word processor more compatible with their planning method in that they could still produce handwritten outlines prior to drafting.

Another study of planning methods and tools expands on the points raised by Bridwell-Bowles et al. Haas (1990) found that 9 of the 10 professional or technical writers in her study made many sorts of notes during the prewriting phase when using pen and paper. These included content notes (e.g., ideas), structure notes (e.g., a rough outline), emphasis notes (e.g., circled key ideas or sections), and procedural notes (e.g., instructions such as "set the stage" or "include examples"). Of the nine note makers, Haas observed that only six of them took any notes when working with a word processor. Moreover, the notes in the pen condition were twice as long as those in the computer condition. Emphasis notes in particular (as in the Kellogg and Mueller experiments) and structure notes to a lesser degree dropped in frequency when writers used word processors. Haas concluded that the word processor alters the way a writer plans, with only content notes emerging with this technology. The writer must combine the pen with the word processor to tap the full range of note making or perhaps use computer tools specifically designed to aid such planning.

The quantitative and qualitative changes in reviewing are also consistent with earlier reports. Several investigators have reported that the ease of making corrections with a word processor encourages writers to polish each sentence as they compose it (Bridwell-Bowles et al, 1987; Card et al., 1984; Daiute, 1985; Ownston et al., 1992). For example, Card et al. found that experienced professionals using a word processor made four and a half times as many modifications as those using longhand. These extra changes increased the time and effort spent reviewing. Interestingly, they found that only 45% of the alterations improved the text, while 10% actually worsened it; the remaining 45% made no difference at all.

Bridwell-Bowles et al. (1987) concluded that the word processor encourages continuous editing of surface features and formatting of the text, but not revision at a deeper or more global level. In fact, without printing pages, writers found it difficult to engage in global editing due to the necessity of scrolling through small sections of a document on a small screen. The writer's ability to get a sense of the text suffers with the small page size of personal computers (Haas & Hayes, 1986). In an attempt to gain what Eklundh (1992) calls a *global perspective of the text,* users of word processors engage in extensive scrolling back and forth through pages and print out numerous drafts. Despite these difficulties, Bernhardt et al. (1989) documented the power of revising on a personal computer for writers who composed a rough initial draft. Presumably the initial draft needed both local and global changes.

Time on Task and Productivity

I have suggested that word processors may enhance productivity even if they have no effect on the availability, accessibility, and application of knowledge. It can be argued that the time spent on a task is the most important factor in productivity. Conceivably, writers might spend more time writing if they use a tool that they enjoy using or one that motivates them in some fashion. There are several reasons to believe that word processors fit this description.

Ease of Typing and Revising

A word processor is a highly automated typewriter. Compared to typing on a manual typewriter, the physical ease of typing on a word processor is attractive, particularly on those that minimize keystrokes and mental load (Card, Moran, & Newell, 1983). Indeed, the task is so easy, with no need to even change paper, that typing on a word processor may pose a health hazard. For example, data entry operators working at video display terminals can generate over 10,000 keystrokes per hour, though such high rates hour after hour may contribute to vision problems, headaches, and potentially repetitive motion disorders.

The typing function of creating words on paper is automated at a level beyond that of electronic typewriters, with memory to store a sentence or two, and markedly beyond that of electric typewriters, manual typewriters, and pen and pencil. It is clearly easier to revise a draft with a word processor than with any other device, assuming that secretarial help is not available or used. I, along with my secretary, greatly prefer updating drafts using a word processor.

My point is not that writers can be more fluent on word processors. Fluency is limited by cognitive factors that go beyond those determining speed of typing and making corrections. Rather, I suspect that writers may enjoy the task of writing more with a superior machine for typing. They may spend more time writing with a machine that makes typing and correcting mistakes more fun and less fatiguing. If that is so, then productivity could well be greater with a word processor.

A related point is that text entered into a word processor can then be evaluated by software designed to check spelling, grammar, usage, readability, and so on. These reviewing aids are examples of systems that attempt to improve a writer's usage of relevant knowledge and are considered in the next chapter. For now it should be noted only that the word processor obviously has advantages over less sophisticated typing devices.

Motivation, Affect, and Technology

Studies of computer hackers (Turkle, 1984) and video game fanatics (Loftus, 1983) point to the alluring, if not addicting, properties of computers. Put aside, for the time being, the novice user who experiences apprehension over learning how to use a computer. Also ignore, for the moment, the typical user, expert as well as novice, who experiences rage and frustration when a power surge or a virus erases the text on a hard disk drive or a network. What is left is the proposition that most people, most of the time, enjoy using computer technology to do their work.

Early evidence suggested that students enjoy using word processors (Woodruff, Bereiter, & Scardamalia, 1982). Reviews of more recent research support the same proposition (Bangert-Drowns, 1993; Hawisher, 1986, 1987b, 1989). For example, Kurth (1987) reported no advantage for word processing on a personal computer in terms of the quantity or quality of writing relative to pen and paper. However, anecdotal evidence suggested that the use of computers enhanced the motivation of student writers because they enjoyed the task more. Students develop a more favorable attitude about writing after using word processors.

Professional writers probably will write with any tool, if necessary, but they too appear to enjoy the task more when using computers (Zinsser, 1983). Curtis (1988) commented on the attachment that university professors develop for their word processors:

> As one instructor observed, "[Composing on the computer] is great fun—we haven't been able to understand why, but it has something to do with the sense of *mastery*. It's rewarding and addictive." So whether or not we are better writers on the machine, we feel we are more "masterful" producers of writing. We are also more attentive, revising more because it's easier, and because we know revision's value. (p. 338)

A full explanation for the positive affect generated by computer usage is elusive. One likely reason is that the ease of entering and modifying text makes the difficult work of writing seem less burdensome and less anxiety-provoking. The draft can more easily be seen as provisional, given the ease of revision. Although such impermanence fails to improve the quality of writing, it may improve the mood of the writer. Further, the immediate feedback of seeing what looks like finished text on the screen may hook writers in the same way that the feedback of video games hooks players. Moreover, writers may believe that the word processor, because it is a high-tech tool, enhances their fluency, quality, or productivity, regardless of whether it actually does so. Alternatively, it may be that in a high-tech society, one expects to use high-tech tools. Work is more fun when the latest technology is part of the job. For whatever reason, most people, most of the time, enjoy writing with computers. The argument, then, is that if they enjoy it more, then they will do it more. Productivity amplification could well follow as a result.

Aesthetics and Tools

The aesthetic appeal of the tools of a craft must also be considered. W. Somerset Maugham, for example, turned each day to a favorite fountain pen (Mulligan, 1983). I presume that the feel and look of the pen, its aesthetic qualities, appealed to him. Ballpoint pens, pencils, typewriters, and word processors all have design features that may or may not appeal to different writers. But word processors possess a feature that the other tools cannot match.

For writing that must eventually appear in a typed or published form, the word processor offers the writer a look at how the document will appear when finished. Advanced workstations with large screens and software that support a "what you see is what you get" approach are especially attractive. Conceivably, the writer may be rewarded by the aesthetic appeal of seeing text in a publishable form as it is being composed. Pens, pencils, typewriters, and dictation machines cannot match this feature. The aesthetic reward may reinforce writing behavior, again pointing to an increase in time spent on the task.

Productivity Studies

Surveys of academic writers in general (Boice & Johnson, 1984), professors in science and engineering departments (Kellogg, 1986a), and professors in departments of psychology (Hartley & Branthwaite, 1989) have tried to evaluate the impact of word processing on productivity. The prediction that the use of a word processor should enhance productivity has not fared well, however. There is no published evidence that reports a reliable correlation between the use of word processors and productivity.

An attempt to establish such a link should not be abandoned yet. The methodological pitfalls in measuring productivity through surveys and accounting for the host of confounding factors that would affect productivity in an academic environment (e.g., laboratory assistants, research colleagues, grant support, institutional prestige, secretarial assistance, to name a few) may have worked against existing studies. Another difficulty with past work is that it may have predated the time when word processors became a common tool for writers. In the early and mid-1980s, word processors were finding their way to writers' desks, but the users may not have been highly experienced. (Of course, by now the technology is so common that it may be difficult to find nonusers.) Finally, studies need to examine the total time spent writing each week. It may be that computers support more efficient writing. But instead of spending more time on the task and producing more, writers may spend less time at the writing table and more time on the golf course, accomplishing no more than usual.

Even so, there is an onerous side to using high-tech tools that may offset in part the motivational-affective advantages noted earlier. Hardware and software failures do occur. Minutes and sometimes hours can be lost fiddling with failed systems. Rare is the writer who has never lost any productive labor to a breakdown in technology.

Another problem is that with a word processor attention must be given to formatting and other problems handled by a secretary working from a handwritten or dictated draft (Gould, 1981; Williams, 1991). Some of the time on task with a word processor is spent doing things that a secretary would normally do, assuming that one is available. That hardly leads to more productive time on the task of being an author. The awesome capabilities of desktop publishing systems demonstrate this point particularly well. These systems allow one individual to handle everything from composing the text to designing the layout to drawing the graphics. Although they give the individual great power, they also place the entire burden of publishing a document on the author. Instead of devoting time and effort to creating documents, the writer spends time formatting them and making them look attractive.

The polished look of the text on the screen may be rewarding to the writer but paradoxically counterproductive. Bridwell-Bowles et al. (1987) found that their research subjects were lured by the polished look of their work to salvage large sections of text that would have been abandoned if handwritten. The Beethovian writers who composed rough drafts to discover their thoughts found this particularly troublesome. The tendency to keep the superficially polished but structurally flawed text could well lead the writer down unproductive paths. Although the computer readily allows deletion of material, the semblance of finished text paradoxically may prohibit writers from making major structural revisions that are sorely needed.

Finally, for children, the ease of revision on a word processor encourages multiple drafts and at times leads to superior quality in the final document (Bernhardt et al., 1989; Daiute, 1985; Hawisher, 1987b). Future research needs to examine whether the same applies to skilled adult writers. It is not at all clear that the conclusions about children apply to all adults. The argument assumes that, without a word processor, adults devote insufficient time to polishing multiple drafts. This conclusion is dubious for professionals with capable secretarial help. On the contrary, it may be that a word processor encourages some adults, those who ordinarily polish several drafts, to tinker with additional drafts, primarily at a local level of sentence structure and diction, beyond the point where quality gains are even noticeable. If that is so, then the word processor may encourage the writer to spend time on one document instead of devoting it to multiple documents. Case (1985) reported this to be a problem for some professors in a study of university faculty working on word processors. Slight gains in quality were offset by no gains or even losses in productivity.

Conclusions

The search for evidence that word processors boost productivity by luring writers to spend more time on the task is worth pursuing further. The results to date, however, are unimpressive. Studies on writing fluency and quality generally show no difference between composing on a computer or with pen and paper. Based on the knowledge-usage hypothesis and the literature, a writer should select whatever tool he or she finds comfortable and useful, given the task assignment, the resource constraints (e.g., access to secretarial help), and the amount of already text produced. Writers may find a mixture of dictation, word processing, and handwriting most conducive to writing, depending on the circumstances. I suspect that the key is to write, no matter with what implement.

The process of writing, as opposed to performance, varies substantially with the tool selected. Planning and reviewing are qualitatively different when drafting on a word processor. Moreover, a clear quantitative shift in cognitive effort occurs. The writer plans and reviews more intensely on a word processor. The greater cognitive effort devoted to these processes on a word processor may partly reflect the difficulties posed by the technology. For example, the word processor limits both the use of graphical modes of planning and the ease of global editing. With more advanced computer systems that address these difficulties, superior performance may well result.

The greater engagement in planning and reviewing on a computer may also be seen as a positive feature, waiting to be exploited by advanced systems or idea processors designed to increase the use of knowledge in writing. Like computer games, the word processor may readily absorb the writer in the difficult work of planning and reviewing. Thus, to conclude that the word processor by itself falls short does not rule out the development of more powerful tools. The next chapter examines computer-based writing aids that aim to augment the availability and accessibility of knowledge.

8

Idea Processors

The most accurate definition of writing, I believe, is that it is the process of using language to discover meaning in experience and to communicate it.

Donald Murray

Word processors may best be thought of as the ultimate tool for a typist. But what might be the ultimate tool for a writer, the one who must discover ideas in the realm of personal symbols and express them through consensual symbols? The knowledge-usage framework suggests the potential value of computer aids that help a writer to retrieve and apply content and discourse knowledge effectively. Theoretically, tools that attempt to help writers make meaning, to use their knowledge to create text, may amplify writing performance as well as restructure the process of writing.

The obstacles facing writers are clear. Content and discourse knowledge may be unavailable. Retrieval of relevant knowledge may be hindered by attentional over-load or affective interference. Applying knowledge inventively to particular rhetorical or content problems may fail for the same reasons. All these problems cause what Graesser, Hopkinson, Lewis, and Brufoldt (1984) called *idea bankruptcy*. They noted that "it is difficult for writers to generate ideas that are informative, interesting, sophisticated, and relevant to a particular pragmatic context" (p. 361).

Tools for Meaning-Making

Designing computer systems that alleviate the problems writers face in making meaning poses a greater challenge than designing computational aids. Spreadsheet, graphics, and word processing software packages automate the computation of numerical, pictorial, and linguistic information. Computation within the realm of various consensual symbol systems is by definition a function well suited to computers. Spreadsheets, graphics, and word processing packages are clever tools that eliminate the need for tedious computations. Certainly, when the writer assumes the role of accountant, drafter, or secretary, these tools are helpful. But when the author confronts his or her defining role as a maker of meaning, then these tools offer little.

161

The word processor, for instance, computes how to position words on a line as the writer creates. Insert, delete, moving text, word wrap, automatic margins and indentations, and so on make for a very slick typewriter. But typing and writing are not identical jobs. Truman Capote immortalized the difference in his critique of the Beat Generation writers: "[It] isn't writing at all—it's typing" (Bartlett, 1992). As argued in the last chapter, ease of typing and a clean copy after retyping are marvelous aids to the secretarial tasks of putting words on paper. But the computations that a word processor performs every time a writer inserts a word, moves a paragraph, and so on do not directly address the need to shape ideas and the text that expresses those ideas. Idea bankruptcy worries and limits the writer more than the computation of page layout.

This chapter examines five functions that potentially do help the writer to make meaning. They address the substance rather than the appearance of a writer's work. I define idea processors as computer-based writing tools that increase the availability, accessibility, and applicability of germane knowledge to writing problems. Idea or knowledge processors have been and should be designed to carry out at least five functions beyond computation. The five functions are those of librarian, editor, attentional funnel, inventor, and therapist.

The first two are knowledge systems that aim to augment directly the availability and accessibility of knowledge. The *librarian* offers content knowledge, and the *editor* provides advice based on discourse knowledge. The *attentional funnel* aims to make the writer concentrate on only one or two processes in an effort to alleviate the attentional overload that commonly occurs when multiple processes are juggled simultaneously. The *inventor* offers heuristics for creating ideas that solve problems in composition. Lastly, the *therapist* aims to help the writer achieve a creative flow state, rather than being overcome by frustration, anxiety, or even boredom. I describe various ways of implementing each of these functions. Next, I address the question of whether idea processors actually can amplify writing performance as hoped.

Functions of Idea Processors

Librarian

To help writers collect knowledge needed for thinking and writing, the computer should serve the function of librarian. Electronic or virtual libraries are now emerging as the standard for research libraries. Human knowledge has outstripped traditional ways of cataloging and storing information. Though text may remain as the largest segment of the knowledge base of electronic libraries, hypermedia technology allows storage of audio and video material as well. *Hypertext* refers to small units of text that are cross-referenced through associative links. Hypermedia extends the network of associative relations to films, photographs, and audio sources stored in digital format.

Gherman (1991) noted that on-line and CD-ROM literature searches are already common in academic environments. A single compact disk holds about 275,000 pages of text (Frase, 1987). Delivery of documents now occurs by mail, express mail, and fax. By the year 2000, much if not most of this delivery could well occur electronically over fiberoptic networks. The National Research and Education Network (NREN), operating at a gigabyte per second rate, aims to link researchers and educators. Under a proposal for a National Information Infrastructure, primary and secondary schools, government, industry, and residential sectors will all be linked for entertainment as well as knowledge access (DeLoughry, 1993a).

DIALOG, SCIMATE, and other bibliographic search systems are widely used tools for collecting information. Using my personal computer in Rolla, Missouri, I can tap the LUMIN card catalog system of the University of Missouri, the catalogs of dozens of other major research libraries including the Library of Congress, and the WORLDCAT system compiled from 15,000 libraries worldwide. Once a volume is identified, I can order it through a loan service. The so-called virtual collection available to me is essentially any book cataloged by numerous major research libraries.

Besides the inclusive collections of the Library of Congress or the British Library, the possibilities for a universal electronic library are under study. The visionary Ted Nelson has proposed a worldwide network, called XANADU, to serve simultaneously millions of users who wish to search and retrieve the stored texts, graphics, and other data (Bolter, 1991). Fiberoptics, CD-ROM, and video disc technology make such a dizzying prospect possible. More knowledge is available to the writer today than at any time in history. To the extent that the availability of knowledge is crucial to quality writing, the electronic library bodes well for the advancement of the human intellect through writing.

However, the very magnitude of available information poses a problem. The writer today may well be swamped rather than enlightened by the extraordinary scope of the electronic library. To avoid information overload, the computer-based librarian must guide the thinker and writer through the maze of information. Two approaches for helping writers search data bases are shown in Table 8.1.

The first approach uses Boolean operators paired with key terms to identify documents relevant to the writer's purposes. Sets and subsets of stored entries are generated by trying various combinations of terms and operators. The aim is to find a combination that generates a usable number of citations. A combination that gen-

TABLE 8.1. Examples of Computers Acting as Librarian

Approach	Method	Example
Boolean search	On-line	DIALOG FIRSTSEARCH WORLDCAT
	CD-ROM	SCIMATE PSYCHLIT PROQUEST
Associative search	Hypertext	PERSEUS XANADU MOSAIC

Source: Adapted from Kellogg, 1986b. Copyright © 1986 by the Psychonomic Society, Inc. Reprinted by permission.

erates hundreds of references probably is too broadly defined and fails to identify only the items of chief interest. Obviously, if no or very few items are generated, then the combination is too narrowly defined.

On-line or network systems using current communications technology include DIALOG, FIRSTSEARCH, and WORLDCAT through a major research library and the Library of Congress. Bandwidth limitations preclude the use of these systems for delivering documents as full text. They are used for searching only, with delivery handled by mail or fax. On-line systems using fiberoptic lines will overcome this limitation (Gherman, 1991).

CD-ROM systems include SCIMATE, which covers physical and biological science journals; PSYCHLIT, which covers behavioral science journals; and PROQUEST, which covers a broad range of general periodicals, as well as technical journals from several disciplines. Theoretically, this technology can support unlimited retrieval of full text. But as a practical matter, many documents have not yet been placed in electronic format. Current systems typically cover only recent years in full text and only a subset of the available journals.

The difficulty with the Boolean search approach is that identifying all and only relevant documents never proceeds quickly. Finding the right key terms and the proper logical combination of these terms are challenging tasks. A possible alternative would be to use a query system modeled on natural language. As the writer describes the information of interest, associative links to relevant citations would be activated using hypertext. Kreitzberg and Shneiderman (1992) described how a knowledge base, such as an encyclopedia, can be structured or linked using hypertext in a way that allows ready access to information on related topics. In theory, such an associative search approach should be more compatible with the structure of human long-term memory and our way of thinking (Pea & Kurland, 1987–88).

Weyer (1982) pioneered the use of associative or relational searching in the development of an interactive social studies textbook at Xerox PARC. The reader browses through a list of topics. As a topic is selected, relevant text is retrieved with key terms marked. Selecting a key term leads to the retrieval of additional text, and the process continues until the reader is satisfied.

One ground-breaking large-scale system is known as the PERSEUS project (Crane, 1988). PERSEUS electronically stores relevant documents and other materials in the field of classical studies. Bolter (1991) notes that PERSEUS now holds "millions of words of ancient texts in Greek and translation with grammatical notes, a 30,000-word Greek dictionary, an historical atlas, diagrams, and even pictures (stored on videodisk) of archaeological sites" (p. 101).

XANADU is Nelson's vision of how to extend the PERSEUS project, in essence, to all domains of knowledge (Bolter, 1991). It comprises a worldwide network containing all available documents, graphics, and other forms of information. The hypertext format of such a universal library would allow a writer to search associatively through vast amounts of material to find relevant knowledge for thinking and writing. Bolter points out that the writer can also record all finished documents or even vague, uninterpretable notes in the same hypertext system. The writer's private library of work could thus merge with the published works of the public library.

Interesting steps in the direction of XANADU have been taken on the Internet, a worldwide electronic network. GOPHER is a software tool that searches data bases linked on the Internet, forwarding the search request to related data bases that may prove fruitful. MOSAIC incorporates GOPHER and similar tools into a relatively powerful hypertext package (DeLoughry, 1993b). Users specify a topic and then view a document, with key words and phrases highlighted in blue. Clicking on or selecting a word or phrase provides other sources available on the Internet. Selected words and phrases, now turned red, are called *hot links*. They are preconnected in the system to all related documents, photographs, films, and other materials. Access time is rapid because of the preestablished connections. Further, the user may retrieve any of the materials and annotate them (DeLoughry, 1993b).

Editor

To provide the writer with discourse knowledge, at least in limited areas, the computer should perform the function of an editor. Checking spelling, diction, punctuation, limited grammatical analysis, readability, and style considerations can now be handled by software.

WRITER'S WORKBENCH is a versatile tool for reviewing diction, punctuation, readability, and style, as well as spelling (MacDonald, 1983). It exemplifies the present approaches and methods of the editor (see Table 8.2). The first approach is proofreading.

Editing for spelling is widely available on word processing systems today. Table 8.2 lists two well-known word processors together with WRITER'S WORKBENCH. Programs are also available to check for wordy phrases (e.g., "accounted for by the fact that"), sexist expressions (e.g., "chairman"), and incorrect constructions (e.g., "must of"). Besides detecting mistakes, these programs can suggest replacements

TABLE 8.2.   Examples of Computers Acting as an Editor

Approach	Method	Example
Proofreading	Spelling check	WRITER'S WORKBENCH WORDPERFECT WORDSTAR
	Diction-punctuation check	WRITER'S WORKBENCH GRAMMATIK EDITOR RUSKIN
	Syntax check	CRITIQUE CORRECT GRAMMAR
Style assessment	Statistical profile	WRITER'S WORKBENCH GRAMMATIK EDITOR RUSKIN
	Readability formula	WRITER'S WORKBENCH EDITOR

Source: Adapted from Kellogg, 1986b. Copyright © 1986 by the Psychonomic Society, Inc. Reprinted by permission.

to improve diction. GRAMMATIK, WRITER'S WORKBENCH, EDITOR, and RUSKIN are the most widely known and most powerful programs. Punctuation errors can be flagged by computer, as can consecutive occurrences of a word (e.g., "the, the") and split infinitives. Electronic thesauruses also aid diction by calling up on the display screen synonyms for a designated term as the writer composes.

The systems discussed thus far operate by checking surface features only for incorrect patterns. A full grammatical analysis requires a syntactic parser, a feature lacking in the editing systems noted above. The EPISTLE system, later renamed CRITIQUE, incorporated a parser in an effort to provide a complete automatic editor for business correspondence (Heidorn, Jensen, Miller, Byrd, & Chodorow, 1982). It detected subject–verb disagreements, wrong pronoun case, noun–modifier disagreement, nonstandard verb forms, nonparallel structures, overuse of the passive voice, excessive use of negatives, and excessive clause complexity. CORRECT GRAMMAR also parses sentences, allowing a more reliable assessment of grammar compared with software that examines surface features only (Ross, 1991).

Style assessment, as opposed to proofreading for errors, represents another approach to the computer-based editor. GRAMMATIK, EDITOR, and WRITER'S WORKBENCH compile numerous statistics. For example, average word length, average sentence length, the frequency of active versus passive voice, and the frequency of simple, compound, and complex sentences are readily tallied. These frequency counts provide a statistical profile of the writer's style. Further, a readability formula can be computed using some of these parameters to provide a single index of style quality. RUSKIN is innovative in its use of style rules. One rule, for example, states that if the educational level of the audience is low, then the text should contain few complex sentences. The program requests information about the intended audience, subject matter, and other aspects of the context in which the writing is done. The program then compares the statistical profile of a text to the style rules (Williams, 1989).

Funnel

To help writers with attentional overload, a computer should serve as a funnel. A funnel, as previously indicated, channels the writer's attention into only one or two processes. By encouraging the writer to ignore reviewing or translating temporarily, attentional overload may be relieved. Three approaches to funneling attention are to hide distracting information, to encourage free writing, and to reduce the physical or mental workload (see Table 8.3).

The first approach is seen in programs that allow the writer to expand and collapse an outline and in programs that selectively display the topic sentences of a document. Such outlining software acts as a funnel by allowing the writer to construct and retrieve a document at different levels of a hierarchical structure. For instance, to plan the main ideas of a document, without concern for translating or reviewing those ideas, the writer could collapse the outline and display only its superordinate levels, hiding all subordinate ones. The subordinate levels might prevent the writer from giving full attention to the superordinate one. Thus, in this

TABLE 8.3. Examples of Computers Acting as a Funnel

Approach	Method	Example
Hiding distractions	Expand and collapse outline	PROMPTDOC THINKTANK FRAMEWORK ACTA BOXWEB
	Topic sentences only	WRITER'S WORKBENCH WANDAH
Free writing	Paced writing	WANDAH WRITER'S HELPER
	Invisible writing	WANDAH
Reducing workload	Listening typewriter	PLAINTALK
	Automatic translation	ANA
	Prompts and suggestions	WRITER'S HELPER STAGE II

Source: Adapted from Kellogg, 1986b. Copyright © 1986 by the Psychonomic Society, Inc. Reprinted by permission.

example, outlining programs encourage the writer to concentrate on high-level planning. Alternatively, to focus on translating a specific subordinate idea, the writer could hide all superordinate levels and expand only the subordinate point of interest at the moment. Once this subordinate point is completely translated, it could be selectively displayed for reviewing as well.

Outlining programs do not necessarily force the writer to plan first, write second, and review third in a linear sequence. On the contrary, they can be quite compatible with the interweaving of processes typically observed. The writer can certainly shift from, say, reviewing a paragraph stored as a subordinate point to planning a new idea at the highest level of the hierarchy. However, by hiding distracting text, such programs do help the writer to finish reviewing the subordinate point before advancing to plan the new superordinate point.

PROMPTDOC and THINKTANK (Owens, 1984), FRAMEWORK (Layman, 1984), ACTA (Kozma, 1991), and BOXWEB (Wayner, 1992) are examples of outlining programs. The BOXWEB program differs from the others in that it forces the writer to grapple with the detailed relations among ideas in the outline; the logic and transitions are made explicit as part of using the outliner. Another interesting variant is the fisheye presentation of text presented by Furnas (1986). Current text appears in full, whereas prior and subsequent text collapse to section headings or keywords. Although procedural details differ, these funnel programs theoretically enable writers to focus attention on one or two processes at a time by expanding and collapsing elements of the developing text.

A second method of hiding distractions is to display only the topic sentences of each paragraph of a document. This method is useful for planning or reviewing the macrostructure of a text while ignoring the details. WRITER'S WORKBENCH

(MacDonald, 1983) displays the first and last sentence of each paragraph. WANDAH (Von Blum & Cohen, 1984) selects the first sentence or any sentence specifically designated by the writer as a topic sentence.

A second funnel approach is to adopt the strategy of free writing. As discussed in Chapter 6, this refers to rapid writing, following whatever meager plan is available, without concern for extensive planning or reviewing (Elbow, 1981). It involves quickly writing off the top of one's head in a stream-of-consciousness manner. The aim of free writing is to put one's thoughts on paper before one's internal editor rejects them as unsophisticated or lacking in style. The product of free writing can and must be scrutinized and edited at a later time.

WANDAH is a software package designed for university-level writing classes, including programs that promote free writing (Von Blum & Cohen, 1984). WAN-DAH does so by flashing the screen when the writer pauses too long, suggesting that the writer was planning or reviewing. The flashing serves as a funnel by reminding the writer to focus on writing rapidly. A similar approach is taken in Wresch's (1984) free writing program that is part of WRITER'S HELPER. His program automatically types a series of Xs if the writer takes more than a second between keystrokes.

Blanking the screen to make the text invisible is another funnel device used by WANDAH to force the writer to ignore reviewing and concentrate on planning and translating. The writer cannot review what he or she cannot read. The aim of invisible writing is to force the writer to put thoughts on paper without worrying about sentence structure, word choice, and other editing concerns. Note that invisible writing precludes reviewing but fails to discourage planning.

The last funnel approach is to reduce the writer's workload by altering the physical or cognitive demands of the task. The listening typewriter is a voice recognition system that allows writers to speak rather than to type their thoughts (Gould, Conti, & Hovanyecx, 1983). For all but the best touch typists, the motor demands of speaking into a microphone are presumably less than those of typing on a keyboard. Eliminating the need to interact with the keyboard may enable writers to focus attention on composing processes. The technical problems of speech recognition pose a serious obstacle to the development of this type of funnel program. To be effective, it must support a large vocabulary, continuous speech, and virtually error-free recognition. The PLAINTALK system developed for giving verbal commands to a Macintosh may fulfill the technical requirements, but that remains to be seen. Presently, PLAINTALK recognizes speech commands, such as "open file." It is not yet designed as a speech-based word processor or listening typewriter (Moran, 1993).

Some funnel programs reduce cognitive workload by generating sentences for the writer. One use for such automatic translation programs is to eliminate the writer altogether in a narrow domain of expertise. For example, ANA generates stock market reports (Kukich, 1983). Whether fully automatic translation programs are technically feasible for anything but routine reports covering a narrow domain of knowledge is doubtful. The knowledge base required to think and write about a broad domain or more than one domain is dauntingly large. Even so, another potential use for automatic translation is to funnel attention to planning and reviewing by allowing the machine to generate a rough first draft from a writer's plan (Heidorn, Jensen, Miller, Byrd, & Chodorow, 1982).

Finally, the use of prompts and suggestions to guide an author through a first draft may similarly reduce cognitive workload. Smith, R. (1982) discussed a program that presents menus and prompts to lead a writer through a standardized genre, such as a monthly business report (e.g., "Please state the objectives of your project") (p. 199). Sharples, Goodlet, and Pemberton (1992) included a similar feature in a comprehensive "cognitive support system for people who create complex documents as part of their professional life" (p. 209). The writer can select a text type, such as company report, and then receive guidance on "the structure of the document and default constraints, such as items to be included, boundaries (such as maximum word length), and context (such as words that should be abbreviated in a consistent manner)" (p. 209). Kozma (1991) noted several programs that include topical and rhetorical prompts (e.g., WRITER'S HELPER; STAGE II) designed to simulate the questions that experts ask themselves spontaneously while composing. Such programs seek to "prompt users to recall, analyze, and integrate topical information; to analyze the predilections and expectations of an audience; and to analyze the relationship between topic and audience and how this relationship will be addressed in the composition" (p. 5). Some of the questions regarding the analysis and integration of topic knowledge would be better regarded as serving an inventive function (see the problem statements in the next section).

Inventor

To assist idea generation, a computer should serve the function of an inventor. These aids attempt to create, clarify, and order a writer's concepts. Inventor devices may be divided into those that aid the writer in forming concepts and those that assist in forming relations among previously established concepts (see Table 8.4). The first approach has been adopted by numerous tutorial programs designed to aid students

TABLE 8.4. Examples of Computers Acting as an Inventor

Approach	Method	Example
Creating concepts	Topics, pentad, tagmemics	INVENT
	Visual synectics	(Unnamed)
	Problem statements	DRAFT
	Exploring	IDEA FISHER
	Nutshelling	WANDAH
	Morphological analysis	BRAINSTORMER
	Electronic conferencing	TALK
Relating concepts	Top-down outlines	FIRSTDRAFT
	Bottom-up networks	WRITER'S HELPER
		NOTECARDS
		WRITER'S ASSISTANT

Source: Adapted from Kellogg, 1986b. Copyright © 1986 by the Psychonomic Society, Inc. Reprinted by permission.

taking college-level rhetoric courses. They could be further developed and employed more generally, however.

Burns (1979, 1984) developed INVENT to serve as a prewriting aid by asking the writer a series of questions about the subject of the document being composed. The program does not understand the writer's responses in any deep sense, but it can detect key words, phrases, and other surface features in order to continue the dialogue. INVENT includes three types of heuristics in different programs (TOPOI, BURKE, and TAGI) for different types of writing. TOPOI assists persuasive writing by using Aristotle's 28 enthymeme topics as the basis for asking questions. The topics are categories of arguments that can be applied to any rhetorical problem. The topics are most suitable for the composer who has no ideas on a subject, only a few underdeveloped ideas or a large collection of vague ideas (Corbett, 1965). The topics point to the kinds of arguments that flesh out a thesis. For example, the topics include a concern for the meaning of terms (definition and ambiguous terms), similarities and differences (opposites, correlative terms), reasoning procedures (division, induction), and consequences (simple and crisscross consequences).

BURKE helps informative writing by drawing on Kenneth Burke's *dramatistic pentad.* The questions concern scene, act, agent, purpose, and agency (Rueckert, 1963). Burke's pentad is a more sophisticated and powerful version of the journalistic pentad of who, what, when, where, and why. The information to be conveyed in a document can be regarded as a dramatic act. To develop the document, it is necessary to specify (1) the scene of the act—where, when, and under what circumstances it was performed, (2) the nature and meaning of the act, (3) the agent who performed the act, (4) the purpose of the agent in performing the act, and (5) the agencies or means by which it was performed. In addition, it is necessary to explore the relationships, or what Burke called the *ratios,* between particular pairs of elements of the pentad, such as scene–act, agency–act, and purpose–act. Burns's program is built on 10 such ratios.

TAGI also aids informative writing by employing the *tagmemic matrix* of Young, Becker, and Pike (1970). The questions prompt the writer to see a concept to be included in a document from three perspectives. The concept can be viewed as a particle (as if it were static), as a wave (as if it were dynamic), or as a field (as if it were part of a larger network). These questions follow from only part of the theory proposed by Young et al. The complete tagmemic matrix consists of nine cells. The rows represent the perspectives of particle, wave, and field. The columns represent three features of any concept to be communicated, namely, its contrastive features (how it differs from other concepts), its range of variation (how it can vary and still remain the same concept), and its distribution in larger contexts (how it fits into a larger system).

To illustrate how these programs operate, consider this brief segment of an actual run of TOPOI (Burns & Culp, 1980, p. 8; the student input is italicized):

> During this exploration process, you will be asked to clarify the purpose of your paper on fear of death. So how would you briefly describe the purpose of your paper by completing this statement: The purpose of this paper is to . . .

Examine the fear of death people have, where we get those fears, and how we may reduce those fears.

Fine, Walt, you and I will talk again about your purpose.
Relax now, Walt, and enjoy this brainstorming session.
What objects do you associate with fear of death?
How might they be included in your theme?

Fear of the unknown, cessation of life, fear of causing pain to our loved ones.

That's the idea, Walt. Give me some more info now.

Pain is another fear causer, knowing we have to die does not relieve the pain/fear of dying.

Super, Walt!
Anything else?
(You can add more info, ask a question, or give a command—whatever you wish.)

How does euthanasia, mercy killing, suicide, murder, and accidental death add to our fears?

I could say that that's for me to know and for you to find out.
Seriously, I cannot pretend to know "how," but you should keep exploring for an answer.

Continue!

(Try explaining a little more, less phrases, more sentences.)
We're moving right along. Here is Question 2. What could be considered a result of fear of death?

Nervousness, depression, suicidal tendencies.

By George, Walt, good one. Write a little more, please.

Hatred for the person who caused the death, or the person who died.

Fantastic, Walt! anything else?

Continue!

Okay.
Do you wish to narrow or change your subject?
(Maybe revise the way it sounds in these questions?) (Yes or No?)

Rodrigues and Rodrigues (1984) described their (nameless) tutorial program that uses visual synectics. *Visual synectics* is a creative invention heuristic based on drawing analogies between the subject being written about and other seemingly unrelated visual concepts. As with any synectics approach, the aim is to spur creativity by forcing one to consider nonobvious relationships (Gordon, 1961). The Rodrigues' program first asks the student to name the writing subject. The student then examines a graphic display or a photograph selected from a collection prepared by the instructors. The program asks the writer to describe objects present in the picture. After eliciting a list of 5 to 10 objects, the program asks the writer to compare the subject with each item on the list. The purpose of visual synectics is to elicit novel views of the subject that the student might never think of without drawing analogies. Rodrigues and Rodrigues (1984, p. 37) illustrated the method with a student writing on nuclear waste disposal who compared the subject to a beach ball ("On the surface, the plans seem solid, but there is a lot of hot air underneath that surface") and to a bathing suit ("We may discover that it offers us very little protection").

Related methods for forming concepts are problem statements, exploring, nutshelling, and morphological analysis. Young et al. (1970) developed heuristic questions for developing *problem statements* or for clarifying the subject of the document and these are embodied in Neuwirth's (1984) DRAFT program. Examples are as follows: "What is the problem? "Are the components of the problem clearly dissonant or incompatible?" *Exploring* refers to working through associative chains among words as a way of stimulating new insights. IDEA FISHER includes 1,000 heuristic questions for developing problem statements and a bank of 61,000 words and 700,000 crosslinks among the words for exploring (Garrison, 1993). *Nutshelling* is a heuristic developed by Flower (1981) for forming concepts about the rhetorical problem facing the writer. WANDAH (Von Blum & Cohen, 1984) employs this method by asking the writer to state the purpose of and audience for the paper and to provide a synopsis of its main ideas. In short, the writer is prompted to put it in a nutshell. Lastly, *morphological analysis* is a heuristic for forming new concepts through a dimensional analysis of old concepts (Stein, 1974). BRAINSTORMER (Bonner, 1984) guides the writer to think of the dimensional structure of two or more concepts concerning the writing subject. The program then establishes a multidimensional matrix of these old concepts. New concepts may be formed through interesting, novel combinations of these dimensions.

The social nature of meaning-making suggests an entirely different approach to brainstorming, one that relies on cooperative thinking and writing using computer networks. Electronic mail, bulletin boards, electronic conferences, and related technologies offer many new approaches to teaching writing, both in and out of the classroom (Hawisher, 1992). Their use as tools for developing one's thinking on a topic seems especially promising. The technology provides a remarkably powerful way of sampling information about one's social environment in the process of generating and honing ideas. One can recruit the thoughts of others to build and modify one's own thinking during prewriting or drafting. The author can send his or her thoughts to one, a dozen, or conceivably thousands of individuals located in the same building, in the same country, or on the other side of the world. They respond individually, at their leisure or not at all, with asynchronous technology such as that used in electronic mail. Synchronous electronic conferencing (e.g., TALK at Carnegie Mellon University) allows multiple writers to send their messages to a common electronic blackboard, where the writers can play off of the responses of all contributors simultaneously (Hartman et al., 1991).

A second type of inventor program aims to clarify and order ideas by forming relations among concepts. The top-down method of organizing is to impose a hierarchical outline or tree structure on ideas. In addition to the outline programs already mentioned in connection with funnel devices, FIRSTDRAFT is worthy of mention. Cole (1985) described it as the quintessential outline processor. A similar program based on tree structures is part of WRITER'S HELPER (Wresch, 1984). The program asks the writer for a list of ideas and then guides the writer in finding the hierarchical category relationships among the ideas. After developing the hierarchy, the program displays the resulting tree structure.

An alternative method of organizing ideas is to work from the bottom up, building a writing structure based on the relations that emerge in thinking about relevant material. No particular form is imposed on the material with this method. Smith, R. (1982) described a nameless program that uses a network method to form relations. The program first asks the writer to list the ideas to be included in a text. Then the program presents all possible pairs of ideas, one at a time, and asks the writer if the pair is related. If it is, the writer is asked to specify the nature of the relation. The program can assist the writer in doing this by displaying a menu of possible relations (e.g., "is an explanation of," "is analogous to"). After the relations are specified, the program displays in a graphical network each idea as a node, the links from each node, and a label indicating the type of relation for each link.

The bottom-up approach to relating ideas is also embodied in hypertext (Marchionini & Shneiderman, 1988). Hypertext enables the writer to go beyond a linear representation of ideas, such as an outline, to a complex nonlinear representation that includes all associative relations among ideas.

NOTECARDS (Halasz, Moran, & Trigg, 1987) is a powerful version of hypertext. The program automates the traditional prewriting strategy of manipulating notecards containing ideas generated by the author or collected from texts. The writer discovers relations among ideas by sorting through the notecards repetitively and categorizing the information. The program permits the writer to label relations, using, for example, the rhetorical relations of evidence, comment, and argument. It then displays the resulting structure as a labeled network that can be used as a guide for drafting text. HYPERCARD includes, among numerous other functions, the ability to shuffle through stacks of cards and link ideas associatively (Williams, 1987).

Several researchers have recognized the need to provide both top-down and bottom-up modes of invention for writers. For example, with Learning Tool the writer constructs relationships among ideas and displays them graphically, either as a tree structure or as a network (Kozma, 1991). Lansman et al. (1990) similarly provided both modes. Sharples et al.'s (1992) WRITER'S ASSISTANT allows the author to work in an unorganized mode (idea labels only), a nonlinear mode (idea labels arranged in a network), and a linear mode (idea labels arranged in a list or table of contents).

Therapist

To deal with affective problems connected with writing, the computer should serve as a therapist. Aids that try to reduce the anxiety, frustration, and lack of confidence of the writer serve the therapist function. At first glance, the notion of computer therapy might strike some readers as hollow. But there is growing interest among clinical psychologists in the use of therapy programs for certain client problems.

A review of the use of computers in psychotherapy admits the complexity of the issues involved but concludes that computers can present questions flexibly and support acceptable client–therapist interactions (Plutchik & Karasu, 1991). Moreover, individuals are often more willing to divulge personal information to a computer than to a human therapist, at least during initial interviews. Hartman (1986) further argued that therapy directed at skill training or behavioral change could be automated with ease. Writing problems may be ideal for testing the value of therapeutic software.

One approach is to embed therapy in a program whose primary function is to serve as a funnel or an inventor. The therapy delivered in this embedded fashion is covert in the sense that the writer is not turning to the program primarily for therapy (see Table 8.5). To illustrate, INVENT (Burns, 1984; Burns & Culp, 1980) positively reinforces the writer by using comments like "good," "fine," "terrific," and "that's the idea" in response to the writer's input. It also makes suggestions to the writer that are primarily affective, not cognitive (e.g., "Relax now and enjoy this brainstorming session" and "We'll have a good time thinking about _____"). Thus, while employing Aristotle's topics as an invention heuristic, the writer covertly receives therapy, however mild, to alleviate anxiety and build confidence. Positive reinforcement and suggestions of positive affect could be embedded in outlining, free writing, and other computerized functions. INVENT seems to be the only extant example of an embedded, covert therapist device.

The use of positive reinforcement in INVENT strikes me as perhaps too contrived to be generally useful. But the program illustrates what may be a powerful method for increasing the fluency and productivity of writers, particularly those who are overly anxious or blocked. Feedback regarding the number of words generated per minute or hour, for example, might provide effective reinforcement. More sophisticated text analyses that measured the rate at which new ideas or propositions or new relationships among ideas are created might provide reinforcement in word processing software not explicitly designed for therapy.

Alternatively, it is possible to design an overt, independent therapist program that the writer uses with the intention of receiving therapy. Neumann (1985) described several programs that implement specific therapeutic techniques and some of the advantages of such programs over human therapists. For instance, MORTON is a program that delivers Beck's cognitive behavior therapy to depressed individuals (Selmi, Klein, Greist, Johnson, & Harris, 1982). Unlike human therapists, MORTON is available any time the user wants it and never gets bored, tired, or angry. Because a main tenet of cognitive therapy is the alteration of debilitating, self-defeating thought patterns, MORTON could perhaps be tailored to deal with procrastination, dysphoria, evaluation apprehension, and other symptoms expressed in the self-talk

TABLE 8.5.　Examples of Computers Acting as a Therapist

Approach	Method	Example
Covert, embedded therapy	Positive reinforcement	INVENT
	Suggestion	INVENT
Overt, independent therapy	Cognitive behavior therapy	MORTON
	Contingency management	(Unavailable)

Source: Adapted from Kellogg, 1986b. Copyright © 1986 by the Psychonomic Society, Inc. Reprinted by permission.

of blocked writers (Boice, 1985). As it happens, Salovey and Haar (1990) reported that cognitive-behavior therapy, when combined with writing process training, successfully overcomes the writing anxiety in college students.

Although a program apparently does not exist, pure behavior therapy offers another viable method for implementing a therapist device. It might be worthwhile to develop contingency management software for writers based on reports of success in treating blocked writers with behavioral therapy (Boice, 1987). Setting up a time schedule for completing the document, monitoring the number of words produced per writing session, and delivering verbal reinforcement are aspects of such therapy that could be readily programmed. Token economies, with rewards determined by the writer, strike this writer as promising.

Functional Integration

The librarian, editor, funnel, inventor, and therapist functions are novel and interesting ways in which computers might facilitate planning and translating for writers. These functions have been presented as if one program carried out a single function. INVENT illustrates the point that a single program can combine functions, in this case the functions of inventor and covert therapist. Conceivably, a writer's workstation that combines all functions—computation, librarian, editor, funnel, inventor, and therapist—would prove most effective. No single program combines all of these to date. However, WRITER'S ASSISTANT (Sharples et al., 1992) and WORD-PROF (Farraris, Caviglia, and Degl'Innocenti, 1992) represent ambitious attempts in this direction.

Effectiveness of Computer Aids

Computer technology will be used for writing regardless of whether it amplifies writing performance. As noted in connection with word processors, the clerical labor of updating drafts is reduced. For student writers and others without secretarial assistance, the savings in typing time and effort make the use of word processors very appealing. Some professionals also prefer handling all aspects of manuscript preparation themselves rather than relying on secretarial assistance. Similarly, the publishing industry saves on typesetting costs when texts are created and stored in digital format. Desktop publishing systems offer the power of the press to a single person. The growing popularity of such systems will further increase computer usage among writers, enabling or, better, requiring them to don the hats of author, secretary, and editor.

Turning the writer into a document designer is but one of the ways that computers are altering the demands placed on writers. Williams (1991, 1992) elucidated several others, such as the "phenomenon of fontitis . . . whereby new users . . . indulge in a riot of visual confusion by mixing multiple fonts upon the page" (p. 12). Creating hypertext and hypermedia requires the writer to think in terms of multiple structures as well as multiple audiences for a document. To the degree that documents will increasingly be written in hypertext, as predicted by Bolter (1991), the difficulties of writing will wax, not wane. Also, electronic mail demands that the writer employ a style that the reader can comprehend and respond to rapidly upon reading, interacting with the writer much more intimately than with traditional texts. Collaborative writing through electronics further heightens this interactivity, with each contributor serving simultaneously and often immediately as writer and editor.

The use of computers as writing tools is merely one part of a broader technological revolution. Computers and telecommunications are rapidly restructuring the nature of our world. The way we write and perhaps the way we think will change as part of this broader cultural evolution (Bolter, 1991). Hawisher and LeBlanc (1992) reflected on the implications of these changes for composition researchers and educators:

> A significant part of the problem we face as a profession attempting to account for dramatically different media, genres, and conventions for written discourse is the speed and breadth of the change and the degree of its impact. In just ten years, we have gone from expensive, underpowered personal computers (Remember the days of 64K memory?) to less expensive, high-powered machines that provide desktop publishing, access to remote databases, e-mail connections to other writers and researchers, on-line dictionaries, handbooks, and editing programs, and most recently, the use of multimedia for teaching and presentations. The use of such systems in both school and business settings is pervasive. Compared to the adoption of other communication technologies and the time it took for their impact to be felt, writing and the printing press for example, the pace at which modern industrial culture is appropriating the microcomputer is breathtaking. . . . We have entered new uncharted waters and navigation can be difficult and dangerous. . . . (pp. 151–152)

In one sense, the outcome of research evaluating the effectiveness of computer-based writing tools is irrelevant. People will use computers and writing technology will progress even if writers are no more effective with computers than they are with pens or even stone tablets. However, for the sake of the overworked writer and for the sake of readers who seek quality writing, the outcome of evaluation research is crucial. Such research is one part of the human factors design process that results in usable and effective tools. Task analysis, user analysis, and iterative design are also important (see Neuwirth & Kaufer, 1992, and Sharples et al., 1992, for informed discussions of development methodology for idea processors). Unhappily, too few studies have been conducted in this area to date to offer adequate guidance in the design process. I will now review a few examples of the existing work on editor, inventor, and funnel programs.

Evaluation Studies

Editor. WRITER'S WORKBENCH has received the most careful evaluation, so we will begin with it. Hartley (1984) compared WRITER'S WORKBENCH and human editors in the task of reviewing a technical article. He found that WRITER'S WORKBENCH was more consistent than humans in detecting errors in spelling, punctuation, diction, and style. Only human editors, however, could detect ambiguities, controversial points, errors of fact, inconsistencies, and other mistakes that required expertise regarding the document's content.

Gingrich (1982) reported the findings of a field study of office workers in which questionnaires, data on program usage, performance on standardized revision tests, and interviews with participants were collected. Key outcomes were that writers enjoyed the immediate feedback and suggestions offered by the programs, and they found more errors using the programs on revision tasks than they did without the help. Similarly, Kiefer and Smith (1983) found that college freshman who trained on WRITER'S WORKBENCH superseded a control group on a test of local editing skill that covered simplicity, directness, and clarity. Nonetheless, Kiefer and Smith failed to observe any improvement in the quality of writing samples of these students as a consequence of using WRITER'S WORKBENCH. A similar negative outcome was reported by Pedersen (1989).

Sterkel, Johnson, and Sjogren (1986) followed business students using the WRITER'S WORKBENCH over three terms in an academic year. A test of editing skills showed no difference between the experimental and control groups across all three terms. Quality judgments of a writing assignment also failed to reveal any difference for the first two terms. But by the third term, the students using WRITER'S WORKBENCH were producing texts of better overall quality compared to those not using the software.

The notable lack of strong effects with editor programs does not surprise Oliver (1985). He noted that WRITER'S WORKBENCH does not detect the grammatical errors that frequently plague student writers, provides a controversial index of readability and style, and may be pedagogically misguided in encouraging writers to conform to quantitative criteria. Reed (1988) countered this argument by validating the revision suggestions provided by another program, WRITER'S HELPER. He found that such quantitative measures as the ratio of words per paragraph or words per sentence, and differentials in actual and intended readability levels, were significantly correlated with subjective quality ratings and syntactic complexity measures. Even so, there is no compelling evidence yet that writers who need help will necessarily understand and heed the suggestions of automated editors.

A promising approach to ensuring that the writer in need in fact heeds the editor's suggestions can be found in MCRUSKIN (MacGowan, 1992). It attempts to duplicate the one-on-one interaction that characterizes a teacher going through a student's document, highlighting problems, explaining why the text may be in error, and offering solutions to the problems that the student can learn from so as to avoid mistakes in the future. As a style program, MCRUSKIN is still rudimentary, but the pedagogical theory underlying its design is an important advance.

Funnel.   The promise of listening typewriter systems hinges on the assumption that output modality constrains writing ability. By allowing the writer to dictate rather than type or write in longhand, the motor demands may decrease, freeing attention for cognitive operations. Consistent with this notion, I found in my survey of science and engineering faculty (Kellogg, 1986a) that the extent to which researchers reported using dictation to compose technical documents correlated positively with their productivity ($r = .39$). This modest relationship apparently emerges only when a wide range of productivity is analyzed (in this case, respondents reported the completion of from 0 to 58 technical articles, proposals, reports, and books over a 3-year period). Hartley and Branthwaite (1989) examined only highly productive psychologists and found no relationship between the use of dictation and productivity.

Gould (1978) calculated that the maximum expected fluency of dictation exceeds that of handwriting by 500%. Yet, his experiments showed that business executives with years of practice at dictation achieved a gain of only 20–65% in fluency in a letter composition task. These experts dictated complex business letters at the same rate as novice dictators but outperformed the novices by 20% on routine letters. Strikingly, the style and content characteristics of the letters failed to vary with the tool used for composition. The quality of the letters could not be reliably distinguished as having been written or dictated.

Gould concluded that the method of composition is of secondary importance, with the limitations of cognitive operations playing a much more important role in determining writing performance. He suggested that these higher-level factors included ''formulation and understanding of the goals of the composition and the problem to be described . . . development of appropriate vocabulary and phrasings, experience at composing the particular type of document, knowledge of recipients (including their expectations and knowledge state), an ability to outline and fill-in, and a secondary working memory not cluttered with irrelevant detail'' (p. 658). An analysis of pause times provides one window on the writer's engagement in these higher-level cognitive operations. Interestingly, Gould's (1980, 1981) extensive research on pause times shows no reliable variation among dictating, speaking (dictating a text meant to be heard, not read), handwriting, and word processing using a keyboard.

Of course, a listening typewriter has the added advantage of providing immediate visual feedback. The writer sees dictated words appearing on the screen, a major difference from dictation machines. The outcome of Gould's (1980) experiments with invisible writing downplayed the significance of this feedback in that composing time, document quality, and error counts were not impacted. Hull and Smith (1983) countered that this null result may have been due to Gould's use of the business letter genre. The writer's schema for composing such letters, particularly Gould's routine letters, may be so well developed that visual feedback diminished in importance. That Gould et al. (1983) found no benefit for writers composing business letters on a listening typewriter cannot, therefore, be taken as definitive evidence that such systems could not help writers in more complex tasks that overload attentional capacity.

Hull and Smith (1983) investigated basic writers and graduate students composing persuasive essays with standard fountain pens and with pens filled with invisible ink that appears only after exposure to a heat source. Both groups of writers successfully generated sentences with the invisible ink. Analyses of cohesive ties, in contrast, revealed that the degree of sentence connectedness suffered under conditions of invisible writing. The graduate students used fewer local ties with invisible ink compared with visible ink; the basic writers actually increased their use of local ties in the absence of visual feedback, but did so in an inappropriate manner that failed to improve coherence. Quality ratings decreased by the same amount with invisible writing for both groups; the more knowledgeable graduate students received markedly higher ratings than the basic writers. Hull and Smith concluded that "the significance of visual feedback lies not in editing or manipulating syntax, but in managing larger units of discourse" (p. 976).

Their conclusion leaves open the door for testing word processors based on speech recognition systems in tasks that challenge the discourse formulation skills of writers. The lessened motor demands of dictation combined with the immediate visual feedback of a word processor may prove to be a useful funnel device in situations that seriously overload a writer's attentional capacity.

Turning to other funnel devices, studies have been conducted on the effectiveness of prompts during drafting. For example, Daiute (1985) evaluated her CATCH program, which includes prompts that vary in form, function, scope, and their relation to the writing process. They include questions about text qualities such as the following: "Does this paragraph have a clear focus?" "Does this paragraph include details to help the reader see, hear, feel, or smell what you're talking about?" The program also analyzes text for problems such as unnecessary words. The writer can ask to see the list of CATCH features at any time.

Daiute (1985) studied eight 12-year-old students, comparing their writing on a computer using CATCH to various control conditions. Her chief interest was in whether use of the program would increase the amount of self-monitoring done, as indicated by frequency and types of revision. Such a result would correspond to other findings that reflective thinking in children can be taught by prompting them to plan out loud in response to cues (Scardamalia & Bereiter, 1985; Scardamalia, Bereiter, & Steinbach, 1984). CATCH was successful in this regard; the students made more changes in first drafts, and these changes involved fewer words after using CATCH. However, the quality of the documents, as measured by subjective ratings, was not affected despite this enhanced revising activity and efficiency. Investigating a similar prompting program with sixth graders, Woodruff, Bereiter, and Scardamalia (1982) reported that students wrote at least as good if not better papers with a pencil than with a computer. Interestingly, however, the students liked writing with a computer better.

Zellermeyer, Saloman, Globerson, and Givon (1991) developed THE WRITING PARTNER in an effort to advance high school students from knowledge-telling approaches to writing to knowledge-transforming approaches. Their software prompted the writer to consider rhetorical goals and the audience, and it guided the writer to develop ideas and attain coherence. Zellermeyer et al. compared performance on five essays written under one of three conditions. The control condition used a word processor. The other two conditions used THE WRITING PARTNER but differed in that in one case the writer had to request guidance from the system. Overall quality scores on the essays proved reliably higher for those using THE WRITING PARTNER compared to the control and request-only groups; the latter two failed to differ. Moreover, those who used THE WRITING PARTNER continued to show superior writing skills on a essay composed with pen and paper 2 weeks after the experimental sessions. Zellermeyer et al. concluded that these writers acquired knowledge transformation skills as a consequence of using the software, enabling them to write better even without the cognitive supports. This is a striking outcome that bodes well for continued development of idea processors that help students learn to compose.

Kozma (1991) studied advanced and novice college-level writers using idea processors that included topical and rhetorical prompts. He found that writers planned more at a conceptual level when using software that included the prompts relative to control conditions. Interestingly, most conceptual planning occurred when the invention prompts were combined with either a bottom-up network organizer or a top-down outliner. These effects occurred at the same level of magnitude for both the advanced and novice students. However, the overall quality of the resulting texts, as well as several analytic quality measures, failed to vary reliably with the type of software used. Stated differently, the time devoted to conceptual planning was uncorrelated with overall quality ($r = -.06$). Advanced writers composed better texts than novices, but the idea processors failed to amplify performance above that seen with a word processor.

Inventor. As noted, Kozma (1991) also compared word processing with two approaches to helping writers invent ideas by relating concepts. The network-based idea organizer and outliner showed no overall differences in the amount of conceptual planning they engendered. But the use of prompts and the type of software interacted reliably. The percentage of time devoted to conceptual planning was markedly greater with the prompts (15%) than without them (6%) when using the idea organizer. This difference diminished when using the outliner (14% versus 11%), suggesting that the top-down mode of relating ideas in an outline serves some of the same functions as the rhetorical and topical prompts. In terms of quality ratings, Kozma noted that advanced writers performed best with the idea organizer plus prompts, whereas novices did best with the outliner plus prompts.

Burns (1979) compared three experimental groups, in which students employed TOPOI, BURKE, and TAGI, with a control group that heard a lecture on the creative process. Burns took several measures of the quality of their prewriting first and then of their composition plan (e.g., a detailed outline); the students did not compose a draft for evaluation. He found that all three experimental groups significantly outperformed the control group in terms of the number of ideas generated; in the factuality, surprise value, insightfulness, and comprehensiveness of those ideas; and in the overall quality impression of their prewriting inquiry. No significant differences were found on any of these measures among the experimental groups. Interestingly, the quality of the composition plans was statistically equivalent among all four groups on all measurements taken. Thus, the benefits seen in the prewriting phase did not carry over to the phase of arranging a plan for a first draft. The attitudes of students toward using the programs were positive. They believed that the programs helped them to think and that the heuristics would be useful for many types of writing assignments.

Two case studies have been reported on NOTECARDS. VanLehn (1985) described how NOTECARDS helped him uncover important flaws in the arguments of a learning theory that he had worked on for several years. The theory had been organized in a tree structure that obscured the errors in reasoning. NOTECARDS readily converted the tree structure to a matrix format that highlighted the flaws, leading to their correction. Although conceivably one could accomplish the same feat manually with paper note cards, VanLehn makes the interesting point that the sheer size of the data base (over 800 cards) made it unlikely that he would have bothered with a matrix structure without the help of the computer.

Trigg and Irish (1987) interviewed 20 users of NOTECARDS in an effort to describe how people use the system. Their work provides many insights that would prove useful in formal evaluations of NOTECARDS or other hypertext systems. For example, the decision to use NOTECARDS for a document depended in part on whether major planning decisions were needed. NOTECARDS was inappropriate for papers that were already well organized in the writer's mind. Also, on long-term projects, the writers capitalized on the power of hypertext to represent multiple organizations of the same material. The same cards were filed in multiple boxes or were associated with several other cards. These multiple, parallel structures best represented the writer's thinking as the product evolved during prewriting and drafting. Eventually, these alternative structures collapsed into one structure for the final draft. Follow-up experiments would now be valuable to determine if NOTECARDS enhances the quality or efficiency of writing when the writing task is novel and long-term. Such conditions are difficult to create in the laboratory, however.

Hartman et al. (1991) examined the use of asynchronous (COMMENTS) and synchronous (TALK) network communications in college composition classes. They found that relative to regular classroom instruction, the use of electronic conferencing increased the interaction of teachers with students. Grades on papers and other assessments of quality apparently failed to show differences attributable to network communications. However, in future work, it would be fruitful to examine ideational fluency during prewriting, which may prove more sensitive to the value of this technology as a brainstorming aid.

Causes for Doubt

Theoretically, idea processors promise to amplify performance as well as restructure writing processes. They could well offer more than word processors in helping writers generate high-quality text with fluency. But the scant research that has been done is not especially encouraging. Moreover, complicating factors remain. Experience in using computers, typing skills, language skills, strategy preferences, and personality variables undoubtedly play a part in determining the efficacy of any computer aid.

Potential Interactions. For example, it may be that only knowledgeable writers can make effective use of particular computer aids, such as outlining programs (see Bryson, Lindsay, Joram, & Woodruff, 1986). Alternatively, some aids, such as Daiute's CATCH program, would be unnecessary for writers whose level of cognitive development obviated the need for enhanced self-monitoring. Similarly, the highly knowledgeable, experienced writer can better handle multiple processes simultaneously because some aspects of the task are performed automatically. Some expert writers may find it possible to concentrate on planning and translating while reviewing automatically, thus eliminating the need for funnel devices. Dorothy Parker (in Cowley, 1958, p. 10) and William Zinsser (1983), both highly accomplished writers, claimed that they carefully constructed every word, phrase, and sentence as they composed a first draft, enabling them to produce a highly polished piece on the first effort.

Similarly, editor functions may be superfluous for an expert writer. Automated checking of spelling, punctuation, diction, and syntax may be necessary only when adequate discourse knowledge is lacking. For the unskilled writer, on the other hand, an automatic editor would appear on the surface to be a godsend. What the writer lacked in knowledge, the editor program could well provide externally. One might even worry that excessive reliance on such tools by novice writers would inhibit their learning of language. The same argument has simmered in mathematics education over the use of hand-held calculators and now powerful programs, such as MATHEMATICA in calculus.

Digging below the surface appeal of editing programs for novices uncovers a still greater danger. Theismeyer (1989) fears that spelling checkers and other automatic editing programs may lead the novice seriously astray. Usage checkers, for instance, flag on the order of 100 to 1,000 items. Even the upper bound falls short of what is needed, according to Thiesmeyer, by at least an order of magnitude. The novice might believe that the program catches a large proportion of troublesome phrases when in fact it may miss most of them. Further, a program that aims to flag a cliche (e.g., "lay it on the line") misses variations on the theme (e.g., "laid the success of his business on the line"). As Theismeyer accurately observed:

> a list that would capture all cases of this one cliche must not only conjugate the verb (remarkably, that is a precaution not always followed by usage-program designers) but must also accommodate the indefinitely large number of nouns and noun phrases that might plausibly be encountered . . . If such a list can be drawn up in principle (and it is not clear that it can), it cannot in practice. (p. 83)

Thus, for the expert, the editor function may be least necessary, whereas for the novice, it may be least suited. Without a sufficient background of discourse knowledge, the unskilled writer may not be able to extend the sample problems caught by the program to the broader class actually encountered in practice. Indeed, if the program is regarded as an authority, the novice may be lulled into believing that broader classes of problems do not even exist.

The writer's method and personality may also limit the value of idea processors. For instance, free-writing programs may fluster more than free individuals who find it very difficult to ignore reviewing while planning and translating. A perfectionist who insists on trying to compose a polished first draft may be most in need of free-writing programs and least able to benefit from them. Similarly, some individuals may prefer the discreetness and anonymity of receiving therapy from a computer, whereas others might regard it as too contrived and impersonal to be of any use. Bridwell-Bowles et al. (1987) reported substantial individual differences in the ease with which writers can compose on a word processor. Related differences for idea processors are likely to emerge.

The specific characteristics of the human–machine interface may also be crucial, as hinted at by the differences observed by Haas (1989) between a personal computer and an advanced workstation. Further studies of large screens with high degrees of legibility, writing tablets that permit drawing and doodling as well as handwriting, graphics programs that support networks as well as hierarchies, and other interfaces are sorely needed (Carroll, 1991; Miller & Thomas, 1977).

Research Directions.   More fundamentally, we need programmatic research on the best approaches and methods for implementing librarian, editor, funnel, inventor, and therapist devices. To illustrate, Burns (1979) selected his invention heuristics on grounds of rhetorical theory, not on the basis of psychological evidence of their power. Our understanding of how well these invention heuristics aid thinkers in their struggle to generate and shape ideas is entirely too thin. Before programming the heuristics, basic research on their usefulness seems in order.

The problem of how to build an electronic librarian shows the need for research in advance of design. The electronic library will amplify thinking and writing to the extent that relevant knowledge is retrieved effectively. It remains to be seen if the associative search procedure using relational links in a network really puts the writer in touch with all and only relevant knowledge more quickly than nested sets of Boolean search. Charney (1991) criticizes relational links in hypertext on the grounds that the lack of logical organization in the form of hierarchies may actually make it more difficult for readers to retrieve and comprehend information. Hypertext designers assume that writers exploring a network data base can organize information in a way that achieves their purpose in finding new, relevant knowledge. The available research on this claim is mixed at best (Charney, 1991). In one carefully executed series of experiments, a hierarchical organization of hypertext nodes supported faster information retrieval than a network linking structure (Mohageg, 1992). Tellingly, a combination condition that included both hierarchical organization and networks was no faster than the hierarchy condition alone.

The sheer size of a project like XANADU underscores the concern raised earlier about drowning in information. Even if highly efficient search procedures are developed, the writer still must discern the truth, validity, and reliability of the information collected. Separating useful knowledge from drivel is difficult even now, when a writer has access only to published, finished products. The thought of authors adding personal libraries of works in progress to catalogs of published materials I find more frightening than liberating. I, for one, would prefer not to tap into the private libraries of thinkers still struggling with how to translate their ideas and private notes into documents meant for public consumption. It is already impossible to keep up with essential reading of finished works in even the most narrowly defined discipline.

Finally, Dobrin (1987) pinpointed an interesting difficulty with outlining programs as invention devices. These forms of idea processors manipulate external symbols referred to here as *consensual symbols*. What is really needed, of course, is creation and manipulation of internal, *personal symbols*. Dobrin phrases it this way:

> Expansive thinking—true idea processing—occurs in the mind, not on paper. It engages the mind's full creative possibilities. If you want to manipulate ideas, help with manipulating symbols is largely beside the point. (p. 96)

Dobrin suggested that the meaning of a term in an outline program is context dependent. It changes as other terms are added to or deleted from the outline. The outline is at best a cryptic structure of consensual symbols that refer to the writer's actual ideas. As the writer's ideas develop in the form of personal symbols, the outline necessarily lags behind. Dobrin noted that "as an outline expands, the meanings of the entries, the relationships among the entries, and the appropriate symbols for the entries all change ... headings become subheadings, topics get split up or eliminated, and ideas or facts that we thought were telling become defanged" (pp. 102–103).

Further research is needed addressing the costs and benefits for writers when they use outlining programs (Kellogg, 1988; Kozma, 1991). Dobrin observed that paper-and-pencil outlines are relatively easy to update because all relevant information remains visible, and they permit more ways to represent relations by underlining, drawing arrows, crossing out, and other notations. Whether a pen-sensitive screen or writing tablet would help is unclear because scrolling from one screen full of information to the next may still be needed.

Conclusions

The knowledge-usage framework adopted in this book suggests that idea processors may succeed in amplifying writing performance, as well as in restructuring the writing process. Idea processors go beyond word processors by attempting to address the thinking aspects of writing rather than the typing aspects. It must be recognized that the theory of designing tools that augment idea generation, organizing, goal setting, sentence generation, revising, and other thinking operations is in its infancy and controversial (e.g., Carroll, 1991). Moreover, reasons for doubting the power of existing instantiations of idea processors are not difficult to enumerate. The chief point I wish to make is the need for programmatic research. The potential of idea processors that empower writers with knowledge overshadows the value of word processors that primarily help writers format documents. To date, though, writers have expressed much more enthusiasm for word processors than for idea processors (Dorner, 1992). Computers have already revolutionized the craft of writing in some respects, but the depth and reverberations of the revolution will hinge on the development and adoption of effective knowledge-based systems.

Chapters 7 and 8 have addressed issues concerning the design of writing tools and have placed these issues in the context of knowledge differences, personality factors, and strategies. I turn now in the penultimate chapter to a discussion of the writer's work environment, schedules, and rituals. These three elements complete the discussion of method and shed further light on the conditions that enable writers to immerse themselves in their work.

9

Work Environments, Schedules, and Rituals

I . . . never acquired the discipline of regular hours for creative work. I write irregularly, and perhaps in that I get more subconscious development of the theme. I find stimulation in solitary walks. An episode in the novel develops, and I come home with much of it perhaps already composed, memorized, and can sit down and write it.

THORNTON WILDER

The study of where, when, and how writers engage in their craft invites the discovery of individual differences. It is difficult to imagine that a particular set of conditions is necessary for all writers for the successful retrieval and application of knowledge relevant to the task of writing. Thornton Wilder's method (see Simon, 1979) is surely but one of many idiosyncratic approaches to writing.

Consider the routine of one legendary writer, as described by Mulligan (1983):

W. Somerset Maugham's day began at 8 a.m. with breakfast on a tray and the morning papers. He shaved in his bath, consulted with his Italian cook about the day's menus and then repaired to his den, where he wrote with a special fountain pen until precisely 12:45 p.m. "My brain is dead after 1 o'clock," Maugham decreed. The rest of the day unfolded with a one-martini lunch, a nap, golf or tennis, the cocktail hour and then a formal black-tie dinner, always with champagne. This rarely varied routine produced 74 novels, plays, collections of essays and short stories in 65 years at his writing desk. (p. B3)

Maugham's approach, civilized as it sounds, is not likely to be any more typical than Wilder's solitary walks. Though we can anticipate differences, whatever approach an individual takes may affect the extent to which knowledge is brought to bear on the task at hand. Obviously, work scheduling and, less obviously, behavioral rituals and work environments affect the amount of time spent trying to write. Moreover, these factors may well influence whether the working time is spent in a state of boredom, anxiety, or creative flow. Theoretically, writers must attain flow in order to engage their tasks fully and use their knowledge optimally.

This chapter examines the evidence that environments, schedules, and rituals restructure the writing process and amplify performance. As is the case with strategies and tools, I expect that the pattern of allocating processing time and cognitive effort to writing processes will vary with the writer's method. Further, the principles of memory retrieval suggest that certain practices should amplify performance. These practices encourage a state of flow rather than one of anxiety or boredom. Like strategies, these other aspects of a writer's method may alleviate the difficulty of attentional overload. The room, time of day, or ritual selected for working may enable or even induce intense concentration or a favorable motivational or emotional state. Moreover, in accordance with encoding specificity, each of these aspects of method may trigger retrieval of ideas, facts, plans, and other relevant knowledge associated with the place, time, or frame of mind selected by the writer for work.

But the study of individual differences in writing environments, schedules, and rituals does not require justification on the grounds that they restructure the process or amplify performance. A look at environments, schedules, and rituals is worthwhile, even though we have only anecdotal reports and surveys as evidence. The evidence is both inherently interesting and essential for understanding the challenges that writing poses to *Homo symbolificus.*

The Writing Environment

One might expect that a quiet work environment would be essential for many writers to enter a state of creative flow. Quiet may produce the concentration needed for superior performance. Even so, the relationship between cognitive performance and level of environmental noise is too complex to allow us to make a strong prediction that silence is necessary for writing.

Background noise improves performance on simple, boring tasks, presumably by raising arousal levels (Sanders & McCormick, 1993). High-intensity noise, at least 95 decibels, can disrupt performance on complex tasks, but more moderate noise levels have no reliable effect. I suspect that individuals who are generally anxious are most bothered by noisy environments. The match between skill level and task difficulty should also enter the equation.

When skills are not up to task demands, a condition that prompts frustration and anxiety, the detrimental effects of noise ought to be easily observable. Laboratory experiments that address general anxiety, skill level, and task difficulty in the context of writing have not yet been done. Even so, we have responses from writers to surveys and interviews to consider.

Anectodes

The classic examples of how quiet spurs fluent, productive, high-quality writing, presumably through a concentration effect, come from Proust and Carlyle. Proust supposedly wrote in a cork-lined room and Carlyle in a noiseproof chamber to ensure silence (Stein, 1974). Nathalie Sarraute, the master of the French genre of *nouveau roman,* illustrates the point that quiet is not necessary (Danto, 1990): "I go every morning to the same cafe: I have my table there, always the same one—when it's free—and I stay for two or two and a half hours. It is a neutral place, and no one disturbs me—there is no telephone" (p. 7)!

However, the lack of interruption in trains of thought may be the critical ingredient in an environment that enables creative flow. As long as a writer can tune out background noise, the decibel level per se may be unimportant. For some writers, the dripping of a faucet may be more disruptive than the bustle of a cafe in the heart of a city.

Robert Creeley recounted his and others' preference for writing environments as follows (Plimpton, 1989):

> Allen Ginsburg, for example, can write poems anywhere—trains, planes, in any public place. He isn't the least self-conscious. In fact, he seems to be stimulated by people around him. For myself, I need a very kind of secure quiet. I usually have some music playing, just because it gives me something, a kind of drone that I like, as relaxation. I remember reading that Hart Crane wrote at times to the sound of records because he liked the stimulus and this pushed him to a kind of openness that he could use. In any case, the necessary environment is that which secures the artist in the way that lets him be in the world in a most fruitful manner. (p. 54)

William Styron also avoided seclusion but found that quiet was needed nevertheless (Cowley, 1959):

> I find it's difficult to write in complete isolation. I think it would be hard for me on a South Sea island or in the Maine woods. I like company and entertainment, people around. The actual process of writing, though, demands complete noiseless privacy, without even music; a baby howling two blocks away will drive me nuts. (p. 271)

John-Steiner (1985) interviewed dozens of writers and other artists and compiled her observations on the creative process in *Notebooks of the Mind.* She observed that sustained, productive work generally is associated with the selection of a special workplace. It typically involves solitude and quiet, though during the apprenticeship phase of a writer's career, almost any environment is workable. For example, the British novelist Margaret Drabble worked at home while her children were young, and her early novels apparently conveyed a sense of confinement (John-Steiner, 1985). More recently, Drabble has written in a hotel room for several days at a time, where she can be alone and uninterrupted, and "her characters expand in that empty space and take possession of the room" (p. 74). Similarly, Catherine Ann Porter wrote any time and any place early in her career. But with success and the financial rewards of recognition, she sought the solitude of rural Connecticut. She wrote *Ship of Fools* there after working for 3 years, with no telephone and few visitors.

Ochse (1990) emphasized the importance of solitude for many creative personalities. In fact, the habit of working alone seems to be a common trait of those who attain distinction in their fields. Solitude minimizes interruptions, which can be devastating to a writer lost in thought, and enables the development of long trains of thought. Ochse cites Walter Cannon's complaint that his creativity was stifled by interruptions or even the fear that they might occur. He also noted Charles Babbage's autobiography, in which he railed against the losses in his creative work brought on by interruptions.

Besides affecting concentration, the environment may induce moods and other retrieval cues that yield relevant knowledge tucked away in long-term memory. Skinner's behavioral concept of stimulus control has application in designing writing environments (Boice, 1990). In a particular environment in which an individual writes and does little else, the environment cues the desired behavior. I believe this phenomenon can be reinterpreted in terms of the cognitive concept of encoding specificity. The abstract ideas, images, plans, tentative sentences, feelings, and other personal symbols that represent the knowledge needed to construct a text are associated with the place and time of the writing environment. These associations are strongest when the writer engages in few if any extraneous activities in the selected environment. Entering the environment serves as a retrieval cue for the relevant knowledge to enter the writer's awareness. Once the writer's attention turns to the ideas that pop into consciousness, the composing process flows again. Particular features of the environment may serve as specific prompts for retrieving, creating, and thinking.

For instance, a scene outside an office window, a painting hanging on the wall, or a plant sitting in the corner may become associated with thinking deeply about a particular text under development. Staring at the feature elicits knowledge representations bearing on the problem at hand.

Boice (1990) has developed a treatment program to help professors and other professionals who must write for a living with the problem of writer's block. A key component of his program is the rearranging of the writing environment. He recommends that the writer "establish one or a few *regular* places in which you do *all* serious writing" and "nothing but serious writing; other writing (e.g., correspondence) would be carried out elsewhere" (p. 76). Boice insists that magazines, novels, and other nonessential reading material be banned, social interactions minimized or eliminated, and cleaning and straightening up of the place delayed until a writing session is completed. By following these recommendations, the writer creates a space solely to think and write, avoiding extraneous activities. This space, therefore, becomes associated with all the mental products of creating meaning and can then serve as a unique retrieval cue for those products.

The point about cleaning up what may become a very messy working environment can, of course, be viewed merely as an admonishment not to procrastinate. But the messy work environment may serve the writer directly as a retrieval cue. For example, in the space I use for my serious writing, the tables and desk are covered with piles of articles, books, computer printouts, and notes of various types. The piles are organized, more or less, according to topic. The physical environment serves as a retrieval cue to content knowledge that I need in writing. By scanning the piles and then sorting through the materials in a given pile, I remember ideas and topics that are needed for a particular section of text.

Will the importance of the environment, if shared by others, make it difficult to rely exclusively on computer systems, at least as presently designed, for the storage of needed information? Without piles of hard copy at hand, the writer may lose a critical aid to memory retrieval. Whether hypertext systems effectively replace this aid or perhaps even improve upon it is uncertain at present. Hansen and Haas (1988) described how paper copies are more tangible to readers and writers than electronic representations of the same information. This tangibility, I suggest, may play an important memorial role in the writing task. Designing high degrees of tangibility into computer tools in the future poses worthwhile challenges.

I close this section with an appeal to authority. Thomas Mann, in a letter to Viktor Polzer, described the features of an environment conducive to writing, some connected with thinking and some with translating ideas into text on paper (John-Steiner, 1985). Take particular note of his comments about the clutter of papers in his working environment:

> For writing I must have a roof over my head, and since I enjoy working by the sea better than anywhere else, I need a tent or a wicker beach chair. Much of my composition, as I have said, has been conceived on walks; I also regard movement in the open air as the best means of reviving my energy for work. For a longer book I usually have a heap of preliminary papers close at hand during the writing; scribbled notes, memory props, in part purely objective—external details, colorful odds and ends—or else psychological formulations, fragmentary inspirations, which I use in their proper place. (p. 76)

Surveys

Boice and Johnson (1984) examined two aspects of the environment selected by faculty for writing. They found that 40% wrote in the same place and 60% selected different places. For amount of distraction, they found that 56% of the sample chose a quiet environment, while the remainder wrote under varying degrees of distraction.

Hartley and Branthwaite (1989), in their study of productive psychologists in Britain, painted a picture of the typical work environment. The psychologists write mainly in a study or office at home. They seek quiet conditions without distractions. These findings corroborated an earlier study of mine that surveyed science and engineering faculty on their work habits and other aspects of writing method in producing technical documents (Kellogg, 1986a).

The results for the survey items concerning the environment are shown in Table 9.1. Each item assessed how often the respondent used a particular method on a 7-point scale. Every method question included a blank "Other" line for respondents to provide additional information not covered clearly in the survey. Specifically, they were asked, "How often do you write in each of the following locations?" and "How often do you write in an environment with the following noise conditions?"

The mean, mode, and standard deviation for the 121 respondents are shown in Table 9.1. There was a strong preference for working in a university office and a home office. The location, however, made no difference in terms of productivity. *Productivity* referred to the number of journal articles, technical reports, books, and grant proposals/reports completed over a 3-year period. Although a library was not a popular alternative site, a variety of locations other than home and university offices

TABLE 9.1.   Analysis of the Writing Environment

Survey Item	Mean	Mode	Standard Deviation	Productivity Correlation (r)
Location				
University office	5.28	6.00	1.36	−.06
Home office	4.58	6.00	1.77	−.01
Library	1.74	1.00	1.12	.09
Noise				
Quiet	4.14	5.00	1.97	.21*
Personnel and equipment	2.88	1.00	1.92	.12
Radio	2.74	1.00	1.87	.08
Television	1.86	1.00	1.46	.14
Stereo music	2.35	1.00	1.63	.11

Note: The response scale ranged from "Never" (1) to "Always" (7).

*$p < .05$.

Source: From Kellogg, 1986a. Copyright © 1986 by Human Sciences Press. Reprinted by permission.

were listed in the blank "Other" space. These included restaurants, airport waiting rooms, and various locations in the home, such the patio and living room.

With regard to background sound, the most frequent response was 5 on a 7-point scale for selecting a quiet environment and 1 for all sources of distraction. The frequency of selecting a quiet environment was reliably related to productivity. The size of this effect is modest at best, however, accounting for only about 4% of the variance in productivity.

The diversity in environments chosen by writers, from Proust's cork-lined room to Sarraute's Parisian cafe, suggests the flexibility of human thought. A person can think in any environment, though some locations become habitual for certain individuals. The key is to find an environment that allows concentrated absorption in the task and maximum exposure to retrieval cues that release relevant knowledge from long-term memory. Thornton Wilder sums up the role of finding the proper writing environment as follows (Cowley, 1959):

> So the only environment the artist needs is whatever peace, whatever solitude, and whatever pleasure he can get at not too high a cost. All the wrong environment will do is run his blood pressure up; he will spend more time being frustrated or outraged. My own experience has been that the tools I need for my trade are paper, tobacco, food, and a little whisky. (pp. 125–126)

Work Scheduling

To begin, consider the following extreme schedules. One writer may sit down in front of a word processor only for brief sessions that never last more than 30 minutes, while another never tries to compose without having at least 3 hours available. I anticipate that the two engage in different writing processes. The long work session should be more conducive to collecting, planning, translating, and reviewing in a recursive fashion. The brief work session, by contrast, should encourage the writer to plan and collect prior to sitting down at the word processor. The 30-minute writing session probably would consist primarily of translating and reviewing. In this example, I assume that two writers perform at the same level of skill and productivity, and that both think and write for the same amount of time in total.

It is hardly surprising that productive writers are those who spend much time at their task. More interesting is that the line between working and not working can be fuzzy indeed. James Thurber commented on his own work scheduling in this way (Cowley, 1958):

> I never quite know when I'm not writing. Sometimes my wife comes up to me at party and says, "Dammit, Thurber, stop writing." She usually catches me in the middle of a paragraph. Or my daughter will look up from the dinner table and ask, "Is he sick?" "No," my wife says, "He's writing something." (p. 96)

Similarly, the musical composer Ellen Zwilich (1985) found herself engaged in work not only at times of directed thinking about a task but also at times of undirected and recurrent thinking throughout the day. She captured the consuming nature of composing in the following observations:

> I spend a few hours a day actively engaged in writing music, but being a composer is like being a writer of any sort—there's never a moment when you're not working. I attend concerts as a composer, think about life as a composer. (p. 29)

Thurbur and Zwilich represent one extreme. The opposite extreme consists of blocked writers who go to great lengths to avoid writing. As noted in Chapter 5, blocking is not uncommon and is deadly for productivity. Between these extremes, one can ask how work time is distributed—massed in binge writing or spaced in regular, shorter sessions? The time of day when writers work is also of interest.

Anecdotes

There is perhaps no better place to begin than with the habits of Ernest Hemingway, who avoided speaking too much about how he wrote for fear it would interfere with the creative process. He told an interviewer that it is "bad for a writer to talk about how he writes" (Plimpton, 1963, p. 3). Plimpton (1989) cited a rare interview with him that revealed his work scheduling:

> When I am working on a book or a story I write every morning as soon after first light as possible. There is no one to disturb you and it is cool or cold and you come to your work and warm as you write. You read what you have written and, as you always stop when you know what is going to happen next, you go from there. You write until you come to a place where you still have your juice and know what will happen next and you stop and try to live through until morning when you hit it

again. You have started at six in the morning, say, and may go on until noon or be through before that. (p. 3)

Carlos Fuentes also found the morning most productive for putting words on paper, but he made use of the afternoon in an interesting way (Plimpton, 1984):

> I am a morning writer; I am writing at eight-thirty in longhand and I keep at it until twelve-thirty, when I go for a swim. Then I come back, have lunch, and read in the afternoon until I take my walk for the next day's writing. I must write the book out in my head now, before I sit down. I always follow a triangular pattern on my walks here in Princeton: I go to Einstein's house on Mercer Street, then down to Thomas Mann's house on Stockton Street, then over to Herman Broch's house on Evelyn Place. After visiting these three places, I return home, and by that time I have mentally written tomorrow's six or seven pages. (p. 346)

But not all well-known writers are so compunctual in the morning and ready to tackle the task. Gore Vidal described his reluctance to begin each day, but once started, a flow state appeared to take hold (Plimpton, 1989):

> I often read for an hour or two. Clearing the mind. I'm always reluctant to start work, and reluctant to stop. The most interesting thing about writing is the way that it obliterates time. Three hours seem like three minutes. (p. 63)

Edward Albee observed that procrastination works only for a while (Plimpton, 1989):

> There's a time to go to the typewriter. It's like a dog—the way a dog before it craps wanders around in circles—a piece of earth, an area of grass, circles it for a long time before it squats. It's like that—figuratively circling the typewriter getting ready to write, and then finally one sits down. I think I sit down to the typewriter when it's time to sit down to the typewriter. (p. 49)

In response to a question about what time of day he found best for writing, William Styron responded (Cowley, 1958):

> The afternoon. I like to say up late at night and get drunk and sleep late. I wish I could break the habit but I can't. The afternoon is the only time I have left and I try to use it to the best advantage, with a hangover. (p. 271)

Not unexpectedly, some find the night hours best for composing. James Baldwin explained (Plimpton, 1989):

> I start working when everyone has gone to bed. I've had to do that ever since I was young—I had to wait until the kids were asleep. And then I was working at various jobs during the day. I've always had to write at night. But now that I'm established I do it because I'm alone at night. (p. 49)

Edmund White carried this issue further, denying that regular schedules are even necessary (Plimpton, 1989):

> Writers say two things that strike me as nonsense. One is that you must follow an absolute schedule every day. If you're not writing well, why continue it? I just don't think this grinding away is useful. (p. 65)

The notion of work schedules in a task as intimate and engrossing as writing is tricky to define clearly, as Thurber implied in his remarks on writing during what seemed like every waking moment. Henry Miller captured this point well in the following statement (Plimpton, 1989):

> Each man has his own way. After all, most writing is done away from the typewriter, away from the desk. I'd say it occurs in the quiet, silent moments, while you're walking or shaving or playing a game or whatever, or even talking to someone you're not vitally interested in. You're working, your mind is working, on this problem in the back of your head. So, when you get to the typewriter it's a mere matter of transfer. (p. 83)

Surveys

Boice and Johnson (1984) found that only 13% of their sample of academicians wrote on a daily basis. Sporadic, binge writing was much more common, with 56% procrastinating until the deadline loomed. They found that the most productive writers adopted a schedule of writing at least once a week. Furthermore, Boice (1982, 1983) found that contingency management programs that require regular writing sessions are effective in overcoming procrastination and blocking.

Hartley and Branthwaite (1989) reported that productive psychologists devoted 2 to 5 hours to writing on a weekly basis. Instead of writing for just short periods of time, they concentrated on a writing project for an extended session, the exact length varying with the nature of the project. The time of day selected for working varied with individuals; essentially any time of the day was fruitful for at least some respondents.

My survey of science and engineering faculty showed a similar pattern for work scheduling (Kellogg, 1986a). Table 9.2 presents the results for the hour of the day, the duration, and the regularity of writing. The respondents tended to work between 8 A.M. and 8 P.M., with the morning hours being the most common time of day; these data correspond well with the interviews of well-known writers in showing a preference for tackling the task first thing in the morning. Interestingly, research on circadian rhythms indicates that performance on intellectual tasks peaks during morning hours, in contrast to the afternoon and evening peaks for perceptual-motor tasks (Folkard & Monk, 1985). Even so, the positive correlations with productivity obtained for these time intervals proved unreliable. Night owls, though rare, were not unique in their productivity.

In terms of the duration of writing sessions, the data indicate a preference for 1 to 3 hours. Working for 1 or 2 hours was reliably correlated with productivity. A

TABLE 9.2. Analysis of Work Scheduling

Survey Item	Mean	Mode	Standard Deviation	Productivity Correlation (r)
Midnight–4 A.M.	1.76	1.00	1.29	.01
4 A.M.–8 A.M.	1.87	1.00	1.49	.04
8 A.M.–noon	4.61	6.00	1.44	.17
Noon–4 P.M.	4.34	4.00	1.33	.15
4 P.M.–8 P.M.	3.60	4.00	1.54	.13
8 P.M.–midnight	3.80	2.00	1.80	.05
Duration				
0–1 hour	3.50	2.00	1.58	.09
1–2 hours	4.46	6.00	1.40	.22*
2–3 hours	4.44	6.00	1.36	.07
3–4 hours	3.49	4.00	1.63	−.04
More than 4 hours	2.76	1.00	1.73	−.12
Regularity				
Every working day	3.01	3.00	1.50	.11

Note: The response scale ranged from "Never" (1) to "Always" (7).

*p < .05

Source: From Kellogg, 1986a. Copyright © 1986 by Human Sciences Press. Reprinted by permission.

multiple regression analysis cast doubt that duration was important; it just happened to correlate with the use of outlines, which clearly did correlate with productivity. Still, the preference for sessions of less than 3 hours fits well with the outcome of a comprehensive study of the time spent in deliberate, highly effortful practice and training by musicians and athletes (Ericsson, Krampe, & Tesch-Römer, 1993).

Highly regular writing schedules was not the rule; the most common response was only a 3 on the 7-point scale. "Write in spurts" and "Marathon writing just before a deadline" were comments listed by respondents that match the pattern commonly observed in Boice and Johnson's (1984) study. In contrast to their results, though, the regularity of working every day was not reliably correlated with productivity.

To summarize, wide individual differences are found in work scheduling. As Samuel Johnson observed, "A man may write at any time, if he will set himself doggedly to it" (Bartlett, 1992). No particular work schedule is associated with high productivity. Even working on a regular basis yields a mixed pattern of results, in contrast to the obvious prediction that the more time spent on a task, the greater the productivity.

Rituals and States of Consciousness

Throughout this book, the difficulty of creating personal symbols and mapping them into consensual symbols of written text has been stressed. One way of shedding light on this difficulty is to consider the rituals that many writers find necessary to avoid procrastination and sustain creative work. I turn here to the role of undirected versus directed thinking and various states of consciousness in the creation of text.

Schiller presumably felt compelled to stock his desk drawer with rotten apples to achieve the right frame of mind. The assault on his olfactory sense heightened his awareness and stimulated his creativity, he believed (Stein, 1974). Balzac wore a monkish garb and drank much strong black coffee, and Mozart composed following exercise (Stein, 1974). The personal, sometimes bizarre rituals that writers use to alter their consciousness in the service of their work are treated in this section.

Anecdotes

Behavioral Rituals.   Thornton Wilder discussed a few of the rituals used by writers in his interview with Cowley (1959):

> Many writers have told me that they have built up mnemonic devices to start them off on each day's writing task. Hemingway once told me he sharpened twenty pencils; Willa Cather that she read a passage from the Bible (not from piety, she was quick to add, but to get in touch with fine prose; she also regretted that she had formed this habit, for the prose rhythms of 1611 were not those she was in search of). My springboard has always been long walks. (p. 103)

Similarly, Joseph Heller found that certain activities yielded fruitful insights (Plimpton, 1989):

> I have to be alone. A bus is good. Or walking the dog. Brushing my teeth is marvelous—it was especially so for *Catch-22*. Often when I am very tired, just before going to bed, while washing my face and brushing my teeth, my mind gets very clear . . . and produces a line for the next day's work, or some idea way ahead. I don't get my best ideas while actually writing . . . which is the agony of putting down what I think are good ideas and finding the words for them and paragraph forms for them . . . a laborious process. (p. 58)

Erskine Caldwell described a couple of unusual ritualistic behaviors (Plimpton, 1989):

> I have a red rug in my room. Wherever I've lived in life, I've carried my red rug with me. I keep it in excellent shape. I have it vacuumed; I have it dry-cleaned. . . . It's a part of my life.

> Another early method I used was to take a trip to write a short story. I'd ride a bus, from Boston to Cleveland, maybe, and get off at night once in a while to write. I'd do a story that way in about a week's time. Then, for a while, I took the night boats between Boston and New York. The Fall River Line, the New Bedford Line, the

Cape Cod Line, all going to New York at night. The rhythm of the water might have helped my sentence structure a little; at least I thought it did. (pp. 50–51)

The poet Richard Wilbur noted the state of intense concentration that he entered when composing (Plimpton, 1989):

I proceed as Dylan Thomas once told me he proceeded—it is a matter of going to one's study, or to the chair in the sun, and starting a new sheet of paper. On it you put what you've already got of the poem you are trying to write. Then you sit and stare at it, hoping that the impetus of writing out the lines that you already have will get you a few ones farther before the day is done. I often don't write more than a couple of lines in a day of, let's say, six hours of staring at the sheet of paper. Composition is, externally at least, scarcely distinguishable from catatonia. (p. 65)

Daydreaming and Dreaming. Undirected thinking also shapes writing, as described by John Hersey (Plimpton, 1989):

When the writing is really working, I think there is something like dreaming going on. I don't know how to draw the line between conscious management of what you're doing and this state. It usually takes place in the earlier states, in the drafting process. I would say it's related to day-dreaming. When I feel really engaged with a passage, I become so lost in it that I'm unaware of my real surroundings, totally involved in the pictures and sounds that the passage evokes. So I think it's a kind of dream state of some sort, though it has baffled most people who've tried to analyze just what takes place in the creative process. (p. 113)

Klinger (1990) argued that daydreams play a particularly important role in creative writing and artistry. The painter Gretchen Lane noted that "often when I paint I am in a state of daydreaming" (p. 300), in which the content and context of the work emerged in undirected thought once the topic had been decided upon. Charlotte Bronte reportedly experienced such intensely vivid daydreams that they bordered on hallucinations. Leo Tolstoy was so enthralled with his daydreams that two of three autobiographical novels had entire chapters titled daydreams. The playwright August Wilson, referring to the character Memphis in his play *Two Trains Running,* said he "just heard him up there talking away in his mind." "Now, whenever Memphis wants to talk, Wilson takes notes" (p. 299, as told to journalist Bob Erlert).

The French playwright Jean Cocteau, according to Klinger (1990), created *The Knights of the Round Table* after a "visitation." Cocteau related that "I was sick and tired of writing, when one morning, after having slept poorly, I awoke with a start and witnessed, as from a seat in a theater, three acts which brought to life an epoch and characters about which I had no documentary information and which I regarded as forbidding" (p. 299).

Even dreaming plays a role in creative work (Stein, 1974). The most commonly cited case is that of Coleridge dreaming the poem that became *Kubla Khan* upon transcription to paper. A more modern example comes from an interview with the composer of popular music, Billy Joel (Berry, 1990):

All the music I write, I've dreamt. I dream music all the time. I don't dream scenes and scenarios like most people do. I dream abstractions—shapes, colors, sounds, symphonies. I wake and I don't remember what I dreamt, but it's in my subconscious like a filing cabinet. When I sit down to write, I try to get into that filing cabinet and once in a while, a little window or drawer will pop open with the music in it and I'll be able to write it very quickly. (p. 3C)

Dreams served as a critical source of inspiration for the music created by Benjamin Britten, particularly for compositions written in the 1950s and 1960s (Wierzbicki, 1992). Britten drew on English poets for descriptions of dreams and what they reveal about the meaning of life. Wierzbicki noted that

for Keats, dreams could be "more serene than Cordelia's countenance, more full of visions than a high romance." For Shelley they amounted to "thought's wilderness," and for Wordsworth they brought "a substantial dread . . . conjured up from tragic fictions." For Shakespeare, the dream state was sometimes a scary pricker of the conscience. . . . At other times, though, the dream for Shakespeare was a blissful retreat. (p. 3C)

Shakespeare, Shelley, Keats, Wordsworth, Tennyson, Middleton, and Wilfred Owen wrote poetry about dreaming that Britten drew upon in composing "Nocturne" and "A Midsummer Night's Dream." Britten's music aimed to reveal the truths that dreams reveal about our lives and explored the notion that reality might be better apprehended in the undirected dream state than in the directed state of waking consciousness (Wierzbicki, 1992).

Recurrent thinking may also enter into creative work. Feldman (1988) gave an account of a dream that he had about once a week for 3 years:

The dream consisted simply of an amusement park ride in motion. I was aware after several repetitions of the dream that this image was somehow related to my work, specifically to my efforts to understand development and creativity. I told almost no one about this dream, although I do remember once discussing it with the small group of research assistants I was working with at Yale. It was clear to me that this image was central and intimate and important, and I was embarrassed that I had no idea what it was. (p. 272)

The answer came to Feldman as a sudden insight while taking a shower in a hotel, sharing a room with a colleague at a professional conference. The insight even sent him out of the shower, in classic form, to tell his roommate of his discovery. He realized: "The ride is not inside, it's outside," meaning that the image referred to a macro-level model of how coinciding forces "set the stage, stimulate, and catalyze change" (p. 275) in development.

Feldman stressed the importance of dreaming and other alternative forms of consciousness in the meaning-making process. He contended that in his anecdote a "series of parallel efforts toward solution of a problem was going on, one set consciously directed toward problem solution through direct application, the other set through less conscious, indirectly applied processes that manifested themselves in certain kinds of dreams, of whose purpose I became increasingly aware'' (p. 287). Eventually, the parallel efforts converge, as when one discusses the dreams with a colleague or reflects upon them in the shower. Feldman continued:

> Essentially, the dreams were showing me that my mind was quite spontaneously *making new things*. That these new things may have been produced in part out of already existing things does not diminish the fact that by the hundreds and thousands, my mind was showing me that it had the ability to produce a virtual torrent of small transformations and to produce them in coherent, organized ways. I was at times transforming things so rapidly and fluidly that it seemed as if my mind were designed to do nothing else. (p. 287)

The interconnection between dreaming and directed thinking may not be the only path to creation of new meanings for writers. For example, the novelist Garcia Marquez diminished the importance of dreams in his own work (Plimpton, 1984):

> In the very beginning I paid a good deal of attention to them. But then I realized that life itself is the greatest source of inspiration and that dreams are only a very small part of that torrent that is life. What is very true about my writing is that I'm quite interested in different concepts of dreams and interpretations of them. I see dreams as part of life in general, but reality is much richer. But maybe I just have very poor dreams. (p. 331)

Alcohol and Drugs.   Besides dreaming and daydreaming, alternate states of consciousness induced by alcohol and other mind-altering substances have been tried as inducements to creative flow. The legendary E. B. White shared the following description of his ritual for beginning the task (Plimpton, 1989):

> I have no warm-up exercises, other than to take an occasional drink. I am apt to let something simmer for a while in my mind before trying to put it into words. I walk around, straightening pictures on the wall, rugs on the floor—as though not until everything in the world was lined up and perfectly true could anybody reasonably expect me to set a word down on paper. (p. 64)

Some writers have taken more than an occasional drink to induce writing. Malcolm Cowley commented on the role of alcohol (Plimpton, 1989):

> One of the reasons why Hart, and many writers, turn into alcoholics is that early in their lives they find that getting drunk is part of the creative process, that it opens up visions. It's a terrible sort of creative device, because three out of four who involve themselves in it become alcoholics. But it does open up doors in the beginning. Hart Crane would even make a first draft when he was drunk; he'd come out and read it, and say, ''Isn't this the greatest poem ever written?'' It wasn't. But then he would work over it patiently, dead sober, for several weeks, and it would amount to something. Not the greatest poem ever written, but still extraordinary. (p. 231)

Tennessee Williams followed a similar pattern of alcoholic creation and sober revision (Plimpton, 1984):

> In Key West I get up just before daybreak, as a rule. I like being completely alone in the house in the kitchen when I have my coffee and ruminate what I'm going to work on. I usually have two or three pieces of work going at the same time, and then I decide which to work on that day. I go to my studio. I usually have some wine there. And then I carefully go over what I wrote the day before. You see, baby, after a glass or two of wine I'm inclined to extravagance. I'm inclined to excesses because I drink while I'm writing, so I'll blue pencil a lot the next day. (p. 99)

But certainly not all well-known writers condone indulgence in alcohol as a stimulant to work. John Irving explained the hazard (Plimpton, 1989):

> The irony is that drinking is especially dangerous to novelists; memory is vital to us. I'm not so down on drinking for writers from a moral point of view; but booze is clearly not good for writing *or* for driving cars. You know what Lawrence said: "The novel is the highest example of subtle interrelatedness that man has discovered." I agree! And just consider for one second what drinking does to "subtle interrelatedness." Forget the "subtle"; "interrelatedness" is what makes novels work—without it you have no narrative momentum; you have incoherent rambling. Drunks ramble; so do books by drunks.

In the same vein, Conrad Aiken added (Plimpton, 1989):

> I've tried it long ago, with hashish and peyote. Fascinating, yes, but no good, no. This, as we find in alcohol, is an *escape* from awareness, a cheat, a momentary substitution, and in the end a destruction of it. With luck, someone might have a fragmentary Kubla Khan vision. But with no meaning. And with the steady destruction of the observing and remembering mind. (p. 229)

Trances and Automatism.   To achieve trance states of consciousness for writing, authors have employed various forms of hypnosis. Aldous Huxley reportedly aided his writing by entering a trance induced by a meditation procedure that he called Deep Reflection. Erickson (1972) stated in describing Huxley, "it was quite common for him to initiate a day's work by entering a state of Deep Reflection as a preliminary process of marshaling his thoughts and putting into order the thinking that would enter his writing later that day" (p. 50). In this state of deep reflection, Huxley focused attention exclusively on the task before him and ignored his surroundings completely. He seemed not to even hear an auditory stimulus such as a telephone ringing.

Gertrude Stein experimented with hypnotic trances to produce automatic writing (Boice & Meyers, 1986). At the turn of the century, spiritualism boasted a strong popular following. Mesmerism induced what appeared to be creative writing and drawing. Ellenberger (1970) chronicled the era of automatic writers whose texts emerged, in theory, from the "other side"; spirits took possession of the hypnotized writer, who presumably translated, without effort, the plans of the spiritual author. Not surprisingly, William James took up the study of such automatisms and sought to relate them to the broader issue of dissociations in consciousness and personality. Gertrude Stein studied with James and co-authored a publication with Leon Solomons reporting their findings on automatic writing (Solomans & Stein, 1896).

Their work purportedly showed that through dissociations induced by distractions, such as that found under the conditions of deep hypnosis, a writer could compose fluently and creatively, without the usual struggle of conscious reflection. They examined various methods for distracting the author from the normally conscious and effortful process of composing and interpreted the automatic writing as a product of a second, dissociated personality. The text produced by this second personality often violated grammatical rules and appeared to represent an unrestrained tapping of a stream of thought. Gertrude Stein parlayed the technique, which she called *experimental writing,* into a celebrated style that drew the attention of the surrealists and others, including Ernest Hemingway (Boice & Meyers, 1986).

Under more controlled laboratory procedures, Spelke, Hirst, and Neisser (1976) documented that writers could be trained to write dictated words while simultaneously reading text with full comprehension. They found that the participants could even categorize the dictated words while maintaining full comprehension of the primary reading task. Although dictating instances of a category wins no literary recognition, the results of Spelke et al. demonstrate, in my judgment, that semantic processing and the motor components of discourse production can occur without conscious awareness and without depleting limited attentional resources (however, see Neisser, 1976, for an alternative interpretation).

The poet James Merrill practiced a similar form of automatic writing using a Ouija board. Merrill explained that he prefers a homemade version (Plimpton, 1984):

> The commercial boards come with a funny see-through planchette on legs. I find them too cramped. Besides, it's so easy to make your own—just write out the alphabet, and the numbers, and your YES and NO (punctuation marks, too, if you're going all out) on a big sheet of cardboard. Or use brown paper—it travels better. (p. 289)

The product using Merrill's method was often nearly illegible. He described the usual outcome as "drunken lines of capitals lurching across the page, gibberish until they're divided into words and sentences. It depends on the pace. Sometimes the powers take pity on us and slow down" (p. 289).

In Chapter 3, I presented the case that writing achieves at most relative automatization. The writer must adopt the perspective of the reader in tackling rhetorical problems, and this necessarily requires conscious reflection. Further, each writing task poses novel problems that demand attention. The extensive interactions among collecting, planning, translating, and reviewing processes also require cognitive effort (McCutchen, 1988). How then can a ritual invoke automatic writing?

The answer comes from an examination of the product. Gertrude Stein's stream-of-consciousness style violated rules of syntax and mechanics. The writer in a trance patently *failed* to retrieve and apply syntactic and rhetorical knowledge. Notice, too, that Merrill's "gibberish" required deciphering into words and sentences through a conscious and effortful process of editing. As Boice (1990) concluded, the surrealists who composed through what they called automatic writing actually employed a ritual-induced version of free writing. By ignoring reviewing, collecting, and all organizational and goal-setting subprocesses of planning, the free writer translates whatever enters the mind. Free writing may be a very useful step in composing, but it must then be followed with attention-demanding interactions among all operations, with special attention given to editing. Thus, rituals for writing in a trance should be viewed only as a preliminary step in the overall process of producing a finished document, at least one that conforms to formal stylistic rules.

Surveys

My survey of science and engineering faculty is a rare attempt to inquire into the rituals and frames of mind needed by professionals to compose (Kellogg, 1986a). The issue is very personal, more so than other questions about writing method, and even these draw complaints. For example, Boice and Johnson (1984) asked innocuous questions about method—none about rituals—and their survey elicited a record number of complaints to the institutional review board about invasions of privacy. Lowenthal and Wason (1977) also noted a general reluctance of academic writers to comment in their survey on writing attitudes.

The survey results are shown in Table 9.3. Many respondents often drink coffee before or during writing. Note, however, that this item showed the highest standard

TABLE 9.3.   Analysis of Rituals and States of Consciousness

Survey Item	Mean	Mode	Standard Deviation	Productivity Correlation (r)
		Rituals		
Prayer or meditation	2.16	1.00	1.87	−.14
Vigorous exercise	2.21	1.00	1.65	.25*
Walking	3.49	1.00	1.99	−.01
Drinking coffee	4.15	6.00	2.17	−.03
Smoking tobacco	1.76	1.00	1.76	.01
		States of Consciousness		
Daydreaming	2.85	3.00	1.52	.08
Mild concentration	3.45	4.00	1.48	.01
Moderate concentration	4.77	5.00	1.32	−.10
Intense concentration	5.23	6.00	1.36	.12
Trance	1.28	1.00	0.89	.08

Note: The response scale ranged from "Never" (1) to "Always" (7).

*$p < .01$.

Source: From Kellogg, 1986a. Copyright © 1986 by Human Sciences Press. Reprinted by permission.

deviation of any question in the study, indicating that a sizable minority never touch the brew, while others drink it constantly (anecdotal observation confirms this). Walking showed a similar pattern. Enough respondents gave high ratings to yield a moderate mean for the walking measure, even though the most frequent response was one. Prayer-meditation, vigorous exercise, and smoking were all idiosyncratic rituals, judging from the means and modes. Five respondents noted various snacks they eat while writing. One noted playing pinball to get in the mood. With the exception of drinking coffee, therefore, the reported rituals were as idiosyncratic as expected.

The correlations with productivity are interesting. On the one hand, the negative, nonsignificant correlation for prayer or meditation offers no support for the belief that, say, Huxley's technique of Deep Reflection would benefit most writers. To be fair, though, the specific technique of meditation may be crucial, and the present survey made no attempt to ascertain this. On the other hand, the frequency of vigorous exercise was positively and significantly correlated with productivity, supporting Mozart's alleged ritual. My own experience and conversations with other academic writers suggest that repetitive vigorous exercise, such as jogging, sometimes enables one to plan mentally what will be translated into text later, and the relaxation and positive affect that come after the workout help one to concentrate. I suspect that any ritual fostering these states, including Huxley's Deep Reflection, could well benefit a writer.

As expected, few academic writers ever enter a trance while writing. However, a state of intense concentration yielded the highest mean and mode for all items concerning states of consciousness. The mean responses were systematically lower for moderate concentration, mild concentration, and daydreaming. These findings are consistent with the view that writing invokes deep concentration, yet none of the items was significantly correlated with productivity. Although daydreaming was not frequently used by most sample participants, one noted that daydreaming was frequent during the early stages of prewriting, while intense concentration dominated draft writing.

Hartley and Branthwaite (1989) found that their two types of writers—thinkers versus doers—differed in the states of consciousness associated with writing. Doers reported daydreaming and experiencing moderate degrees of concentration more often than thinkers.

Writing and thinking are effortful endeavors, and the methods used to encourage both offer an intriguing picture of human beings as symbol creators and manipulators. We have now examined the literature on how knowledge, personality, strategies, tools, work environments, schedules, and rituals influence the writing process and writing performance. It is time to reflect back on the theoretical framework proposed in this book and to address its problems and implications.

10

The Psychology of Symbol Creation

The fact is that several major lines of thought have arrived almost simultaneously at the recognition of the basic mental function that distinguishes man from non-human creatures—the use, in one way or another, of symbols to convey concepts.

SUZANNE LANGER

I defined thinking as the creation and manipulation of personal symbols that provide an internal model of our world. Meaning-making is a significant form of thinking that entails work not only in the private domain of mental experience but also in the public domain of shared discourse. We render experience meaningful by creating consensual symbols that refer to objects and events, beliefs and intentions, memories and fantasies. *Acts of meaning*, to use Bruner's (1990) phrase, define the scope of human behavior and culture. We take the experiences encountered in life and imbue them with significance. We achieve this by creating consensual symbol systems that express the personal symbols of thoughts, feelings, recollections, fantasies, and dreams. Through these consensual symbol systems, we communicate with one another about the significance of our experience. Through these systems, we develop both shared and conflicting beliefs and goals that take us beyond the private, isolated world of our own personal symbols.

Cognitive psychology to date has focused on the processing of information rather than the making of meaning. We process information from the world of natural objects and events and from the artifactual world of consensual symbols, such as text, speech, art, and music. Questions about how we create meaningful information have been too often slighted. Although research on the comprehension and production of speech shows balance, cognitive psychologists have been more concerned with how we read texts than with how we write them in the first place. I envision a psychology of human cognition that places the creative aspects of oration, musical composition, painting, sculpting, and dancing, as well as writing, at its center, for these are the very activities that set our species apart.

A large and rapidly expanding literature on the process of writing has developed primarily from the efforts of scholars in education and the humanities. The failure of cognitive psychologists to take much interest in this work is ironic given that the cognitive models advanced by Flower and Hayes and by Bereiter and Scardamalia have proved so influential. This book has treated the intersection of thinking, meaning-making, and writing while recognizing that a full account of any one of these topics lies beyond the scope of a single volume. My dual intent has been to interest the cognitive psychologist in the topic of writing and to interest the educator and composition researcher in a broader view of what cognitive psychology has to offer them.

In this final chapter, I integrate the key themes of the book and speculate about some of their implications. I begin with the mindfulness of writing and contrast this with the mindlessness observed in so many other forms of human thought and behavior. Second, I examine some implications of and problems for the view that consciousness is organized by a constructive narrator. Third, I discuss some practical applications of the views set forth here in education and in psychotherapy. I conclude with a brief look at the niche occupied by *Homo symbolificus* in the realms of animal and artificial intelligence.

Mindfulness in Writing

The act of writing often reveals the human mind in its most mindful state. We have seen that the highly interactive components of writing require large investments of attention. Even when a writer satisfices on performance in an attempt to lessen the investment of cognitive effort in a writing task, the degree of automatization obtained is only relative. In sharp contrast to what is seen in the development of other skills, as writers mature and gain expertise, they invest more effort and reflective thought in the task. As one becomes an expert typist, the task demands less attention; not so with original composition. The shift from knowledge-telling to knowledge-transforming represents, if anything, a shift to more effortful writing. We have seen that amplifying the quality of text produced depends on engaging the process of writing fully and mindfully in a state of creative flow.

The effortful labor of writing can perhaps best be seen in the cycle of cognition that underlies knowledge transformation. The cycle shows us that the process of exploring our environment and transforming our knowledge is continuous and never-ending. As an act of meaning-making, composing a text is as much a form of learning as it is a form of communicating. The determination of when the final draft of a text is finished is in a sense arbitrary; the deadlines imposed by others or self-imposed by the author stop the cycle of thinking, exploring, and learning. But in principle, an author could revise a text endlessly, continuously gaining new insights and reshaping the text for ever more effective communication with an increasingly well-understood audience.

The picture of *Homo symbolificus* in the act of making meaning through writing reveals an active, engaged, intelligent, and mindful creature. But not all human behavior fits this picture. Indeed, Ellen Langer (1989) has suggested that much adult behavior is characterized by mindlessness. We often think and act without any deliberation or reflection on what we are doing or about the consequences of our actions.

Certainly in infants and young children, mindless behavior is not only common, it may well be inevitable. Karmiloff-Smith (1990) concluded, from studies of drawing, that the thinking and behavior of young children are restricted to automatic routines. A 5-year-old can mindlessly draw a stick figure of a man, for example, but lacks the capacity to reflect on the figure and alter it in a deliberate and creative fashion. Drawing a two-headed man or a bizarre, nonexistent man is virtually impossible at that age. The young child has an implicit schema for a person that may automatically trigger motor movements needed to draw a normal man, but has not yet developed a sufficiently explicit representation or personal symbol. Without such an explicit representation, mindful, flexible thinking is not possible. By the ages of 8 to 10, children can mindfully consider a mental image of a man and imagine how to add new elements or alter the orientation or position of the figure.

Mindlessness takes three forms: entrapment by categories, automatic behavior, and acting from a single perspective (Langer, 1989). When we rely too much on remembering or reproducing old concepts and categories and not enough on creating new ones, we fall prey to entrapment. Social prejudice and confirmation bias—the tendency to seek evidence that confirms our hypotheses about the world—illustrate *category entrapment*. *Automatic behavior* refers to habits entrenched through practice. We act without thinking of alternative actions because of the force of habit. *Acting from a single perspective* refers to following a rule slavishly, without reflecting on alternatives. We limit our sampling of features from the environment to those needed to invoke the rule in question. For instance, cooking by recipe, with no variations on the rule, illustrates mindless action in this sense.

Although the phenomenon of mindlessness seems at odds with the view that thinking and creating lie at the heart of human nature, a careful examination suggests otherwise. First of all, the phenomena described by Langer should not be surprising in light of the assumption that people seek to satisfice and minimize the expenditure of cognitive effort. We settle for at best satisfactory but mediocre levels of performance in exchange for economizing attentional resources. Certainly entrapment by categories and acting from a single perspective limit the creative application of knowledge to the problems and situations created by our environment. We doubtless meet those challenges less effectively than we might if a more mindful approach were adopted. Still, we get by, bumbling on to the next situation, perhaps happy in knowing implicitly that we have conserved our attentional resources for the crisis that may be waiting around the corner.

Because the cognitive demands of writing and other forms of making meaning are great, mindless behavior may well be adaptive for us. If writers sought to mindfully engage every problem posed by their environment—those in the physical, social, and cultural realms, as well as those posed by immediate tasks—then depletion of resources and exhaustion would seem inevitable. An image comes to mind here of the frenetic perfectionist whose neurotic behavior exhausts his creative ability.

Furthermore, carrying out activities mindlessly, particularly the automatic behaviors described by Langer, allows one to focus exclusively on the task of creating meaning. Entering a state of creative flow in writing may well be more likely when routine social interactions and other daily needs proceed automatically. My image here is of the so-called absentminded professor whose forgetfulness in the realm of the mundane enables superior mindfulness in the creative realm.

Langer (1989) called for people to develop a state of mindfulness as a way to think and act more intelligently. Although I doubt that being mindful about everything is wise, the general point is well taken and wholly consistent with a theme of this book. Achieving one's full potential as a writer calls for total absorption in the task. It may well be that writing often represents a sure path to developing mindfulness in general. Ornstein (1991) placed the concept of mindfulness in the context of evolutionary theory, suggesting that further development of our species requires greater mindfulness, greater conscious reflection, and the ability to actively choose our destiny. Perhaps writing and other acts of meaning already have been to an extent and shall increasingly become the primary tools for further advances in human intelligence.

The Constructive Narrator

The constructive narrator embodies ideas that are under discussion in assorted scholarly tribes of psychologists, anthropologists, literary theorists, and philosophers. The core idea is that the construction of the contents of consciousness typically conforms to a narrative structure. A theoretical narrator habitually weaves stories from the events of perception, imagination, and memory as a means of establishing coherence and meaning. As Fuller (1979) noted: "The need to make life coherent, to make a story out of it, is probably so basic that we are unaware of its importance" (p. 224). I turn now to four critical issues for this point of view.

Relation to Narrative Discourse

I begin by considering what theorists know about the structure of narrative discourse and its relation to the narrator of consciousness. The issue of what makes a story has resisted the formalizations of scholars; it is best regarded as a natural concept with fuzzy boundaries. Specifying the defining features that enable one to draw a sharp boundary between what is and is not a story has proved difficult (Leitch, 1986). It is generally agreed, first and foremost, that stories are dynamic and sequential in nature.

Simple narrative relates events chronologically, whereas narrative with plot may deviate from strict chronology, with remembered past and imagined future events intertwined with present events. A narrative begins with one situation, and a series of changes occurs through time that are causally linked. The setting, theme, plot, and resolution emerge from the sequence. The constituents of narrative are the "unique sequence of events, mental states, happenings involving human beings as characters or actors" that acquire their meaning "by their place in the overall configuration of the sequence as a whole—its plot or *fabula*" (Bruner, 1990, p. 43).

A second characteristic of narrative is that the distinction between "real" and "imaginary" is unimportant (Bruner, 1990). The plot is determined by the sequence of events, not the truth or falsity of each one. Consider the work of an empirical historian, a historical novelist, and a fictional novelist. All three can yield powerful stories, regardless of their varying degrees of truth.

A third characteristic of narrative is the way it handles ordinary and exceptional events. The story readily assimilates events that fit the plot and highlights those that do not as requiring special attention (Bruner, 1990). In reading a narrative, a person searches for some explanation or set of reasons as to why the unexpected took place. Causality and order reign; an individual finds meaning by discovering, imposing, or creating sequential and causal relationships.

Lastly, stories possess a dramatic quality. Burke's (1945) pentad of an actor, an action, a goal, a scene, and an instrument sets the stage, and imbalances between pairs of these elements yield the drama. Specifically, Burke proposed that stories relate to moral values. When an action deviates from the goal, it must be rectified. Drama emerges from the troubles that occur in the story that demand resolution in a moral world. Once again, narratives emphasize the importance of establishing causal relations and order, as defined by an individual's knowledge and beliefs.

Kintsch (1974), Mandler (1984), Thorndyke (1977), Meyer (1975), and others have provided detailed models of the comprehension of and memory for discourse structures. Story processing has received the most attention. A narrative schema may operate by establishing a setting, theme, plot, and resolution of conflict according to a grammar such as that proposed by Thorndyke. Alternatively, a narrative schema may operate along the lines proposed by Trabasso and van den Broek (1985) in their reading model.

Trabasso and van den Broek suggested that the reader first establishes a setting or context and then revises this context as new information emerges. The circumstances of the context create a large set of causes and conditions wherein connections are either necessary or necessary and sufficient. To illustrate, I quote from Trabasso and van den Broek (1985):

> In identifying a causal relation between event A and event B as necessary in the circumstances, a counterfactual criterion is applied: Event A is said to be necessary for event B, in the circumstances, in that if event A had not occurred, then event B also would not have occurred. A causal relation, by these criteria, defines a logical dependency between A and B. An event is sufficient, in the sense that if event A is put into the circumstances and the events are allowed to go on from there, event B will occur. (p. 617)

Discourse-processing models may shed light on the means by which the narrator establishes sequences and causal relations. Wholesale adoption of a particular model of discourse processing is misguided, however. Reading romances, fairy tales, fables, and other forms of stories calls for nuances and twists that need not characterize a narrator of everyday experience. If a narrative system in fact constructs conscious experience, then it must surely be a general one. The narrator hypothesis sheds light on why and how people go about seeking and discovering meaning in all its forms, not merely in how they read and write narrative texts.

Writing Narratives

Although the narrator is not the same as the schema for processing narrative discourse, the composition of narratives may be privileged in a sense. Perhaps the narrator provides a scaffold for the early acquisition of narrative schemata. Perhaps the practice that individuals receive with narratives from an early age results in a higher degree of expertise with this type of text relative to others. If that is so, then one would expect to find that writing a narrative text is less effortful than writing descriptive, expository, and persuasive texts. This prediction is predicated on holding equal the other factors affecting the expenditure of effort, such as the degree of topic knowledge.

Engelhard, Gordon, and Gabrielson (1991) reported that college students compose higher-quality narrative texts than they do descriptive and expository texts. Mature writers certainly possess schemata for persuasive, expository, descriptive, and narrative writing tasks (Flower & Hayes, 1984). Yet, in the absence of intensive instruction in descriptive, expository, and persuasive writing, I would expect to find that the narrative text structure is most engrained.

Consistent with this line of reasoning, Britton, Burgess, Martin, McLeod, and Rosen (1975) reported an advantage for narrative composition. They studied writers composing with inkless pens and carbon paper. The writers were handicapped by being unable to read the text produced, a key component of the task environment. Under these adverse conditions, the participants struggled greatly in composing persuasive essays. But the inkless pens did not appear to interfere with the composition of narratives. Similarly, Ransdell (1989) reported that participants judge persuasive expositions to be subjectively more difficult to write than narratives.

One difficulty with these studies is that one cannot safely conclude that narratives are specially privileged. Without a third type, such as descriptive text, the pattern is unclear. Equally one could argue that persuasive writing is especially difficult rather than stating that narrative writing is especially easy. This alternative appears plausible; addressing the doubts of the reader may be less troublesome in telling a story than in arguing a position (though holding a reader's interest in storytelling certainly is not trivial). It is also important to assess directly the engagement of cognitive effort during composition.

Reed, Burton, and Kelly (1985) examined three types of writing and measured overall cognitive effort using secondary RTs. Although narratives tended to demand the least cognitive effort for most writers, their results were statistically unreliable, probably because of the low statistical power of their design. My colleagues and I continued this line of research by borrowing the narrative, descriptive, and persuasive writing tasks from Reed et al. (1985) in an experiment designed with adequate statistical power (Kellogg, Krueger, & Blair, 1991). As in my previous research, directed introspection and secondary RTs indexed the cognitive effort devoted to planning, translating, and reviewing. We anticipated that the composition process would be least effortful in the narrative condition.

Each participant composed two texts, one in longhand and one on a word processor. The students wrote on test taking and drinking alcohol; both topics were familiar to them, and the drinking topic was previously used by Reed et al. (1985).

We also borrowed from Reed et al. a dozen questions posed to the participants as a prewriting activity lasting for 5 minutes. These questions prompted the writers to think about the topic in the form of a narrative, descriptive, or persuasive composition. We instructed them to use the questions as much as they wished, but not to feel compelled to answer all the questions in their writing.

We held the topics constant across composition types to avoid confounding type with the nature of the topic. To illustrate, students in the narrative condition gave a chronological account of an event that involved drinking or taking a test, depending on the topic. Those in the descriptive condition described a person or place involved in drinking or taking a test. Finally, those in the persuasive condition took a stand for or against a proposition. In one case, the proposition was that the legal drinking age should be lowered to 18. In the other case, it was that all graduating seniors must pass a test in their major field in order to graduate.

The degree of interference in RT, relative to baseline times obtained when the participants were not writing, reflected the cognitive effort devoted to the writing process. The means for cognitive effort, in terms of reaction interference in milliseconds, are shown in Figure 10.1 as a function of composition type and composing process. Narrative writing demanded significantly less effort than both descriptive and persuasive writing across all three processes. The narrative advantage observed in Figure 10.1 was obtained when writing both with a word processor and in longhand.

Thus, despite obvious differences among individuals in the availability of content and discourse knowledge, knowledge of narrative text structures may be possessed by all people at a relatively high level of expertise. This is not to say that one cannot develop exceptional expertise about narratives—storytellers, novelists, and narrativity scholars do exactly that. Moreover, this is not to say that the weaving of a good short story or novel comes effortlessly. It surely does not. This is to say that narrative writing appears to be privileged in relation to cognitive effort. The relative ease with which this type of text is written follows from the view that people acquire narrative schemata in the natural course of early cognitive development. I turn to the developmental evidence on this point in the next section.

Nonnarrative Thinking

Bruner (1986) distinguished the narrative mode of thinking from the paradigmatic or logico-scientific mode and contended that neither can be reduced to the other. As Bruner explained:

> There are two modes of cognitive functioning, two modes of thought, each providing distinctive ways of ordering experience, of constructing reality. The two (though complementary) are irreducible to one another. Efforts to reduce one mode to the other or to ignore at the expense of the other inevitably fail to capture the rich diversity of thought. (p. 11)

The paradigmatic mode invokes the arrangement of propositions in the form of a logical argument that strives to convince others of general truths. Scientific, legal,

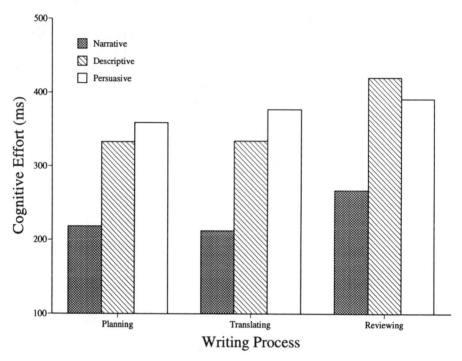

FIGURE 10.1. Cognitive effort as indexed by interference with secondary task reaction time in milliseconds for narrative, descriptive, and persuasive composition. (From Kellogg, 1993. Copyright © 1993 by *Composition Studies*, Texas Christian University. Reprinted by permission.)

and, still even on occassion, political discourses take shape through the work of paradigmatic thought. Formal reasoning and empirical proof constitute the procedures for establishing truth in this mode of thinking. By contrast, narrative thinking aims not to establish truth but rather lifelikeness or verisimilitude. As Bruner noted, a well-formed argument is structured to establish a condition of abstract truth. A well-formed story is structured to draw the reader into a convincing world of human goals, intentions, emotions, and motivations.

Bruner may be correct in his assertion that the paradigmatic mode of thinking cannot be reduced to some version of narrativity. If that is so, then where does that leave the hypothesis that conscious experience finds its structure through the actions of a narrator? The answer emerges from a consideration of cognitive development. Although paradigmatic thinking perhaps cannot be reduced to narrative thinking, it is equally plain that narrative thinking comes first in cognitive development and dominates the mental life of most people throughout life.

There are several indications that narrative thinking emerges naturally and unavoidably with linguistic and cognitive development (Lucariello, 1990). Nelson's (1986) work on learning concepts and structuring events suggests that young children are predisposed to arrange their experience in terms of sequence and causality. Work on story comprehension by Stein and her colleagues also underscore the early emergence of the narrative mode of thinking. For example, Stein and Policastro (1984) reported that second-grade children recognize that a story must contain an animate protagonist and a causal sequence of events. Their rankings of the degree to which texts displayed "storiness" correlated highly with the rankings of their teachers, suggesting the presence of narrative thinking in the children as well as the adults. Stein and Glenn (1979) found that children recall stories in the order dictated by a narrative schema, with a mere 7% of the recalled statements occurring at a time other than the investigators predicted.

Further, according to Piagetian theory, by the age of 9 months, infants develop the concept of object permanence and the distinction between means and ends. Mancuso (1986) noted that these basic notions lay the groundwork for understanding causality and comprehending stories. He emphasized the early development of narrative understanding this way:

> Story structure develops epigenetically out of these structures whose early manifestations are observable in a child aged about nine months. One need not be surprised, then, at the observation that two-year-old children can understand the idea of story. (p. 101)

In contrast, logico-scientific thinking emerges only slowly, as well illustrated by the late acquisition of formal operations in the context of Piagetian theory. The abstract thinking and hypothesis-testing of formal operations are delayed at least until early adolescence (Flavell, Miller, & Miller, 1993). Thinking logically and formulating experience into well-reasoned arguments hardly come naturally or early in life. With education and with a cultural setting that prizes paradigmatic thought, the individual certainly possesses the flexibility to learn and use logical and persuasive schemata. Graduate and professional schools aim to cultivate exactly that, as exemplified by the law school refashioning the student to "think like a lawyer." But the addition of paradigmatic thinking skills surely does not displace the fundamental narrative structure of consciousness nor does it overpower the primacy of narrative thinking.

In fact, scholars are beginning to take seriously the idea that narrative thinking plays a pivotal role even in science, the bastion of paradigmatic thought. Scientific claims may not be facts but rather beliefs held for various reasons (Olson, 1992). The narrative form can serve as the glue that holds these reasons together. The gifted writings of Lewis Thomas and Stephen Jay Gould amply demonstrate that the narrative form has a clear place in scientific writing. And its place is not limited to popular scientific writing. Myers' (1990) investigation of the technical writings of two biologists pointed to the role of narrative thinking in science. Journet's (1991) analysis of scientific texts in ecology led her to conclude that the narrative serves as a powerful interpretive and rhetorical strategy in science. Thus, the narrative mode seems to slip its way into tasks that traditionally have constituted the bulwark of logico-deductive thought.

In any case, that some individuals some of the time think about and construct their conscious experience in the form of logical and scientific arguments certainly cannot be doubted. I merely point out here the fundamental nature of the narrator and the primacy of narrative thinking. Narrative thinking emerges early in development, persists throughout life, and seems to intrude even when it is less than welcome.

Dennett's Denials

Daniel Dennett (1991) addressed the fundamental question of how the brain and mind are related in *Consciousness Explained*. His primary concern was the classic philosophical issue of dualism versus monism, an issue tangential to the points I wish to make about meaning-making, thinking, and writing. Dennett took the reductionist road to his destination of monistic materialism. The mind, he contended, is nothing but a complex machine—in our case, a machine composed of neural matter. One argument he made about the nature of these neural processes challenges, or so it seems, the hypothesis of a contructive narrator.

The notion of a neuronal center that serves the role of narrator struck Dennett as "the most tenacious bad idea bedeviling our attempts to think about consciousness" (p. 108). He claimed that the narrator implies a "Cartesian Theatre," a notion that Dennett rightfully disdained. Yet his claim hinges on equating the narrator with a homunculus who sits in the audience and interprets the on-stage activity of other schemata. The term *narrator*, as explained in Chapter 2, carries this danger of misunderstanding. When schemata operate, *personal symbols* are generated; the experience of these symbols *is* the experience of consciousness. Personal symbols cannot be viewed by a homunculus, even if one existed, or by anyone else. Dennett joins Neisser (1976) and others in confusing personal and consensual symbols. There is no Cartesian Theatre and no homunculus in the audience because consensual symbols that may be scrutinized do not exist in the brain or the mind.

In place of "the" narrator, Dennett envisions the simultaneous construction of "multiple drafts" of narratives that continually undergo revision and are distributed throughout the brain. The specialized schemata or processing modules envisioned, for example, in Baars's (1988) theory of consciousness need not be centrally coordinated, according to Dennett. The automatic operations of specialist modules in perception, memory, and cognition instead generate multiple versions of consciousness that "yield, over the course of time, something *rather like* a narrative stream or sequence, which can be thought of as subject to continual editing by many processes distributed in the brain" (p. 113).

I have no quarrel with Dennett's position on this point as long as the discussion focuses on how a fundamental cognitive function can be, and often is, distributed among multiple neuronal structures and involve multiple component processes. There may be no central location in the brain where the narrator resides, piecing together the output of specialist modules scattered throughout the cortex and other brain structures (Calvin, 1990). However, at a cognitive level of description, the role for a functional narrator clearly remains. A rudimentary narrative system is still needed to organize the personal symbols of consciousness.

Dennett leaves us without a clear explanation of how multiple narrative drafts coalesce into the unitary stream of consciousness that most of us experience most of the time. Dissociative states, hallucinations, thought disorders, and even multiple personalities would be common without the action of the narrator, it seems to me. Given that we typically experience a coherent stream of personal symbols, a cognitive system is needed to account for the order. I would not insist on or even expect to find a single place in the brain where the narrator resides, any more than I would expect a localized representation of any other cognitive system. Such localization is possible but hardly necessary.

Applications in Education and Psychotherapy

I have addressed the psychology of writing from a theoretical and empirical point of view. Yet virtually every issue that I have considered contains the seeds of practical applications in the teaching of writing, in the use of writing in teaching other subjects, and in other domains. To illustrate, I briefly relate this discussion to a few of the current practices and issues in education and psychotherapy.

How well a writer composes depends in theory on the availability, accessibility, and application of relevant knowledge to the task. Teaching writing entails much more than teaching students how to use language. To be sure, students must acquire knowledge of semantics, syntax, pragmatics, rhetoric, and text structure. Yet they must also develop a rich repertoire of content knowledge, knowing the detailed facts and procedures of specialized domains and disciplines. They must further acquire the metacognitive knowledge that is essential for developing a model of their audience, for reflecting on rhetorical and content problems posed by a writing assignment, and for monitoring their progress and success in meeting goals. The emphasis placed on knowledge availability carries a sobering implication for writing instruction. To be successful, the instructor must teach the student how to think as well as write, and to do so within the specific domains called upon by a specific writing assignment.

Four instructional methods follow from the above point of view. First, writing must be incorporated into courses that teach specific domains of knowledge; it should not be isolated in composition courses. Fulwiler and Young (1989) have reviewed effective programs for writing across the curriculum. Well-educated college students must have some sense of how to write like a historian, an economist, a biologist, a journalist, and a manager, as well as like a novelist, a poet, or a literary critic, to name a few. The student needs exposure to the various subcultures of writing. Extensive reading in each discipline not only provides relevant content knowledge, it also provides models for composing quality work within that discipline.

Modeling the experts has always been an important way to acquire writing skills. However, the number of models that must be emulated has now multiplied. One concern with the multidisciplinary method is when and how to expose the developing writer to different subcultures of writing. Are some vital and others less so? Will any be learned well if the learner is taught multiple ways of communicating through text? Moreover, the subcultures of writing are constantly evolving. New technologies of writing, such as computer-based collaborative writing, hypertext, and multimedia, foretell uniquely rapid changes. How can multiple models of writing be taught when the models themselves, at the level of individual disciplines, are in flux?

Second, instructors should use writing in and out of the classroom as a tool for learning. A written text is more than a vehicle for communication with others. It is also a vehicle for expanding and transforming one's own knowledge base. The student profits from putting words on paper in order to understand a concept better. The writing may be entirely personal, or it may be used to explain the concept to another student. Exercises that focus on the learning potential of writing fit well with writing across the curriculum. Schumacher and Nash (1991) reported that such exercises track the growth of a student's content knowledge in ways that other forms of assessment miss.

One concern with the learning tool method is the danger of forgetting that students must master discourse knowledge. In using writing as a way of acquiring the content knowledge of a discipline, matters of grammar, diction, usage, mechanics, and so forth are sometimes treated as secondary concerns. The student and instructor of a content area should rightfully focus on the use of writing as a means of learning the content knowledge at hand. But trouble arises if the student wrongly concludes that discourse knowledge is less important than content knowledge. Ideally, writing as learning must seek to integrate discourse and content knowledge.

Third, although models are important, writing instruction must do more than merely present students with texts that function as prototypes for document schemata. In addition, it should teach students general strategies, such as brainstorming and free writing, that help them cope with the demands of the writing process. The use of idea processors functioning as attentional funnels and inventors may prove especially useful in teaching such general procedural knowledge.

Fourth, general procedures, though important, are again not enough by themselves. As advocated by Hillocks (1986) in his environmental mode of teaching, writing instruction should provide students with task-specific procedures tailored to a particular type of writing. The teacher must identify critical types of writing, such as argumentation, teach the procedures relevant to these types, and then guide the student in composing arguments on a task that engages the student's interest. Supporting Hillocks's position, Smagorinsky (1991) reported empirical findings on the inadequacies of presenting models alone compared to teaching general and task-specific procedures.

One concern with teaching such procedures is knowing which ones ought to be focused upon, given the limited amount of instructional time available. Smagorinsky addressed the profound challenges faced by writing instructors who must ideally cover both general and task-specific procedures. As argued here, knowledge in all its facets and multiple methods of applying this knowledge are what make a writer. Educating a writer is truly a daunting task, perhaps the broadest challenge in education.

Writing instruction is an obvious application of the psychology of writing, but it is not the only one of interest. Psychotherapists have also looked to writing as a means of personal restoration. This is not surprising in light of the themes of this book. People seek meaning in their lives. Not all must write in order to find meaning, but the mindfulness required by writing could well serve as a tool for therapy.

Pennebaker (1993) and his colleagues have documented in several studies the therapeutic value of writing about traumatic experiences that disrupt physical and psychological health. Their work showed that participants who addressed their emotional difficulties in their narrative writing had fewer visits to their health centers, missed fewer days of work, and, remarkably, exhibited signs of stronger immune system functioning.

Moreover, Pennebaker has isolated interesting differences in the content of the narrative texts created by those whose health showed strong improvement through writing. Specifically, those who improved used many negative emotional words in their writing. They also shifted from infrequent to frequent use of cognitively oriented terms, such as *understand, realize, because,* and *reason.* Over several days of writing, Pennebaker observed improvements in the organization and clarity of the stories written only by those who also improved in health. As makers of meaning, human beings need to express themselves—their emotions, insights, and efforts—to find coherence, using both oral and written forms of language. Full health may come to those who can express themselves in this manner. As Pennebaker intriguingly noted: ''The body expresses itself linguistically and biologically at the same time'' (p. 546).

Expressively writing about upsetting life events seems to help people adjust to current difficulties and appears to improve health. Spera, Morin, Buhrfeind, and Pennebaker (1993) studied professionals who had lost their jobs. They randomly assigned them either to write about the trauma of losing their jobs, to write about their specific plans for finding new work, or to not write at all. Spera et al. theorized that disclosing in writing their personal feelings and thoughts about finding themselves unemployed would change their view of their old jobs and orient them positively to finding new work.

Their results confirmed this prediction. Within 8 months of the writing treatment, only 14% of those who did not write had found full-time jobs. Strikingly, 53% of those who expressed their trauma had accepted jobs compared to 24% of those who only wrote about plans for finding work. The magnitude of this difference is impressive and its direction is counterintuitive. On the surface, one might think that putting search plans on paper would most help the job seeker. Indeed, it did help to a small degree compared with not writing at all. However, expressing feelings and thoughts of anger, confusion, and disappointment helped the job seekers in a much deeper and more powerful way; such writing enabled these subjects to develop new meanings and purposes in life.

Homo Symbolificus Revisited

Our species makes meaning, finds order in the human condition, and creates consensual symbols that communicate the significance of what we discover in our private experience. Over a half-century ago, Suzanne Langer (1942) focused attention on the fundamental drive to invent meanings and conjure stories about the human condition. Yet the quotation from Langer that opened this chapter may strike today's reader as out-of-date and sadly misinformed. After all, contemporary studies on animal cognition have painted an intriguing picture of sophisticated signing systems throughout the animal kingdom and the prospect that our primate relatives might be able to learn languages designed by us. Further, the past 50 years have witnessed the computer revolution, including artificial intelligence systems that manipulate symbols with alacrity. Where does all this leave *Homo symbolificus* in a world filled with sentient creatures and machines?

I close with some brief observations about the unique features of our species, features that seem to endure even in the face of current knowledge. I suggest that we are alone on this planet as makers of meaning and reject the charge that we are simply too vain to accept the alternative. My comments aim to provoke discussion about the implications of the views set forth in the preceding chapters, particularly those concerned with personal and consensual symbols. These implications are too complex to settle conclusively in a few pages of observations, but they are too important to ignore altogether.

Artificial Intelligence

To apprehend the difference between humans and machines that I wish to highlight here, it is instructive to examine the most radical or strongest claim of artificial intelligence (AI). The strong AI position holds that, in principle, a machine can be programmed to think, feel, and act in a manner that is indistinguishable from a human being (Penrose, 1989). If that is so, then there is no reason to deny that machines are capable of making meaning, just as humans do. The views advanced in this book conflict with the strong AI view in two ways. One follows from the distinction between personal and consensual symbols. The other concerns the drive of people to seek ultimate purpose, to find the meaning of life as a whole.

I must emphasize that neither point diminishes in the slightest the value of AI research directed at the design of expert systems, robots, and other tools that augment the intellectual and physical functioning of human beings. Virtually all workers in AI and related fields of cognitive science identify with such valuable research, not with the strong AI hypothesis. Even the development of expert systems that can compose a text, a musical score, or a picture are feasible and worth developing as aids for writers and artists. The computational power of computers, including connectionist systems or so-called neural nets, has many useful applications in human endeavors. But to say that the computer can be an intelligent and powerful processor of information is not tantamount to concluding that it can create meaning in a manner indistinguishable from that of human beings.

Personal and Consensual Symbols

First, the fundamental distinction made in Chapter 1 between personal and consensual symbols raises problems for the strong AI view. Conscious experience consists of personal symbols such as internal dialogue, imagery, daydreams, memories, fantasies, feelings, and other phenomenal events. Personal symbols are dense and unarticulated; they are a product of mental/neural operations and exist only for the individual experiencing them. These private events must be mapped onto the consensual symbol systems that human beings create to communicate with each other and to express the meanings we find in the personal symbols of consciousness.

The formal languages used to program a computer are articulated consensual symbol systems (Kolers & Smyth, 1984). The symbols can be scrutinized and understood by anyone who knows the syntactic rules of the language. It makes no difference whether the software embodies a natural language, a high-level computer language, a low-level assembly language, or all these. It makes no difference whether the examiner looks at a display screen or a computer printout. The point is that when a computer executes a line of code, the exact events that occur can be copied onto a screen or piece of paper and examined by a programmer.

The symbols manipulated by a central processing unit or a neural network may appear to be hidden from an observer watching a machine in action. At one level of analysis, the observer's blindness parallels the inability of one person to see the exact perceptions and thoughts—the personal symbols—of another person. An analysis based on the distinction between personal and consensual symbols reveals a striking difference in these two situations. The symbols manipulated by a computer can *always*, in principle, be rendered in a form that can be observed and understood by anyone who understands the articulated consensual symbol system in question. This does not mean that understanding the behavior of a sophisticated AI system complete, say, with sensing, motor, and learning abilities, is trivial. It means instead that with sufficient time and effort, the machine's workings can be understood because the necessary information is fully encoded in a symbol system that can be scrutinized.

In contrast, the symbols manipulated by the mind of a human being (and other biological systems) can *never*, in principle, be copied, observed, or understood by anyone except the individual generating them. According to the concepts espoused here, observers see the mind of another individual only through the lens of translation—from a mapping of personal symbols to consensual symbols. The neural workings of the brain give rise to personal symbols that possess subjective and inherently private qualities, known as *qualia* in the jargon of the philosophy of mind. These qualities are *not* observable nor can they ever be made observable. Brain imaging methods may enable one to examine neural structures and processes, but the experience, the qualia correlated with neural activity, remains hidden.

Although the formal language of a computer is consensual, one might counter that the machine experiences dense personal symbols as it executes a step in its program. The philosophical view of functionalism indeed ascribes "mental states to beings whose brains may be structurally similar to ours, but who differ from us in material compositions" (Hill, 1991, p. 45). The functionalist view holds that neuronal activity is unnecessary for the qualia of human mental life, such as pain, and may be duplicated by any sufficiently sophisticated android. As long as there is a "one-to-one structure-preserving correspondence between neurons of the android and the real neurons of a human brain" (p. 45), the functionalist expects to find personal symbols in both or perhaps in neither.

The present view, and the one advocated and defended by Hill, disagrees, holding that neural activity is *necessary* for the personal symbols of conscious experience, which in turn are *necessary* elements of a psychological theory of the mind. Certainly, one can imagine or project such mental experiences into the workings of the machine, but to do so adds nothing to our understanding of how the machine operates. The observable symbols of formal programming languages provide a complete description. The thinking and intelligent behavior of the computer is entirely understandable in terms of its manipulation of consensual symbols. Adding a Rylean ghost in the machine adds nothing of consequence for computers.

Assuming that the symbols of machines *are* wholly consensual, it follows that human beings and all other biological species that generate personal symbols differ fundamentally from machines. First, the process of translating personal symbols into consensual symbols loses meaning in the context of computers. At most, computers need only translate from one consensual system—say, machine language—to another—say LISP. This algorithmic, painless form of translation bears scant resemblance to the birthing pains of a writer trying to translate a personal thought into a sentence that expresses that thought clearly.

Second, Searle's (1987) well-known Chinese Room argument illuminates a related point about the limitations of operating entirely with consensual symbol systems. When computers manipulate symbols according to the rules of a program, they allegedly exhibit no more understanding than Searle does in following a set of instructions on manipulating Chinese characters without knowing Chinese. Searle questioned, in essence, what it means to say that a person or a machine understands a consensual symbol system. He concluded that the intentionality and semantics of human understanding require more than a set of syntactic rules for manipulating consensual symbols.

For example, for a computer to really understand the symbol RED, it is necessary on this view to ground the symbol with sensory experiences—that is, experiences embodied in personal symbols. Similarly, grounding the symbol FEAR in a manner that allows true understanding would require a bevy of perceptions, memories, and bodily sensations and reactions. Johnson (1987) offered a compelling analysis that sensory, motor, and other bodily experiences provide the grounding for human understanding of all linguistic symbols. If one accepts that any "bodily experience" that a computer scientist can provide to a computer—such as a television camera image or pressure detectors—is necessarily coded in the format of consensual symbols (digital or analog), then computers may be incapable of grounding language in the same way that a person does.

Meaning-making, as seen in writing and art, entails by definition the mapping between personal symbols and consensual symbols. Assuming that personal symbols provide the basis for true understanding, and further assuming that computers operate only in the realm of consensual symbols, the vision of meaning-making machines is clouded considerably. I say this knowing that philosophers and computer scientists can imagine machines that violate both assumptions. It may be in our nature, as makers of meaning, to see characteristics of ourselves in the artifacts we create. Certainly, the ability to fantasize and write about our fantasies is an essential part of *Homo symbolificus*. It does not follow that we can always build what we can describe. Describing a meaning-making machine is much like drawing an impossible figure, along the lines of Escher, I suspect. One can put it on paper, but building it is another matter altogether.

Reference versus Purpose

Finally, humans make meaning not only in the sense of reference but also in the sense of purpose (Csikszentmihalyi, 1990). People order and interpret their experiences to uncover causal connections that lead to some final purpose. The meaning of LIFE occupies our thoughts as doggedly as the meaning of RED or FEAR. Computers, I suggest, do not make meaning in this sense of discovering ultimate purpose. For the sake of the argument, grant that the strong AI contention that RED, FEAR, and any other symbol can be grounded in a sufficiently sophisticated robotic system and thus given meaning in the sense of reference. Does it follow that the machine would then make meaning about its purpose in existing? Or is a concern with the ultimate significance of existence a separate matter, one that only biological creatures or perhaps even only human creatures address?

These questions may not be answerable on theoretical grounds. Perhaps only building the robot (which may be impossible) and seeking the answers will suffice. Certainly, it is not difficult to *imagine* a machine that seeks to understand the significance of its "life," as science fiction writers have done many times. But my own intuition about the matter is that the prospect of death underscores the human drive to find purpose, significance, and ultimate meaning in life in a fashion that cannot be matched, in principle, by artifacts of any form.

Nonbiological forms of intelligence, I presume, would not fret over death in the sense that all biological forms of intelligence must, if they are capable. Exact copies of machines can be made. As parts of a machine wear out, they can always be replaced. The articulated consensual symbol systems of computers are by definition copiable. Personal symbols, the product of biological brains and minds, are by definition unique and noncopiable. Pulling the plug on a robot or even dismantling it piece by piece always leaves open the possibility of reversing the operations or creating a duplicate. Such cannot be said for *Homo symbolificus*. The human mind, comprised of noncopiable personal symbols, must confront its own demise, whereas the copiable mind need not. Not even human cloning provides an escape to the extent that mutations, the mechanisms of gene expression, and the influence of a novel environment will alter the brain and mind of the cloned descendent. I suspect that this difference—the knowledge of inescapable death—will separate us as makers of meaning, in the fullest sense, from our wisest artificial counterparts.

Animal Cognition

The cognitive revolution in American psychology spurred by Jerome Bruner, George Miller, and their colleagues in the late 1950s broke the lock of behaviorism on theorizing about human cognition, thinking, and consciousness. Slowly but surely, the same questions raised about the processing of information in the human mind began to be asked about other animals. Inevitably, but only with great resistance, the issue of conscious awareness in infrahuman species has made its way to the center of cognitive ethology (Griffin, 1991).

Turning once again to Suzanne Langer's quotation, today's readers must question whether their views have not been overturned by the animal research of the past five decades. Our uniqueness has been traditionally cast in terms of tool usage and language usage. Cracks in this formulation, however, are now apparent, as will be mentioned.

Moreover, the observation that machines are limited to consensual symbols, and are therefore inherently different from human beings, carries far less weight in the case of our fellow members of the animal kingdom. Granted, Kennedy (1992) provided a compelling critique of the work of cognitive ethologists who impute conscious experiences—personal symbols of some form—to infrahuman species. Surely there must be some boundary, fuzzy though it may be, along the phylogenetic scale below which we fail to find such symbols of consciousness. Although composed of the right material, the neural structures of other organisms presumably must meet a criterion of complexity before conscious experiences of the sort that you and I would recognize can be presumed. Where to place such a criterion or boundary is clearly a matter of legitimate debate (Kennedy, 1992).

Even so, it is clear that other animals can model their environment in some fashion. Apes, in particular, may well achieve this modeling through personal symbols bearing some continuity with our own, given our close evolutionary history (Leakey & Lewin, 1992). Further, that animals use at least rudimentary consensual symbols in the form of signaling systems in nature is well established. Moreover, apes apparently can learn, at least to a limited degree, consensual symbols designed by people for communication in an experimental setting. What then does the present approach to humans as the makers of meaning, par excellence, suggest about how we differ from infrahuman species?

The answer has two parts. First, the tool and language usage found elsewhere in the animal kingdom is fascinating, but it cannot be taken as definitive evidence against the proposition that consensual symbol usage sets our species apart. Our tool and language usage far exceeds that of any other species, and they are only the beginning of the symbols that comprise human culture. Second, unlike the symbols of other species, the consensual symbols that we create are subject to the forces of cultural evolution. Human ideas—which Dawkins (1976) refers to as *memes*—coexist with genes in the evolutionary history of *Homo symbolificus*. Unlike any other biological system, we have in a sense taken charge of our own evolution as an intelligent form of life. We do so by making consensual symbols that are copied through imitation and other forms of learning; the copied ideas succeed in an evolutionary sense by becoming a permanent fixture of our culture.

Tools, Language, and Other Artifacts

The unique biological features of our species and our evolutionary history fall well beyond the scope of my brief comments here (Leakey & Lewis, 1992; Ornstein,

1991). Our large brains, upright posture, and relatively small bodies distinguish us from other primates. Our prehensile hands, so marvelously designed for making artifacts, distinguish us from cetaceans—whales and dolphins. I leave the full story to the anthropologists and zoologists, and focus here on tools and language. Before doing so, I wish to duck the charge of anthropocentric chauvinism. Our uniqueness in no way justifies an attitude that only human needs count. A concern for animal welfare is not at odds with the view that only humans are makers of meaning. All species are unique in some way. Seeing the worth of other species should not depend on attributing human traits to them. Sadly, we have too often depended on anthropomorphism as a way of elevating other forms of life into our sphere of concern.

Griffin (1984) described several intriguing examples of tool usage uncovered in recent years by ethologists. What is especially interesting is the phylogenetic range of such behavior. Ant-lions are one of two insects that dig pits to capture prey; hermit crabs attach anemones to their shells to gain the protective benefit of the anemones' stinging projectiles; nesting ravens pry loose rocks and drop them on intruders; sea otters use stones to open shellfish; and chimpanzees "fish" for termites using a branch that has been fashioned to fit into the termite mound. Even so, Griffin noted that tool use is relatively rare in the animal kingdom and is sometimes limited to certain populations or even certain individuals of a species. Further, those that use tools "do so only when it is important to them, usually when food can be obtained only with the aid of some implement" (p. 118). Although it could be argued that people use tools only when it is important to them, the range of situations in which such use is important is vast indeed.

Similarly, the study of symbolic communication in nonhuman species has allowed remarkable insights into animal cognition (Griffin, 1984; Parker & Gibson, 1990). The waggle dance of honey bees, the antennae and head gestures of weaver ants, the alarm calls of vervet monkeys, and the complex signaling of cetaceans suggest the distinct possibility that signaling and symbolic communication of various forms occur throughout the animal kingdom. Moreover, laboratory efforts to teach chimpanzees, orangutans, and gorillas American Sign Language and other consensual symbol systems have been instructive in revealing dramatically the evolutionary links that we share. Even so, the results of these investigations have spurred more controversy than definitive conclusions.

Terrace (1984), one of the strongest critics of this work, contended that modeling and other behavioral learning better account for the findings more satisfactorily than the hypothesis that the animals have internalized a semantic and syntactic system. Moreover, there has been no suggestion to date that primates or ceteceans possess the large vocabularies and productivity or generativity of human language. Checklist comparisons of human language with vocalizations and gestures of other species, as well as theoretical analyses of the energy levels emitted and received in animal communication systems, point to the uniqueness of human language (Morton & Page, 1992). In short, like tool usage, language usage and the brain structures underlying it assume an importance in our species unparalleled in evolutionary history (Corballis, 1991).

Finally, tools and language are only two—albeit highly visible and important—illustrations of consensual symbol usage by human beings. All artifacts forged by human creativity and thought are symbolic, and are part of the texture of cultures and subcultures. Clothing, homes, building architecture, and art, to name just four examples, are designed for symbolic reasons just as much as for practical reasons. The necktie that I all too often wear and the lawn and roses that I tend communicate rough forms of meaning in a public domain. Such forms of communication do not match the sophistication and complexity of language, but neither can they be ignored as further evidence of human symbol use (Whitehead, 1927).

Cultural Evolution

The zoologist Richard Dawkins (1976) explained that the evolution of life depends on differences in the survival rates of replicating entities. Genes are the replicating material in biological evolution. Dawkins contended that ideas—or, in the language used here, the consensual symbols that refer to ideas created by an individual—are also replicating entities. Dawkins called these idea units *memes*. He contended that the principles of natural selection apply equally to genes and memes:

> Examples of memes are tunes, ideas, catch-phrases, clothes fashions, ways of making pots or of building arches. Just as genes propagate themselves in the gene pool by leaping from body to body via sperms or eggs, so memes propagate themselves in the meme pool by leaping from brain to brain by a process, which, in the broad sense, can be called imitation. If a scientist hears, or reads about, a good idea, he passes it on to his colleagues and students. He mentions it in his articles and his lectures. If the idea catches on, it can be said to propagate itself, spreading from brain to brain. (p. 206)

Homo symbolificus makes meaning in essentially all activities. Meme evolution, like gene evolution, is a natural and inevitable process resulting from our need to think, create, signify, and find purpose. Unlike the pattern of other species, meme evolution has allowed our species to evolve at an astonishing rate of speed. The brain organization of humans 10,000 years ago differed little, if any, from our own; yet, witness the cultural differences from the hunter-gatherer to the modern urban dweller. Considering language alone, Dawkins (1976) noted that "Geoffrey Chaucer could not hold a conversation with a modern Englishman, even though they are linked to each other by an unbroken chain of some twenty generations of Englishmen, each of whom could speak to his immediate neighbors in the chain as a son speaks to his father" (p. 203). Thus, it is the importance that we place on consensual symbol use that separates us from infrahuman species. Unlike others in the animal kingdom, we seek to replicate our thoughts—in the form of consensual symbols—as well as our genes.

The relationship between cultural and biological evolution is controversial and lies well beyond the scope of this closing chapter. Anthropologists and zoologists envision the possibility of a coevolutionary framework in which certain ideas work to enhance genetic reproductive success (Goldsmith, 1991). Still, there is no reason to suppose that genetic success is the sole or even primary benchmark for judging the value of ideas. Celibacy, as Dawkins (1976) pointed out, is a remarkably enduring idea in some religious orders, despite the fatal consequences it carries for genetic reproduction. Beethoven's Ninth Symphony has succeeded because of its aesthetics, not its genetics. Truth and beauty surely rank among the benchmarks used to position ideas in the landscape of cultural evolution.

Cultural evolution, then, can be viewed as the replication of memes embodied in the personal symbols of mental experience and the consensual symbols of social interaction. Dawkins (1976) argued, correctly I believe, that cultural evolution sets us apart from other species in a fundamental way. Humans are "survival machines" no different from any other life form when viewed solely in terms of the selfish gene. But unlike any other life form of which we know, *Homo symbolificus* privately generates ideas and shares these ideas through sophisticated and pervasive modes of communication.

Concluding Remarks

By this point, I hope you are convinced that the study of writing takes us to the heart of what it means to be human. Suzanne Langer's observation about the uniqueness of our symbol use, however, remains fresh even in light of the past 50 years of animal research, AI, and, surprisingly, even the cognitive revolution in psychology. Cognitive psychology seems long overdue in focusing on the study of writing and other meaning-making activities.

A central distinction in the psychology of thinking and writing is between personal and consensual symbols. Personal symbols—the memories, perceptions, fantasies, and dreams of mental life—are unique, private events that exist only as a product of the mental operations that generate them. The consensual symbols of public discourse, in contrast, are copiable and open to scrutiny and comprehension by all who understand the culturally and biologically defined rules governing their use. Human intelligence, unlike animal intelligence and AI, depends on the creation and manipulation of both personal and consensual symbols.

The challenge in writing comes from the difficulties involved in both creating coherent ideas and rendering these ideas in coherent texts. The mapping between the private world of thought and the public world of text probably always falls short of what the author would like. As Pagels (1988) tells us: "Beethoven once remarked that the music he had written was nothing compared with the music that he had heard" (p. 331). The depth of this challenge is what makes the writing task so compelling to the writer and so interesting to the psychologist.

References

Ahern, S. & Beatty, J. (1979). Pupillary responses during information processing vary with Scholastic Aptitude Test scores. *Science, 205*, 1289–1292.

Alexander, P. A., Schallert, D. L., & Hare, U. C. (1991). Coming to terms: How researchers in learning and literacy talk about knowledge. *Review of Educational Research, 61*, 315–343.

Allport, A. (1984). Alternatives to the computational view of mind: The baby or the bathwater? *Journal of Verbal Learning and Verbal Behavior, 23*, 315–324.

Amabile, T. M. (1983). *The social psychology of creativity.* New York: Springer-Verlag.

Amabile, T. M. (1985). Motivation and creativity: Effects of motivational orientation on creative writers. *Journal of Personality and Social Psychology, 48*, 393–399.

Anderson, J. (1990a). *Cognitive psychology and its implications.* New York: W.H. Freeman and Company.

Anderson, J. (1990b). *The adaptive character of thought.* Hillsdale, NJ: Lawrence Erlbaum Associates.

Andreason, N. C. (1987). Creativity and mental illness: Prevalence rates in writers and their first-degree relatives. *American Journal of Psychiatry, 144*(10), 1288–1292.

Applebee, A. N. (1982). Writing and learning in school settings. In M. Nystrand (Ed.), *What writers know* (pp. 365–381). New York: Academic Press.

Arnheim, R. (1986). *New essays on the psychology of art.* Los Angeles: University of California Press.

Atkinson, J. W., & Raynor, J. O. (1978). *Personality, motivation, and achievement.* New York: Halsted Press.

Attneave, F. (1957). Transfer of experience with class schema to identification learning of patterns and shapes. *Journal of Experimental Psychology, 54*, 81–88.

Baars, B. J. (1988). *A cognitive theory of consciousness.* Cambridge: Cambridge University Press.

Baddeley, A. D. (1986). *Working memory.* Oxford: Oxford University Press.

Bandura, A. (1978). The self-system in reciprocal determinism. *American Psychologist, 33*, 344–358.

Bangert-Drowns, R. L. (1993). The word processor as an instructional tool: A meta-analysis of word processing in writing instruction. *Review of Educational Research, 63*, 69–93.

Baron, J. (1982). Personality and intelligence. In R. J. Sternberg (Ed.), *Handbook of human intelligence* (pp. 308–351). Cambridge: Cambridge University Press.

Baron, J. (1985). What kinds of intelligence components are fundamental? In S. F. Chipman,

J. W. Segal, & R. Glaser (Eds.), *Thinking and learning skills. Volume 2. Research and open questions* (pp. 365–390). Hillsdale, NJ: Lawrence Erlbaum Associates.

Barrett, E. (1989). Textual intervention, collaboration, and the online environment. In E. Barrett (Ed.), *The society of text* (pp. 305–321). Cambridge, MA: MIT Press.

Barron, F. (1969). *Creative person and creative process.* New York: Holt, Rinehart, and Winston.

Barron, F. (1988). Putting creativity to work. In R. J. Sternberg (Ed.), *The nature of creativity: Contemporary psychological perspectives* (pp. 76–98). Cambridge: Cambridge University Press.

Barron, F., & Harrington, D. M. (1981). Creativity, intelligence, and personality. *Annual Review of Psychology, 32,* 439–476.

Barsalou, L. W. (1983). Ad hoc categories. *Memory & Cognition, 11,* 211–227.

Bartlett, F. C. (1932). *Remembering: A study in experimental and social psychology.* London: Cambridge University Press.

Bartlett, F. C. (1958). *Thinking: An experimental and social study.* New York: Basic Books.

Bartlett, J. (1992). *Familiar quotations: A collection of passages, phrases, and proverbs traced to their sources in ancient and modern literature* (16th ed., Justin Kaplin, General Editor). Boston: Little, Brown and Company.

Bazerman, C. (1990, April). The nature of expertise in writing. In G. Schumacher (Chair), *The nature of expertise in writing.* Symposium conducted at the meeting of the American Educational Research Association, Boston.

Beaugrande, R. de (1984). *Text production.* Norwood, NJ: Ablex.

Beck, A. T. (1991). Cognitive therapy: A 30-year retrospective. *American Psychologist, 46,* 368–375.

Becker, H. S. (1986). *Writing for social scientists: How to start and finish your thesis, book, or article.* Chicago: University of Chicago Press.

Beeman, C. A. (1990). *Just this side of madness: Creativity and the drive to create.* Conway, AR: UCA Press.

Benton, S. L., Kraft, R. G., Glover, J. A., & Plake, B. S. (1984). Cognitive capacity differences among writers. *Journal of Educational Psychology, 76,* 820–834.

Bereiter, C., & Scardamalia, M. (1987). *The psychology of written composition.* Hillsdale, NJ: Lawrence Erlbaum Associates.

Berlyne, D. E. (1965). *Structure and direction in thinking.* New York: John Wiley.

Berman, M. (1988). The two faces of creativity. In J. Brockman (Ed.), *The reality club* (pp. 9–38). New York: Lynx Books.

Bernhardt, S. A., Edwards, P., & Wojahn, P. (1989). Teaching college composition with computers: A program evaluation. *Written Communication, 6,* 108–133.

Berry, W. (1990, December 9). Seeing red: Billy Joel is still angry, but now he's broke. *St. Louis Post Dispatch,* Arts and Entertainment, p. 3C.

Bettleheim, B. (1976). *The uses of enchantment: The meaning and importance of fairy tales.* New York: Alfred A. Knopf.

Bloom, L. Z. (1985). Anxious writers in context: Graduate school and beyond. In M. Rose (Ed.), *When a writer can't write* (pp. 119–133). New York: Guilford Press.

Blumenthal, A. L. (1977). *The process of cognition.* Englewood Cliffs, NJ: Prentice-Hall.

Bobrow, J. (1979). *Barron's new guide to the Law School Admissions Test.* Woodbury, NY: Barron's Educational Series.

Bock, J. K. (1982). Toward a cognitive psychology of syntax: Information processing contributions to sentence formulation. *Psychological Review, 89,* 1–47.

Boden, M. A. (1990). *The creative mind: Myths and mechanisms.* London: Basic Books.

Bodker, S. (1989). A human activity approach to user interfaces. *Human–Computer Interaction, 4,* 171–195.

Boice, R. (1982). Increasing the writing productivity of "blocked" academicians. *Behavior Research and Therapy, 20,* 197–207.

Boice, R. (1983). Clinical and experimental treatments of writing block. *Journal of Consulting and Clinical Psychology, 51,* 183–191.

Boice, R. (1985). Cognitive components of blocking. *Written Communication, 2,* 91–104.

Boice, R. (1987). A program for facilitating scholarly writing. *Higher Education Research and Development, 6,* 9–20.

Boice, R. (1990). *Professors as writers: A self-help guide to productive writing.* Stillwater, OK: New Forums Press.

Boice, R., & Johnson, K. (1984). Perception and practice of writing for publication by faculty at a doctoral-granting university. *Research in Higher Education, 21,* 33–43.

Boice, R. & Meyers, P. E. (1986). Two parallel traditions: Automatic writing and free writing. *Written Communication, 3,* 471–490.

Bolter, J. D. (1991). *Writing space: The computer, hypertext, and the history of writing.* Hillsdale, NJ: Lawrence Erlbaum Associates.

Bonner, P. (1984, March). Make a new plan, Stan. *Personal Software,* pp. 120–123.

Boorstin, D. J. (1985). *The discoverers.* New York: Vintage Books.

Boorstin, D. J. (1992). *The creators.* New York: Random House.

Bourne, L. E., Jr. (1966). *Human conceptual behavior.* Boston: Allyn & Bacon.

Bourne, L. E., Jr. (1982). Typicality effects in logically defined categories. *Memory and Cognition, 10,* 3–9.

Bower, G. H. (1981). Mood and memory. *American Psychologist, 36,* 129–148.

Bracewell, R., Scardamalia, M., & Bereiter, C. (1978, October). *The development of audience awareness in writing* (Report No. CS 204 174). Paper presented at the annual meeting of the American Educational Research Association (Toronto, March 27–31, 1978). *Resources in Education* (ERIC Document Reproduction Service No. ED 154 433).

Brand, A. G. (1989). *The psychology of writing: The affective experience.* New York: Greenwood Press.

Branthwaite, A., Trueman, M., & Hartley, J. (1980). Writing essays: The actions and strategies of students. In J. Hartley (Ed.), *The psychology of writing* (pp. 98–109). London: Nichols Publishing.

Breland, H., & Jones, R. J. (1984). Perceptions of writing skills. *Written Communication, 1,* ·101–109.

Bridwell-Bowles, L., Johnson, P., & Brehe, S. (1987). Composing and computers: Case studies of experienced writers. In A. Matsuhashi (Ed.), *Writing in real time: Modeling production processes* (pp. 81–107). London: Longman.

Britton, J., Burgess, T., Martin, N., McLeod, A., & Rosen, H. (1975). *The development of writing abilities.* London: Macmillan Education Ltd.

Britton, B. K., Glynn, S. M., Meyer, B. J. F., & Penland, M. J. (1982). Effects of text structure on use of cognitive capacity during reading. *Journal of Educational Psychology, 74,* 51–61.

Britton, B. K., Gulgoz, S., & Tidwell, P. (1990, November). *Shaped mental representations of original versus principled revisions of text.* Paper presented at the meeting of the Psychonomic Society, New Orleans.

Britton, B. K., Holdredge, T. S., Curry, C., & Westbrook, R. D. (1979). Use of cognitive capacity in reading identical texts with different amounts of discourse level meaning. *Journal of Experimental Psychology: Human Learning and Memory, 5,* 262–270.

Britton, B. K., & Tesser, A. (1982). Effects of prior knowledge on use of cognitive capacity in three complex cognitive tasks. *Journal of Verbal Learning and Verbal Behavior, 21*, 421–436.

Britton, B. K., Van Dusen, L., Glynn, S. M., & Hemphill, D. (1990). The impact of interference on instructional text. In A. C. Graesser & G. H. Bower (Eds.), *The psychology of learning and motivation* (Vol. 25) (pp. 53–70). New York: Academic Press.

Brown, A. S., & Murphy, D. R. (1989). Cryptomnesia: Delineating inadvertent plagiarism. *Journal of Experimental Psychology*: Learning, *Memory, and Cognition, 15*, 432–442.

Brown, J. S. (1985). Idea amplifiers: New kinds of electronic learning environments. *Educational Horizons, 63*, 8–112.

Brown, J. S., McDonald, J. L., Brown, T. L., & Carr, T. H. (1988). Adapting to processing demands in discourse production: The case of handwriting. *Journal of Experimental Psychology: Human Perception and Performance 14*, 45–59.

Bruce, B., Collins, A., Rubins, A. D., & Gentner, D. (1982). Three perspectives on writing. *Educational Psychologist, 17*, 131–145.

Bruner, J. S. (1966). On cognitive growth II. In J. S. Bruner, R. R. Oliver, & P. M. Greenfield (Eds.), *Studies in cognitive growth* (pp. 30–67). New York: John Wiley & Sons.

Bruner, J. S. (1986). *Actual minds, possible worlds*. Cambridge, MA: Harvard University Press.

Bruner, J. S. (1990). *Acts of meaning*. Cambridge, MA: Harvard University Press.

Bruner, J. S., Goodnow, J. J., & Austin, G. A. (1956). *A study of thinking*. New York: John Wiley & Sons.

Bryson, M., Lindsay, P., Joram, E., & Woodruff, E. (1986, April). *Augmented word processing: The influence of task characteristics and mode of production on writer's cognition* (Report No. CS-209–362). Paper presented at the meeting of the American Educational Research Association (ERIC Document Reproduction Service No. ED 276 016).

Burke, K. (1945). *A grammer of motives*. New York: Prentice-Hall.

Burns, H. L. (1979). Stimulating rhetorical invention in English composition through computer-assisted instruction. *Dissertation Abstracts International, 40*, 3734A. (University Microfilms No. 79–28268).

Burns, H. L. (1984). Recollections of first-generation computer-assisted prewriting. In W. Wresch (Ed.), *The computer in composition instruction* (pp. 15–33). Urbana, IL: National Council of Teachers of English.

Burns, H. L., & Culp, G. H. (1980, August). Stimulating invention in English composition through computer-assisted instruction. *Educational Technology*, pp. 5–10.

Buzan, T. (1991). *Use both sides of your brain* (3rd Ed.). New York: E. P. Dutton

Caccamise, D. J. (1987). Idea generation in writing. In A. Matsuhashi (Ed.), *Writing in real time: Modeling production processes* (pp. 224–253). Norwood, NJ: Ablex.

Calvin, W. H. (1990). *The cerebral symphony: Seashore reflections on the structure of consciousness*. New York: Bantam Books.

Campbell, J. (1988). *The power of myth*. New York: Doubleday.

Caramazza, A., McCloskey, M., & Green, B. (1981). Native beliefs in "sophisticated" subjects: Misconceptions about trajectories of objects. *Cognition, 9*, 117–123.

Card, S., Moran, T. P., & Newell, A. (1983). *The psychology of human-computer interaction*. Hillsdale, NJ: Lawrence Erlbaum Associates.

Card, S. K., Robert, J. M., & Keenan, L. N. (1984). On-line composition of text. In B. Shackel (Ed.), *Human–computer interaction—INTERTACT'84* (pp. 51–56). Amsterdam: North-Holland.

Carroll, J. M. (Ed.). (1991). *Designing interaction: Psychology at the human–computer interface*. New York: Cambridge University Press.

Carter, M. (1990). The idea of expertise: An exploration of cognitive and social dimensions of writing. *Composition and Communication, 41*, 265–286.

Case, D. (1985). Processing professorial words: Personal computers and the writing habits of university professors. *College Composition and Communication, 36*, 317–322.

Catano, J. V. (1985). Computer based writing: Navigating the fluid text. *College Composition and Communication, 36*, 309–316.

Cattell, R. B. (1963). Theory of fluid and crystallized intelligence: A critical experiment. *Journal of Educational Psychology, 54*, 1–22.

Chafe, W. (1990). Some things that narratives tell us about the mind. In B. K. Britton & A. D. Pellegrini (Eds.), *Narrative thought and narrative language* (pp. 79–98). Hillsdale, NJ: Lawrence Erlbaum Associates.

Chambers, J. A. (1964). Relating personality and biographical factors to scientific creativity. *Psychological Monographs: General and Applied, 78* (Whole No. 584), 1–20.

Chang, T. M. (1986). Semantic memory: Facts and models. *Psychological Review, 99*, 199–220.

Charney, D. (1984). The validity of using holistic scoring to evaluate writing: A critical overview. *Research in the Teaching of English, 18*, 65–81.

Charney, D. (1991). The impact of hypertext and processes of reading and writing. In S. J. Hilligross & C. L. Selfe (Eds.), *Literacy and computers* (pp. 1–32). New York: Modern Language Association.

Clark, H. H., & Clark, E. (1977). *Psychology and language.* New York: Harcourt Brace Jovanovich.

Cleary, L. M. (1991). Affect and cognition in the writing processes of eleventh graders: A study of concentration and emotion. *Written Communication, 8*, 473–507.

Cochran-Smith, M. (1991). Word processing and writing in elementary classrooms: A critical review of the literature. *Review of Educational Research, 61*, 107–155.

Cole, B. C. (1985). *Beyond word processing: Using your personal computer as a knowledge processor.* New York: McGraw-Hill.

Collins, A. M. & Gentner, D. (1980). A framework for a cognitive model of writing. In L. W. Gregg & E. R. Steinberg (Eds.), *Cognitive processes in writing* (pp. 51–72). Hillsdale, NJ: Lawrence Erlbaum Associates.

Conte, M. L., & Ferguson, L. W. (1974). Rated effectiveness of antidrug letters by drug users and nonusers. *Journal of Psychology, 86*, 355–359.

Corballis, M. C. (1991). *The lopsided ape: Evolution of the generative mind.* New York: Oxford University Press.

Corbett, E. P. J. (1965). *Classical rhetoric for the modern student.* New York: Oxford University Press.

Coughlin, E. K. (1989, May 10). Walker Percy, a physician turned novelist, chastises the sciences for failing to explicate the human mind. *The Chronicle of Higher Education,* A5, A7.

Cowley, M. (Ed.). (1958). *Writers at work: The Paris Review interviews* (Vol. 1). New York: Viking Press.

Craik, F. I. M., & Tulving, E. (1975). Depth of processing and the retention of words in episodic memory. *Journal of Experimental Psychology: General, 104*, 268–294.

Crane, G. (1988). Redefining the book: Some preliminary problems. *Academic Computing, 2*(5), 6–11, 36–41.

Crowhurst, M. & Piché, G. (1979). Audience and mode of discourse effects on syntactic complexity in writing at two grade levels. *Research in The Teaching of English, 13*, 101–109.

Csikszentmihalyi, M. (1990). *Flow*: *The psychology of optimal experience*. New York: Harper & Row.

Csikszentmihalyi, M., & Csikszentmihalyi, I. S. (Eds.). (1988). *Optimal experience*: *Psychological studies of flow in consciousness*. New York: Cambridge University Press.

Culpepper, M., & Ramsdell, R. (1982). A comparison of a multiple choice and an essay test of writing skills. *Research in the Teaching of English, 16*, 295–297.

Curtis, M. S. (1988). Windows on composing: Teaching revision on word processors. *Written Communication, 39*, 337–344.

Daiute, C. A. (1984). Performance limits on writers. In R. Beach and L. S. Bridwell (Eds.), *New directions in composition research* (pp. 205–231). New York: Guilford Press.

Daiute, C. A. (1985). *Writing and computers*. Reading, MA: Addison-Wesley.

Daly, J. A. (1978). Writing apprehension and writing competence. *Journal of Educational Research, 2*, 10–14.

Daly, J. A. (1985). Writing apprehension. In M. Rose (Ed.), *When a writer can't write*: *Studies in writer's block and other composing-process problems* (pp. 43–82). New York: Guilford Press.

Daniels, G. H. (1972). Acknowledgment. *Science, 175*, 124–125.

Danto, G. (1990, November 18). Me, my selves, and I. *The New York Times Book Review*, p. 7.

Dawkins, R. (1976). *The selfish gene*. New York: Oxford University Press.

Day, R. (1992, November). *Very long-term encoding specificity*. Paper presented at the annual meeting of the Psychonomic Society, St. Louis.

Deely, J. (1986). The coalescence of semiotic consciousness. In J. Deely, B. Williams, & F. E. Kruse (Eds.), *Frontiers in semiotics* (pp. 5–34). Bloomington: Indiana University Press.

Dembo, L. S. (Ed.).(1983). *Interviews with contemporary writers*. Madison: University of Wisconsin Press.

DeLoughry, T. J. (1993a, January 20). Clinton urged to give highest priority to computer network. *Chronicle of Higher Education*, pp. A17, A19.

DeLoughry, T. J. (1993b, July 7). Software designed to offer Internet users easy access to documents and graphics. *Chronicle of Higher Education*, p. A23.

Dennett, D. C. (1991). *Consciousness explained*. Boston: Little Brown and Co.

DiPardo, A. (1990) Narrative knowers, expository knowledge: Discourse as a dialetic. *Written Communication, 1*, 59–95.

Dobrin, D. N. (1987). Some ideas about idea processors. In L. Gerrard (Ed.), *Writing at century's end*: *Essays on computer-assisted composition* (pp. 95–107). New York: Random House.

Duffy, T. M., Curran, T. E., & Sass, D. (1983). Document design for technical job tasks: An evaluation. *Human Factors, 25*, 143–160.

Dorner, J. (1992). Authors and information technology: New challenges in publishing. In M. Sharples (Ed.), *Computers and writing*: *Issues and implementation* (pp. 5–14). Dordrecht: Kluwer Academic Publishers.

Duffy, T. M., & Kabance, P. (1982). Testing a readable writing approach to text revision. *Journal of Educational Psychology, 74*, 733–748.

Durst, R: K. (1989). Monitoring processes in analytic and summary writing. *Written Communication, 6*, 340–363.

Eich, J. E. (1980). The cue-dependent nature of state-dependent retention. *Memory and Cognition, 8*, 157–173.

Einstein, G. O., & Hunt, R. R. (1980). Levels of processing and organization: Additive effects of individual item and relational processing. *Journal of Experimental Psychology: Human, Learning, and Memory, 6,* 588–598.

Eklundh, K. S. (1992). Problems in achieving a global perspective of the text in computer-based writing. In M. Sharples (Ed.), *Computers and writing: Issues and implementation* (pp. 73–84). Dordrecht: Kluwer Academic Publishers.

Elbow, P. (1981). *Writing with power.* New York: Oxford University Press.

Ellenberger, H. (1970). *Discovery of the unconscious.* New York: Basic Books.

Emig, J. (1971). *The composing processes of twelfth graders.* National Council of Teachers of English Research Report No. 13, Urbana, IL.

Englart, C. S., & Hiebert, E. H. (1984). Children's developing awareness of text structures in expository material. *Journal of Educational Psychology, 76,* 65–74.

Englehard, G., Gordon, B., & Gabrielson, S. (1991). The influences of mode of discourse, experiential demand, and gender on the quality of student writing. *Research in the Teaching of English, 26,* 315–336.

Englert, L. S., Stewart, S. R., & Hiebert, E. H. (1988). Young writer's use of text structure in expository text generation. *Journal of Educational Psychology. 80,* 143–151

Erickson, M. H. (1972). A special inquiry with Aldous Huxley into the nature and character of various states of consciousness. In C. T. Tart (Ed.), *Altered states of consciousness* (pp. 47–54). Garden City, NY: Doubleday.

Ericsson, K. A., & Krampe, R. T., & Tesch-Römer (1993). The role of deliberate practice in the acquisition of expert performance. *Psychological Review, 100,* 363–406.

Ericsson, K. A., & Simon, H. A. (1980). Verbal reports as data. *Psychological Review, 87,* 215–251.

Eysenck, H. J. (1987). Speed of information processing, reaction time, and the theory of intelligence. In Phillip A. Vernon (Ed.), *Speed of information processing and intelligence* (pp. 21–67). Norwood, NJ: Ablex.

Faigley, L. (1979). Another look at sentences. *Freshman English News, 7*(3), 18–21.

Faigley, L. (1986). Competing theories of process: A critique and a proposal. *College English, 48,* 527–542.

Faigley, L., Cherry, R. D., Jolliffe, D. A., & Skinner, A. M. (1985). *Assessing writers' knowledge and processes of composing.* Norwood, NJ: Ablex.

Faigley, L., & Miller, T. P. (1982). What we learn from writing on the job. *College English, 44,* 557–559.

Faigley, L., & Witte, S. (1981). Analyzing revision. *College Composition and Communication, 32,* 400–414.

Feldman, C. F., Bruner, J., Renderer, B., & Spitzer, S. (1990). Narrative comprehension. In B. K. Britton & A. D. Pellegrini (Eds.), *Narrative thought and narrative language* (pp. 1–78). Hillsdale, NJ: Lawrence Erlbaum Associates.

Feldman, D. H. (1988). Creativity: Dreams, insights, and transformations. In R. J. Sternberg (Ed.), *The nature of creativity: Contemporary psychological perspectives.* New York: Cambridge University Press.

Ferraris, M., Caviglia, F., & Degl' Innocenti, R. (1992). Word prof: A writing environment on computer. In. J. Hartley (Ed.), *Technology and writing: Readings in the psychology of written communication* (pp. 221–232). London: Jessica Kingsley Publishers.

Fields, A. (1982). Getting started: Pattern notes and perspectives. In D. H. Jonassen (Ed.), *The technology of text: Principles for structuring, designing, and displaying text* (pp. 29–52). Englewood Cliffs, NJ: Educational Technology Publications.

Flavell, J. H. (1987). Speculation about the nature and development of metacognition. In F. E. Weinert & R. H. Kluwe (Eds.), *Metacognition, motivation, and understanding* (pp. 21–29). Hillsdale, NJ: Lawrence Erlbaum Associates.

Flavell, J. H., Miller, P. H., & Miller, S. A. (1993). *Cognitive development* (2rd ed.). Englewood Cliffs, NJ: Prentice-Hall.

Flower, L. S. (1981). *Problem-solving strategies for writing*. New York: Harcourt Brace Jovanovich.

Flower, L. S., & Hayes, J. R. (1977). Problem-solving strategies and the writing process. *College English, 39*, 449–461.

Flower, L., & Hayes, J. R. (1980a). The cognition of discovery: Defining a rhetorical problem. *College Composition and Communication, 2*, 21–32.

Flower, L., & Hayes, J. R. (1980b). The dynamics of composing: Making plans and juggling constraints. In L. W. Gregg & E. R. Steinberg (Eds.), *Cognitive processes in writing* (pp. 31–50). Hillsdale, NJ: Lawrence Erlbaum Associates.

Flower, L. S. & Hayes, J. R. (1981). The pregnant pause: An inquiry into the nature of planning. *Research in the Teaching of English, 15*, 229–243.

Flower, L. S., & Hayes, J. R. (1984). Images, plans, and prose: The representation of meaning in writing. *Written Communication, 1*, 120–160.

Folkard, S., & Monk, T. H. (1985). Circadian performance rhythms. In S. Folkard & T. H. Monk (Eds.), *Hours of Work* (pp. 37–52). Chichester: John Wiley & Sons.

Frase, L. T. (1987). Creating intelligent environments for computer use in writing. *Contemporary Educational Psychology, 12*, 212–221.

Fredericksen, C. H., & Dominic, J. F. (Eds.). (1981). Writing: The nature, development, and teaching of written communication. *Volume 2, Writing: Process, development, and communication*. Hillsdale, NJ: Lawrence Erlbaum Associates.

Freedman, A., Clarke, L., Carey, J., DePaul, S., & Miller, A. (1988). *The effect of computer technology on composing processes and written products of grade 8 and grade 12 students*. Toronto: Queen's Printer for Ontario.

Freedman, S. W. (1983). Student characteristics and essay test writing performance. *Research in the Teaching of College English, 17*, 313–325.

Freedman, S. W., & Calfee, R. C. (1983). Holistic assessment of writing: Experimental design and cognitive theory. In P. Mosenthal, L. Tamor, & S. A. Walmsley (Eds.), *Research in writing: Principles and methods* (pp. 75–98). New York: Longman.

French, E. G., & Thomas, E. H. (1958). The relation of achievement motivation to problem-solving effectiveness. *Journal of Abnormal and Social Psychology, 56*, 46–48.

Freud, S. (1900). *The interpretation of dreams*. In Standard Edition (Vols. 4–5). London: Hogarth Press.

Fuller, R. (1979). Teaching reading with stories vs. cognitive hierarchy. *Journal of Suggestive-Accelerated Learning and Teaching, 4*, 220–226.

Fulwiler, T., & Young, A. P. (1990). *Programs that work: Models and methods for writing across the curriculum*. Portsmouth, NH: Boynton/Cook Publishers.

Furnas, G. W. (1986). Generalized fisheye views. *Proceedings of CHI '86*, 16–23.

Galbraith, D. (1992). Conditions for discovery through writing. In M. Sharples (Ed.), *Computers and writing: Issues and implementations* (pp. 45–71). Dordrecht: Kluwer Academic Publishers.

Gardner, H. (1982). *Art, mind and brain: A cognitive approach to creativity*. New York: Basic Books.

Gardner, H. (1983). *Frames of mind: The theory of multiple intelligences*. New York: Basic Books.

Gardner, H. (1991). *The unschooled mind: How children think and how schools should teach*. New York: Basic Books.

Garrison, A. (1993, January). Idea Fisher 2.0. *MacWorld*, p. 199.

Gazzaniga, M. S. (1985). *The social brain: Discovering the networks of the mind*. New York: Basic Books.

Gherman, P. M. (1991, August 14). Setting budgets for libraries in electronic era. *Chronicles of Higher Education*, p. A36.

Gibson, J. J. (1966). *The senses considered as perceptual systems*. Boston: Houghton Mifflin.

Gibson, J. J. (1979). *The ecological approach to visual perception*. Boston: Houghton Mifflin.

Gilhooly, K. J. (1982). *Thinking: Directed, undirected, and creative*. London: Academic Press.

Gilhooly, K. J. (1987). Mental modeling: A framework for the study of thinking. In D. N. Perkins, J. Lochhead, & J. Bishop (Eds.), *Thinking: The second international conference* (pp. 19–32). Hillsdale, NJ: Lawrence Erlbaum Associates.

Gilliland, K., Schlegel, R., Dannels, S., & Mills, S. (1989). Relationship between intelligence and criterion task set performance. *Proceedings of the Human Factors Society 33rd Annual Meeting* (pp. 888–890). Santa Monica, CA: Human Factors Society.

Gingrich, P. S. (1982). The UNIX writer's workbench software: Results of a field study. *Bell System Technical Journal, 62*, 1909–1921.

Gleitman, L. R., Gleitman, H., & Shipley, E. F. (1972). The emergence of the child as a grammarian, *Cognition, 2*, 137–163.

Glynn, S. M., Britton, B. K., Muth, D., & Dogan, N. (1982). Writing and revising persuasive documents: Cognitive demands. *Journal of Educational Psychology, 74*, 557–567.

Godshalk, F., Swineford, F., & Coffman, W. (1966). *The measurement of writing ability*. Princeton. NJ: English Testing Service.

Goldsmith, T. H. (1991). *The biological roots of human nature: Forging links between evolution and behavior*. New York: Oxford University Press.

Goodman, N. (1976). *Languages of art*. Indianapolis: Hackett Publishing Company.

Gordon, C. (1990). Changes in readers' and writers' metacognitive knowledge: Some observations. *Reading, Research, and Instruction, 30*, 1–14.

Gordon, C. J., & Braun, C. (1985a). Learning to write and writing to learn in elementary school. In A. K. Petrosky & D. Bartholomae (Eds.), *Teaching of writing: Eighty-fifth yearbook of the National Society for the Study of Education* (pp. 131–147). Chicago: University of Chicago Press.

Gordon, C. J., & Braun, C. (1985b). Metacognitive processes: Reading and writing narrative discussion. In D. L. Forrest-Pressley, G. E. Mackinnon, & T. G. Waller (Eds.), *Metacognition, cognition and human performance (Vol. 2)*. (pp. 1–75). New York: Academic Press.

Gordon, W. J. J. (1961). *Synectics*. New York: Harper & Row.

Gorell, R. M. (1983). How to make Mulligan stew: Process and product again. *College Composition and Communication, 34, 272–277*.

Gould, J. D. (1978). How experts dictate. *Journal of Experimental Psychology: Human Perception and Performance, 4*, 648–661.

Gould, J. D. (1980). Experiments on composing letters: Some facts, some myths, and some observations. In L. W. Gregg & E. R. Steinberg (Eds.), *Cognitive processes in writing* (pp. 97–127). Hillsdale, NJ: Lawrence Erlbaum Associates.

Gould, J. D. (1981). Composing letters with computer-based text editors. *Human Factors, 23*, 593–606.

Gould, J. D., Conti, J., & Hovanyecz, T. (1983). Composing letters with a simulated listening typewriter. *Communications of the ACM, 26*, 295–308.

Gradwohl, J. M., & Schumacher, G. M. (1989). The relationship between content knowledge and topic choice in writing. *Written Communication, 6*, 181–195.

Graesser, A. C., & Clark, L. F. (1985). *Structures and procedures of implicit knowledge*. Norwood, NJ: Ablex.

Graesser, A. C., Hopkinson, P. L., Lewis, E. W., & Bruflodt, H. A. (1984). The impact of different information sources on idea generation: Writing off the top of our heads. *Written Communication, 1*, 341–364.

Graves, D. H. (1983). Writing: Teachers and children at work. Exeter, NH: Heinemann Educational Books.

Green, D. W., & Wason, P. C. (1982). Notes on the psychology of writing. *Human Relations, 35,* 47–56.

Greeno, J. G. (1989). A perspective on thinking. *American Psychologist, 44,* 134–156.

Grice, H. P. (1989). *Studies in the ways of words.* Cambridge, MA: Harvard University Press.

Griffin, D. R. (1984). *Animal thinking.* Cambridge, MA: Harvard University Press.

Griffin, D. R. (1991). *Progress toward a cognitive ethology. Cognitive ethology: The minds of other animals.* Hillsdale, NJ: Lawrence Erlbaum Associates.

Grobe, C. (1981). Syntactic maturity, mechanics, and vocabulary as predictors of quality ratings. *Research in the Teaching of English, 15,* 75–85.

Gruber, H. (1974). *Darwin on man.* Chicago: University of Chicago Press.

Guilford, J. P. (1967). *The nature of human intelligence.* New York: McGraw-Hill.

Gustin, W. C. (1985). The development of exceptional research mathematicians. In B. S. Bloom (Ed.), *Developing talent in young people* (pp. 270–331). New York: Ballantine Books.

Haas, C. (1989). Does the medium make a difference? A study of composing with pen and paper and with a computer. *Human–Computer Interaction, 4,* 149–169.

Haas, C. (1990). Composing in technological contexts: A study of note-making. *Written Communication, 7,* 512–547.

Haas, C., & Hayes, J. R. (1986). What did I just say? Reading problems in writing with the machine. *Research in the Teaching of English, 20,* 22–35.

Halasz, F. G., Moran, T. P., & Trigg, R. H. (1987). Note cards in a nutshell. *Proceedings of the ACM CHI and GI 1987 Conference: Human Factors in Computing Systems and Graphics Interface,* Special Issue, 45–52.

Halliday, M. A. K. (1987). Spoken and written modes of meaning. In R. Horowitz & S. J. Samuels (Eds.), *Comprehending oral and written language* (pp. 55–82). New York: Academic Press.

Halliday, M. A. K., & Hasan, R. (1976). *Cohesion in English.* London: Longman.

Hansen, W. J. & Haas, C. (1988). Reading and writing with computers: A framework for explaining differences in performance. *Communications of the ACM, 31,* 1080–1089.

Harris, M. (1979). *Cultural materialism.* New York: Random House.

Hartley, J. (1984). The role of colleagues and text-editing programs in improving text. *IEEE Transactions on Professional Communication, 27,* 42–44.

Hartley, J. (1991). Psychology, writing, and computers: A review of research. *Visible Language, 25,* 339–375.

Hartley, J., & Branthwaite, A. (1989). The psychologist as wordsmith: A questionnaire study of the writing strategies of productive British psychologists. *Higher Education, 18,* 423–452.

Hartman, D. E. (1986). Artificial intelligence or artificial psychologist? Conceptual issues in clinical microcomputer use. *Professional Psychology: Research and Practice, 17,* 528–534.

Hartman, K., Newwirth, C. M., Kreisler, S., Sproull, L., Cochran, C., Palmquist, M., & Zubrow, D. (1991). Patterns of social interaction and learning to write: Some effects of network technologies. *Written Communication, 8,* 79–113.

Havelock, E. (1991). The oral–literate equation: A formula for the modern mind. In D. R. Olson & N. Torrance (Eds.), *Literacy and orality* (pp. 11–27). Cambridge: Cambridge University Press.

Hawisher, G. E. (1986). Studies in word processing. *Computers and Composition, 4,* 6–31.

Hawisher, G. E. (1987a). The effects of word processing on the revision strategies of college freshmen. *Research in the Teaching of English, 21,* 145–159.

Hawisher, G. E. (1987b). Research update: Writing and word processing. *Computers and Composition, 5,* 7–23.

Hawisher, G. E. (1989). Research and recommendations for computers and composition. In G. E. Hawisher & C. L. Selfe (Eds.), *Critical perspectives on computers and composition instruction* (pp. 44–69). New York: Teachers College Press.

Hawisher, G. E. (1992). Electronic meetings of the mind: Research, electronic conferences, and composition studies. In G. E. Hawisher & P. LeBlanc (Eds.), *Re-imagining computers and composition: Teaching and research in the virtual age* (pp. 81–101). Portsmouth, NH: Boynton/Cook Publishers.

Hawisher, G. E., & LeBlanc, P. (1992). *Re-imagining computers and composition: Teaching and research in the virtual age.* Portsmouth, NH: Boynton/Cook Publishers.

Hayes, J. R. (1981). *The complete problem solver.* Philadephia: Franklin Institute.

Hayes, J. R., & Flower, L. S. (1980). Identifying the organization of writing processes. In L. W. Gregg & E. R. Steinberg (Eds.), *Cognitive processes in writing* (pp. 3–30). Hillsdale, NJ: Lawrence Erlbaum Associates.

Hayes, J. R., & Flower, L. S. (1986). Writing research and the writer. *American Psychologist, 41,* 1106–1113.

Hayes, J. R., Flower, L. S., Schriver, K., Stratman, J., & Carey, L. (1985). *Cognitive processes in revision* (Technical Report No. 12). Pittsburgh: Carnegie Mellon University, Communcations Design Center.

Hayes-Roth, B., & Hayes-Roth, F. (1979). A cognitive model of planning. *Cognitive Science, 3,* 275–310.

Heidorn, G. E., Jensen, K., Miller, L. A., Bird, R. J., & Chodorow, M. S. (1982). The EPISTLE text critiquing system. *IBM Systems Journal, 21,* 305–326.

Hill, C. S. (1991). *Sensations: A defense of type materialism.* New York: Cambridge University Press.

Hillocks, G. (1986). *Research on written composition: New directions for teaching.* Urbana, IL: National Council of Teachers of English.

Horton, S. R. (1982). *Thinking through writing.* Baltimore: Johns Hopkins University Press.

Howard, G. S. (1991). Culture tales: A narrative approach to thinking, cross-cultural psychology, and psychotherapy. *American Psychologist, 46,* 187–197.

Hull, G. A., & Smith, W. L. (1983). Interrupting visual feedback in writing. *Perceptual and Motor Skills, 57,* 963–978.

Hunt, E. (1987). The next word on verbal ability. In P. A. Vernon (Ed.), *Speed of information processing and intelligence* (pp. 347–392). Norwood, NJ: Ablex.

Hunt, K. W. (1965) *Grammatical structures written at three grade levels.* NCTE Research Report No. 3. Champaign, IL: National Council of Teachers of English.

Huot, B. (1990). The literature of direct writing assessment: Major concerns and prevailing trends. *Review of Educational Research, 60,* 237–263.

Husen, T., & Tujinman, A. (1991, October). The contribution of formal schooling to the increase in intellectual capital. *Educational Researcher, 20,* 17–25.

Hyman, R. J. (1989). *Information access: Capabilities and limitations of printed and computerized sources.* Chicago: American Library Association.

Iran-Nejad, A., & Ortony, A. (1984). A biofunctional model of distributed mental content, mental structures, awareness, and attention. *Journal of Mind and Behavior, 5,* 171–210.

James, C., & Garrett, P. (Eds.). (1992). *Language awareness in the classroom.* London: Longman.

Jaynes, J. (1976). *The origin of consciousness in the breakdown of the bicameral mind.* Boston: Houghton Mifflin.

Jensen, A. R. (1987). Individual differences in the Hick paradigm. In P. A. Vernon (Ed.), *Speed of information-processing and intelligence* (pp. 101–175). Norwood, NJ: Ablex.

Jensen, G. H., & DiTiberio, J. K. (1989). *Personality and the teaching of composition.* Norwood, NJ: Ablex.

Johnson, M. J. (1987). *The body in the mind: The bodily basis of meaning, imagination, and reason.* Chicago: University of Chicago Press.

John-Steiner, V. (1985). *Notebooks of the mind: Explorations of thinking.* Albuquerque: University of New Mexico Press.

Joram, E., Woodruff, E., Bryson, M., & Lindsay, P. H. (1992). The effects of revising with a word processor on written composition, *Research in the Teaching of English, 26,* 167–193.

Journet, D. (1991). Ecological theories as cultural narratives: F. E. Clement's and H. A. Gleason's "stories" of community succession. *Written Communication, 8,* 446–472.

Jung, C. G. (1921) *Psychological types* [trans. 1923]. Princeton, NJ: Princeton University Press.

Kahneman, D. (1973). *Attention and effort.* Englewood Cliffs, NJ: Prentice-Hall.

Karmiloff-Smith, A. (1986). From meta-processes to conscious access: Evidence from children's metalinguistic and repair data. *Cognition. 23,* 95–147.

Karmiloff-Smith, A. (1990). Constraints on representational change: Evidence from children's drawings. *Cognition, 34,* 57–83.

Kaufer, D., Hayes, J. R., & Flower, L. S. (1986). Composing written sentences. *Research in the Teaching of English, 20,* 121–140.

Kean, D., Glynn, S. M., & Britton, B. K. (1987). Writing persuasive documents: The role of students' verbal aptitude and evaluation anxiety. *Journal of Experimental Education, 55,* 95–102.

Kellogg, R. T. (1986a). Writing method and productivity of science and engineering faculty. *Research in Higher Education, 25,* 147–163.

Kellogg, R. T. (1986b). Designing idea processors for document composition. *Behavior Research Methods, Instruments, & Computers, 18,* 118–128.

Kellogg, R. T. (1987a). Effects of topic knowledge on the allocation of processing time and cognitive effort to writing processes. *Memory & Cognition, 15,* 256–266.

Kellogg, R. T. (1987b). Writing performance: Effects of cognitive strategies. *Written Communication, 4,* 269–298.

Kellogg, R. T. (1988). Attentional overload and writing performance: Effects of rough draft and outline strategies. *Journal of Experimental Psychology: Learning, Memory, and Cognition, 14,* 355–365.

Kellogg, R. T. (1989). Idea processors: Computer aids for planning and composing text. In B. K. Britton & S. M. Glynn (Eds.), *Computer writing environments: Theory, research, and design* (pp. 57–92). Hillsdale, NJ: Lawrence Erlbaum Associates.

Kellogg, R. T. (1990). Effectiveness of prewriting strategies as a function of task demands. *American Journal of Psychology, 103,* 327–342.

Kellogg, R. T., (1992, November). *Topic knowledge and verbal knowledge in writing.* Paper presented at the annual meeting of the Psychonomic Society, St. Louis.

Kellogg, R. T., (1993). Observations on the psychology of thinking and writing. *Composition Studies, 21,* 3–41.

Kellogg, R. T., Krueger, M., & Blair, R. (1991, November). *The relative ease of writing narrative text.* Paper presented at the annual meeting of the Psychonomic Society, San Francisco.

Kellogg, R. T., & Mueller, S. (1993). Performance amplification and process restructuring in computer-based writing. *International Journal of Man-Machine Studies, 39*, 33–49.

Kelly, G. A. (1955). *The psychology of personal constructs.* (Vols. 1 and 2). New York: Norton.

Kennedy, J. S. (1992). *The new anthropomorphism.* Cambridge: Cambridge University Press.

Kennedy, M. L. (1985). The composing process of college students writing from sources. *Written Communication, 2*, 434–456.

Kerek, A., Daiker, D., & Morenberg, M. (1979). The effects of intensive sentence combining on the writing ability of college freshman. In D. McQuade (Ed.), *Linguistics, stylistics, and the teaching of composition* (pp. 142–149). Akron, OH: L & S Books.

Kiefer, K. E., & Smith, C. R. (1983). Textual analysis with computers: Tests of Bell Laboratories' computer software. *Research in the Teaching of English, 17*, 201–214.

Kieras, D. E. (1989). An advanced computerized aid for the writing of comprehensible technical documents. In B. K. Britton & S. M. Glynn (Eds.) *Computer writing environments: Theory, research, and design* (pp. 143–168). Hillsdale, NJ: Lawrence Erlbaum Associates.

Kincaid, J. P., Hagard, J. A., O'Hara, J. W., & Cottrell, L. K. (1981). Computer readability editing system. *IEEE Transactions on Professional Communications, 24*, 38–41.

King, L. (1990). *Tell me more.* New York: G. P. Putnam's Sons.

Kinneavy, J. L. (1971). *A theory of discourse.* New York: Norton.

Kintsch, W. (1974). *The representation of meaning in text.* Hillsdale, NJ: Lawrence Erlbaum Associates.

Kintsch, W., & van Dijk, T. A. (1978). Toward a model of text comprehension and production. *Psychological Review, 85*, 363–394.

Klare, G. R. (1963). *The measurement of readability.* Ames: Iowa State University Press.

Klare, G. R. (1976). A second look at the validity of readability formulas. *Journal of Reading Behavior, 8*, 129–152.

Klinger, E. (1990). *Daydreaming: Using waking fantasy and imagery for self-knowledge and creativity.* Los Angeles: Jeremy P. Tarcher.

Kolers, P. A., & Roediger, H. L. (1984). Procedures of mind. *Journal of Verbal Learning and Verbal Behavior, 23*, 425–449.

Kolers, P. A., & Smythe, W. E. (1984). Symbol manipulation: Alternatives to the computational view of mind. *Journal of Verbal Learning and Verbal Behavior, 23*, 289–314.

Kozma, R. B. (1991). The impact of computer-based tools and embedded prompts on writing processes and products of novice and advanced college writers. *Cognition and Instruction, 8*, 1–27.

Kreitzberg, C. B., & Schneiderman, B. (1992). Restructuring knowledge for an electronic encyclopedia. In J. Hartley (Ed.), *Technology and writing: Readings in the psychology of written communication* (pp. 169–178). London: Jessica Kingsley Publishers.

Kroll, B. M. (1985). Social-cognitive ability and writing performance: How are they related. *Written Communication, 2*, 293–305.

Kubie, L. S. (1958). *Neurotic distortion of the creative process.* Lawrence: University of Kansas Press.

Kukich, K. (1983). Ana's first sentences: Sample output from a natural language stock report generator. In M. E. Williams & T. H. Hogan (Eds.), *Proceedings of the Fourth National Online Meeting* (pp. 271–280). Medford, NJ: Learned Information.

Kurth, R. (1987, January). Using word processing to enhance revision strategies during student writing activities. *Educational Technology*, pp. 13–19.

L'Amour, L. (1989). *Education of a wandering man.* New York: Bantam.

Langer, E. J. (1989). *Mindfulness.* Reading, MA: Addison-Wesley.

Langer, J. A. (1984). The effects of available informtion on responses to school writing tasks. *Research in the Teaching of English, 18,* 27–44.

Langer, J. A., & Applebee, A. N. (1987). *How writing shapes thinking: A study of teaching and learning.* NCTE Research Report No. 22, No. 21802–519. Urbana, IL: National Council of Teachers of English.

Langer, S. (1942). *Philosophy in a new key.* Cambridge, MA: Harvard University Press.

Lansman, M., Smith, J. B., & Weber, I. (1990). *Using computer-generated protocols to study writers' planning strategies.* Technical Report No. TR90–033. Chapel Hill: University of North Carolina, Department of Computer Science.

Larsen, R. (1988). Flow and writing. In M. Csikszentmihalyi & I. S. Csikszentmihalyi (Eds.), *Optimal experience: Psychological studies of flow in consciousness* (pp. 150–171). Cambridge: Cambridge University Press, 1988.

Layman, D. (1984, August 7). Framework: An outline for thought. *PC Magazine,* pp. 119–127.

Leakey, R., & Lewin, R. (1992). *Origins reconsidered: In search of what makes us human.* New York: Doubleday.

Lehman, D. (1986, August 18). Yale's insomniac genius. *Newsweek,* pp. 56–57.

Leitch, T. M. (1986). *What stories are: Narrative theory and interpretation.* University Park: Pennsylvania State University Press.

Lipman, M. (1991). *Thinking in education.* Cambridge: Cambridge University Press.

Loftus, G. (1983). *Mind at play: The psychology of video games.* New York: Basic Books.

Logan, G. D. (1992). Shapes of reaction-time distributions and shapes of learning curves: A test of the instance theory of automaticity. *Journal of Experimental Psychology: Learning, Memory, and Cognition, 18,* 883–914.

Lowenthal, D., & Wason, P. C. (1977, June 24). Academics and their writing. *Times Literary Supplement,* p. 282.

Lucariello, J. (1990). Canonicality and consciousness in child narrative. In B. K. Britton & A. D. Pellegrini (Eds.), *Narrative thought and narrative language* (pp. 131–150). Hillsdale, NJ: Lawrence Erlbaum Associates.

Lutz, J. A. (1987). A study of professional and experienced writers revising and editing at the computer and with pen and paper. *Research in the Teaching of English, 21,* 398–421.

MacDonald, N. H. (1983). The UNIX writer's workbench software: Rationale and design. *Bell System Technical Journal, 62,* 1891–1908.

MacDonald, N. H., Frase, L. T., Gingrich, P. S., & Keenan, S. A. (1982). The writer's workbench: Computer aids for text analysis. *Educational Psychologist, 17,* 172–179.

MacGowan, S. (1992). Ruskin to McRuskin—Degrees of interaction. In P. Holt & N. Williams (Eds.), *Computers and writing: State of the art* (pp. 297–318). Oxford: Intellect Books.

MacKinnon, D. W. (1978). *In search of human effectiveness.* New York: Creative Education Foundation.

Maimon, E. P. (1986). Knowledge, acknowledgement, and writing across the curriculum: Towards an educated community. In D. A. McQuade (Ed.), *The territory of language: Linguistics, stylistics, and the teaching of composition* (pp. 89–100). Carbondale: Southern Illinois University Press.

Mancuso, J. C. (1986). The acquisition and use of narrative grammar structure. In T. R. Sarbin (Ed.), *Narrative psychology: The storied nature of human conduct* (pp. 91–110). New York: Praeger.

Mandler, J. (1984). *Stories, scripts, and scenes: Aspects of schema theory.* Hillsdale, NJ: Lawrence Erlbaum Associates.

Marchionini, G., & Shneiderman, B. (1988). Finding facts vs. browsing knowledge in hypertext systems. *Computer, 21*, 70–81.

Markus, H., & Wurf, E. (1987). The dynamic self-concept: A social psychological perspective. *Annual Review of Psychology, 38*, 299–337.

Massimini, F., Czikszentmihalyi, M., & Delle Fave, A. (1988). Flow and biocultural evolution. In M. Czikszentmihalyi & I. S. Czikszentmihalyi (Eds.), *Optimal experience: Psychological studies of flow in consciousness* (pp. 60–81). New York: Cambridge University Press.

Matsuhashi, A. (1982). Explorations in the real-time production of written discourse. In M. Nystrand (Ed.), *What writers know: The language, process, and structure of written discourse* (pp. 269–290). New York: Academic Press.

Matsuhashi, A. (Ed.). (1987). *Writing in real time: Modeling production processes.* Norwood, NJ: Ablex.

Matus, I. (1991, October). The case for Shakespeare. *Atlantic Monthly*, pp. 64–72.

May, R. (1975). *The courage to create.* New York: Norton.

Mayer, R. E. (1983). *Thinking, problem solving, and cognition.* San Francisco: W. H. Freeman and Company.

Mayer, R. E. (1987). *Educational psychology: A cognitive approach.* Boston: Little, Brown, and Company.

McClelland, D. C. (1961). *The achieving society.* Princeton, NJ: Van Nostrand.

McCutchen, D. (1986). Domain knowledge and linguistic knowledge in the development of writing ability. *Journal of Memory and Language, 25*, 431–444.

McCutchen, D. (1988). Functional automaticity in children's writing: A problem of megacognitive control. *Written Communication, 5*, 306–324.

McCutchen, D., & Perfetti, C. A. (1982). Coherence and connectedness in the development of discourse coherence. *Text, 2*, 113–139.

Mellon, J. C. (1979). Issues in the theory and practice of sentence combining: A twenty year perspective. In D. Daiker, A. Kerek, & M. Morenberg (Eds.), *Sentence combining and the teaching of writing* (pp. 1–38). Akron, OH: L & S Books.

Messer, S. B. (1976). Reflection-impulsivity: A review. *Psychological Bulletin, 83*, 1026–1052.

Meyer, B. J. F. (1975). *The organization of prose and its effect on memory.* Amsterdam: North-Holland.

Michotte, A. (1963). *The perception of causality.* (Trans. by T. R. Miles & E. Miles). London: Methuen.

Miller, G. A., Galanter, E., & Pribram, K. H. (1960). *Plans and the structure of behavior.* New York: Holt, Rinehart, & Winston.

Miller, J. R., & Kintsch, W. (1980). Readability and recall of short prose passages: A theoretical analysis. *Journal of Experimental Psychology: Human Learning and Memory, 6*, 335–354.

Miller, L. A. (1985, July). Computers for composition: A stage model approach to helping. *IBM Research Report, Computer Science*, No. RC 11261.

Miller, L., & Thomas, J. (1997). Behavioral issues in the use of interactive systems. *International Journal of Man-Machine Studies, 9*, 509–536.

Minsky, M. (1977). Frame-system theory. In P. N. Johnson-Laird & P. C. Wason (Eds.), *Thinking: Readings in cognitive science* (pp. 355–376). Cambridge: Cambridge University Press.

Mischel, W. (1968). *Personality and assessment.* New York: John Wiley & Sons.

Mohageg, M. P. (1992). The influence of hypertext linking structures on the efficiency of information retrieval. *Human Factors, 34*, 351–367.

Monaghan, P. (1989, December 6). Psychologist specializes in counseling graduate students who seem unable to finish their doctoral dissertations. *Chronicle of Higher Education*, pp. 13, 16.

Moran, C. (1983, March). Word processing and the teaching of writing. *Electronic Media*, pp. 113–115.

Moran, N. (1982). Subjective mental workload. *Human Factors, 24*, 25–40.

Moran, T. (1993, September). AV cyclone and the tempest. *MacWorld*, pp. 34–35.

Morris, N. W., & Murphy, G. L. (1990). Converging operation on a basic level in event taxonomies. *Memory & Cognition, 18*, 407–418.

Morton, E. S., & Page, J. (1992). *Animal talk: Science and the voices of nature*. New York: Random House.

Moses, J. D. (1986). The effects of differing levels of background knowledge on the writing process. *Dissertation Abstracts International, 46*, 3584-B.

Mulligan, H. A. (1983, May 15). Travis McGee's creator takes on TV evangelists. *St. Louis Post-Dispatch*, B3.

Murphy, G. L., & Medin, D. L. (1985). The role of theories in conceptual coherence. *Psychological Review, 92*, 289–316.

Murray, D. M. (1982). *Learning by teaching: Selected articles on writing and teaching*. Montclair, NJ: Boynton/Cook Publishers.

Murray, D. M. (1985). The essential delay: When a writer's block isn't. In M. Rose (Ed.), *When a writer can't write* (pp. 219–226). New York: Guilford Press.

Myers, D. G. (1987). *Social Psychology* (2nd ed.). New York: McGraw-Hill.

Myers, G. (1990). *Writing biology: Texts in the social construction of scientific knowledge*. Madison, WI: University of Wisconsin Press.

Myers, H. F. (1991, November 25). Das Kapital. *Wall Street Journal*, pp. 1, 10.

Navon, D. (1984). Resources—A theoretical soup stone? *Psychological Review, 91*, 216–234.

Neisser, U. (1976). *Cognition and reality: Principles and implications of cognitive psychology*. San Francisco: W. H. Freeman and Company.

Neisser, U. (1983). Components of intelligence or steps in routine procedures? *Cognition, 15*, 189–197.

Nelson, K. (1986). *Event knowledge: Structure and function in development*. Hillsdale, NJ: Lawrence Erlbaum Associates.

Newell, A., & Simon, H. A. (1972). *Human problem solving*. Englewood Cliffs, NJ: Prentice-Hall.

Neumann, D. (1985, November). *Computer applications in psychotherapy*. Paper presented at the meeting of the Society for Computers in Psychology, Boston.

Neuwirth, C. M. (1984). Toward the design of a flexible, computer-based writing environment. In W. Wresch (Ed.), *The computer in composition instruction* (pp. 191–208). Urbana, IL: National Council of Teachers of English.

Neuwirth, C. M., & Kaufer, D. S. (1992). Computers and composition studies: Articulating a pattern of discovery. In G. E. Hawisher & P. LeBlanc (Eds.), *Re-imagining computers and composition: Teaching and research in the virtual age* (pp. 173–190). Portsmouth, NH: Boynton/Cook Publishers.

Nickerson, R. S. (1981). Thoughts on teaching thinking. *Educational Leadership, 39*(1), 21–24.

Nickerson, R. S. (1988–89). On improving thinking through instruction. *Review of Research in Education, 15*, 3–57.

Nickerson, R. S., Perkins, D. N., & Smith, E. E. (1985). *The teaching of thinking*. Hillsdale, NJ: Lawrence Erlbaum Associates.

Nicklin, J. L. (1993, January 13). Colleges that helped spawn Michener's career are the beneficiaries of his philanthropy. *Chronicle of Higher Education*, pp. A27-A28.

Nold, E. W., & Freedman, S. W. (1977). An analysis of readers' responses to essays. *Research in the Teaching of English, 11,* 164–174.

Norman, D. A. (1989). Cognitive artifacts. In J. M. Carroll (Ed.), *Designing interaction: Psychology at the human–computer interface* (pp. 17–38). New York: Cambridge University Press.

North, S. M. (1987). *The making of knowledge in composition: Portrait of an emerging field.* Portsmouth, NH: Boynton/Cook Publishers.

Nystrand, M. (1982). Rhetoric's "audience" and linguistics' "speech community." Implications for understanding writing, reading, and text. In M. Nystrand (Ed.), *What writers know: The language, process, and structure of written discourse* (pp. 1–28). New York: Academic Press.

Nystrand, M. (1986). *The structure of written communication: Studies in reciprocity between writers and readers.* Orlando, FL: Academic Press.

Nystrand, M. (1989). A social-interactive model of writing. *Written Communication, 6,* 66–85.

Ochse, R. (1990). *Before the gates of excellence.* New York: Cambridge University Press.

Odell, L., & Goswami, D. (1984). Writing in a nonacademic setting. In R. Beach & L. S. Bridwell (Eds.), *New directions in composition research* (pp. 233–258). New York: Guilford Press.

Odell, L., & Goswami, D. (Eds.). (1986). *Writing in nonacademic settings.* New York: Guilford.

Oliver, L. J. (1985). The case against computerized analysis of student writings. *Journal of Technical Writing and Communications, 15,* 309–322.

Olson, D. R. (1976). Culture, technology, and intellect. In L. B. Resnick (Ed.), *The nature of intelligence* (pp. 189–202). Hillsdale, NJ: Lawrence Erlbaum Associates.

Olson, D. R. (1977). From utterance to text: The bias of language in speech and writing. *Harvard Educational Review, 47,* 257–281.

Olson, D. R. (1992, May). The mind according to Bruner. *Educational Researcher, 21,* 29–31.

Ornstein, R. (1991). *The evolution of consciousness: The origins of the way we think.* New York: Simon & Schuster.

Owens, P. (1984, April). Thinktank and Promptdoc. *Popular Computing, 3*(6), 186–189.

Ownston, R. D., Murphy, S., & Wideman, H. H. (1992). The effects of word processing on students' writing quality and revision strategies. *Research in the Teaching of English, 26,* 249–276.

Pagels, H. (1988). *The dreams of reason.* New York: Simon & Schuster.

Parini, J. (1991). On being prolific. In R. Pack & J. Parini (Eds.), *Writers on writing* (pp. 199–206). Hanover, NH: Middleburg College Press.

Parker, S. T., & Gibson, K. R. (1990). *"Language" and intelligence in monkeys and apes: Comparative development perspectives.* New York: Cambridge University Press.

Pea, R. D. (1985). Beyond amplification: Using the computer to reorganize mental functioning. *Educational Psychologist, 20,* 167–182.

Pea, R. D., & Kurland, D. M. (1987–88). Cognitive technologies for writing. *Review of Research in Education, 14,* 227–325.

Pedersen, E. L. (1989). The effectiveness of WRITER'S WORKBENCH and MACPROOF. *Computer-Assisted Composition Journal, 3,* 92–100.

Pelz, D. C., & Andrews, F. M. (1976). *Scientists in organizations.* Ann Arbor: Institute for Social Research, University of Michigan.

Pennebaker, J. W. (1993). Putting stress into words: Health, linguistic, and therapeutic implications. *Behavior Research and Therapy, 31,* 539–548.

Pennington, N., & Hastie, R. (1988). Explanation-based decision making: Effects of memory structure on judgements. *Journal of Experimental Psychology: Learning, Memory and Cognition, 14,* 521–533.

Penrose, R. (1989). *The emperor's new mind: Concerning computers, minds, and the law of physics.* New York: Oxford University Press.

Percival, E. (1966). The dimensions of ability in English composition. *Educational Review, 18,* 205–212.

Perkins, D. N. (1987). Thinking frames: An integrative perspective on teaching cognitive skills. In J. B. Baron & R. J. Sternberg (Eds.), *Teaching thinking skills: Theory and practice* (pp. 41–61). New York: W. H. Freeman and Company.

Perl, D. (1979). The composing processes of unskilled college writers. *Research in the Teaching of English, 13,* 317–336.

Peterson, C. & Seligman, M. E. P. (1987). Causal explanations as a risk factor for depression: Theory and evidence. *Psychological Review, 91,* 347–374.

Pianko, S. (1979). A description of the composing processes of college freshman writers. *Research in the Teaching of English, 13,* 5–22.

Plimpton, G. (Ed.). (1963). *Writers at work: The Paris Review interviews. Second Series.* New York: Viking Press.

Plimpton, G. (Ed.) (1984). *Writers at work: The Paris Review interviews. Sixth Series.* New York: Viking Press.

Plimpton, G. (1989). *The writer's chapbook: A compendium of fact, opinion, writ, and advice from the 20th century's preeminent writers.* New York: Viking Press.

Plutchik, R., & Karasu, T. B. (1991). Computers in psychotherapy: An overview. *Computers in Human Behavior, 7,* 33–44.

Powers, W. T. (1973). *Behavior: The control of perception.* Chicago: Aldine Publishing.

Rafoth, B. A. (1985). Audience adaptation in the essays of proficient and nonproficient freshman writers. *Research in the Teaching of English, 19,* 237–253.

Rafoth, B. A. (1988). Discourse community: Where writers, readers, and texts come together. In B. A. Rafoth & D. L. Rubin (Eds.), *The social construction of written communication* (pp. 131–146). Norwood, NJ: Ablex.

Rafoth, B. A. (1989). Audience and information. *Research in the Teaching of English, 23,* 273–290.

Rafoth, B. A., & Rubin, D. L. (1984). The impact of content and mechanics on judgments of writing quality. *Written Communication, 1,* 446–458.

Rafoth, B. A., & Rubin, D. L. (1988) (Ed.). *The social construction of written communication.* Norwood, NJ: Ablex.

Ransdell, S. E. (1989). Producing ideas and text with a word processor. *The Computer-Assisted Composition Journal, 4,* 22–28.

Ransdell, S. E., & Levy, C. M. (in press). Writing as process and product: The impact of tool, genre, audience knowledge, and writer expertise. *Computers in Human Behavior.*

Raphael, T. E., Englert, C. S., & Kirschner, B. W. (1989). Students' metacognitive knowledge about writing. *Research in the Teaching of English, 23,* 343–379.

Redd-Boyd, T. M. & Slater, W. H. (1989). The effects of audience specification on undergraduates' attitudes, strategies, and writing. *Research in the Teaching of English, 23,* 77–108.

Reed, W. M. (1989). The effectiveness of composing process software: An analysis of *Writer's Helper*, *Computers in the Schools, 6,* 67–82.

Reed, W. M., Burton, J. K., & Kelly, P. P. (1985). The effects of writing ability and mode of discourse on cognitive capacity engagement. *Research in the Teaching of English, 19,* 283–297.

Richardson-Klavehn, A., & Bjork, R. A. (1988). Measures of memory. *Annual Review of Psychology, 39,* 475–543.

Rico, G. L. (1983). *Writing the natural way.* Los Angeles: Tarcher.

Rodrigues, D., & Rodrigues, R. J. (1984). Computer-based creative problem solving. In W. Wresch (Ed.), *The computer in composition instruction* (pp. 34–46). Urbana, IL: National Council of Teachers of English.

Roe, A. (1952). A psychologist examines 64 eminent scientists. *Scientific American, 187*(5), 21–25.

Roen, D. H., & Willey, R. L. (1988). The effects of audience awareness in drafting and revising. *Research in the Teaching of English, 22,* 75–88.

Rosch, E. (1973). Natural categories. *Cognitive Psychology, 4,* 328–350.

Rosch, E., & Mervis, C. B. (1975). Family resemblances: Studies in the internal structure of categories. *Cognitive Psychology, 7,* 573–605.

Rosch, E., Mervis, C. B., Gray, W., Johnson, D., & Boyes-Braem, P. (1976). Basic objects in natural categories. *Cognitive Psychology, 8,* 382–439.

Rose, M. (1980). Rigid rules, inflexible plans, and the stifling of language: A cognitivist's analysis of writer's block. *College Composition and Communication, 31,* 389–401.

Rose, M. (1984). *Writer's block: The cognitive dimension.* Carbondale: Southern Illinois University Press.

Rose, M. (1985). *When a writer can't write: Studies in writer's block and other composing-process problems.* New York: Guilford Press.

Rosenberg, H., & Lah, M. I. (1982). A comprehensive behavioral-cognitive treatment of writer's block. *Behavioral Psychotherapy, 10,* 356–363.

Rosenberg, R. A., Israel, P. B., Nier, K. A., & Andrews, M. (1991). *The papers of Thomas A. Edison: From workshop to laboratory (Vol. 2).* Baltimore: Johns Hopkins University Press.

Rosenberg, S., Lebowitz, R., Penningroth, S., & Wright, R. E. (1992, May). *Correlates of the quality of expository writing.* Paper presented at the meeting of the Midwestern Psychological Association, Chicago.

Rosenberg, S., & Wright, R. E. (1988, November). *Ideas in writing: Effects of topic familiarity.* Paper presented at the annual meeting of the Psychonomic Society, Chicago.

Ross, D. (1991). Prospects for writers' workstations in the coming decade. In G. E. Hawisher & C. L. Selfe (Eds.), *Evolving perspectives on computers and composition studies Questions for the 1990s* (pp. 84–110). Urbana, IL: National Council of Teachers of English.

Rowan, K. E. (1990). Cognitive correlates of explanatory writing skill: An analysis of individual differences. *Written Communication, 7,* 316–341.

Ruas, C. (1985). *Conversations with American writers.* New York: Alfred A. Knopf.

Rubin, D. L. (1984). Social cognition and written communication. *Written Communication, 1,* 211–245.

Rubin, D. L. (1988). Introduction: Four dimensions of social construction in written communication. In B. A. Rafoth & D. L. Rubin (Eds.). *The social construction of written communication* (pp. 1–33). Norwood, NJ: Ablex.

Rubin, D. L., Piche, G. L., Michlin, M. M., & Johnson, F. L. (1984). Social cognitive ability as a predictor of the quality of fourth-graders' written narratives. In R. Beach & L. S. Bridwell (Eds.), *New directions in composition research* (pp. 297–307). New York: Guilford.

Rubin, D. L. & Rafoth, B. A. (1986). Social cognitive ability as a prediction of the quality of the expository and persuasive writing among college freshmen. *Research in the Teaching of English, 20*, 9–21.

Rueckert, W. H. (1963). *Kenneth Burke and the drama of human relations.* Minneapolis: University of Minnesota Press.

Rumelhart, D. E. (1980). Schemata: The building blocks of cognition. In R. J. Spiro, B. C. Bruce, & W. F. Brewer (Eds.), *Theoretical issues in reading comprehension* (pp. 33–58). Hillsdale, NJ: Lawrence Erlbaum Associates.

Rumelhart, D. E., & Norman, D. A. (1978). Accretion, tuning, and restructuring. Three models of learning. In J. W. Cotton & R. Klatzky (Eds.), *Semantic factors in cognition* (pp. 37–53). Hillsdale, NJ: Lawrence Erlbaum Associates.

Rushdie, S. (1989). *Satanic verses.* New York: Viking Penguin.

Rymer, J. (1988). Scientific composing processes: How eminent scientists write journal articles. In D. A. Jollife (Ed.), *Advances in writing research, Volume 2: Writing in academic disciplines* (pp. 211–250). Norwood, NJ: Ablex.

Saloman, G., & Globerson, T. (1987). Skill may not be enough: The role of mindfulness in learning and transfer. *International Journal of Educational Research, 11*, 623–638.

Salovey, P., & Haar, M. D. (1990). The efficiency of cognitive-behavior therapy and writing process training for alleviating writing anxiety. *Cognitive Therapy and Research, 14*, 515–528.

Sanders, M. S., & McCormick, E. J. (1993). *Human factors in engineering design* (7 ed.). New York: McGraw-Hill.

Sarbin, T. (1986). The narrative as a root metaphor for psychology. In T. Sarbin (Ed.), *Narrative psychology: The storied nature of human conduct* (pp. 3–21). New York: Praeger.

Scardarmalia, M., & Bereiter, C. (1991). Literate expertise. In K. A. Ericsson & J. Smith (Eds.), *Toward a general theory of expertise: Prospects and limits.* (pp. 172–194) Cambridge: Cambridge University Press.

Scardamalia, M., Bereiter, C., & Steinbach, R. (1984). Teachability of reflective process in written composition. *Cognitive Science, 8*, 173–190.

Schank, R. C., & Abelson, R. P. (1977). *Scripts, plans, goals, and understanding: An inquiry into human knowledge structures.* Hillsdale, NJ: Lawrence Erlbaum Associates.

Schmandt-Besserat, D. (1988). From accounting to written language: The role of abstract counting in the invention of writing. In B. A. Rafoth & D. L. Rubin (Eds.) *The social construction of written communication* (pp. 119–130). Norwood, NJ: Ablex Publishing Corporation.

Schriefers, H. (1990). Lexical and conceptual factors in the naming of relations. *Cognitive Psychology, 22*, 111–142.

Schriver, K. A. (1989). Evaluating text quality; the continuum from text focused to reader focused methods. *IEEE Transactions on Professional Communication, 32*, 238–255.

Schumacher, G. M., Klare, G. R., Cronin, F. C., & Moses, J. D. (1984). Cognitive activities of beginning and advanced college writers: A pausal analysis. *Research in the Teaching of English, 18*, 169–187.

Schumacher, G. M., & Nash, J. G. (1991). Conceptualizing and measuring knowledge change due to writing. *Research in the Teaching of English. 25*, 67–96.

Scribner, S. (1984). Studying working intelligence. In B. Rogoff & J. Lave (Eds.), *Everyday cognition: Its development in social context* (pp. 9–40). Cambridge, MA: Harvard University Press.

Searle, J. (1987). Minds and brains without programs. In C. Blakemore & S. Greenfield (Eds.), *Mindwaves* (pp. 209–233). Oxford: Basil Blackwell.

Segal, J. W., Chipman, S. F., & Glaser, R. (1985). *Thinking and learning skills: Volume 1. Relating instruction to research*. Hillsdale, NJ: Lawrence Erlbaum Associates.

Seligman, M. E. P., & Yellen, A. (1987). What is a dream? *Behavior Research Therapy, 25,* 1–24.

Selmi, P. M., Klein, M. H., Greist, J. H., Johnson, J. H., & Harris, W. G. (1982). An investigation of computer-assisted cognitive-behavior therapy in the treatment of depression. *Behavior Research Methods and Instrumentation, 14,* 181–185.

Sharples, M. (1985). *Cognition, computers, and creative writing*. Chichester, West Sussex: Ellis Horwood Limited.

Sharples, M., & Evans, M. (1992). Computer support for the development of writing abilities. In M. Sharples (Ed.), *Computers and writing: Issues and implementations* (pp. 99–108). Dordrecht, The Netherlands: Kluwer Academic Publishers.

Sharples, M., Goodlet, J., & Pemberton, L. (1992). Developing a writer's assistant. In J. Hartley (Ed.), *Technology and writing: Readings in the psychology of written communication* (pp. 209–220). London: Jessica Kingsley Publishers.

Shephard, R. N. (1990). *Mind sights*. New York: W. H. Freeman and Company.

Simon, H. A. (1990). Invariants of human behavior. *Annual Review of Psychology, 41,* 1–19.

Simon, H. A. & Chase, W. G. (1973). Skill in chess. *American Scientist, 61,* 394–403.

Simon, L. (1979). *Thorton Wilder: His world*. Garden City, NY: Doubleday.

Simon, R. J. (1974). The work habits of eminent scientists. *Sociology of Work and Organizations, 1,* 327–335.

Simonton, D. K. (1988). *Scientific genius: A psychology of science*. Cambridge: Cambridge University Press.

Singer, J. L. (1975). *Daydreaming and fantasy*. London: Allen and Unwin.

Skinner, B. F. (1983). Intellectual self-management in old age. *American Psychologist, 38,* 239–244.

Smagorinsky, P. (1991). The writer's knowledge and the writing process: A protocol analysis. *Research in the Teaching of English, 25,* 339–364.

Smith, F. (1982). *Writing and the writer*. Hillsdale, NJ: Lawrence Erlbaum Associates.

Smith, R. N. (1982). Computerized aids to writing. In W. Frawley (Ed.), *Linguistics and literacy* (pp. 189–208). New York: Plenum Publishing Corporation.

Smith, S. M., Glenberg, A., & Bjork, R. A. (1978). Environmental context and human memory. *Memory and Cognition, 6,* 342–353.

Solomans, L. M. & Stein, G. (1896). Normal motor automatism. *Psychological Review, 3,* 492–512.

Sommers, N. I. (1979). The need for theory in composition research. *College Composition and Communication. 30,* 46–49.

Spelke, E., Hirst, W., & Neisser, U. (1976). Skills of divided attention. *Cognition, 4,* 215–230.

Spera, S. P., Buhrfeind, E. D., & Pennebaker, J. W. (in press). Expressive writing and coping with job loss. *Academy of Management Journal.*

Spivey, N. N., & King, J. R. (1989). Readers as writers composing from sources. *Reading Research Quarterly, 24,* 7–26.

Stallard, C. K. (1974). An analysis of the writing behavior of good student writers. *Research in the Teaching of English, 8,* 206–218.

Stanzel, F. K. (1984). *A theory of narrative*. Cambridge: Cambridge University Press.

Staton, J., & Shuy, R. W. (1988). Talking our way into writing and reading: Dialogue journal practice. In B. A. Rafoth & D. L. Rubin (Eds.), *The social construction of written communication* (pp. 195–217). Norwood, NJ: Ablex.

Stein, M. I. (1974). *Stimulating creativity: Volume. 1. Individual procedures.* New York: Academic Press.

Stein, N. L., & Glenn, C. G. (1979). An analysis of story comprehension in elementary school children. In R. O. Freedle (Ed.), *New directions in discourse processing* (Vol. II, pp. 53–120). Norwood, NJ: Ablex.

Stein, N. L., & Policastro, M. (1984). The concept of story: A comparison between children's and teacher's viewpoints. In H. Mandl, N. L. Stein, & T. Trabasso (Eds.), *Learning and comprehension of text* (pp. 113–155). Hillsdale, NJ: Lawrence Erlbaum Associates.

Sterkel, K. S., Johnson, M. I., & Sjorgren, D. (1986). Textual analysis with composites to improve the writing skills of business communication students. *Journal of Business Communication, 23,* 43–61.

Sternberg, R. J. (1977). *Intelligence, information processing, and analogical reasoning: The componential analysis of human abilities.* Hillsdale, NJ: Lawrence Erlbaum Associates.

Sternberg, R. J. (1985a). All's well that ends well, but it's a sad tale that begins at the end: A reply to Glaser. *American Psychologist, 40,* 571–572.

Sternberg, R. J. (1985b). *Beyond IQ: A triarchic theory of human intelligence.* New York: Cambridge University Press.

Sternberg, R. J. (1988a). Mental self-government: A theory of intellectual styles and their development. *Human Development, 31,* 197–224.

Sternberg, R. J. (Ed.). (1988b). *The nature of creativity: Contemporary psychological perspectives.* New York: Cambridge University Press.

Sternberg, R. J., & Lubart, T. I. (1989, November). *Buy low, sell high? An investment model of creativity.* Paper presented at the annual meeting of the Psychonomic Society, Atlanta.

Stiggins, R. (1982). A comparison of direct and indirect writing assessment methods. *Research in the Teaching of English, 16,* 101–114.

Stillings, N. A., Feinstein, M. H., Garfield, J. L., Rissland, E. L., Rosenbaum, D. A., Weisler, S. E., & Baker-Ward, L. (1987). *Cognitive science: An introduction.* Cambridge, MA: MIT Press.

Stotsky, S. (1990). On planning and writing plans—Or beware of borrowed theories. *College Composition and Communication, 41,* 37–57.

Stratman, J. F. (1990). The emergence of legal composition as a field of inquiry: Evaluating the prospects. *Review of Educational Research, 2,* 153–235.

Sullivan, F. J. (1987, March). *Negotiating expectations: Writing and reading placement tests.* Paper presented at the meeting of the Conference on College Composition and Communication, Atlanta.

Sutton-Smith, B. (1986). Children's fiction making. In Theodore R. Sarbin (Ed.), *Narrative psychology: The storied nature of human conduct* (pp. 67–90). New York: Praeger.

Tanaka, J. W., & Taylor, M. (1991). Object categories and expertise: Is the basic level in the eye of the beholder? *Cognitive Psychology, 23,* 457–482.

Taylor, C. W., & Barron, F. (Eds.). (1963). *Scientific creativity: Its recognition and development.* New York: Wiley.

Taylor, S. E. & Brown, J. (1988). Illusion and well-being: A social psychological perspective on mental health. *Psychological Bulletin, 103,* 193–210.

Terrace, H. S. (1984). Apes who "talk": Language or projection of language by their teaching? In J. De Luce & H. T. Wilder (Eds.), *Language in Primates* (pp. 19–42). New York: Springer-Verlag.

Theismeyer, J. (1989). Should we do what we can? In G. E. Hawisher & C. L. Selfe (Eds.), *Critical perspectives on computers and composition instruction* (pp. 75–93). New York: Teachers College Press.

Thines, G., Costall, A., & Butterworth, G. (1991). *Michotte's experimental phenomenology of perception.* Hillsdale, NJ: Lawrence Erlbaum Associates.

Thorndyke, P. W. (1977). Cognitive structures in comprehension and memory of narrative discourse. *Cognitive Psychology, 9,* 77–110.

Thurstone, L. L. (1938). *Primary mental abilities.* Chicago: University of Chicago Press.

Trabasso, T., & van den Broek, P. (1985). Causal thinking and the representation of narrative events. *Journal of Memory and Language, 24,* 612–630.

Transition. (1992, April 20). *Newsweek,* p. 85.

Trigg, R. H., & Irish, P. M. (1987, November). Hypertext habitats: Experiences of writers in NoteCards. Chapel Hill, NC: *Proceedings of Hypertext '87.*

Tulving, E. (1985). How many memory systems are there? *American Psychologist, 40,* 385–398.

Tulving, E., & Thomson, D. M. (1973). Encoding specificity and retrieval processes in episodic memory. *Psychological Review, 80,* 352–373.

Turkle, S. (1984). *The second self: Computers and the human spirit.* New York: Simon & Schuster.

Tyler, S. W., Hertel, P. T., McCallum, M. C., & Ellis, H. C. (1979). Cognitive effort and memory. *Journal of Experimental Psychology: Human Learning and Memory, 5,* 607–617.

VanLehn, K. (1985, July). *Theory reform caused by an argumentation tool.* Palo Alto, CA: Xerox Palo Alto Research Center.

Vitz, P. C. (1990). The use of stories in moral development: New psychological reasons for an old education method. *American Psychologist, 45,* 709–720.

Von Blum, R., & Cohen, M. E. (1984). WANDAH: Writing aid and author's helper. In W. Wresch (Ed.), *The computer in composition instruction* (pp. 154–173). Urbana, IL: National Council of Teachers of English.

Voss, J. F., Vesonder, G. T., & Spillich, G. J. (1980). Text generation and recall by high-knowledge and low-knowledge individuals. *Journal of Verbal Learning and Verbal Behavior, 17,* 651–667.

Vygotsky, L. S. (1962). *Thought and Language.* (E. Haufmann & G. Vakar, Eds. and Trans.). Cambridge, MA: MIT Press.

Wayner, P. (1992). Boxweb: A structured outline program for writers. In P. Holt & N. Williams (Eds.), *Computers and writing: State of the art* (pp. 78–89). Oxford: Intellect Books.

Weil, T. (1992, January 5). London country: Jack London's memory lives in California. *St. Louis Post-Dispatch,* p. 2T.

Weisberg, R. W. (1986). *Creativity: Genius and other myths.* New York: W. H. Freeman and Company.

Weiskrantz, L. (Ed.). (1988). *Thought without language.* Oxford: Clarendon Press.

Wertheimer, M. (1959). *Productive thinking.* New York: Harper & Row.

Weyer, S. A. (1982). The design of a dynamic book for information search. *International Journal of Man-Machine Studies, 17,* 87–107.

Whitehead, A. N. (1927). *Symbolism: Its meaning and effect.* New York: Macmillan.

Wickens, C. (1984). *Engineering psychology and human performance.* Columbus, OH: Merrill.

Wierzbicki, J. (1992, June 7). Britten's magnificent dream: "Drowsy" music permeates "Midsummer Nights Dream." *St. Louis Post-Dispatch,* Arts and Entertainment, pp. 3C, 9C.

Williams, G. (1987, December). HyperCard. *Byte*, pp. 109–129.

Williams, N. (1989). Computer assisted writing software: RUSKIN. In N. Williams & P. Holt (Eds.) *Computers and writing: Models and tools* (pp. 1–16). Norwood, NJ: Ablex.

Williams, N. (1991). *The computer, the writer, and the learner*. Berlin: Springer-Verlag.

Williams, N. (1992). New technology. New writing. New problems? In P. Holt & N. Williams (Eds.), *Computers and writing: State of the art* (pp. 1–19). Oxford: Intellect Books.

Witte, S. P. (1983). Topical structure and revision: An exploratory study. *College Composition and Communication, 34,* 313–339.

Witte, S. P. (1987). Pre-text and composing. *College composition and communication, 38,* 397–425.

Witte, S. P. (1992). Context, text, and intertext: Toward a constructivist semiotic of writing. *Written Communication, 9,* 237–308.

Witte, S. P., & Cherry, R. D. (1986). Writing processes and written products in composition research. In C. R. Cooper & S. Greenbaum (Eds.), *Studying writing: Linguistic approaches* (Vol. 1) (pp. 112–153). Beverly Hills CA: Sage Publications.

Witte, S. P., & Faigley, L. (1981). Coherence, cohesion, and writing quality. *College Composition and Communication, 32,* 189–204.

Woodruff, E., Bereiter, C., & Scardamalia, M. (1982). On the road to computer assisted compositions. *Journal of Educational Technology Systems, 10,* 133–149.

Wresch, W. (1984). Questions, answers, and automated writing. In W. Wresch (Ed.), *The computer in composition instruction: A writer's tool* (pp. 143–153). Urbana, IL: National Council of Teachers of English.

Wright, R. E., & Rosenberg S. (1993). Knowledge of text coherence and expository writing: A developmental study. *Journal of Educational Psychology, 85,* 152–158.

Young, R. E., Becker, A. L., & Pike, K. L. (1970). *Rhetoric: Discovery and change*. New York: Harcourt Brace Jovanovich.

Zbrodoff, N. J. (1985). Writing stories under time and length constraints. *Dissertation Abstracts International, 46,* 1219A.

Zellermeyer, M. G., Soloman, T., Globerson, T., & Givon, H. (1991). Enhancing writing related metacognitions through a computerized writing partner. *American Educational Research Journal, 28,* 373–391.

Zinsser, W. (1983). *Writing with a word processor*. New York: Harper & Row.

Zuckerman, H. (1977). *Scientific elite*. New York: Free Press.

Zwilich, E. (1985, July 14). American classical composer. *New York Times Magazine*, pp. 29–30.

Index